I0883775

Crete, 20 May 1941. The first campaign-sized airborne assault is launched. Many books have been written about this famous invasion, with the emphasis mainly on the battles for Maleme and Chania. The battle for Heraklion, an epic struggle, remained largely forgotten and widely unstudied. Yet the desperate fight for Heraklion had everything: street fighting in the town; heroic attacks against well-fortified positions and medieval walls; heavy losses on all sides; and tragic stories involving famous German aristocratic families like the von Blüchers and members of the Bismarck family. This book highlights personal stories and accounts.

The author's access to records from all three sides allowed accounts to be placed in their correct place and time. Finally, the history of the battle is written with the added perspective of extensive Greek accounts and sources. In contrast, earlier books were based solely on British and German sources, totally ignoring the Greek side. Many of these accounts are from people who were fighting directly against each other and some reveal what the enemies were discussing and thinking while they were shooting at or attacking each other. Some accounts are so accurate and detailed that we can even identify who killed whom. In addition, long lost stories behind both well-known and previously unpublished pictures are revealed. For the first time 75 year-old mysteries are solved: What were the names of the paratroopers in the planes seen crashing in famous pictures? What was the fate of soldiers seen in pictures taken just before the battle?

The author has studied the battlefield in every detail, thus giving the reader the opportunity to understand actions and incidents by examining what happened on the actual field of battle. For example, how was it possible for a whole platoon to be trapped and annihilated as in the fate of Wolfgang Graf von Blücher? Such a question is not easily answered even by people with a military background. How was it possible for the paratroopers to fail in their attempt to occupy the town? The answers to questions like these became very clear when the author walked through the battlefields, following the accounts of the people from all sides who had fought there and which describe the same incidents.

The author's extensive research is vividly presented via detailed maps and photographs, both from the era of the battle and today; even battlefield archaeology plays a role in revealing what really happened on the battlefield. The author's approach addresses two different types of readers: those who are largely unfamiliar with the battle, hence the emphasis on personal stories, accounts and pictures; and the researcher who wants a reliable source of first-hand material and perhaps a different point of view, such as is offered by Greek accounts and sources, and by the writer's detailed analysis of the battle. This fresh account of one of the Second World War's most memorable battles is given added authority by the writer's military background, together with his deep knowledge of the battlefield and his access to Greek accounts and sources.

Yannis Prekatsounakis was born in 1974 in Heraklion, Crete and joined the Hellenic Naval Academy in 1994. He graduated in 1998 as a 2nd Lieutenant and served on various warships – mainly frigates and fast patrol boats – as well as in several commands of the fleet and the Hellenic National Defence General Staff; he is a graduate of the staff courses appropriate to his rank. In 2015, he was appointed to HS Degiannis as Commanding Officer. He has a Masters Degree in Military Electronic Systems Engineering from the Defence College of Management and Technology in the UK. His keen interest in history – and particularly the Battle of Crete – was the main motive for his detailed research over many years (focusing on his birthplace, Heraklion).

# THE BATTLE FOR HERAKLION. CRETE 1941

## The Campaign Revealed Through Allied and Axis Accounts

Yannis Prekatsounakis

Helion & Company

Helion & Company Limited
Unit 8 Amherst Business Centre
Budbrooke Road
Warwick
CV34 5WE
England
Tel. 01926 499 619
Email: info@helion.co.uk
Website: www.helion.co.uk
Twitter: @helionbooks
blog.helion.co.uk

Published by Helion & Company 2016. Reprinted in paperback 2020
Designed and typeset by Mach 3 Solutions Ltd (www.mach3solutions.co.uk)
Cover designed by Paul Hewitt, Battlefield Design (www.battlefield-design.co.uk)



ISBN 978-1-913336-01-1

British Library Cataloguing-in-Publication Data.
A catalogue record for this book is available from the British Library.

# Contents


Preface iv
Acknowledgements vi
Glossary and Abbreviations vii
Introduction ix

1. Destination Crete 13
2. The Invasion Begins 27
3. The Drops on Gournes and the Battle at Kopsas Hill 94
4. The Battle at the Airfield and Blücher 113
5. The Attack on the Town 161
6. The Battle Continues 209
7. The Final Attack and the Evacuation 242
8. After the Battle 261

Epilogue 286

Bibliography 287
Index 289

# Preface

I have always been fascinated by the epic Battle for Crete – and it was, therefore, my great fortune to meet Constantinos E. Mamalakis and Nikos Valasiadis: two people with a passion for history (and especially for the Crete campaign). After a long period of collecting information, accounts and books about the battle, I decided some years ago to begin detailed research focusing on Heraklion, which is my hometown. My aim then was to answer the many questions about aspects of the battle that remained unclear or widely debated.

Why Heraklion? This is a good question, since the best-known battlefields on Crete are Maleme, Galatas, Souda and Chania. I am well aware that many books have been written about this famous Second World War battle, so one more would have had little new to add. I realised that most of the books focused on the Maleme-Chania sector, with some minor discussion of Heraklion and Rethymnon. Additionally, I felt that the Crete campaign was too extensive to be successfully studied in detail in just one book, so I chose to focus on only one sector, with the aim of covering every aspect in the greatest possible detail – including clearing up less understood features and unexplained incidents.

The Battle for Heraklion was an event of major proportions, as it had everything: street-fighting in the town (uniquely in the Battle for Crete); heroic attacks against well-fortified positions and medieval walls; heavy losses (mainly by the paratroopers); and tragic stories involving famous German aristocratic families like the von Blüchers and members of the Bismarck family. What I have also noticed is that all of the previously published books are based solely on British and German sources – totally ignoring the Greek side. This is a major deficiency, given that two Greek infantry regiments and the local population fought in and around Heraklion. Also, histories of battles are usually written in a narrative style and tell the story of the conflict – and its sequence of events – from a broad perspective without giving due importance to the personal views and experiences of the people who participated in those events. I have always wondered about the names and the faces of the people who fought in this battle… what they were thinking, what influenced their decisions and what their personal stories were.

As I have mentioned, this book emphasises personal stories and accounts. Having access to records from all three sides (British, German and Greek), the stories can be placed in their correct place and time. It is too often the case that many different accounts are published, but in most instances, the presentation of these accounts is not constructed so as to show the exact place, time and phase of the battle where the stories occurred. In this book, the intention is to provide explanations from all sides to describe the same incident. On many occasions, these explanations are from people who were fighting directly against each other – and many incidents reveal what the enemies were discussing and thinking while they were shooting at or attacking each other. For some actions, we can even identify who killed whom.

In this book, the Greek side is presented through official sources and personal accounts for the first time. In previous books published in English and in German, where the Greek side is absent, incorrect conclusions have been drawn based upon faulty assumptions or by totally ignoring important events in the battle. My research aimed to fill this gap and present a complete picture of the battle by studying all three sides. It is this element that distinguishes this work from other accounts.

Since I live in Greece, I was able to examine the battlefield and the landscape very carefully, and understand actions and incidents by studying what happened on the actual field of battle. We usually read about battles on mountains, hills and in valleys, but readers are expected to imagine the scene without being presented with sufficient information to picture the actual dimensions of the battlefield; maps can be of very little help in imagining a battlefield. During my research, I was often surprised by the topography, since what I had originally imagined as a tall hill or a wide valley or a great distance actually turned out to be something much smaller and more familiar. This made it difficult for one to believe that such a feature was an important objective – costing many lives during the battle. By walking the battlefields, I was able to better understand the decisions taken by commanders and soldiers during the battle; for example, how was it possible for a whole platoon to be trapped and annihilated, as in the fate of Wolfgang *Graf* von Blücher? Such a question is not easily answered even by people with a military background. How was it possible for the paratroopers to fail in their attempt to occupy the town? The answers to questions like these became very clear when I walked through the battlefields, following the accounts of the people who had fought there and, more revealingly, accounts from the different sides which describe the same incidents.

My belief is that the battlefield is, essentially, the same place that we can walk through today and everything is there waiting to be discovered. A general description of an attack or a fight is not sufficient for this book, so I have tried to include explanations from the people who participated. I have also tried to discover the exact places on the battlefield where events occurred, and I have taken 'then and now' photographs – so verifying my research. Having walked the exact steps of the soldiers at the actual locations where they fought, I was able to understand their thoughts, the conditions under which they acted and their decisions. In this way, many events and actions which originally, were incomprehensible to me and to most other historians, finally became clear. My research allows me to explain and present my point of view – thus revealing some important errors made in books written soon after the battle.

In endeavouring to find the exact locations where incidents occurred, I have managed to discover the spots where Wolfgang *Graf* von Blücher and his brother, Hans Joachim, were killed and buried; this book includes photographs of these places as they are today. Many previously unidentified pictures have now been placed at their correct place and time – also identifying the persons pictured in them. Photographs are therefore very important for this book and they complement the text and the stories that are related in it. Also, regarding maps, a great effort has been made for those included to be as informative and relevant to the story as possible.

I hope that I have managed to fulfil my aims and present the reader with a comprehensive view of the battle: one which clarifies issues that have remained unclear through all the years since it took place. In writing this book, I have had in mind two different types of readers: those who are largely unfamiliar with the battle – hence the emphasis on personal stories, accounts and pictures – and the researcher who wants a reliable source of first-hand material and perhaps a different point of view, such as is offered by Greek accounts and sources, and by my own analysis of the battle.

# Acknowledgements

Apart from Constantinos E. Mamalakis, who played a key role in the development of this book, I would also like to thank all the people who helped me in many different ways in my efforts to gather information and material for the book: Nikos Valasiadis for his contributions to every aspect of my research, as well as for his unstinting work on detailed maps; Colonel (retired) of the *fallschirmjäger* Steffen Rhode, of *BDF Suchdienst*, who managed to discover rare reports and accounts – some of which were considered missing, or their existence was not known; Adrian Nisbett for his invaluable help in the editing of the text and his advice regarding the content based on his own study and knowledge of the battle – and especially the story of the von Blücher brothers; Mike Smythe for putting me in contact with valuable sources of information – including veterans and their families; Shaun Winkler, who very generously provided material and pictures from his great collection; Jose Ramon Artaza Ivanes for data on individuals and the unique pictures which he provided; Dimitris Skartsilakis for the material and pictures from his personal collection; David Lenk, who is a unique source of information through his contact with veterans and his thorough study of the battle; Mike Kennedy for keeping his father's accounts – thus preserving some unique stories from the battle; Menelaos Pratikakis, whose knowledge of the battlefield and the area around Heraklion proved a valuable guide to my research and a great help for the 'then and now' pictures; Mrs Eva Grammatikaki and Mrs Deniz Chloe Alivizou from the Society of Cretan Historical Studies for the extracts from their relevant publications; Colonel Ioanis Gemenetzis of the Hellenic Army History Directorate; and Mrs Emma Halford-Forbes from the Black Watch Museum and Mr Rod Mackenzie from the Argylls Museum. My thanks also to G.W. Cone, Stephan Janzyk, Dieter Frieß and Paul Bernhard.

Very special thanks are due to the veterans of the battle, who despite their advanced age, provided their accounts and memories. I was very fortunate to meet, or be in contact with them, and this was a great honour for me. I am especially grateful to Theodoros E. Kallinos (†), David Hutton, Dr Eberhard Boerger (†) and Gerhard Broder (†).

Last but not least, I would like to thank Mr Duncan Rogers – publisher of Helion & Company – for the acceptance of my work from its earliest stage and his flawless co-operation and support.

# Glossary and Abbreviations

| | | |
|---|---|---|
| AA | | Anti-Aircraft |
| Bde | | Brigade |
| *BDF* | *Bund Deutscher Fallschirmjäger* | German Paratroopers' Association |
| Bn | | Battalion |
| BW | | Black Watch |
| CO | | Commanding Officer |
| Coy | | Company |
| Cpl | | Corporal |
| *DDF* | *Der Deutsche Fallschirmjäger* | *The German Paratroopers'* Magazine |
| *Feldw* | *Feldwebel* | Staff Sergeant |
| | *Fliegerkorps* | Air Corps |
| | *Flieger* Division | Air Division |
| *FschFlaMGBtl* | *Fallschirm Flugabwehr Maschinengewehr Bataillon* | Parachute Anti-Aircraft Machine Gun Battalion |
| *FschJg* | *Fallschirmjäger* | Paratrooper |
| *FschJgRgt* | *Fallschirmjäger* Regiment | Paratrooper Regiment |
| *FschPiBtl* | *Fallschirm Pionier Bataillon* | Parachute Engineer Battalion |
| *FschSanAbt* | *Fallschirm Sanitäts Abteilung* | Parachute Medical Battalion |
| | *Gebirgsjäger* | Mountain troops/hunters |
| *Gefr* | *Gefreiter* | Lance Corporal |
| | *Generalmajor* | Major General |
| | *Generalleutnant* | Lieutenant General |
| *Hptm* | *Hauptmann* | Captain (Army) |
| | *Hauptfeldwebel* | Sergeant Major (Warrant Officer Class I) |
| HQ | | Headquarters |
| *K.G.z.b.V.* | *Kampfgruppe zur besonderen Verwendung* | Special-Purpose Battle Group |
| *KG* | *Kampfgeschwader* | Bomber Wing |
| KIA | | Killed in action |
| *LL* | *Luftlande* | Air-Landing |
| Lt | | Lieutenant |
| *Ltn* | *Leutnant* | 2nd Lieutenant |
| | *Oberst* | Colonel |
| *Oblt* | *Oberleutnant* | 1st Lieutenant |
| *Objg* | *Oberjäger* | Senior Private |

| | | |
|---|---|---|
| *Obgfr* | *Obergefreiter* | Senior Lance Corporal |
| *Obfw* | *Oberfeldwebel* | Master Sergeant (Warrant Officer) |
| POW | | Prisoner of war |
| RN | | Royal Navy |
| Sgt | | Sergeant |
| | *Staffelkapitän* | Squadron Commander |
| *StG* | *Sturzkampfgeschwader* | Dive-Bomber Wing |
| | *Sturmregiment* | Assault Regiment |
| | *Stabsarzt* | Medical Officer (Captain) |
| *Uffz* | *Unteroffizier* | Junior NCO (Sergeant/Corporal) |
| *ZG* | *Zerstörergeschwader* | Fighter Wing |
| | *Zug* | Platoon |

The designation of the German units follows the rule of the alteration between Roman and Arabic numerals from one level of unit to the next. More specifically, the battalions and *abteilungen* are designated with Roman numerals, while one level down, the companies are designated with Arabic numerals. Moving further down, the platoons (*zug*) are designated with Roman numerals, while moving one level above battalions, the regiments are designated with Arabic numerals; for example, *III./FschJgRgt.1* denotes the 3rd Battalion of the 1st *Fallschirmjäger* Regiment, *5./FschJgRgt.2* denotes the 5th Company of the 2nd *Fallschirmjäger* Regiment and *III. Zug 14* denotes the 3rd Platoon of the 14th Company.

In the *Luftwaffe*, the term '*gruppe*' was a unit comprised of three squadrons. Each *gruppe* was designated by a Roman numeral (I, II, III, IV), followed by the abbreviated *geschwader* (combat wing) designation; for example, *II/ZG 26* means *II Gruppe* of *Zerstörergeschwader 26*.

# Introduction

The storm of the Second World War arrived over Greece on 28 October 1940 and began with the Greek word '*OXI*'.[1] This was the answer the Greek prime minister, Ioannis Metaxas, gave to the Italian ambassador when the latter asked for unopposed entry of Italian troops into Greek territory; however, the war with Greece did not develop according to Mussolini's plans and by the spring of 1941, the Italians were on the defensive and in retreat – having completely lost the initiative to the Greek Army.

At this stage of the war, the Germans were busy preparing for the invasion of the Soviet Union, but they were also forced to keep an eye on their Italian allies, who appeared to require German assistance in both North Africa and Greece. To bolster their faltering ally, the German Army invaded Greece on 6 April 1941 and had, in a few days, managed to break the exhausted Greek defence. Where this was not possible, the Greek defences were outflanked, as German forces cut through Yugoslavia and Bulgaria. Within a short time, the Germans entered Athens (27 April 1941) and on 26 April, the first paratroop operation in Greece took place at Corinth, where the men of the *FschJgRgt.2* occupied the Corinth Canal. Despite this success, the operation did not succeed in blocking the escape route of the retreating Allied troops.

After the Germans had broken through the main line of Greek defences – and especially the outflanking of the Metaxas Line – the Greek Army was in a state of disintegration; however, despite the difficulty of the situation – and on the initiative of their officers – some units managed to flee to Crete after retreating through the islands of the Aegean and Peloponnese. The Greek Army General Staff had also very wisely transferred to Crete all new recruits from training camps in central Greece. The V Division of Crete – consisting of Cretan soldiers – had unfortunately remained on the mainland and could not be dispatched to Crete. The Allied force – comprising British and Commonwealth troops – had very effectively retreated through the Greek mainland, and many of these men now found themselves on Crete preparing the defence of the island.

On 29 April, General Freyberg – commander of the New Zealand Division – arrived on Crete with his staff aboard the British cruiser HMS *Ajax*. The next day, Freyberg was appointed commander of Allied forces on Crete (CREFORCE) by General Wavell, the commander-in-chief Middle East. From the first day of his new duties, Freyberg understood the difficulties of his assigned mission, as well as being aware of the severe shortages of supplies and, more importantly, of weapons and communication facilities.

The defence of the island was assigned to four combat groups allocated to the sectors of Heraklion, Souda-Chania, Maleme and Rethymnon, with the defence focused on the north coast, where the larger towns with airfields and ports were located. Immediately upon their arrival on the island, the Allied forces began their efforts to improve the infrastructure and strengthen their defensive positions, despite continuous strafing and bombing by the *Luftwaffe*. Fresh British and Commonwealth forces also arrived, with Freyberg's command reaching a total of 1,512 officers and 30,000 NCOs and soldiers by the day of the invasion.

On 16 May, Freyberg reported that his defence plan for Crete was complete and that he was very optimistic about the outcome of the approaching battle. Since 4 May, the Greek Ministry of

1 Pronounced 'OCHI' – meaning 'NO'.

the Army had divided Crete into four military districts, as follows: District I in Chania, District II in Rethymnon, District III in Heraklion and District IV in Neapolis. Each district had, under its command, training battalions, regimental depots, garrison posts and *gendarmerie* units. On 9 May, the 1st and 2nd Greek Military Commands were established, with the 1st comprising Districts I and II and the 2nd made up of Districts III and IV. All these units and commands were subordinated to the British commander in each sector. In total, the Greek Army force on the island was 474 officers and 11,000 enlisted men; Greek units deployed in the Heraklion sector were the Regimental Depot Battalion,[2] the 3rd and 7th Infantry Regiments[3] and local *gendarmerie* units.

Command of the Allied forces in Heraklion was assigned to Brigadier B.H. Chapell, the CO of the 14th Infantry Brigade, with the following units: the 2nd Battalion of the Leicestershire Regiment; the 2nd Battalion of the York & Lancaster Regiment; the 2nd Battalion of the Black Watch Regiment; and the 2/4 Australian Infantry Battalion. On the evening of 19 May, the 1st Battalion of the Argyll & Sutherland Highlanders arrived at Tymbaki, accompanied by three medium tanks. This force remained close to the south coast of the island.

Artillery units in the Heraklion sector were the 234th Medium Battery, Royal Artillery, with 13 Italian and French 75mm and 100mm guns; one section with two 4" guns of the 15th Coastal Regiment, Royal Artillery; six 40mm Bofors guns of the 7th Australian Light Anti-Aircraft Battery; four Bofors guns from the 156th Light Anti-Aircraft Battery, Royal Artillery; four 3" guns from 'C' Heavy Anti-Aircraft Battery, Royal Marines; and a section of the 23rd Light Anti-Aircraft Battery, Royal Marines. The 7th Medium Regiment, Royal Artillery was positioned and used as infantry. The above-mentioned forces were supplemented and supported by other small auxiliary units, such as engineers and medical services. There were some RAF units on the island with a small number of mostly outdated fighters, which had suffered losses and damage during bombing raids and in air combat before the battle. On 19 May, the few remaining aircraft departed for Egypt.

In December 1940, a *Führer* Directive had ordered that the British strongholds on the Greek islands should be occupied by the use of paratroopers. By 15 April, the operational plan for the invasion of Crete had been completed by *General* Kurt Student's *XI Fliegerkorps* and submitted through the *IV Luftflotte* of *General* Alexander Löhr to the commander-in-chief of the *Luftwaffe*, *Reich* Field Marshal Göring. Hitler gave final approval on 25 April with the issue of Directive No.28 for Operation '*Merkur*'. Operational command was assigned to *General* Löhr, while further planning and the execution of the operation was passed to *General* Student (the commander of the *XI Fliegerkorps*). The *VIII Fliegerkorps*, under *General* Wolfram von Richthofen, was assigned the air support operations, while logistical support and the transport of the required forces was the responsibility of *Generalmajor* Conrad. Logistical support for this operation was extremely complex, as all the men and their equipment would have to be transferred by train from Germany to Greece. Equipment included vehicles and even the gliders, which were disassembled and packed for transportation by train. Suitable airfields and camps had to be found or created from scratch in Greece, and the required amounts of fuel, ammunition and supplies were to be stockpiled ready for use.

The staff of the *OKW*[4] - and especially the army – did not approve of the operation proceeding totally under *Luftwaffe* control. It was felt that the *Luftwaffe* staff was inexperienced and not properly trained for ground operations of this scale. As events were to demonstrate, the army was

2 Garrison Battalion.

3 Each of these Greek regiments was more like a reinforced battalion – consisting mainly of a recruit battalion and supplemented by some additional companies – having a total strength of approximately 700-800 men. Each regiment also had 10 outdated Saint Etienne machine guns.

4 *Oberkommando der Wehrmacht* (*Wehrmacht* High Command).

probably right, but this was only proven some days later, when losses mounted and the battle was heading towards disaster during the first two days of the operation.

The units allocated for the invasion were: the airborne forces of *General* Student's *XI Fliegerkorps* (comprising the *Flieger*[5] *Division.7* and the *Sturmregiment*); air transport elements of *XI Fliegerkorps* under *Generalmajor* Conrad; and the 5.*Gebirgs* Division – reinforced by units from the 6.*Gebirgs* Division[6] (both under the command of *Generalmajor* Julius Ringel). The air assault would be launched by 750 men in gliders and 10,000 more dropped by parachute. After capturing and securing the airfields and ports of Maleme/Chania, Rethymnon and Heraklion on the first day, 7,000 more troops from the mountain divisions would arrive by sea and 5,000 more would be landed on the airfields on the second day. This was the plan.

Air transport and support missions would be conducted by 600 transports, 100 gliders, 180 fighters, 150 dive-bombers, 280 bombers and 60 reconnaisance planes. For the sealift, 70 vessels were assembled under the protection of a small number of Italian destroyers. Three assault groups were formed for the attack: *Gruppe West* – codenamed '*Komet*' – tasked with capturing Maleme Airfield; *Gruppe Mitte* – codenamed '*Mars*' – ordered to capture Chania, Souda and Rethymnon; and *Gruppe Ost* – codenamed '*Orion*' – whose mission was to capture the town, port and airfield of Heraklion. The 1st Parachute Regiment (*FschJgRgt.1*), with the 7th and 8th Companies of the 2nd Parachute Regiment (*FschJgRgt.2*) – supported by machine gun and medical units – were under the command[7] of *Oberst* Bruno Bräuer and formed *Gruppe Ost*. Topolia and Tanagra Airfields were the assembly and starting points for the forces of *Gruppe Ost*, which had been dispersed at various camps and airfields around Athens.

The supporting naval forces of *Admiral* Karlgeorg Schüster were to carry the mountain troops, heavy guns, vehicles and tanks. The fleet was actually a collection of Greek steamers, caiques and minor Italian warships. According to the operational plan, two convoys were to be formed – escorted by Italian destroyers. The intention was for the first convoy to arrive in Maleme on 21 May and the second to arrive at Heraklion 24 hours later. The Germans occupied the island of Milos (just 80 miles north of Crete) for use as a naval base and as an assembly point for the convoys.

Since 16 April, the *VIII Fliegerkorps* had been intensively active over the Aegean Sea – interdicting any movement by sea and making communication between the islands and the mainland extremely difficult. Crete could be reached only under the cover of darkness and the island was essentially isolated. Since 14 May, a systematic bombing and strafing campaign had attacked the island's defensive positions and infrastructure. Continued bombing of the island by the *Luftwaffe* no doubt strengthened the belief of the Cretan population that the Germans were an enemy who should be opposed by any means possible. In addition, the rest of the country had already been occupied and Crete appeared to be the Greeks' last hope for freedom and for continuing the fight against the enemy of the motherland.

On the eve of the battle, both sides appeared ready for what may come. The Greeks, both soldiers and civilians – with their long martial tradition dating from ancient times – were eager to face the invaders; the battle would be just one more to add to the thousands fought through Greece's long history. The British, whose soldiers enjoyed a reputation for toughness, probably wanted to avenge their retreat through Greece's mainland and teach the 'Jerries' a lesson. The Germans, with their iron discipline and strong sense of duty, were ready to follow their leaders and prove once and

5 7th Airborne Division.

6 Both of these divisions comprised mountain troops. The units from the 6th Division were mainly AA and field artillery units.

7 According to the initial planning, the commander of *Gruppe Ost* was General Ringel of the mountain troops, but in the end, he and his forces were deployed in the Maleme-Chania area.

for all their fighting quality and the value of their lengthy and highly demanding training. The German Staff's estimation was that in the first two days, all the operation's main goals would have been achieved, given that the few demoralised British and Greek forces would not be able to offer any serious resistance. The testing time finally arrived on the morning of 20 May; the soldiers now had to face the steel of their enemy's weapons. Epic stories of past battles heard during training and preparation were now to give way to a reality where death was as much a prospect as glory.

# 1
# Destination Crete

"TO CRETE!" This was the decision – and the final destination – of the young Greek infantry lieutenant Theodoros E. Kallinos on 13 April 1941, while he was on the island of Chios. There he was informed that having broken the Greek Army defensive lines, the German forces were advancing on the mainland of Greece.

In April 1941, during the German attack against northern Greece, Lieutenant Kallinos was a company commander in Fortress Kali on the Metaxas Line. At 0200 on 9 April, when the commanding officer of the fortress announced to him via telephone that the city of Salonika had been occupied by the Germans and there was no choice left other than to surrender, Kallinos answered: "I will not surrender, nor have I the right to leave my company to the Germans. I still have 20,000 cartridges for each machine gun. Either we will fight till the last bullet, or we will march southwards in order to fight in a new defensive line."

On the morning of 9 April at 0800, Kallinos and his company set off for Agion Oros (Mount Athos). They arrived at the harbour of Dafni after four days of marching from the Metaxas Line – having managed to avoid the German units advancing in the area (see Map 1.1). There, Kallinos was informed that the Germans were not very far from Athens, so he decided to go even further south – to the island of Crete – in order to continue the fight. In small boats, they passed in succession from Mount Athos to the island of Lemnos and then to Lesvos – finally ending up in Chios. There, apart from Kallinos' men, 300 more soldiers and officers arrived progressively – many of them managing to reach Crete as a result of Lieutenant Colonel Kitsos' initiative. As Kallinos knew about the presence of the *Luftwaffe* over the Aegean Sea, he understood that the trip to Crete was very dangerous for his men.

Having in mind the German statement from an Athens radio station that Greek soldiers were not considered prisoners – and so were free to return to their families – he addressed his soldiers:

> Officers, NCOs and soldiers: I didn't leave you to the Germans in the front line and I brought you all here to Chios. I gave an oath as a cadet in 1933, and then again as a 2nd lieutenant in 1937, to defend the homeland even with my blood. I must not forget the oath that I gave and I will go to Crete to defend our country. You are conscripts and you have served the homeland very bravely so far, but now you must return to your families that are waiting for you.

Then the soldiers shouted: "All together to Crete!" and Kallinos ordered: "ATTENTION! I give you a direct order to return to your families and there you will have the chance to work and fight for the freedom of our country. I will go to Crete, which will be a stronghold and the turning point for the freedom of all of Greece."

Kallinos' soldiers boarded two big caiques destined for Euboea and Peloponnese. Kallinos himself, along with Sergeant Ioannis Papageorgopoulos from Argos (who had refused to obey the order to return to his home), Lieutenant Avlitis and a Cretan major with 15 more Cretan soldiers, set out for Crete in a small motorboat. They reached the island of Tinos before dawn and the next

**Special Presentation I: Theodoros E. Kallinos**

Theodoros E. Kallinos here as a young lieutenant in 1941. (Author's collection)

Theodoros E. Kallinos (1914-2014) was born in Tsaritsani Elassonas and graduated from the 'Evelpidon' Military Academy in 1937. He assumed duties as a company commander in the 19th Infantry Regiment in Serres, where he remained until 1939, when he was transferred to Fortress Kali on the Metaxas Line.

During the Battle of Crete, he was a company commander in Heraklion and he led his men in battle against the *I./FschJgRgt.1* on the hills east of the airfield in the area of Gournes. Being at the point of the counterattack against the paratroopers on Kopsas Hill, he managed to defeat the Germans and change the outcome of the battle. Many years later, he used to say: "I still cannot understand how I wasn't killed during this charge, where I was totally exposed to the German fire."

During the German occupation of Greece (1941-1944), Kallinos joined the Resistance and he participated in the struggle against the Germans. Although he was never arrested, he was sentenced to death by an Italian court martial, while his father and his three younger brothers were jailed.

In the early post-war period in Greece, he was involved in the turbulence of the civil war. In 1947, he was discharged from the army; finally, he officially retired in 1962 as a colonel. After the war, he continued his struggle for democracy and Greek Independence; even at the age of 97, he used to say: "Why am I continuing my struggle at this age? Because I deeply believe that as long as the mind works, one must keep on fighting for his ideas."

night, they passed Naxos and then proceeded to Santorini (Thera). Since the boat was not able to cover the distance from Santorini to Crete during the night and before the following dawn, the captain of the boat refused to go to Crete – fearing the *Luftwaffe* was sinking everything that approached Crete during daylight. After the Cretan major threatened the captain and forced him to take them to the island, they finally departed and disembarked on a beach east of Heraklion (near Chersonnisos).

In Heraklion, Lieutenant Kallinos presented himself to Major Kasimatis from the Regimental Depot Battalion and he was assigned the role of organising a company comprising mainly local soldiers. One week later, Kallinos' company marched flawlessly along the main road of Heraklion in front of the Heraklion Guard HQ – in the town centre – with an astonished Major Kasimatis watching from the balcony. After that display, Kasimatis assigned Kallinos' company to cover the town and the airfield from the east against possible landings by sea or air. During the night of 19/20 May, Kallinos' company settled into defensive positions on Kako Oros Hill and prepared for battle.[1]

1 Interview with the author, April 2012.

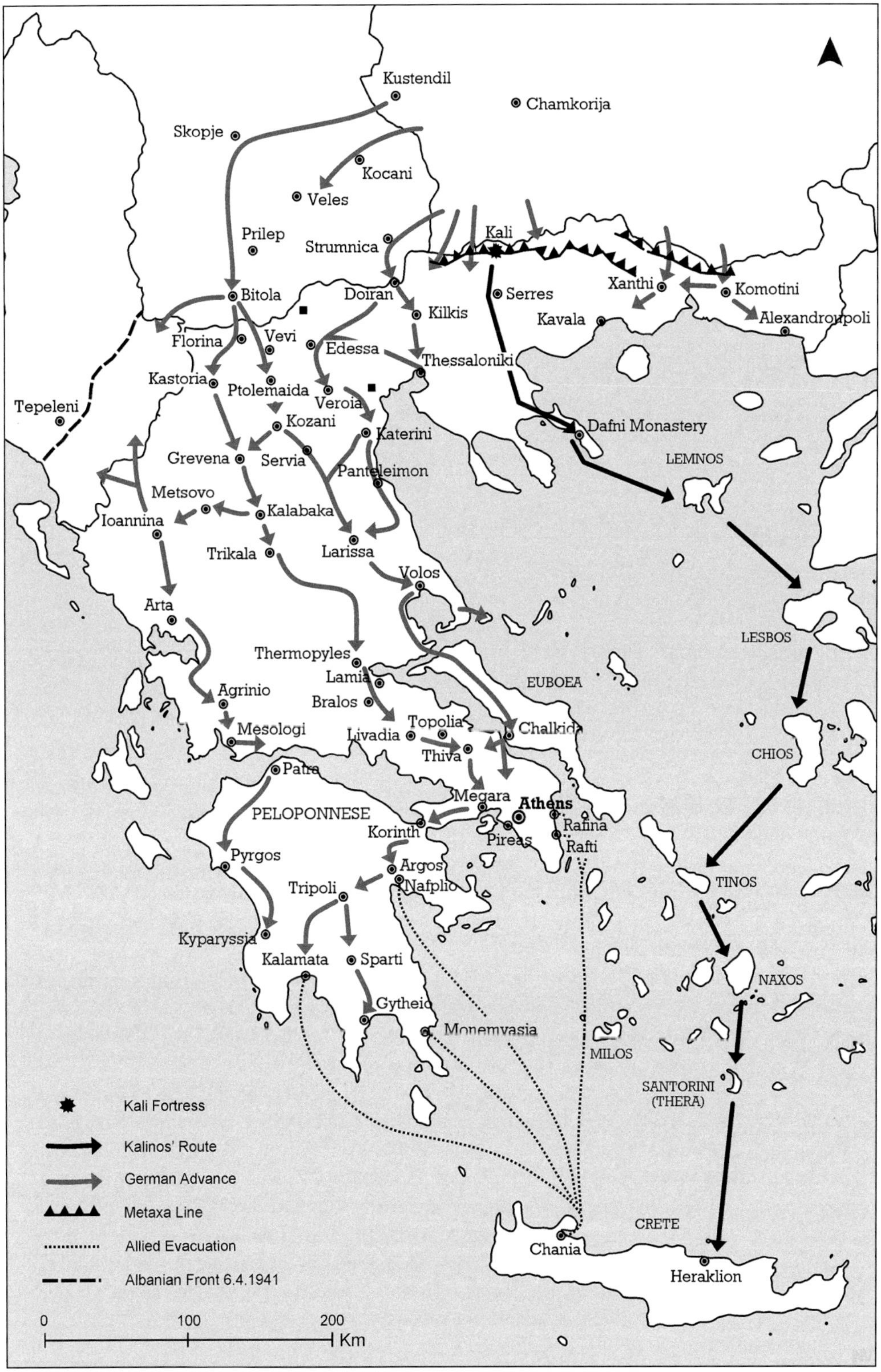


Map 1.1 The Greek Front in April 1941 and Lieutenant Kallinos' route. (N. Valasiadis, 2015)

The HQ building of the Heraklion Guard and Regimental Depot Battalion (right) in the centre of Heraklion. Opposite to it (left) is the Dialynas Building. (Author's collection)

> Attention all passengers: the mountains away on the horizon and the villages that can barely be seen are Crete. Yes, now you all know that our final destination is Crete. In a while, we will get off in the big harbour of Souda Bay. The city of Chania is just five kilometres away from Souda.

The announcement by the captain of the boat that transported the Greek soldiers from Nafplion (in Peloponnese) echoed throughout the boat and on the upper decks. It was the morning of 20 April 1941: the day of the Orthodox Easter.

Among the recruits was Private Christos Roussopoulos, who had set out on 3 April from his village, Neo Cheimonio, in Thrace. Now, for the first time, he heard that he was heading to Crete. Christos Roussopoulos recorded in his diary:

> We all began climbing like ants onto the upper deck from each of the boat's hatches and finally there didn't remain even one inch of empty space on the deck. As the time passed, the mountains came closer to us. We could see very clearly a few villages. The sea was full of boats from the convoy, four cargo and three warships. From the soldiers who stayed all night on the upper deck we heard that during the night the alarm was raised three times and each time they had to lie on the deck in order to make room for the anti-aircraft guns and the gunners.
>
> After a while we entered the big natural harbour of Souda. It looked like the entire war fleet of Greece had been assembled there. From a distance it was not possible to see their names but the guns on the bow, the stern and on the sides could be clearly seen. In the harbour there were also submarines and even hydroplanes and many cargo ships [...]

[...] As soon as the companies began leaving the harbour, the alarm sirens started sounding and right away the anti-aircraft guns both from the shore and the warships opened fire. German *Stukas* appeared in the sky like little swallows. We were ordered to scatter. We scattered, everyone finding and lying down in a trench. The German planes were flying in circles high in the sky and some of them were diving, then releasing their bombs above the harbour. Two of the aircraft were hit and crashed far away while one ship in the harbour was on fire.

Private Christos Roussopoulos in 1941. (Courtesy of the Society of Cretan Historical Studies)

Things quietened for a moment and we came out of the trenches. We dusted the thorns from our clothes and we began laughing, pointing at some lads, in order to show that we were not afraid at all. It was pure hypocrisy. The truth was that we had been afraid, and very much so indeed. Then we were assembled again in our platoons and companies [...]

[...] On 21 April at 9 p.m. we were assembled again. We were told that the next morning we were to leave on foot for Heraklion. That night indeed we didn't see anyone drunk. The songs and the discussions continued into the late evening. Finally, 22 April dawned. In the camp there weren't any bugles, nor loudspeakers, so all the announcements were made with a loud voice. At 6 a.m. we were told to start packing our things. At 7 a.m. we were given some bread, a little cheese and a few olives. As soon as the distribution had been finished, we were again assembled in our companies and after a while we were given the order to march [...]

[...] Today, 23 April, is the celebration of Saint George but none of my friends has the name Giorgos [George] to wish him well... In the street we saw empty English vehicles. I suppose that they were going to pick up the English soldiers marching to Heraklion as well. As soon as we walked down the slope of the last hill, the city of Heraklion appeared. Even from a distance it looks like it is one of the biggest cities of Greece.

The town of Heraklion is surrounded by big walls that were built by the Venetians. At the point where the road from Chania meets these walls there is a gate like an arch. It is called 'The door to Chania'. We turned right and after a short distance we got off the roads. On the walls there were old wooden buildings used as barracks. After a while more English lorries came, bringing the rest of the troops. The officers told us that they didn't ask the English to transport us by lorries in order not to show that we were afraid to walk. When the night fell we entered those old barracks to sleep but in an hour we all went out to escape from the bugs and we lay down outside the buildings [...]

[...] Today is 5 May. Early in the morning we assembled in platoons with our belongings and waited in lines. We passed through the city... In a short time we passed outside the barracks of the 43rd Greek Infantry Regiment of the V 'Crete' Division. Those barracks are now given to our English allies so we camped in the fields under the olive trees and under the sky and the stars. We were lucky and it didn't rain. After a while we passed the airport of Heraklion which is full of English soldiers with their anti-aircraft guns, surrounded by sandbags for protection from the bombs falling on the airfield. At the end of the airfield there is a down-slope with a small church in a cave and then the valley of Karteros. Far away on the opposite side of the valley there is a mountain with strange black stones. We have the impression that this is an 'evil mountain' and we are right since this mountain is called Kako

Oros (Evil Mountain). There, at the foothill of this mountain we stopped. Each company was assigned to cover a certain area away from the other companies and each platoon respectively away from the other platoons of the company.

When the German bombers come and bomb the airfield, they leave flying over the slopes of this mountain right above our positions. While they fly over us, the English anti-aircraft guns keep firing and the shrapnel from the shells falls on us. The officers tell us to build trenches covered with stones [...]

[...] Even from the first day some are wounded, fortunately not badly. We improve the trenches by putting flat stones above our heads. The bombings occur many times during the day and the officers advise us not to walk around without reason.

One day while the aircraft were leaving two of them were hit and I saw them crashing into the sea.[2] The next day pieces from the planes along with four corpses of the crew members were washed ashore on the sandy beach.[3] The next day, the guys from our company who went to Heraklion for supplies saw the entire ceremony of their burial by the Greek authorities. An honour guard even presented arms and fired a farewell salute. According to international law a proper burial should be given to each soldier, even for enemies when they fall doing their duty. Greece totally conforms to those rules [...]

[...] Today is 16 May. During an afternoon bombing raid some of our aircraft, those old types with double wings, were scrambled together with some English aircraft. A dogfight began in the sky right over our heads. The sky was full of noises from the engines of the planes and the firing of the machine guns. We found the courage to come out of our trenches in order to see this not so pleasant 'spectacle'. They played like sparrows that play thieves and policemen except that those twit pleasantly, while the planes roar and spew hot metal. In time they were so mixed up that we couldn't say which was a friend and which was the enemy. Suddenly a plane was on fire. White smoke and red flames sparkled in the sunlight. We began cheering, believing that it was a German plane. From the smoke a white object like a handkerchief appeared. Soon this handkerchief took the shape of a small white umbrella and under this was hanging a black spot like a mouse. The flame became stronger and a trail of smoke was left. The plane began to fall and crashed very far from us, behind some hills. The umbrella was getting bigger and we clearly saw that it was the pilot of the plane.

The officers took the opportunity to explain to us that the German paratroopers would arrive the same way. We started shouting 'At arms!' in order to arrest the German who jumped and descended to the ground. Our officers stopped us and said that he landed a long way from us in other company areas and they were going to take care of him. Some hours later we were told that when the pilot landed and the Greek soldiers shouted 'Halt!', he responded, 'English, English', so it turned out that he was English and the plane was English as well. Up to the evening we had two more bombing raids on the airfield. During the following hours we were instructed on how to deal with the paratroopers. We were told that it was certain that the Germans were planning to attack in order to occupy Crete. From now on we are on alert day and night and ready with guns in hand [...][4]

2 This was the plane of *Oberleutnant* Sophus Baagoe, who was shot and crashed into the sea on 14 May. Baagoe was a *Luftwaffe* ace with 14 aerial victories. He was posthumously awarded the Knight's Cross on 14 June 1941. He is one of the two pilots credited with the kill of the RAF top ace Pat Marmaduke Pattle. Baagoe was serving with *8./ZG 26* – flying Bf 110 D-3 (W.Nr. 4290). His gunner, *Oberfeldwebel* Daniel Becker, was also killed.

3 The beach of Karteros (East Beach), east of the airfield.

4 C. Roussopoulos, *The Battle of Crete - Testimonies 5*, pp.48-73.

**Special Presentation 2: David Hutton**

David Hutton, 'A' Coy, 2nd Bn, BW. (Courtesy of David Hutton)

David Hutton was born in 1917 in Liff, near Dundee. His grandfather had also served in the Black Watch. He left school at 14 to start work initially at a market garden in Liff; then on a poultry farm, but at the age of 16, he decided to join the army.

Having been turned down by the Royal Scots Greys due to being under 18, he went to another recruiting office, lied about his age and was taken on by the Black Watch in 1934 at the age of 17. He was sent to Palestine with the 2nd Battalion and later, he was promoted to corporal and sent to Somaliland; then to Egypt and finally, to Crete. Hutton and his platoon leader, Lieutenant Michael Fairly, were seriously injured during an attack on the second day of the battle, while their machine gunner, Private James Reekie, was killed. Hutton was transferred to a field hospital in Villa Ariadne in Knossos, where after the battle, he was taken prisoner by the Germans. He was then transferred to a POW camp in Germany, where he remained for the rest of the war.

David Hutton from 'A' Company, 2nd Battalion of the Black Watch Regiment recalls:

> I had joined the army before World War Two. I joined in 1934 and knew that I would be engaged in battles overseas. We were moved from Somaliland back to Egypt for desert training at the end of 1940. We did not know why or where we would need these skills; everything was kept secret. It was around February/March 1941 when one morning, we were told to collect our belongings; we were always ready to be deployed somewhere at a moment's notice.
>
> We were loaded onto trucks to move from Cairo to Alexandria. In Alexandria, we boarded HMS *York* and we sailed at dawn. About half way across the Mediterranean Sea, we were attacked by two torpedo-carrying aircraft: they missed us! We arrived in Souda Bay and moved into the village of Galatas. We dug trenches around the hill overlooking Souda Bay. We were later transferred to Heraklion and continued to dig trenches along the coast, as it was thought the Germans would attack from the sea. We were well trained for the job – therefore, going to Crete was part of the job we had signed up to do. We were relatively comfortable going into hotspots, maybe a little apprehensive. We had three years' experience of war in Palestine and extensive battles in Somaliland before moving to Crete, so we just got on with the job.[5]

5 Interview with – and letter to – the author, November 2013.

> '*KRETA!*' The decision was announced as soon as the company commanders came out of the commanding officer's tent. Only one night is left and tomorrow we begin against the enemy at last. A general agitation prevails in the camp. The messengers come and go from everywhere carrying last minute orders. Afterwards, briefings about the operation follow. The island of Crete is roughly 260 km long and 30 to 40 km wide and will be invaded by air.
>
> Paratroopers are going to be used with strong air support. Since the English forces with the remaining Greek soldiers have been on the island for many months, strong resistance is expected. It is likely that the Royal Navy will try to impede our flight to the island. Our regiment [*FschJgRgt.1*] has as its mission the occupation of the town of Heraklion and the airfield east of the city. Heraklion has a population of 40,000 and it is the biggest town on the island. We will be dropped east of the airfield with the task of occupying a radio station almost 12 km from the town. Everything is clear. Everything will go well. When evening fell in the camp calm prevails. It is not possible to sleep. Thoughts hang around in my mind. One year before, in exactly the same month, we were heading to Narvik. Tomorrow we will jump on Crete! Thousands of kilometres separate these two places. In the north, rocks, ice and sleet. Here, tropical heat, dry landscape with sandy and dry areas and fields. I wonder what 20 May 1941 is going to bring? Will I taste victory? Or will my comrades dig a grave for me?[6]

These were the thoughts of NCO Dr Günther Müller of *FschJgRgt.1's* sanitary unit on the eve of the battle.

Paratroopers carrying a map of Crete during Operation '*Merkur*'. (G. Müller & F. Scheuering, *Sprung über Kreta*)

6 G. Müller & F. Scheuering, *Sprung über Kreta*, p.42.

### Special Presentation 3: Dr Günther Müller

Dr Günther Müller. (Author's archive)

Dr Günther Müller (1911-1962) served in the *FschJgRgt.1* from 1939 in Poland until 1943 on the Eastern Front. From 1 March 1943, he served with the 2nd *FschJg* Division in Russia and in Italy. He was taken prisoner by the Americans on 18 September 1944 in Brest, France along with the famous *fallschirmjäger general* and veteran of the Prison Valley battle, Bernhard Ramcke. He was released from captivity on 19 September 1946.

In addition to his duties as a medical NCO, Müller used his camera to record the battle east of the airfield in the area of the command post of the *FschJgRgt.1*. Later, with Fritz Scheuering, he wrote a book describing their memories of – and experiences in – the battle, titled *Sprung über Kreta* (*Jump Over Crete*), which was published in 1944. Today, this book is one of the main sources for the battle in Heraklion – and especially for the area east of the airfield.

*Sprung über Kreta* and *Sieg der Kühnsten* were the two main books about the Battle of Crete published during the war. They are both excellent sources of pictures, accounts and evidence, but since they were published during the war, they were censored and, in some respects, supported German propaganda, so they must be approached with some caution. (Author's collection)

Pictures taken by Dr Günther Müller during the battle, but never published in his book. (Author's collection)

Paratrooper Gerhard Broder from the *2./ FschJgRgt.1* remembers:

Gerhard Broder. (Courtesy of Gerhard Broder)

> In Stendal[7] we are alerted that we are going to be used against Greece. We will be transported by land or air but wearing only the standard *Luftwaffe* uniform without any paratrooper insignia. The exact destination is unknown to us. The trucks are loaded on trains. The railway transport is rather cosy and comfortable. The landscape passes at a slow speed. I always find a corner in which to sleep in the wagons, on a truck or in a cargo net. The locomotives transport large troop units with great reliability over long distances. From the train I see the beautiful and fertile Hungarian land and Budapest [...]
>
> [...] We approach the Balkan Mountains at the Greek border and we drive through the Rupel[8] pass along the Sturma [Strimonas River valley] in order to reach Salonika [see Map 1.1]. In the valley immediately past the border, we meet Greek fortifications which are the so-called Metaxas Line. The concrete bunkers are similar to the Maginot Line. It strikes me that often the firing directions look backwards and the bunkers provide cover to each other. Near the bunker is a German military cemetery with birch crosses and still fresh graves. In my mind I imagine the attack of the *Gebirgsjäger* [German mountain troops] and the conquest of the fortifications. Soon we reach Salonika at last... The convoy continues further to the gulf of Thermaikos and to the south [...]
>
> [...] At the beach, in the gulf of Volos or perhaps the gulf of Euboea, we build an idyllic camp. Some drivers have captured a turtle and they have drilled a hole on the shell. The animal is tethered on a cord and it grazes in grass. We knock the sand in front of our tents gently with sticks, to drive away any snakes. The sea is beautiful and the water is clear. I experience the idyllic beauty of the southern landscape [...]
>
> [...] But now the idyll in the gulf is over and it has been replaced by the operational orders. Aerial photographs have been distributed to the company and it has been officially announced that the Greek island of Crete is going to be captured by an airborne assault. This island lies in the eastern Mediterranean Sea, its waters are controlled by the British fleet and it has approximately 480,000 inhabitants [...]
>
> [...] Our company is in the second wave of the attack and our mission is to neutralise the anti-aircraft guns and then attack and secure Heraklion's airfield from the east. According to the aerial photographs, the approach will be over a small island near the coast [the island of Dia]. Crete will be approached in a low altitude flight over the sea and the jump will take place over the coastal road at a height of approximately 80 metres. After a fall of 30 metres, when the canopy is deployed, the speed of descent will be 5-8 metres per second. In this phase the defenceless paratrooper will be exposed to the enemy, but for only a very short time.[9]

7 The training school and the German paratroopers' barracks were in Stendal.
8 Rupel is a fortress on the Metaxas Line.
9 G. Broder, *Guerre Mondiale Contre Moi*, pp.74-81.

German paratroopers at the Topolia Camp, just before the battle. (Courtesy of Dimitris Skartsilakis)

Men of the *2./FschSanAbt.7* at Megara Airfield in a relaxed moment, just before the battle. *Gefreiter* Otto Loop – pictured here sitting second from the left – was killed in Heraklion on 27 May, just a few days after this photo was taken. (Courtesy of Jose Ramon Artaza Ivañez)

Men of the *11./FschJgRgt.1* photographed a few days before the invasion. Half of them were killed on the first day of the battle. Seen here (from left to right): Fleischhauer, *Jäger* Alfred Lange (KIA 20.05.1941), *Gefreiter* Otto Erlhöfer (KIA 26.05.1941), *Oberjäger* Johann Brüns (KIA 20.05.1941), Gottwald, *Gefreiter* Walter Hoppe (KIA 20.05.1941), *Jäger* Wilhelm Dorfner (KIA 20.05.1941) and Harmuth. (Courtesy of Dr Eberhard Boerger)

*Oberleutnant* Wolfgang *Graf* von Blücher of the *2./FschJgRgt.1* wrote to his mother just a few days before the battle:

> *On the way in Hungary*
> *L 33450, LGP. Vienna, 3.5.1941*
> [Posted from Athens on 19 May 1941]
>
> My beloved Mother,
> I have to thank you for your letter of the 24th [April], which I received before our departure. At the moment we are in very good spirits. I know from last year the excitement of preparing for action, but you should see Lebs [Lebrecht] and Jochen [Hans Joachim]![10] Their delight in being soldiers is even stronger than previously. However, I am only guessing about Lebs, because the last time I met him was in Tangermünde. I think I mentioned that to you already. It will probably be a long time before you receive this letter, because it will only be sent to you from the place where we leave for our mission. A year ago it was Dortmund![11] More than eight days ago we were ordered from Altengrabow ahead of schedule and we left Stendal on the morning of 4 April. Lebs had already left two days earlier.
>
> Hatta [stepfather] phoned me at Stendal one or two days beforehand and learned that we are still there! I can imagine that you thought that we had arrived in Greece after listening to the special announcements[12] on the radio. But unfortunately this is not the case. We strongly hope that our mission will come about and that we can push the Tommies [British troops] somewhere else [. . .]
>
> [...] I cannot send home information, as I have a feeling that the mission might begin very soon. One has to obey the rules of secrecy. So I will end. A thousand best wishes to all of you and a big kiss for you,
>
> Yours
> Wölfe[13]

Nobody could imagine what fate awaited the three brothers, just two days after the letter was sent.

*Oberleutnant* Wolfgang *Graf* von Blücher. (Courtesy of the von Blücher family)

10 The two younger brothers of Wolfgang were also in the *FschJgRgt.1* and participated in the Battle of Heraklion.

11 He refers to the operation in Holland in May 1940 – during which Wolfgang *Graf* von Blücher was awarded the Knight's Cross.

12 The first paratroopers' operation in Greece took place in Corinth on 26 April, where the men of the *FschJgRgt.2* occupied the Corinth Canal.

13 Adrian Nisbett Archive.

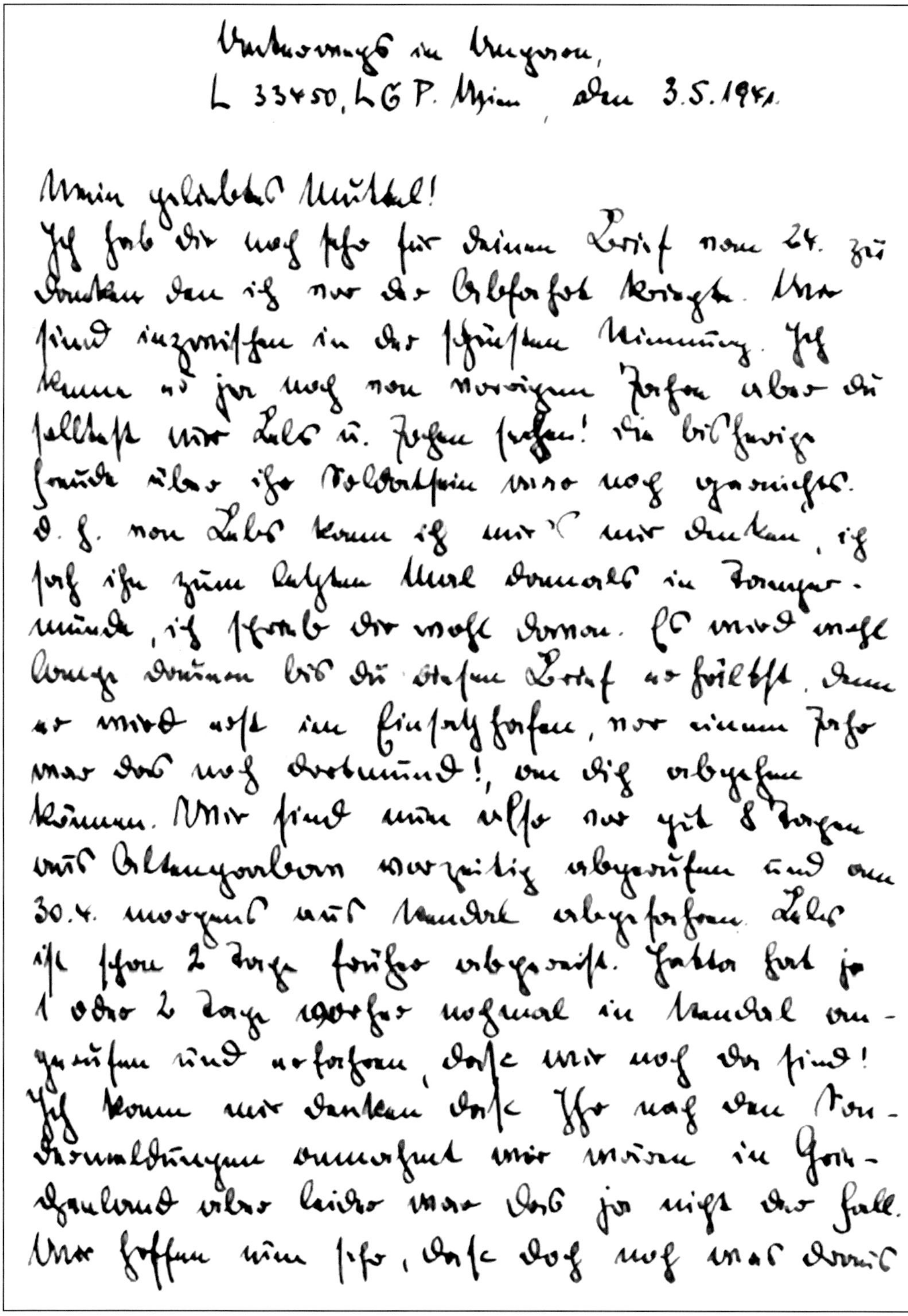

Unterwegs in Ungarn,
L 33450, LGP. Wien, den 3.5.1941.

Mein geliebtes Muttel!
Ich hab Dir noch sehr für Deinen Brief vom 24. zu danken den ich vor der Abfahrt kriegte. Wir sind inzwischen in der schönsten Stimmung. Ich kenne es ja noch vom vorigen Jahre aber Du solltest mal Lolo u. Jochen sehen! Die bisherige Laune über ihr Soldatsein war noch gemischt. D.h. von Lolo kann ich mir's nur denken, ich sah ihn zum letzten Mal damals in Travemünde, ich schrieb Dir wohl davon. Es wird wohl lange dauern bis Du diesen Brief erhältst, denn er wird erst im Einsatzhafen, vor einem Jahr war das noch Dortmund!, an Dich abgehen können. Wir sind nun also vor gut 8 Tagen aus [illegible] vorzeitig abgerufen und am 30.4. morgens aus [illegible] abgefahren. Lolo ist schon 2 Tage früher abgereist. [illegible] hat ja 1 oder 2 Tage vorher nochmal in [illegible] angerufen und erfahren, dass wir noch da sind! Ich kann mir denken dass Ihr nach den Sondermeldungen annahmt wir wären in Griechenland aber leider war das ja nicht der Fall. Wir hoffen nun sehr, dass doch noch was daraus

The original letter sent by *Oberleutnant* Wolfgang *Graf* von Blücher. (Courtesy of Adrian Nisbett)

**Special Presentation 4: Wolfgang *Graf* von Blücher**

*Oberleutnant* Wolfgang *Graf* von Blücher belonged to the *2./FschJgRgt.1* under *Hauptmann* Gröschke. He was from a Prussian aristocratic family with a deep military tradition, since he was related to Field Marshal Blücher, who fought Napoleon at Waterloo.

He had been awarded the Knight's Cross in May 1940 for his actions during the invasion of Holland. During the operation in Crete, he was serving in *FschJgRgt.1* along with his two younger brothers, Lebrecht and Hans Joachim.

Wolfgang *Graf* von Blücher here as a *Leutnant*. (Courtesy of the von Blücher family)

Finally, 19 May arrived. The Allied troops and the Greeks were wondering when this teasing routine of bombing and alarms was going to become a real battle. When night fell, the paratroopers gathered around bonfires – discussing the operation and thinking about what the next morning would bring. The most experienced men knew very well what it was like to jump into a real fight, while the unexperienced ones were anxious to test their courage against the enemy and prove their bravery. Despite the revelation that the paratroopers were seriously vulnerable to the enemy during several stages of previous operations, these men were the pioneers of airborne assault tactics, so no one could imagine or predict what was about to occur during the following days on Crete.

# 2

# The Invasion Begins

According to the operational plan, the assault was to be conducted in two waves, since there were just not enough transport planes available to carry all the airborne forces in only one sortie. This compromise would eliminate the element of surprise for the second wave, which according to the rehearsals and the calculations, would be dispatched some hours later than the first one.

The *XI Fliegerkorps* staff chose to dispatch first the groups with objectives in the western sectors of the island – in Maleme, Chania and Souda – while the second wave would follow later and assault Rethymnon and Heraklion. The airborne forces were divided into three groups – named according to their respective areas of deployment:

### First wave

*Gruppe West*, under *Generalmajor* Meindl: This battle group consisted mainly of the *LL-Sturm-Regiment* (minus *1./LL-Sturm-Rgt and 2./LL-Sturm-Rgt)*, the *3./FschFlaMGBtl*, *1./FschArtAbt.7* and *I. Zug/FschSanAbt.7*. They departed early in the morning (around 0600) from Eleusis Airfield to allow the first drop to be made at 0720. This group's objectives were the Maleme Airfield and the surrounding country as far as Kasteli to the west and Galatas to the east.

*Gruppe Mitte* (Middle), under *Generalleutnant* Süssmann: This battle group actually consisted of two forces split into two waves and in two different sectors: the force in the first wave included the *FschJgRgt.3*, with the 1.*/LL-Sturm-Rgt* and *2./LL-Sturm-Rgt*, *3./FschMGBtl.7*, *FschPiBtl.7*, and *1./FschSanAbt.7*. They also flew from Tanagra Airfield early in the morning, with their main objectives being the village of Galatas, the town of Chania and finally, Souda.

### Second wave

*Gruppe Mitte's* second force included *I./FschJgRgt.2*, *III./FschJgRgt.2*, *2./FschArtAbt.7*, *1./FschMGBtl.7* and *2./FschFlaMGBtl.7*. They departed from Megara Airfield at 1330 and jumped on Rethymnon between 1530 and 1630.

*Gruppe Ost*, under *Generalleutnant* Ringel (*Oberst* Bräuer was the commander of the *FschJgRgt.1*): This battle group consisted mainly of the *FschJgRgt.1*, accompanied by *II./FschJgRgt.2* (see page 60), *1./FschFlaMGBatl.7* and *2./FschSanAbt.7*. They took off from Topolia Airfield in the afternoon and jumped between 1630 and 1830[1] near Heraklion – tasked with occupying the airfield, the town, the port and the radio station in Gournes. They were also ordered to secure the coast in order to allow landing operations from the sea by the *Gebirgsjäger*.

The airborne assault was to be supported by escort fighters and bombers, whose task was to provide close air support to the paratroopers and suppress the enemy's air defences. The co-ordination of this great variety of aircraft types – all operating from different airfields and having

1 German time: the same applies for the time mentioned above for each wave.

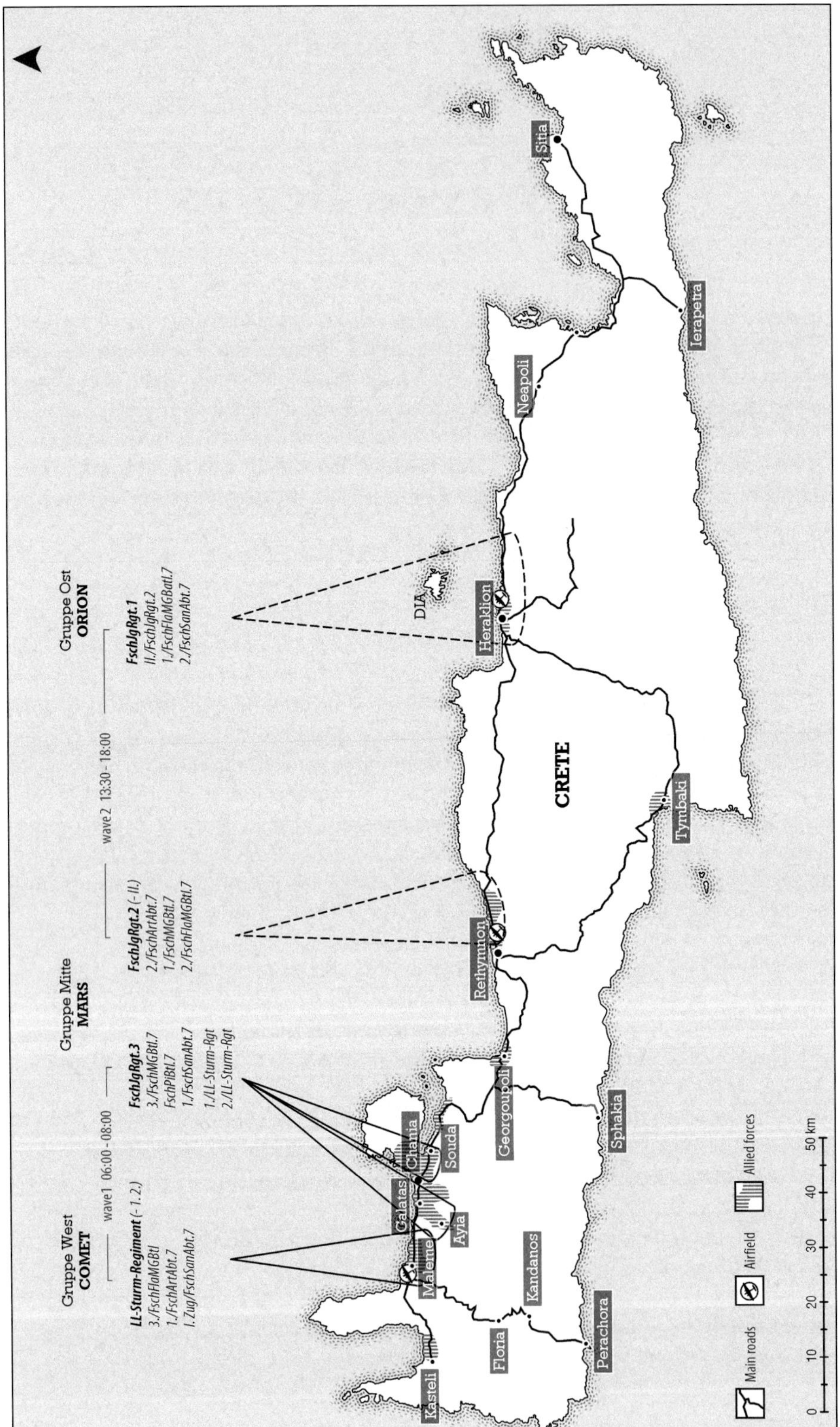


Map 2.1 The German airborne assault on 20 May 1941. (N. Valasiadis, 2015)

The airfield and the paratroopers' camp in Topolia, from which the *FschJgRgt.1* set off for Heraklion. (Courtesy of Dimitris Skartsilakis)

different times on task – was a real nightmare for the staff of the *XI Fliegerkorps.* Even today, with all the available state-of-the-art communications, this type of operation presents a high level of risk and difficulty.

Early in the morning of 20 May, in line with the operational plan, the paratroopers began their final preparations for boarding the planes. Paratrooper Bernd Bosshammer, of *5./FschJgRgt.1,* wrote in his diary:

> Early in the morning we were transferred in Opel Blitz lorries to the neighbouring airfield in Topolia. I do not feel well because of the vegetable soup and grapes that we had for breakfast. The butter is very 'heavy' in my stomach. It's already noon and we sweat in the heavy jump-smocks that we wear, carrying medicines, guns, munitions and the heavy parachute.
>
> The airfield is wrapped in a cloud of dust. We must refuel the Ju-52s, using hand pumps and 200 litre fuel barrels. Finally, the required number of planes for the transport of our company is assembled, and each platoon leaves a group behind, which later was dropped in Maleme.
>
> At around 16:00[2] we board the planes and the heat is intolerable. We take off and the planes are assembled after flying in circles over the airfield. During the flight we do not face any threat from the enemy and our fighters protect us. We fly very low above the sea, roughly 30 to 40 metres. Everything is OK![3]

2 The time zone adhered to by the Germans during the operations in Greece was German time, which was actually one hour earlier than the local time used by the British and the Greeks. In this study, only the German accounts refer to German time, while in all other cases, local time is used (unless otherwise stated).

3 B. Bosshammer's war diary, BDF e.v. Archiv, Freiburg/Breisgau.

*Oberst* Bräuer, with men of *FschJgRgt.1*, waiting for the beginning of the operation at Topolia Airfield. The preparations for the second wave took much longer than planned – causing considerable delays, which cost the paratroopers at Heraklion dearly. (Courtesy of Shaun Winkler)

Paratroopers from the *2./FschSanAbt.7* boarding a Ju-52 at Topolia. (Courtesy of Jose Ramon Artaza Ivañez)

Paratrooper Gerhard Broder, of *2./FschJgRgt.1*, described the scene:

> Hectic activity prevails on the airfield. Very early in the morning of May 20 1941 the engines roar when 500 heavily-laden Ju-52s begin their mission to the west part of the island, against the airfield of Maleme and the city of Chania. Before the paratroopers' drop, a heavy bombardment by the planes of the *VIII Fliegerkorps* takes place. We wait for the return of the Ju-52s for our dispatch as a second wave.
>
> The jump takes place in tropical temperatures but with the same uniforms and equipment as were used for icy Narvik. We were never trained how to fight in tropical conditions like these. After considering the whole situation, *Hauptmann* Gröschke [the company commander] gives the order to drink the coffee ration. Life jackets are distributed for the flight over the sea [...]
>
> Instinctively, there is scepticism among the soldiers about the extensive technical measures and organisational instructions. Are all those things going to work properly as planned? Do we rely again too much on luck? I feel very small and weak and completely dependent on fate and luck, which now cannot be stopped. However, that strengthens the feeling of self-preservation! We are ready for the mission. We have no hesitation, we feel no weakness, we do not think of possible casualties.
>
> The second wave is to depart at 13:00 and we are going to jump after a bombardment. Only seven out of the 500 Ju-52s that departed in the morning failed to return. By between 10:00 and 11:00 all the planes have landed.
>
> The available time for servicing and refuelling the planes is too short. The ground personnel use primitive hand-pumps for refuelling. The men are exhausted. An enormous dust cloud rises over the airfield, which makes take-off and landing very difficult or almost impossible.
>
> The telephone connections have been destroyed by sabotage and it is not possible to rearrange the time schedule of the attack. Without radio communications only planes and dispatch riders can be used to carry the messages. At 15:00, the *VIII Fliegerkorps*, our flying artillery, bombs our objectives and the drop areas. These attacks were a total failure, however, since no paratroop drops followed immediately after the raids.[4]

The planes were flying in tight 'V' formations at a very low altitude (roughly 30 metres above the sea) in order to avoid detection by the enemy. The paratroopers – wearing the distinctive life-vests of the *Luftwaffe* that were very uncomfortable over the harness of the parachute, but compulsory due to safety regulations – were waiting patiently for the arrival over their destination, with some of them joking and others thinking about what might lie ahead of them.

While the paratroopers were on the airfields of the Greek mainland preparing for the jump, for the defenders of Heraklion, the morning of 20 May started with the usual raid by German bombers and fighters. These had become almost a daily routine for the past few weeks.

Private Christos Roussopoulos of the 7th Greek Infantry Regiment wrote in his diary:

> Finally, 20 May 1941 dawned. We look around and we see that we are roughly 500 metres away from the town and a bit south of the Chanioporta [West Gate] in a suburban area called Mastabas.
>
> It is still early in the morning and even before the alarm is sounded, we see over our positions a German plane flying so low that I thought that the wings would hit the olive trees. The officers ordered us not to come out of our cover under the olive trees. However we are curious

4 G. Broder, *Guerre Mondiale Contre Moi*, pp.81-84.

A Ju-52 takes off for Crete from Topolia Airfield. (Courtesy of Mike Smythe)

Ju-52s take off from Topolia Airfield – creating vast clouds of dust. (Courtesy of Mike Smythe)

Ju-52s on their way to Crete. (Courtesy of Shaun Winkler)

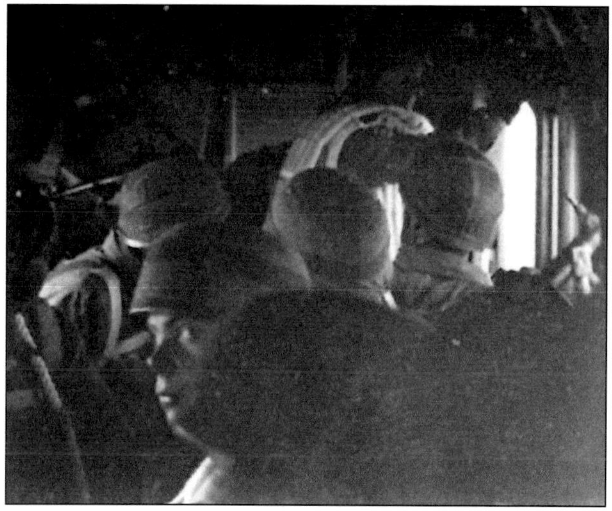

Gefreiter Otto Loop, with his comrades from the *2./FschSanAbt.7*, in their Ju-52 on the flight to Crete. He was killed in action seven days later. (Courtesy of Jose Ramon Artaza Ivañez)

Wolfgang *Graf* von Blücher in one of the planes of the *2./FschJgRgt.1*, on the way to Crete, waiting for the moment to jump. One year after the operation in Holland – and having been promoted to *oberleutnant* – he was to lead his platoon in combat for the second time. The first occasion in Holland was totally successful and he had been awarded the Knight's Cross. What would fate bring in Crete? These thoughts were no doubt in his mind during the flight to Crete. Fewer than 20 hours after this photo was taken, Blücher's platoon had been in heavy combat and he had met his fate. (Courtesy of Adrian Nisbett) Note: The photo was taken by paratrooper Rudolf Jacobs during the flight to Crete. The photo is of poor quality because shortly after the jump, Jacobs' camera was hit by a bullet while he was trying to take cover from the fire of a British tank, in the area east of the airfield.

and we want to have a better view, so we disobey the orders. As a matter of fact it was later proved that because of that action our positions were spotted by the enemy. After 10 minutes the alarm sirens started sounding. The anti-aircraft fire can't hit the German plane because it flies very low. After many passes over our positions, the plane changes course to return to its base and leaves, firing at the road that leads to Rethymnon and Chania, and blowing up the small bridge of Xeropotamos. As soon as the aircraft reaches the open sea, the anti-aircraft guns started firing from everywhere but without any success.

At 11:00 we were given some bread. In order to avoid leaving our positions and assembling every day for food, we were given rations for four days. Before we returned to our positions under the olive-trees, we had already eaten some bits of bread. We tried to control our hunger in order to have enough food for four days, but we ate all the bread at once. We were farmers and we were used to eating a lot of bread. In order to forget the bread and our hunger and since we did not have any drills or training, we decided to tell a story before dinner-time.[5]

5 C. Roussopoulos, *The Battle of Crete – Testimonies 5*, pp.76-77.

In Heraklion at 1603, the radio-location station AMES[6] that was installed on Hill 182 (roughly 2km south-east of the airfield) signalled 'Red Alarm'. Almost immediately, a large number of bombers appeared over Heraklion – coming from the sea. They started bombing and machine gunning the Allied positions – mainly in the area of the airfield.

At 1613, 50 Ju-87 *Stukas* were overhead. These were the aircraft of *Hauptmann* Brucker's *III Gruppe* of *StG 2* from Karpathos (Scarpanto), and they were followed by the He-111s of the *II/KG 26*. Two of the He-111s were hit as they came in at low level. These aircraft were 1H+ZP flown by *Oberleutnant* Kurt von Stetten and 1H+MP – and both of these planes crash-landed on the airfield. Kurt von Stetten and two of his crew were killed, while one was wounded and taken prisoner. The crew of the other aircraft managed to evade capture. When the He-111s left, strafing by Bf-109s followed.

At 1634, the *Messerschmitt* BF-110s of *II/ZG 26* appeared over the airfield – their task being to destroy any surviving gun sites. Two of these aircraft from 4 *Staffel* were shot down into the sea. The *staffelkapitän*, *Oblt* Reinhold Heubel (3U+AM), and his gunner were killed, while *Uffz* Otto Stein and *Gefr* Dietrich Hermann managed to ditch 3U+CN and reach the shore, where they were captured.[7]

The beginning of the attack on Heraklion is well recorded in the war diary of the 2nd Bn, Black Watch:

> 14:30 – Area[8] informed us that enemy parachute troops had been dropped at Maleme [...]
> 16:00 – A large formation of enemy aircraft approached and machine-gunned the drome. The mouth of the gorge[9] was also bombed.
> 16:03 – SUPER RED alarm.
> 16:13 – Dive bombing begins. Heavy fire on drome.
> 16:26 – Bombing towards west.
> 16:39 – C. Coy reports a nearby Bofors believed to be wiped out.[10]
> 16:34 – Australian positions strafed by M.E. 110s.

Brigadier Chappel had been the Crete garrison commander before the arrival of General Freyberg. During the invasion, he was the commanding officer of the 14th Infantry Brigade – responsible for the defence of the Heraklion sector. (Author's archive)

The planes were flying so low that the soldiers on the Two Charlies[11] were able to see the faces of the pilots. According to some accounts, the British troops had filled the space between the Two Charlies with barbed wire strung tautly between their tops, but did not manage to trap any planes.

The air raid passed without any substantial casualties for the Allied forces. Brigadier Chappel imposed no restrictions on opening fire by AA guns, but all other weapons and positions were to be concealed until the preliminary bombardment was over. The field guns were not to open fire on the airfield until ordered – an order which is very often wrongly interpreted by historians as a general order to include the AA guns. The brigade commander's intention

6 Air Ministry Experimental Station – an experimental radio-location device (radar).
7 C. Shores, B. Cull & N. Malizia, *Air War for Yugoslavia, Greece and Crete 1940-41*, p.351.
8 Codeword for the 14th Infantry Brigade command post in the Katsabas area.
9 The term 'gorge' refers to the narrow passage at the east end of the airfield, where the road to Karteros passes next to the church of Agios Ioannis (Saint John).
10 Refers to a 40mm AA gun in the area west of the airfield held by 'C' Coy.
11 The twin hills south of the airfield – also known in Greek as 'Dyo Orakia'.

was to use the field guns only if troop carriers landed in numbers, or the anti-aircraft guns were knocked out.

The British had deployed AA and field guns, mortars and tanks around the airfield. Four Bofors 40mm AA guns of the 156th Light AA Battery were sited on the airfield, while six more Bofors of the 7th Australian Light AA Battery were positioned on the defensive perimeter. The artillery force also included four 3-inch guns and a number of Pom-Poms of the Heavy AA Battery of the Royal Marines, one machine gun platoon of the 23rd Light AA Battery of the Royal Marines and thirteen 75mm and 100mm field guns of the 234th Medium Battery. The 75mm and 100mm field guns were spoils of the war captured from the Italians in North Africa. These guns had been abandoned by the Italians without their sights and then transferred by the British to Crete as a last-ditch measure due to the lack of heavy field guns.

After the war, two of the Italian 75mm guns were placed at the Battle of Crete Memorial in Heraklion. Here, Frank Unwin – a British veteran from the 234 Medium Battery that was positioned at the airfield – inspects one of the guns 70 years after the battle. (Courtesy of C.E. Mamalakis)

A paratrooper photographed immediately after the battle on a 100mm Italian gun. (Author's collection)

The British soldiers – famous for staying cool under fire – waited patiently for the raid to finish. At 1730, when the air raid was over, the alarm was raised again and 'Red Alarm' was signalled – meaning that the drop of paratroopers was imminent. Before long, the Ju-52s that had crossed the Aegean Sea from the Topolia Airfield appeared on the horizon and the characteristic noise of their engines was heard.

Ju-52s flying at low altitude over the Aegean Sea, on the way to Crete. Each transport could carry 12 paratroopers with their gear, and a group of 53 transports could carry a regular paratrooper battalion. (Courtesy of Shaun Winkler)

Paratroopers inside a Ju-52 on the way to Crete. (Courtesy of Shaun Winkler)

## The airfield sector

The aircraft that were carrying the *II./FschJgRgt.1* passed over the small island of Dia (north of the coast of Heraklion) and gained height – starting the parachute drops as soon as they reached the coast. *Hauptmann* Burckhardt and his men dropped in an area extending from Nea Alikarnassos to the Two Charlies, the Karteros Valley (East Wadi), the airfield and the area south of it. Some drops (probably miss-drops) were conducted near Brigadier Chappel's command post, which was located in a small cave at the base of a prominent rock formation in the Katsabas area, between the port and the airfield.

The war diary of Black Watch recorded the drop:

> 17:29 – Large number of Dorniers, Messerschmitts and Junkers 88s overhead.
> 17:31 – Enemy parachute troops dropping by Greek barracks and "Charlies".[12]
> 17:50 – C. Coy reports enemy parachute troops landed west of Heraklion.[13]
> 18:00 – More enemy parachute troops dropping south-west of "Charlies", estimated strength 30.
> 18:19 – Nine planes dropped a large number of enemy parachute troops near Greek barracks.
> 18:25 – "I" Tanks [Matilda] cruising in vicinity of Greek barracks. More troops dropped on west side of Heraklion.[14]

The paratroopers were leaving the burning planes in a hurry in order to save their lives – resulting in harrowing scenes: some men's parachutes did not open because of the low altitude; others came down in flames; and still others hit the ground, with their parachutes twisted into a candle shape, because of the too-rapid exit from the aircraft.

The burning engines of the planes were trailing long flames that reached the exit doors of the fuselage – thus setting fire to any parachute that was emerging from the door. Perhaps those who were killed by a bullet were the lucky ones. Paratrooper Karl Heinz Schneider from *II./FschJgRgt.1* realised that his Ju-52 was in flames, but managed to jump and land intact by pure luck: he soon discovered that most of his comrades were dead or wounded. The jump altitude was low in order to minimise the time of descent and exposure to the enemy fire, but in the process making the Ju-52s an easy target for the AA guns. Many planes were shot down around the airfield that day.

The units of *Hauptmann* Burckhardt's *II./FschJgRgt.1*, which dropped around the airfield, suffered the heaviest casualties, since they landed right on top of the British defensive positions. A battle group – consisting of the *6./FschJgRgt.1* and the *7./FschJgRgt.1*, with a company of AA machine guns (*1./FschFlaMGBatl.7*) and one platoon from the 14th (anti-tank) Company (*III. Zug 14*), under *Hauptmann* Dunz – was dropped at Nea Alikarnassos and at Buttercup Field on the western edge of the airfield. These units were quickly swept up by the British – being almost eliminated in 20 minutes. The airfield was very quickly secured by the Scottish soldiers of the Black Watch and only isolated groups and snipers remained, while some of the Germans managed to infiltrate the abandoned Greek barracks. The Australians of 2/4 Bn, under Captain Rolfe, cleared their area and the barracks of the enemy – killing some 90 paratroopers – with the loss of three dead and nine wounded.

Among the dead paratroopers was the CO: *Hauptmann* Werner Dunz. According to the British reports, in the area west of the airfield, the gunners of 234th Medium Battery killed 175

12 All the records about the drops at the airfield and the barracks refer to the 6th and 7th Companies of *II./FschJgRgt.1*, along with the 3rd Platoon of 14th (anti-tank gun) Company (*III. Zug 14*).
13 The drop of the 9th and 11th Companies of *III./FschJgRgt.1*.
14 The drop of the rest of *III./FschJgRgt.1*.

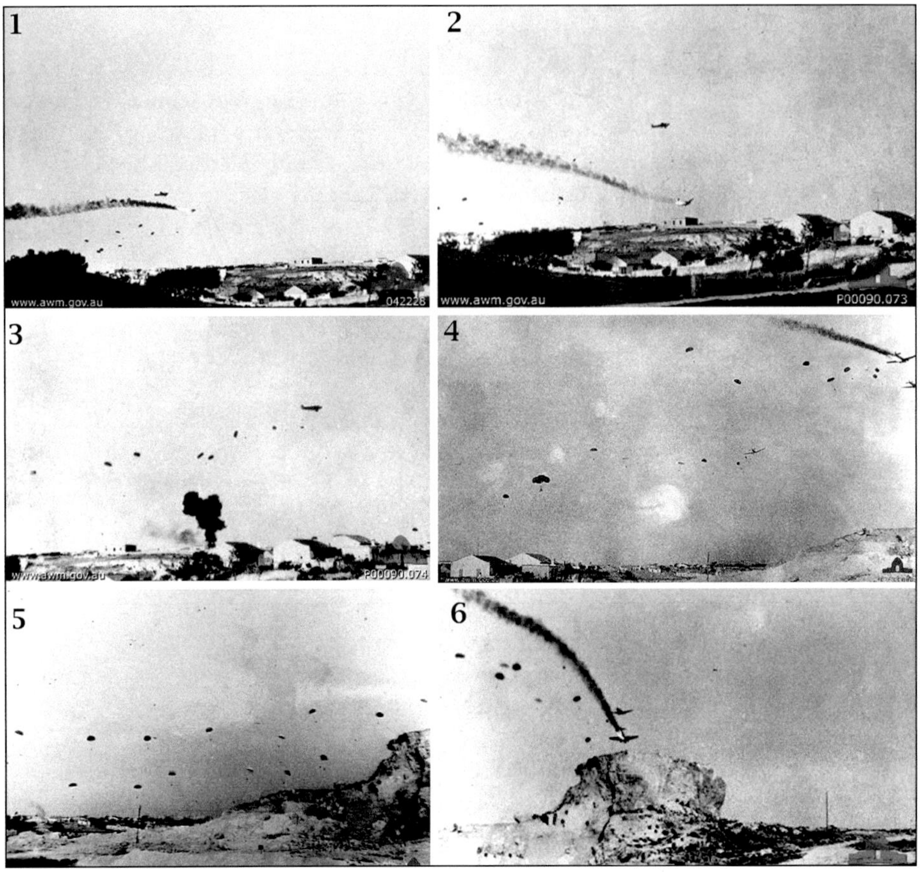


Lieutenant Gordon Hope-Morley, the information officer of the 14th Brigade (who was carrying his camera with him), took a series of photos of the first paratroopers' drops west-south-west of the airfield. The anti-tank gun attached to five parachutes seen in the fourth picture indicates the drop of the *III. Zug 14* in the area of Nea Alikarnassos, west of the airfield. Lieutenant Hope-Morley was standing a short distance from Brigadier Chappel's command post (the rock formation in the last frame) – looking towards the airfield. The plane shown in the picture going down behind the rock (frames 4, 5 and 6) is the G6+EK of *Uffz* Helmut Biewendt, while the one seen crashing in the picture (frames 1, 2 and 3) is the G6+KL of *Oblt* Hans Rehrmann (*Hptm* Dunz was also on board this plane), both from *K.G.z.b.V.101.* (AWM Archive) Note: The G6+GK of *Ofw* Heinz Otto has also been reported to have crashed near Nea Alikarnassos.

paratroopers. That is quite consistent with the German records, which list 74 dead from the *6./FschJgRgt.1* and 71 dead from the *7./FschJgRgt.1* in the first hours of the battle, to which the dead from the *III. Zug 14* and the *1./FschFlaMGBatl.7* must be added. Only three men from the *6./FschJgRgt.1* and two from the *1./FschFlaMGBatl.7* managed to escape by reaching the coast and swimming to Amnissos in Karteros Valley, east of the airfield.

The *7./FschJgRgt.1* was the last of *Gruppe* Dunz's to arrive. According to post-war accounts from 234th Medium Battery stationed in and around Nea Alikarnassos, some of this last wave of paratroopers penetrated into the town and seriously wounded Major Snook[15] – the CO of 7th Medium Regiment.

15 Major R.J.B. Snook DSO was wounded when a German lobbed a grenade into the HQ located in a school building.

Lieutenant Hope-Morley's images were digitally combined into one for this reconstruction of the 1941 landscape. The same place was photographed from approximately the same angle in May 2008, in the Katsabas area. The rock formation, where Chappel's HQ was located, has undergone some major changes since 1941, but still stands. (Courtesy of Nikos Valasiadis)

The small caves at the bottom of the rock formation, where the 14th Brigade command post was situated during the battle, photographed in 1984. The caves have been filled and sealed since then and are no longer visible today. (Courtesy of C.E. Mamalakis)

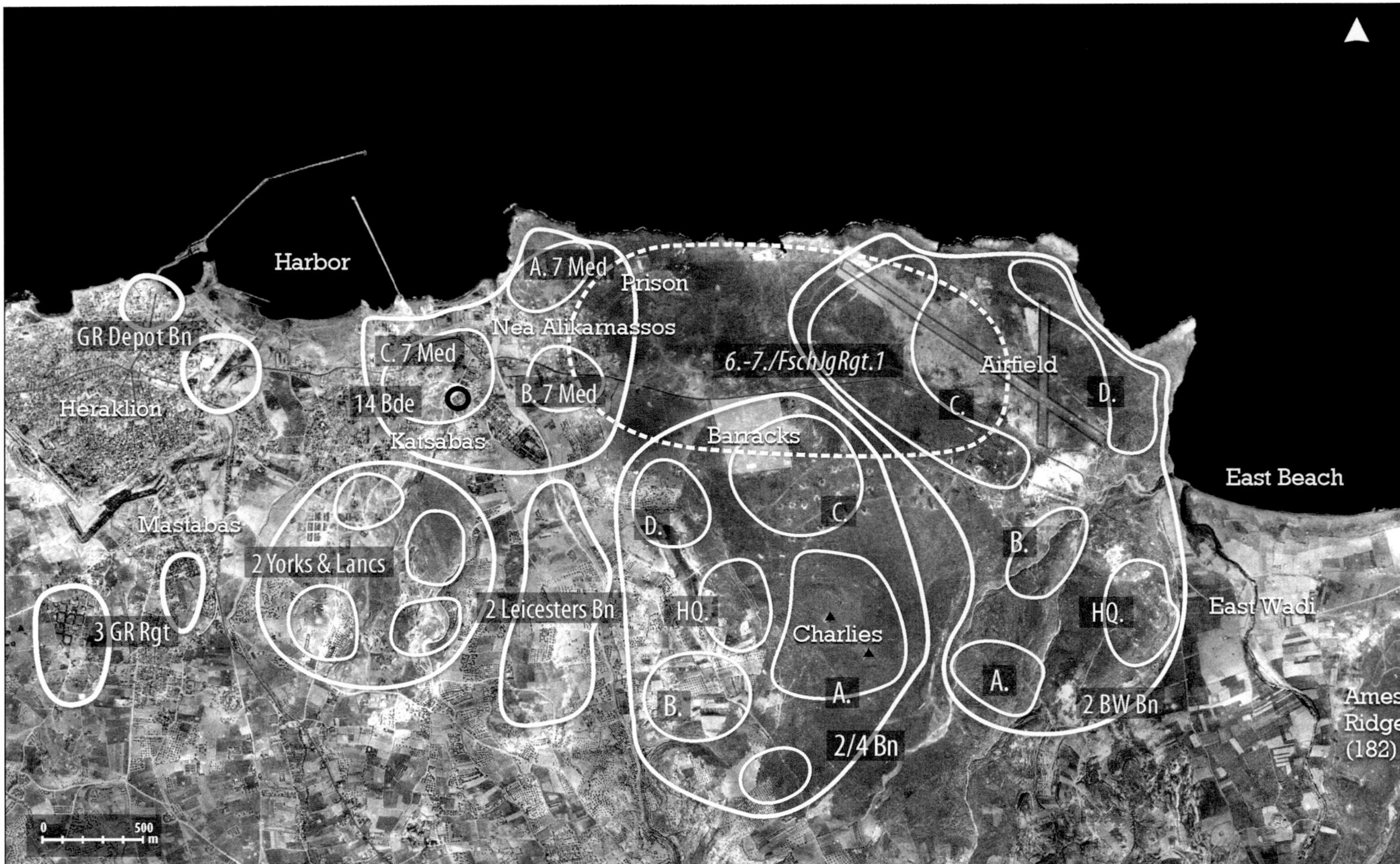


Map 2.3 The airfield sector and the drop zone of *Gruppe* Dunz (*6-7./FschJgRgt.1*). Both Ju-52s seen crashing in Lieutenant Hope-Morley's photos ended up in the Nea Alikarnassos and barracks area. (N. Valasiadis, 2015)

Due to multiple aircraft problems on 20 May, three groups from *7./FschJgRgt.1* were stranded at their allotted airfield in Greece (*Gruppe Obfw* Neumann, *Gruppe Objg* Sandhof and *Gruppe Oblt* Götte – later under the command of *Objg* Schaper – while *Oblt* Götte[16] himself joined *Gruppe Obfw* Lüsing at the last minute and left his group behind). Two groups crashed-landed on Milos before reaching Crete (*Gruppe Obfw* Estenfeld and *Gruppe Objg* Steber). A third aircraft also crashed-landed on Milos on its return journey. This plane carried the two men from *Gruppe Obfw* Lüsing, who later claimed that they had not jumped because the pilot had totally missed the drop zone and they were flying over an urban area instead of the area of the airfield. This would explain the off-target drops near the 14th Brigade command post, as this urban area was actually the area of Katsabas and Nea Alikarnassos, between the town of Heraklion and the airfield.

Erich Reinhardt, a survivor from the *7./FschJgRgt.1* who was on board the Ju-52 of *Gruppe* Estenfeld, wrote in his memoirs:

> We were suddenly torn from our dreams. The rear gunner had received a note; he shouted out wildly that we should throw everything out of the plane as two engines had failed. At the same time we received the signal to prepare to jump, after which we heard that land was in sight and that we should prepare ourselves for an emergency landing. We had unhooked the weapon containers and thrown them into the sea. What a situation! I thought: 'Crete in view and no weapons.' With profound relief we heard the pilot shouting: 'Land in sight. Prepare for an emergency landing!'
>
> The machine touched down and rushed towards a pile of stones. We felt the wheels falling away and the machine nearly turned over, but at last it came to a stop and the only thought was to get out as quickly as possible. No one was injured but the fuselage was split. A German officer came running up to our pilot. We were of the opinion that we were on Crete, but this was not so, we were on Milos, which had been under German occupation for only a few days.
>
> The officer shouted to the pilot that he would be brought in front of a court-martial, because he had deliberately or negligently landed on a pile of stones.[17] I was privately suspicious that the engines were in no way defective. It was clear that the first flight over Crete had badly disturbed our pilot and perhaps he thought five minutes of cowardice was preferable to a lifetime of death.[18]
>
> 15 HOURS ON MILOS
>
> Several Ju-52s returning from Crete made an emergency landing on Milos, where a Ju-52 collided with a damaged Ju-88 causing a terrible explosion. We ran off as fast as we could away from the inferno. Another Ju-52 landed and we saw to our surprise two men from our company who had not jumped. When it comes to a crunch, there is nothing in human nature that can be called impossible. That was certainly also the case in the *Wehrmacht*. The two soldiers had a great deal of experience, having seen active service in Norway and Holland. They claimed that the rest of the paratroopers had been dropped over the wrong area and that

16 It was *Oberleutnant* Götte, together with *Oberjäger* Schaper (the company welfare officer), who compiled the list of jumpers for the *7./FschJgRgt.1* several days prior to the invasion. *Oberjäger* Schaper later explained that there had been an almighty row while compiling the final list. Erich Reinhardt reported that the body of *Oberleutnant* Götte was found after the battle, on the outskirts of Nea Alikarnassos.

17 The suggestion here is that by destroying the aircraft on purpose, the pilot would also destroy any evidence proving the condition of the aircraft before landing.

18 The pilots of the second wave had already completed a sortie to Maleme and back, and had gone through a hail of anti-aircraft fire, so were well aware of the situation on Crete.

they had obtained written confirmation from the pilot that he had missed the target area over Heraklion and had seen several houses, which did not suggest that they were anywhere near an airfield. For some unknown reason no action was taken against the two soldiers. I met one of them later, who had become a captain in the *Luftwaffe*. Hopefully neither of them related their stories of heroism on Crete afterwards. In war there is a fine dividing line between heroism and cowardice.

A lot of stories were doing the rounds on Milos that our 7 Company was going through a terrible trial of fire, as one of the two that did not jump explained excitedly. We were soon to discover that the reality was even worse, so much so that it could not conceivably be worse.

[...] The two men who had not jumped were probably highly satisfied to be safe with our group, after two men had been taken ill. They therefore would be able to avoid any disagreeable repercussions. And indeed, this proved to be so. The two of them were often the victims of our ribbing – *Ich sehe Haüser* (I see houses) – which caused the *Uffz* to keep a special eye on me on the parade ground. I almost lost my nerve at one time and certainly would have done, if he had belonged to our squad [...]

[...] Of the 93 soldiers of our company, who first jumped over Iraklion [Heraklion], only four, I repeat, ONLY 4, had survived.[19]

The area of Katsabas, south-west of the airfield, as seen from the top of the rock where the 14th Brigade HQ was situated. That this is the place where the mis-drops of the *7./FschJgRgt.1* took place has also been confirmed by British veterans. At the top-right of the picture, the Two Charlies can be seen, while in the far background, the Greek barracks located south of the airfield can also be seen. (Courtesy of Shaun Winkler)

The bombing in the area of the 14th Brigade HQ, just before the arrival of the paratroopers. Because of the confusion that prevailed at the beginning of the battle, with the paratroopers landing all around, the capture of prisoners was not the first priority of the adversaries. As a consequence, many cases of executions of surrendering soldiers and paratroopers were recorded. An example of this was what happened in the yard of the Kastelakis Brothers' pasta factory, just a few metres away from the 14th Brigade HQ. The paratroopers killed in this incident were buried in the yard and it is not known whether their bodies were later collected or not. The factory is seen here (first building on the left). (AWM Archive)

19 E. Reinhardt, 'Memoirs of a Former German Paratrooper', David Lenk Archive.

The area west of the airfield was virtually devoid of structures – no doubt the reason it was selected as a suitable landing zone. The most prominent buildings were the aforementioned Greek barracks, the abattoir and the prison building. During 1941, the ground between these structures and between the airfield and the area of Nea Alikarnassos was largely flat and without cover, so it is unsurprising that the surviving paratroopers (those not killed in the air or on the ground immediately after landing) sought refuge in these buildings.

According to British and Australian records, by around 1930 hours a small force of paratroopers had established themselves in two blocks of the Greek barracks, the abattoir and the prison. Initial attempts to remove these paratroopers proved unsuccessful. On 21 May, it was estimated that 60-100 paratroopers were in the Greek barracks and that by the evening of the 22nd, these men had either been killed in the barracks or shot down while trying to escape to the abattoir when the barrack area was shelled by mortar fire. There were also multiple British patrols sent out to the abattoir area between 21 and 24 May. On each occasion, paratroopers were found and killed.

The *14./FschJgRgt.1* was the anti-tank company and was under the direct command of the regiment, rather than belonging to any of the battalions. During the Battle for Heraklion, the 1st Platoon (*I. Zug 14*), under *Leutnant* Fleischmann, dropped with *Major* Walther's *I./FschJgRgt.1*; the 2nd Platoon (*II. Zug 14*), under *Leutnant* Wiener, dropped with the *III./FschJgRgt.1* (*Major* Schulz[20]); and the 3rd Platoon (*III. Zug 14*), under *Leutnant* Schamberger, dropped at the airfield with *Gruppe* Dunz. Unluckiest of all was *III. Zug 14*, which dropped into the intense fire of the defenders, in an area extending from the coast to the south-south-west of the airfield, with most of the paratroopers being killed while still in the air.

By the end of the next day – and after offensive action by the Australians and the British at the airfield – only four out of the 35 paratroopers survived, with *III. Zug 14* suffering a loss rate of 90 percent. Among the dead was the platoon leader, *Leutnant* Otto Schamberger. After the battle, a makeshift memorial for the 31 dead of *III. Zug 14* was erected in the area south of the airfield.

*III. Zug 14's* dead are actually the paratroopers pictured in Lieutenant Hope-Morley's photos, and they are:

*Jäger* Alois Alzinger (also mentioned as 'Atzinger')
*Gefr* Herbert Berger
*Jäger* Josef Bernlochner
*Objg* Erwin Bohlander
*Gefr* Otto Börner (also mentioned as 'Dörner')
*Obgfr* Willi Brandt
*Jäger* Hans Chrzibek
*Jäger* Gerhard Dittrich
*Gefr* Karl Fanbold
*Gefr* Wilfried Gersonde
*Feldw* Gunther Gottschald
*Obgfr* Hans Greben
*Gefr* Gustav Heide
*Obgfr* Rudolf Herzog
*Objg* Hugo Köhler
*Gefr* Wilhelm Krause
*Obgfr* Willi Lutter
*Obgfr* Walter Orlik
*Objg* Werner Ramminger
*Gefr* Paul Rösch
*Gefr* Rudi Rother
*Gefr* Heinrich Silberhorn
*Ltn* Otto Schamberger
*Gefr* Christian Schreinemaker
*Gefr* Alois Schneider
*Objg* Hans Stroinski
*Gefr* Rudi Schulze
*Objg* Josef Weimann
*Objg* Horst Wittke
*Objg* Rolf Wollin
*Gefr* Frank Zeidler

20 *II. Zug 14* also supported *Gruppe* Schirmer with *7 and 8./FschJgRgt.2*.

The common grave of 14 paratroopers from the 6th and 7th Companies of *II./* FschJgRgt.1, west of the airfield, in the Buttercup Field area. In the background are the barracks – home of the 43rd Greek Infantry Regiment. The buildings are still used by the Greek military today. (Courtesy of Dimitris Skartsilakis)

A temporary grave of two men from the *II./FschJgRgt.1*, who were killed in the barracks-airfield area. Mount Stroumboulas can be seen in the background towards the right. (Author's archive)

A Ju-52 shot down by light weapons fire of the 2/4 Australian Battalion – in the area north-east of the Two Charlies – on 20 May. (Courtesy of David Lenk)

Andenken
an
Otto Schamberger

Lehrer von Pfarrkirchen
Leutnant in einem Fallschirmjäger-Regiment
Teilnehmer am Polenfeldzug und Einsatz Holland

welcher am 20. Mai 1941 bei den Kämpfen um Kreta für Führer, Volk und Vaterland im Alter von 24 Jahren gefallen ist.

R. I. P.

Mein Jesus Barmherzigkeit (300 Tage Ablaß)

Süßes Herz Mariä sei meine Rettung! (300 Tage Ablaß)

Barmherziger Jesus, gib ihm die ewige Ruhe! (300 Tage Ablaß).

Buchdruckerei J. Kramer, Pfarrkirchen

Otto Schamberger, here as an NCO; and his death card. (Courtesy of David Lenk)

The original grave of *Leutnant* Schamberger – the platoon leader of *III. Zug 14* – on the rocky coast alongside the airfield. (Author's archive)

The plain at the end of the runway, where the men of *III. Zug 14* and of *6* and *7./FschJgRgt.1* were dropped. This is also the rocky coast where *Leutnant* Schamberger was buried. In the background (on the right), the barracks can been seen. (G. Müller & F. Scheuering, *Sprung über Kreta*)

Also killed was *Feldwebel* Günther Gottschald from *III. Zug 14*. His plane (G6+EK) was set on fire and crashed while approaching Heraklion Airfield, as shown in Lieutenant Hope-Morley's photos (the aircraft in flames passing over the rock). His body was never identified. Also in the same plane were *Ojäg* Josef Weimann and *Obgfr* Willi Lutter, while other paratroopers from *III. Zug 14* who remained unidentified – and most probably were in the same aircraft that crashed – are *Jäger* Alois Atzinger, *Objg* Erwin Bohlander, *Gefr* Paul Rösch and *Gefr* Wilhelm Krause. (Courtesy of Shaun Winkler) Note: The bodies of Willi Lutter and Josef Weimann hadn't been identified and are buried in common graves 445-446 with the crew of the plane, which are *Uffz* Helmut Biewendt – *flugzeugführer* (pilot), *Uffz* Werner Kirmse – *bordfunker* (radio operator) and *Feldw* Erich Mählig – *bordmechaniker* (flight engineer).

The crash site of the Ju-52 G6+EK that carried the men of *III.Zug 14*. In the previous pictures, it is seen passing over the rock and going down in flames. On the right, the Pak 35 that was being transported in the plane can be seen upended, with its carriage arms vertical. Mount Jouhtas is in the background – indicating that the area of the crash is just south of the airfield. (Courtesy of Flemming Melin Christiansen)

The crash site in a picture taken from another angle. In the background (on the right), the rock of the 14th Brigade HQ can be seen. (Courtesy of Dimitris Skartsilakis)

The memorial for the 31 dead of *III. Zug 14*, south of the airfield at the area of the crash site of the Ju-52. (Courtesy of David Lenk)

### Special Presentation 5: Rudi Rother – the lost brother

One of the dead of *III. Zug 14* was *Gefreiter* Rudi Rother. He was born on 19 February 1919 in Thuringian Zeulenroda and was the first of eight children. Before joining the armed forces in July 1939, he worked in a butcher's shop. He volunteered for the paratroopers and the following year, participated in operations in Holland, where he was awarded the Iron Cross 2nd Class.

Rudi Rother in 1940. (Courtesy of Shaun Winkler)

Rudi visited his family for the last time at the beginning of 1941, during his holiday leave. In his last letter to his family in the spring of 1941, he described how tough life in the military was and expressed his hope for an early end of the war. His family received no more news of him until June 1941, when a paratrooper informed them that Rudi was missing in action after the jump on Crete. His plane had been under heavy fire during the jump. His parents tried to find out what had happened to their son, but after the war, they were living in East Germany and were unable to communicate with the Western world.

His younger brother Heinz, who saw his brother for the last time in 1941 when he was eight, finally managed to visit the war cemetery in Maleme in 1994. Looking at the list of the dead, he found Rudi's name and soon he was standing in front of his brother's grave in Block I, No.839.

The plaque with the names of the fallen paratroopers from *III. Zug 14*. (Courtesy of Shaun Winkler)

With his comrades in training during a jump in Germany. (Courtesy of Shaun Winkler)

Private Selby Dean – of the 2/4 Australian Battalion – described the drop of the paratroopers south of the airfield on 20 May 1941:

> We were in this position for some days getting heavily bombed and machine-gunned all the time. About midday some German paratroopers arrived and dropped right in on top of us.
>
> It was absolute carnage as we were just waiting for them. I'm not sure how many landed but we had our area cleaned out by nightfall. The Black Watch did the same.
>
> One of our blokes scored a German codebook, which set out the procedures for getting supplies. We put it into action and they dropped us some supplies, which was marvellous.
>
> When we tried it a second time all we got was a planeload of bombs as they had woken up to us. Jerry then started to drop the paratroopers back into the hills so that we couldn't get to them. We had to commence patrolling. Now, this lot is as clear to me as if it happened yesterday. You will have to excuse the language. One of these patrols was on a mountain and we were following a track when we came to a spot where the track took a right hand turn around a corner. This held us up, as it was an ideal place for an ambush. Blue Benson was again in charge and couldn't make up his mind what to do. Silly me volunteered to take a dive around the corner to see what would happen. As soon as I did this Jerry opened up with machine gun and rifle fire. Luckily, I was able to find protection in a split in the rock and wasn't shot. After a while things quietened down and the following conversation took place. I said, "Hey, Blue. Hey Blue". Blue said, "You stupid f...... idiot. What do you want"? "Hey Blue", I said, "That frightened the shit out of me. I'll wait till dark and then get out". I didn't have to wait until dark though as another patrol further up the hill tackled the Germans and I was able to get out. It was all pretty terrifying though.[21]

A similar fate also awaited the 5th and 8th Companies, as they dropped at the east end of the airfield and along the Karteros Valley (East Wadi), in front of the defensive positions of the HQ, 'A', 'B' and 'D' Companies of the Black Watch and the Bren Carriers.

Private Selby Dean of the 2/4 Australian Battalion. (Courtesy of C.E. Mamalakis)

The *5./FschJgRgt.1* lost 35 men during the battle – 25 of them during the first 24 hours, while the *8./FschJgRgt.1* had 47 dead (45 of whom were lost on the first day of the battle). The *8./FschJgRgt.1* was dropped close to the British positions south-east of the airfield, while a large portion of the *5./FschJgRgt.1* was dropped well into the Karteros Valley, away from the British positions – resulting in far fewer casualties than the companies which dropped around the airfield.

There is a strange story of what took place at the east edge of the airfield, based on the account of a Black Watch soldier: right at the drop zone of the *5./FschJgRgt.1*, Alex Kennedy – a soldier of 'D' Company of the Black Watch – was acting as a messenger during the battle. 'D' Company was stationed on the eastern edge of the airfield, and when the drops started, Kennedy

21 C.E. Mamalakis' archive.

was ordered to carry a message to another company on the East Hill. While he was running close to the rocks below the eastern end of the runway, a German officer suddenly stood up from behind the rocks, challenged Kennedy and then shot him with his pistol – wounding Kennedy in the shoulder. The German led the wounded Kennedy into a cave, where he was looked after and his wounds were dressed, so saving the life of the British soldier. According to Kennedy, this German was a high-ranking officer – and most probably the officer in charge of that area.

Late in the evening, the German officer decided to attack the Black Watch positions above – using the weapons and the ammunition that Kennedy was carrying with him: a .303 rifle with a grenade launcher and a bag of grenades. After his attack, he returned to the cave and shortly afterwards – when a platoon of the Black Watch was sent down to investigate the source of the attack – the German officer was spooked into breaking his cover, and while running away, he was killed by a machine gun burst. Kennedy, who was stripped to the waist because of the shoulder injury, maintained that it was the large Union Jack tattooed on his chest and his frantic Scottish accent that saved him from a similar fate. He was evacuated to a field hospital the following day, and later he was made a POW after the Allies evacuated the island.

Alex Kennedy. (Courtesy of Mike Kennedy)

The cave where Alex Kennedy was kept prisoner and the spot where the German officer was killed. This particular cave is located at the rocks right below the eastern edge of the airfield. (Courtesy of Mike Kennedy)

*Leutnant* Dietrich Platow's 8th Company also dropped in the same area, south of 5th Company's drop zone. Platow tried to take the Scots on East Hill by surprise and attacked with his men immediately after landing. After the battle, he was found dead near Prassas, at the south edge of East Hill.

The men who followed Platow in the attack – and who fell alongside their leader – were:

*Gefr* Herbert Morgenroth
*Gefr* Heinz Schmidt
*Gefr* Josef Brendelbergen
*Gefr* Siegfried Biener
*Jäger* Paul Syda
*Gefr* Harry Sonnemann
*Gefr* August Betz
*Jäger* Franz Haid
*Gefr* Herbert Dietrich
*Jäger* Hans von der Wehd
*Gefr* Rudi Schneider

The graves of paratroopers from the *8./FschJgRgt.1*, who were killed on 20 May: *Jäger* Johann Galek (on the top of East Hill – probably killed during the drop); *Gefreiter* Herbert Morgenroth (in the Karteros Valley, right in front of East Hill); *Gefreiter* Heinz Schmidt; *Gefreiter* Josef Brendelbergen; and *Gefreiter* Siegfried Biener, *Oberjäger* Otto Brück, *Leutnant* Otto Rothe, *Gefreiter* August Barlage and an unknown *fallschirmjäger* (at the south/south-east end of East Hill). These men were dropped at exactly the same area where the Bren Carriers were stationed. (Courtesy of Jose Ramon Artaza Ivañez and the author)

The remains of a paratrooper's grave at the drop zone of the *8./FschJgRgt.1* – today, very close to the positions of the Black Watch. (Author's collection)

Paratrooper Bernd Bosshammer from the *5./FschJgRgt.1* continues his narrative:

> Our mission was to occupy the Heraklion airfield. At around 17:30 Crete appeared on the horizon. When we approached the coast, the planes gained altitude and flew over the island of Dia. It was 17:50 already and suddenly we were in the middle of AA and heavy machine-gun fire. The order to jump was given and I was last in the line.
>
> My platoon leader, *Leutnant* Georg von Berlepsch jumped first. *Gefreiter* von Suttner in front of me collapsed right in front of the door. I pushed him out and jumped behind him.[22] With the opening of the parachute canopy, my sub-machine-gun hit me hard on the forehead and I started bleeding. *'I saw stars.'* I landed very badly in a vineyard. I could barely see anything. Very quickly I got rid of the parachute harness and swept the blood from my face.
>
> A new formation of Ju-52s was already over us. A drop-container whose parachute didn't open crashed noisily to the ground. We were taking fire from everywhere. I jumped up and ran forward because our aim was to occupy the hill next to the airfield[23] which was 800 metres from my current position. I had covered almost 200 metres when I found a drop-container with mortars and rifles in it and I met *Obergefreiter* Franzl Kopp.
>
> I shouted and told him about the container. I ran forward towards the hill and I observed a heavy bombardment at a distance of roughly 120 metres in front of me. I saw Karl Hein Siebert with two others that I did not know. We shouted to each other and I ran forward for

22 Rudolf von Suttner was shot in the heart at the moment he tried to jump out of the plane. The paratroopers of the 5th Company really didn't have any other option than to jump, since any delay could result in jumping over the sea, which meant certain death by drowning; this was the case for many casualties in this area.

23 He means Agios Ioannis Hill (East Hill).

30 metres, but while trying to get over a barbed-wire fence, I collapsed, feeling intense pain and burning in my leg.

My left leg was hit and I had not even fired a bullet yet. After a few minutes and having recovered from the shock, I shouted to Siebert and told him about my injury. I tried to stay calm despite the heavy bombardment. I had the feeling that I was right in the middle of the cross-fire.

My comrades believed that I was an Englishman and the English shot at me too. A shooting contest began. I remained frozen as if dead and after 8 to 10 minutes that seemed like an eternity to me, the shooting stopped. My water-bottle as well as my uniform were full of bullet-holes. I rolled into a hollow, covered with blood. At around 20:00 a medic came. It was Blumlein, who dressed my wound in a hurry and left. After an hour, I was transferred to a small ditch along with nine wounded paratroopers.

At around 21:30 an English tank [a Bren Carrier] approached and swept the ditch with machine-gun fire. I played dead. The tank went about 1000 metres away and then returned and shot again into the ditch. Cries were heard and later I learnt that Fiedler was killed by a bullet in the head. The tank turned away, met three other tanks and they all moved towards the airport.

We all breathed a sigh of relief when darkness fell. In the ditch there were 16 paratroopers, two of whom were dead. The comrades that were not badly wounded carried us, since we could not walk, into a stable. The rest tried to find their units. Bienta, Reuter and Hannes Caspers arranged for us to have medical care. We were in the stable, I, Gulden and Rohe. The night was cold and we covered ourselves with a parachute. We could not help each other and whenever we tried to move we were in great pain.[24]

Bosshammer was left injured in the stable for nine days until he was found by other paratroopers on 29 May, when the battle was over. Later, he was transferred to Olympia Hospital in Athens.

Bernd Bosshammer in 2001 at the drop zone, near the spot where he stayed injured for nine days. East Hill, where the British positions were, can be seen in the background to the right. All fire against the men of *5./FschJgRgt.1* was coming from these heights. (Author's archive)

Paratrooper Bernd Bosshammer, *5./FschJgRgt.1.* (B. Bosshammer, BDF e.v. Archiv, Freiburg/Breisgau)

24 Bosshammer.

The drop of the *5./FschJgRgt.1* took place in Karteros Valley, east of the airfield. The hill of Agios Ioannis (East Hill) was a formidable obstacle. Since the hill and control of the road were dominated by strong British forces, the paratroopers never managed to overrun it and then approach the airport from the east (via the Amnissos-Karteros-Heraklion Road).

Some of the paratroopers – either because of miscalculation or because of their efforts to escape from burning planes and enemy fire – were dropped at sea, where they drowned. They stood no chance of survival, since they were weighed down by so much heavy gear and supplies.

David Hutton from the Black Watch recorded:

> I was with 'A' Company. Our platoon was sent to the end of the airfield on the first day, as it was initially assumed that the Germans would arrive here by sea. As I recollect it, communications were fairly dreadful.
>
> Little was happening on the ground at the airport, but we could see *fallschirmjägers* landing to our right in the bay and in the sea, where many must have drowned. The area we saw the paratroopers landing was to the east, at what was referred as 'East Wadi' / 'East Beach'.
>
> Many landed short of the beach and we saw several parachutes floating in the water. Many must have been carrying too much weight to survive. They were out of our range and, as a consequence, we were moved south to the Charlies that evening.
>
> German aircraft were flying in very low over the bay, then rising up quickly to drop *fallschirmjägers* over the Charlies and immediate surroundings. We tried to dig in as we went along, but the ground was hard and we felt quite exposed.[25]

The body of a drowned paratrooper, still wearing his harness and parachute, washed ashore on the coast of Crete. (Author's archive)

25 Interview with – and letter to – the author, November 2013.

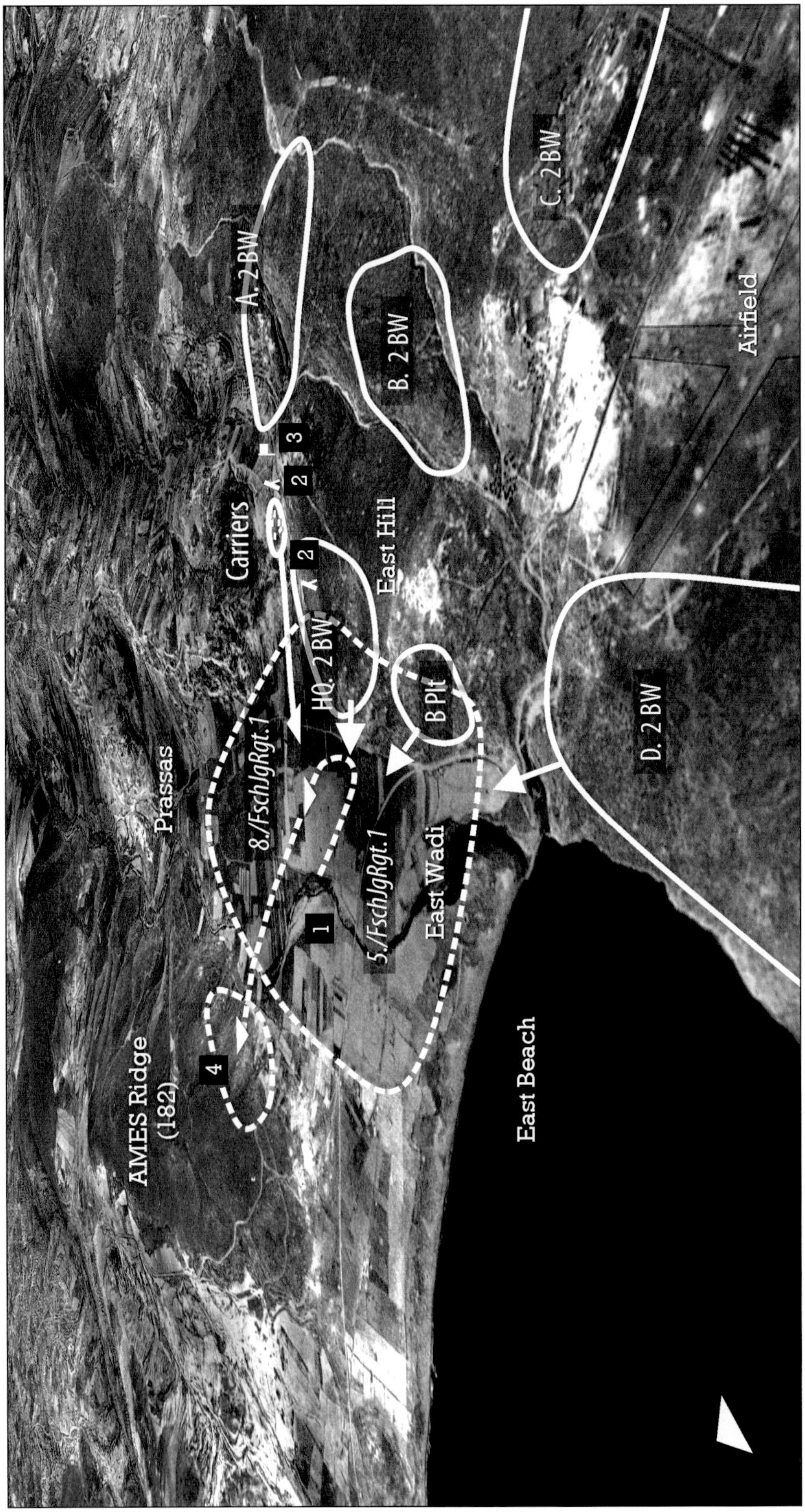


Map 2.4 The drop of *Kampfgruppe* Burckhardt and the retreat area after the drop and the decimation of the 5th and 8th Companies. (N. Valasiadis, 2015)

David Hutton's platoon, while preparing for the battle, taking their positions on the hills south of the airfield. Hutton (right, with the large dent in his helmet) is pictured here with his Bren gunner, Private Reekie, who was killed at the Charlies. (Courtesy of David Hutton)

The paratroopers of the *5./FschJgRgt.1* were dropped in the valley east of the airfield and in front of the British lines, but they were one of the few units to be carrying their weapons with them when they jumped; this proved to be a great benefit, since in most cases, it was not possible for paratroopers to approach the drop containers because of enemy fire. Carrying weapons during the parachute jump was at an early and experimental stage at that time, and the safest technique had not yet been developed. The *5./FschJgRgt.1* was one of the units that participated in pre-battle training jumps carrying weapons, and it is noteworthy that Bernd Bosshammer himself was injured on the head by his own sub-machine gun during the jump on Crete.

Major Pitcairn's Scottish soldiers, who had established defensive positions on the East Hill and had an excellent field of fire and observation post, unleashed a counter-attack and cleared the East Wadi – forcing the paratroopers to retreat and establish their positions at the foot of Hill 182. The retreat to Hill 182 allowed the paratroopers to regroup, but only about 70 men managed to assemble. On 20 May, approximately 300 men and 12 officers of the *II./FschJgRgt.1* were killed, and in the supporting units, eight officers and 100 men were injured.

The war diary of the Black Watch recorded:

> 18:30 – Large number of enemy parachute troops landed in East Wadi.
>
> 18:32 – Carriers [Bren Carriers] ordered to move out and destroy them. Subsequently ascertained that two carriers were unable to get out of their ditch. One carrier with 2/Lt. Snowden ran into wire near A. Coy's cook-house. 2/Lt. Snowden killed whilst trying to rescue his driver.
>
> 18:42 – One platoon B. Coy takes up position on east edge of East Hill between HQ position and Gorge platoon of D. Coy. Own mortars open fire on enemy concentrations in East Wadi.

The drop of *Kampfgruppe* Burckhardt in the Karteros Valley (East Wadi). East Hill can be seen in the background. (Author's collection)

Lieutenant Gerald Barry, who was on the East Hill in the trenches of the HQ Coy, 2nd Bn, BW, described what he witnessed:

> At about 5 p.m. a lot of German troop carriers arrived and proceeded to empty parachutists all round, among us, behind us, and in the valley below us [East Wadi]. All of a sudden, there were about 200 men dangling on their lines, descending from a height of about 300 feet [100 metres] all round us, and masses more up the valley. A tremendous scrimmage then occurred.
>
> I was far too occupied in our immediate vicinity to notice what was going on elsewhere. Three men on parachutes dropped within a few yards of our shelter, and Bill and I polished them off with revolvers and Mills bombs. Bill was splendid and went quite wild!
>
> In the meantime, there was a hell of a lot of shooting going on, and having cleared our immediate area, I grabbed a rifle and looked out over the valley. The vineyard in front of us was full of green parachutes, also several large cylinders, containing their gear, guns, etc., and men running about all over the place. All the enemy, except a few who managed to crawl away in the vines, were shot by us and A Coy, on our right, was also having the hell of a shoot.
>
> Suddenly I saw one man crawling immediately in front of us. Bill and I polished him off with rifles. On looking round, I noticed that a parachute had descended on a fir tree to our right, on top of the A/A post beneath it. In the little garden in front of the pioneer platoon, several more were to be seen, and I knew I need have no worry as to the fate of their occupants. Away over the river,[26] among the vineyards there, were several more to be seen, and a lot of shooting went on for some time before they were mopped up. Further up the valley, we could hardly deal with them, and a whole lot escaped.
>
> By 8 p.m., the situation was well in hand, and the shooting died down. At this moment, a figure suddenly appeared below us at the bottom of our road, running wildly towards us, dressed in civilian clothes and unarmed. We thought he was a German and debated whether

26 Karteros River.

A wide-angle view of the Karteros Valley (East Wadi), as seen from the positions of the Black Watch HQ Company. (Author's collection)

we should shoot him. I said No, and fortunate it was, for it turned out to be L/C Eddie, of the Mortar Platoon, who had taken his washing up to the village in the valley and suddenly found himself cut off by the blitz. He had hidden in a house, been given a suit of civilian clothes, and dodged his way back to us. A good stiff whisky restored him to the proper frame of mind.

By darkness, our line was still completely intact, as also that of A Coy on our right. The Germans were very brave in the way they tried to collect their gear and shoot back at us. All this time, of course, I had no idea how our own men had fared, but reports of casualties began to come in. Poor Snowy[27] was killed, as he tried to bring his carrier into action, also Cpl Nicol, Sgt Hindmarsh, Cpl Chiles, Leithen, Dalgarus, and a few others. They had been shot by parachutists with tommy guns, firing down on them while still in the air. A Coy had three killed.

After dark, we could hear all the Germans who had escaped calling to each other all round us in the darkness, just like a dispersed covey of partridges after a day's shoot! We had to be very careful, not knowing how many there were, or exactly where they were. I formed a close perimeter in our area, and no one had any sleep that night.[28]

27 2nd Lieutenant Snowden.
28 C.E. Mamalakis, Ian Powys Archive.

Some of the Black Watch HQ Company trenches, as they are today. (Author's collection)

When taken prisoner by the British at El Alamein in 1942, *Hauptmann* Burckhardt admitted to his interrogators that despite his careful study of aerial photographs taken just two days before the battle, he concluded that there weren't any tanks or AA guns in the area. The careful camouflage of the defensive positions by the British was very effective.

This description by Sergeant Wharton from the Bren Carrier Platoon is illustrative:

> I was a sergeant in the carriers, moved by road with Lt Snowden in charge. I think it took us a couple of days to move from Souda Bay to Heraklion. So when we got to Heraklion and the position was shown to the Carrier Platoon officer, what we'd to do, we started preparing for the invasion. Slit trenches, burying the carriers so they could come out on a run. Bush branches to wipe away the tracks for the aerial photographs. It was well planned. Very well planned. If we moved at all from the station with the carriers in the slit trenches we again got the brush-wood and covered our tracks and just sat still, the planes were high over us.[29]

Burckhardt also considered that due to bad staff work and planning, the close air support by the *Stukas* came long before the drops – hence the defenders were not stunned and were ready for the paratroopers when they arrived. The AA guns were intact and Burckhardt lost two of his Ju-52s before the men could jump.

The German Staff later explained the delay in the drops and the change in the initial planning and time schedule of the operation: 'Because of delays in refuelling, these planes (transports) arrived too late over the designated drop-points and the paratroopers were therefore without direct

29 C.E. Mamalakis, Ian Powys Archive.

One of the Bren Carriers in the hands of the paratroopers, in the airfield area, soon after the battle. Kako Oros Hill can be seen in the background. (G. Müller & F. Scheuering, *Sprung über Kreta*)

fighter and bomber support'.[30] Part of the problem had been the dust at the airfields in Greece, which had disrupted all the flight schedules.

When Burckhardt's men landed in the Karteros Valley, there was another unpleasant surprise (apart from the mortars and the machine gun fire): Bren Carriers. These were even more dangerous than the heavy tanks, since they offered a very good view for their crew and they were especially fast and agile. In order to destroy the Bren Carriers, the paratroopers ambushed them – killing their crews, but at a high cost.

*Hauptmann* Burckhardt reported:

> The camouflage of these AFVs had been perfect. I had been sure when we jumped that we should have only infantry to deal with. That was my first surprise. The second was when I discovered who the infantry were.[31]
>
> I had never expected such bitter fighting and we began to despair of ever gaining our objective, or indeed of surviving at all. The Bren carriers were particularly dangerous to us, for they were not as blind as the tanks, and faster, and we had no armour-piercing weapons. The only thing to do was to ambush and storm each one separately, jumping on them and killing the crew with machine pistols. They never surrendered. In this way we destroyed many carriers, but for each one I lost at least twenty men, sometimes more.[32]

Erich Reinhardt reported:

> [...] our Battalion Commander, Burckhardt, who was often mocked as a cocktail party soldier, showed great courage in the assault on Iraklion [Heraklion]. He had in the two or three days during which he played hide and seek in the mountains, recovered from the onslaught and spoke only of revenge.[33]

30 *XI Fliegerkorps*, *Gefechtsbericht* '*Einsatz KRETA*' 1941, Anlage III, p.5.
31 The Black Watch was considered one of the toughest units of British Army.
32 WO 231/3, National Archives.
33 David Lenk Archive.

## The town sector (west)

The *II./FschJgRgt.2*, under *Hauptmann* Schirmer, was dropped west of Heraklion at 1700 in the area of Gazi-Tsalikaki, with the largest group dropped around Hill 67 (Stavromenos, or Chalepa Hill). They encountered relatively weak resistance – mainly by the inhabitants of the nearby villages of Gazi, Rodia, Krousonas, Tylissos, Agios Myron and Voutes. The total strength was 350 paratroopers and consisted of the Battalion HQ plus a platoon (in four planes), the 7th Company (in nine planes), the 8th Company (in nine planes) and the 2nd Platoon of the *14./FschJgRgt.1* (*II. Zug 14./FschJgRgt.1*, in three planes).

The *8./FschJgRgt.2* was dropped west of Hill 67 and moved westwards in order to secure the area, while the *7./FschJgRgt.2* was dropped east of the hill and moved south-east/eastwards towards the city as far as the Giofyros River. The men of *II./FschJgRgt.2* occupied the main bridge over the Giofyros River on the road to Heraklion, and there they were providing medical care for the wounded paratroopers who were gathered near the bridge.

Paratrooper Adolf Strauch of the *II./FschJgRgt.2* described the situation:

> The 7th and 8th Companies under *Hauptmann* Schirmer were tasked to cover the 1st Regiment from the west [...] The enemy fire was weak. We found all the pre-planned points and we collected our supplies. Exactly at that moment the 1st Regiment arrived.[34]

A snapshot of the *II./FschJgRgt.2* command post at Hill 67. (Author's collection)

The old bridge over the Giofyros River, on what was in 1941 the main road to Heraklion. (Author's collection)

34 A. Strauch, BDF e.v. Archiv, Freiburg/Breisgau.

**Special Presentation 6: Gerhard Schirmer**

Gerhard Schirmer (9 January 1913-5 September 2004) volunteered for the paratroopers on 1 May 1939. He participated in operations in Poland, Holland and Norway.

During the Greek campaign, he was the commander of the *6./FschJgRgt.2*, but assumed the duties of *II./FschJgRgt.2* commander due to the serious injury suffered by *Major* Pietzonka during the Corinth Canal operation on 26 April 1941.

Schirmer's battalion successfully captured the airfield at Argos and took a large number of Allied troops prisoner as they were retreating. On Crete, he jumped west of the town of Heraklion and later, he and his men managed to occupy the very important Hill 296 (south of the airfield), which was the turning point for the battle in this area. For his actions, he was awarded the Knight's Cross.

*Hauptmann* Gerhard Schirmer, commander of the *II./FschJgRgt.2* on Crete. (Author's archive)

Later, Schirmer fought in Russia, Tunis, Italy and again on the Eastern Front. He was captured by the Americans in April 1945 in Hamburg, and then handed over to the Russians, who held him in captivity. In 1956, he returned to West Germany and served in the *Bundeswehr* until his retirement in 1971.

Odysseas Vamvoukakis, from the village of Marathos, described the battle against the paratroopers of the *II./FschJgRgt.2*, west of Heraklion:

> We moved to Tsalikaki where we were pressing the Germans. My comrades were a policeman named Pavlos from Chania who was later arrested and executed by the Germans, Thomas Maris from Marathos who had a rifle (which was later sent to Cyprus for the struggle against the Turks), Lysimachos Ladas with a pistol, Gregoris Moulakakis, Giorgis Livas and many more villagers who were in groups that I can't recall and say what exactly groups they were. I'm saying only the names of those who were with me.
>
> Well, we were in a location in a field with olive trees and the Germans were shooting on us and first they were aiming high at the top of the olive tree, lowering the shot gradually.
>
> I was lying on the ground but my water bottle and my rucksack were full of bullet-holes and when I felt the cold water on my chest I said: 'Be careful because

Odysseas Vamvoukakis from the village of Marathos, photographed in 1941. (Courtesy of C.E. Mamalakis)

> they are going to kill us all.' Next to the field was a vineyard and I saw a parachute there so I went and took a few strings to hang my pistol on my belt.
>
> About 15 metres away a German was hiding who, if I had seen him, I would have killed right away but we moved back very carefully on a small road to the west. As soon as we got to this small road, we heard shooting and I thought that it should be Lysimachos who shoots against the Germans in order to cover our retreat but then I looked and saw the German at the olive tree where we were before, shooting at us. Then I shot him and we retreated without any other threat.[35, 36]

Among the armed civilians from the nearby villages who gathered to fight the paratroopers of the *II./FschJgRgt.2* west of the city was Nikolaos Kyrikakis from the village of Voutes:

> I was 19 years old during the battle of Crete. On the first day of the battle that started with bombings in the city of Heraklion, I was working with my father in our vineyard.
>
> I immediately dropped everything and after taking from our house in Voutes a short-barrel single shot rifle with 38 rounds and a pistol (not in good condition at all) with 50 rounds I left alone for the battlefield in the area of Tsalikaki - Chalepa.
>
> Exactly at that moment three planes started dropping paratroopers. At first and before the parachutes opened, I thought that they were dropping bombs. When the parachutes deployed I started shooting at them. I shot 10-15 rounds without knowing whether I got someone or not. Since there were so many paratroopers I retreated southwards to Pigadi Arkalou.
>
> Along with an officer we moved to my village where we formed a group under the senior police officer of the nearby village of Agios Myron named Nikolaides: nine Gendarmerie men, an old man called Giorgis Polychronakis, with the nickname 'Katsa-Katsa', Michalis Alogdiannakis, Giannis and Christoforos Merdoulakis, the 15 year old Manolis Stivaktakis, Manolis Kavalos, Apostolis Polychronakis from Krousonas with the nickname 'Kikirikos' and an English sergeant.[37]
>
> We were armed with anything that we could find available: shotguns, old pistols, swords, Mannlicher rifles. We engaged in combat with the Germans in the area of Konstantinidis Metochi[38] and the battle lasted till dark.
>
> On the second day of the battle, very early and alone again I left my village in order to go to the battlefield. The Germans had abandoned Konstantinidis Metochi and were assembled in Chalepa Agakou and Sfakianakis Metochi. The last one was a two-storied house with tile-roof that still exists abandoned today and belonged to the Sfakianakis family.
>
> When I got there by following the noise of shooting, I saw two men taking cover behind a pile of stones in an old demolished house. They were shooting at the house in Sfakianakis Metochi, in the first floor of which were some Germans, firing at those two Cretans with a machine-gun from the west window, at a distance of 180-200 metres.

35 The area where this incident took place is at the edge of the drop zone of the *8./FschJgRgt.2*. According to the German Archives, on 20 May there was only one dead paratrooper from this company: *Obergefreiter* Eberhard Fiedler. Most probably, this was the paratrooper that Odysseas Vamvoukakis shot. It is worth noting that the corpse of Eberhard Fiedler was never found, since he was isolated from the rest of his company at the edge of the drop zone and the locals buried his body in order to avoid German retaliation.

36 Interview with C.E. Mamalakis.

37 The presence of the English sergeant in this area west of the city, where no English units were, means that he was a member of John Pendlebury's team, who had links in Krousonas Village.

38 Konstantinidis' farm; the word 'metochi' in Greek means 'farm'.

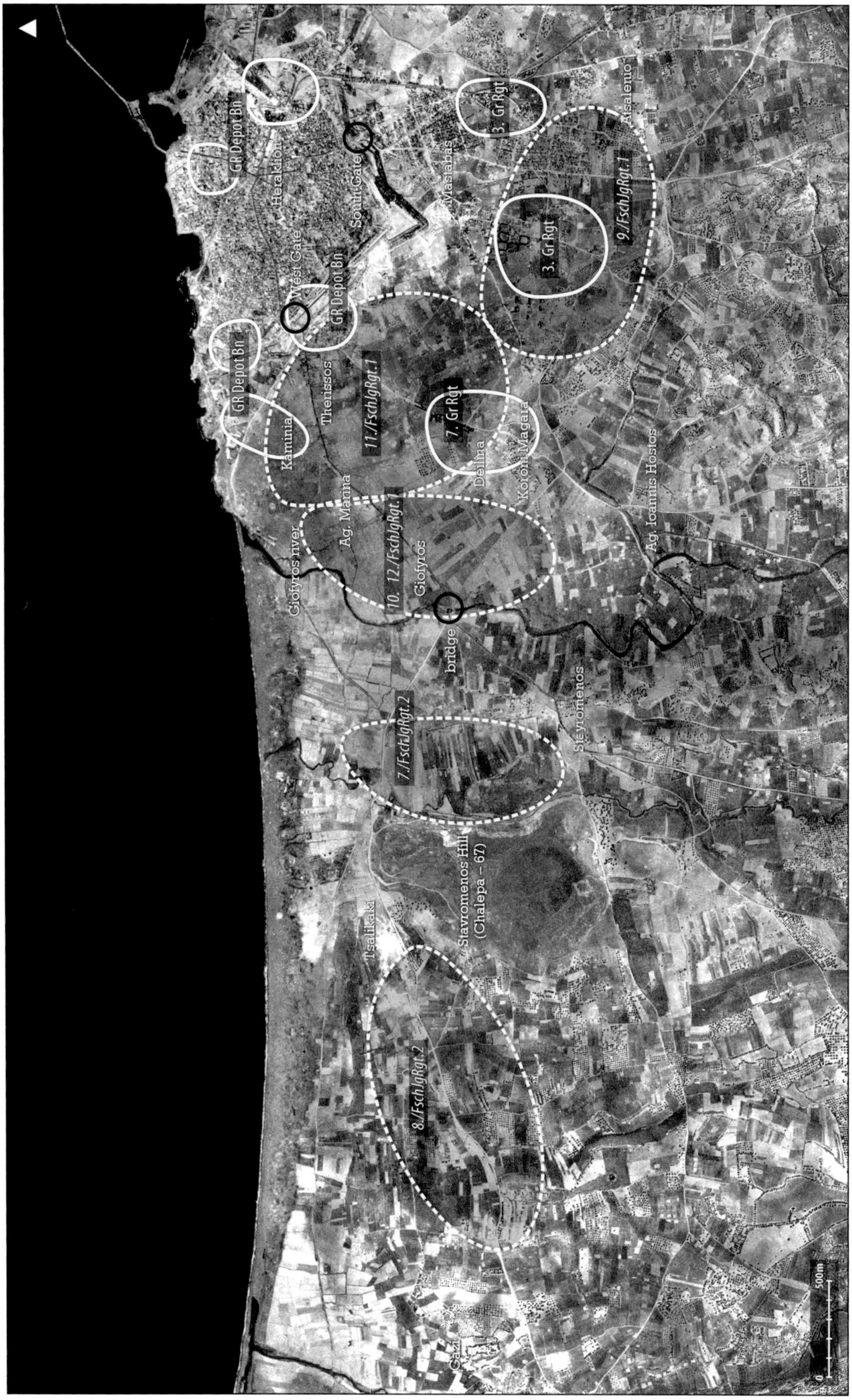


Map 2.5 The area west of Heraklion, with the drop zones and Allied positions. (N. Valasiadis, 2015)

The drop of the *8./FschJgRgt.2*, west of the town in the area that Odysseas Vamvoukakis describes. (Courtesy of Shaun Winkler)

Three Ju-52s in standard 'V' formation drop men from *8./FschJgRgt.2* on Hill 67, west of Heraklion Town. The peak of Mount Stroumboulas can be seen in the background. (Author's collection)

The same area photographed in 2014. The wartime photographer stood in the *7./FschJgRgt.2* drop zone at the top of Hill 67, some several hundred metres east of *8./FschJgRgt.2*. (Author's collection)

I came close to them and asked them who they were. They replied that they were from the village of Anogia. The older one told me that his name was Skoulas and the other Cheretis. Cheretis was wearing army trousers and shirt while Skoulas had a strange appearance, wearing traditional riding boots and breeches, on his head he had something black like a monk's hat and he had a short beard and a thick moustache. Skoulas asked me: 'Who are you and where are you coming from? Why you are alone? Where are the others?' I joined them and together we started shooting at the Sfakianakis house. From time to time the machine-gun from the house was firing on our position.

After some time of shooting, Skoulas' rifle was jammed and was useless. Skoulas tried hard to release the cartridge that was stuck in the rifle by hitting the rifle on a rock but without any success. He asked me to give him my gun but then he said that it was not fair and besides there only were a few rounds left. So he said that he was going to find another gun. I must say that each time that he was trying to release the stuck cartridge he was standing up in order to hit the rifle hard, leaving his cover and giving a very good target to the Germans. When we tried to warn him to take cover he replied: 'The German bullets don't kill.' Finally he decided to leave and search for another gun in Gazi.

What I saw then, I never saw or heard in my life again. He left walking without taking cover and every time he found a stone he was standing and hit the rifle. The Germans were shooting at him and he was giving contemptuous gestures to them while following a path of 80-100 metres long in open field, without cover from trees or bushes. Cheretis and I were trying to cover him but the Germans were shooting short bursts. While Cheretis was watching Skoulas leaving he was shouting at him to take cover but in vain. Finally Cheretis told me: 'He is absolutely crazy.' After a while the Germans stopped shooting and I searched for Skoulas but I didn't find him and I thought that he was probably dead somewhere. I returned in tears to Cheretis where he was fighting along with two other men from Krousonas.

I met this man many years after the battle, completely different, with the name Papagiannis Skoulas, without beard, wearing suit and tie.[39]

At 1730, the *III./FschJgRgt.1 Battalion* – under *Major* Schulz – was dropped in the area of Deilina-Kaminia-Therissos-Mastabas, west and south-west of the city and outside the Venetian walls.

The British soldier Reg Spurr of the 2nd Battalion, the York & Lancaster Regiment describes in a very vivid way the drop of the *III./FschJgRgt.1* paratroopers and especially of the 9th Company, that dropped in this specific area at the beginning of the battle. Reg Spurr was well away from his combat post – being on leave in a tavern in the Mastabas-Therissos area. Unaware of the imminent German attack, he was caught by surprise when the invasion began. His account confirms the lack of awareness of the invasion, which had already begun in Chania and Rethymnon, among Heraklion-based units.

Private Reg Spurr of the 2nd Battalion, the York & Lancaster Regiment, in 1940. (Courtesy of the Society of Cretan Historical Studies)

39 C.E. Mamalakis' archive.

The abandoned house in Sfakianakis Metochi today, as seen from the north. (Courtesy of C.E. Mamalakis)

A view of the house from the rocky area, where Kyrikakis and his comrades were fighting against the paratroopers. (Courtesy of C.E. Mamalakis)

The west side of the house, where the MG-34 was placed by the paratroopers – covering the whole area with fire. (Courtesy of C.E. Mamalakis)

The *9./FschJgRgt.1*, that was dropped in this area, was among the most unfortunate, since it dropped right on the positions of the 3rd Greek Infantry Regiment and the 2nd Battalion of the York & Lancasters. The unit was virtually annihilated in a few hours. Among the dead was the company commander, *Oberleutnant* Wilhelm Singer, who is buried next to men of the *11./FschJgRgt.1.* This indicates that he was killed not far from the West Gate. The *9./FschJgRgt.1* losses were so devastating that the rest of the *III./FschJgRgt.1* heard nothing of the fate of this company during the first days of the battle.

The following account by Reg Spurr is very characteristic of what had happened in the Mastabas-Therissos area, south of Heraklion:

> [...] The next day arrived, and Robbo and myself set out at the appropriate time, 1 o'clock. There were no enemy planes about, so we looked forward to a few drinks and examining the town, which was only the other side of the shallow valley. We found a nice little *taverna* in which were a couple of chaps from the Black Watch and a couple of Royal Engineers. We got a glass of beer each and sat with the other chaps. A few Cretans came in and we bought them a drink each. They started asking us if we thought the Germans would come, when we heard the bombers come. We couldn't see them as the windows were high up. The bombing got more and more ferocious. We could hear what sounded like buildings going up all round us, but we were not prepared to leave our drinks. The noise was horrific, there were waves of *Stukas* which screamed as they dived, then the heavy bombers, then *Stukas* again. One of the Black Watch said, 'I thought the clear skies were too good to last.' Then after about an hour it suddenly went quiet. Suddenly there was the roar of possibly hundreds of fighters, very low indeed, zipping about all over the place with machine guns and cannons blazing. Then they veered off, followed by the roar of hundreds of bigger aircraft.
>
> The next thing was, two Cretans dashed into the *taverna* shouting, 'Umbrella! Umbrella!' I then heard a bugle call from the direction of our position, as we were nearest to the town. I said, 'Sh-sh-sh-sh' and we all sat and listened. Sure enough, our buglers could be heard sounding the alarm followed by three 'Gs', which was the signal for paratroopers.
>
> Immediately there came the sound of thousands of rounds of small arms fire. I jumped on the seat to look out of the window. It looked a wonderful sight really, hundreds of three-engine planes and parachutes. The parachutes seemed to be coming down all over the place. I was surprised to see how low the planes were when their passengers baled [*sic*] out [...]
>
> For a few seconds we all stood on the seats and watched as all these hundreds of parachutes floated down. It was fascinating for a moment. Then Robbo said, 'Come on lads, we've got to get back to our units.' So we all dashed for the door. I can't remember what the others did, but I recall having a last gulp of beer. When we got out into the street, the first thing I did was look up at the sky. There were still what looked like at least 100 three-engine planes, which were Junkers 52s. One was flying much lower than the others and making for the open sea, the opposite direction to the others. In fact, it was so low one could see the corrugations in the body, it looked as if it was made of corrugated iron. I suspect it was flying so low because a parachute was caught on the tail and the poor bloke wearing the chute was trailing along behind like a streamer. A couple of Greek soldiers were firing at him with their rifles. I recall being tempted to do the same, then thought there must be a lot of bullets going in that direction.
>
> Parachutes were coming down everywhere. Three dropped about twenty feet away, two in the street were already dead. The one who straddled the wall seemed to try to balance himself, then it looked as if he was pulled down from the other side of the wall and there was an agonizing scream. Robbo got to a gateway in the wall near where the para had gone first. I was a couple of paces behind. Just inside the gateway was a woman of about forty. She had a wicked-looking carving knife in her hand, the German's throat was cut wide open. He was

still making a gurgling noise. The woman, far from being afraid, looked very, very angry and started slashing at the parachute cords, then started to cut open the German's clothes, obviously looking for weapons to substitute for her carving knife. She was dressed in traditional Cretan dress and looked up only to scream something in Greek with a quick point further up the street.

One of the Cretans from the *taverna* spoke a little English and said, 'Come on English, she said there's a lot of them up here,' and went running up the street. He only went a few yards, then turned back saying, 'I'll get a gun first.' There was Robbo, the two Black Watch chaps and myself, where the others had gone I don't know. Robbo said 'Spread out and you two stay a few yards behind,' indicating myself and one of the Black Watch. Like that we advanced cautiously up the narrow street and reached a passage running off to the right. He signalled stop, which we did whilst he checked carefully round the corner. I looked round and saw the Cretan who had done the interpreter bit for us, stood by one of the 'dead on arrival' Germans. He had found a *Schmeisser* automatic pistol, and I think he was trying to find out how it worked [...]

Most of the noise now was from small arms fire and it was mainly coming from the right, where we had come from. Suddenly from the road junction emerged about 15 Jerries who opened fire on us. Robbo got hit in the chest with a hand grenade. The two Jocks and myself lay flat where we were as there was no cover and returned the fire. The Jerries seemed to be making a running fight of it, as if they were in a hurry to get somewhere, or were being chased by someone else. I think I fired about 10 shots but after about five I thought, 'Those Jocks are taking their time.'

[...] I went to look at Robbo. I couldn't recognize him but I was amazed, he was still alive but only just. I recall feeling very sick. I told him I'd fetch the stretcher-bearers and they'd soon have him tucked up in bed in hospital. I don't know if he heard me, but he would not have believed it any more than I did. There was a lot of blood all around him. I stayed with him for a minute or two, I think it was really because I didn't know what to do, but I like to think it was to be with him when he died.[40]

A wartime image of Heraklion – illustrating the labyrinth-like narrow streets. (Author's collection)

40 R. Spurr, *To Have and to Lose – Testimonies 1*, pp.185-193.

The participation of the Cretans in the battle from the very beginning was a key factor in the outcome. Patrick Leigh Fermor remembered:

Patrick Leigh Fermor in 1942. (C.E. Mamalakis' archive)

> For the Allies the most strange and strong memory from those 10 days was the participation of the Cretan population. It made a great impression on us. Nothing similar had happened in the other countries which had been attacked and occupied. In the rest of Europe the resistance was not yet born while in Crete the resistance was born at the moment that the first paratrooper landed on the ground of Crete. I was then just a lieutenant in the command post of the 14th Brigade in the caves between the town and the airfield. I was the only one who had served in the Albanian front [during the war against the Italians in 1940-1941] as a liaison officer hence I had seen by myself the incomparable bravery of the Greeks beating the divisions of Mussolini in the mountains of Epirus.
>
> It was one of the miracles of war and virtually the first victory of the Allies. There, a strong friendship was developed between me and the soldiers of the 5th Division 'Crete' which unfortunately during the battle of Crete, remained on the mainland of Greece. How much we all wanted to have them with us in Crete![41]

The Regimental Depot (Garrison) Battalion of Heraklion, under Major Demetrios Kasimatis, was deployed in Chanioporta (West Gate) on the west walls and westwards as far as the Giofyros River, and from the coast to the north and Therissos to the south. The 7th Greek Infantry Regiment was stationed in Therissos as a reserve (minus two companies, which were deployed at Kako Oros, about 4km east of the airfield) under Lieutenant Colonel Evangelos Cheretis. South of Therissos and in the Mastabas area, the 3rd Greek Infantry Regiment – commanded by Lieutenant Colonel Antonios Beteinakis and with its command post in Mastabas – was deployed as far as Phoinikia (south-west of the town); this unit controlled the Heraklion-Knossos and Heraklion-Phoinikia Roads.

2nd Lieutenant Filotas Adamides of the 3rd Greek Infantry Regiment described the drop of the *III./FschJgRgt.1* – and particularly the *9./FschJgRgt.1*:

> One of the paratroopers landed a distance of 100-150 metres ahead of me in a field with high wheat, between me and my platoon. The situation demanded that I act immediately. With a few jumps I went close to him with two other chaps from my platoon, one of which was the staff sergeant of the company. He was full of joy when he saw me and having already killed the German who was lying covered with his parachute, he said, making a joke: 'You are coming second and too late lieutenant and as you can see we have already replaced our armament with German-made, hence I let you have the weapons of this paratrooper.' Actually the first thing I did was to take the pistol and the binoculars of the dead German, leaving the rest for the soldiers of the platoon.

41 P.L. Fermor, *Speech in the Vikelaia Library* (Heraklion, 21 May 1994), C.E. Mamalakis' archive.

> After the initial sweep, the soldiers started returning to their positions again, exactly as they had been trained to fight the paratroopers. Some soldiers from Sfakia came back much later in the evening loaded with German weapons and gear, having a piece of cloth tied on their heads and a knife in the mouth according to the old Cretan custom,[42] after we thought that they were missing or dead.[43]

The CO of the 3rd Greek Infantry Regiment, Lieutenant Colonel Antonios Beteinakis, described his experience:

> [...] The whole evening of 20 May passed in the middle of a huge struggle. Our soldiers, after having run out of ammunition, charged with bayonets and [rifle] butts against the Germans. For about two hours they were chasing the dispersed Germans from house to house and fence to fence till late at night. Not one of the Germans would have survived without the approach of nightfall. Uncountable guns, rounds, machine-guns, hand grenades and anti-tank guns came to our possession and in that way resupplied our units. In only a few minutes my soldiers learned how to use those weapons and we were able to continue the fight. At around 7pm and after finding by accident many American guns (Springfield rifles) stored in the Battalion's depot, I attacked the Germans[44] left at the east edge of Mastabas with 150 men and in a short time I cleared the area of the paratroopers.[45]

Private Christos Roussopoulos of the 7th Greek Infantry Regiment wrote in his diary:

> [...] After three hours of bombing and machine-gunning, the big German carrier planes called Junkers began arriving. As soon as they reached the coast the paratroopers were jumping according to the plan I assume. Every 10 minutes another formation of 13 planes was coming [...] In a while the sky south of Heraklion and to a distance of 500 metres from the town[46] was full of colour but mostly white parachutes [...]
>
> All this time our guns were exposed to the dust and dirt of the countryside, under the olive-trees and on the rocks. With the first shot, the bolt was stuck and didn't open. We had to hit the bolt with a rock and put another cartridge in the chamber. This was a big delay and a huge handicap at that crucial moment of the battle.
>
> On our first charge against the Germans, just with the first steps we made, we started seeing dead paratroopers all around. On a plateau I saw 10 dead paratroopers and among them were two Greek soldiers lying dead. While I started the fight feeling hate for the German invaders and I was shooting to kill them either on the ground or still in the air, now I see them dead next to each other and some of them disfigured by the hit of some anti-aircraft shell, with a hand or a leg severed or even the head smashed [...] Those who were killed just by a bullet seem like they are still alive, having a sad expression because of the things that they saw happening around them before they died. A paratrooper is dead next to a Greek soldier. Their faces are against each other as if they were saying: 'Why have we killed each other? Why?' [...]

42 The Cretans have a grand war-tradition and customs directly related to the ancient Greeks.

43 *Cretan Panorama* Magazine, March-May 2011, p.130.

44 The men of the *9./FschJgRgt.1.*

45 Lt Col A. Beteinakis, *After Action Report concerning the battle in Heraklion, 20-29 May 1941*, p.4.

46 The drop zone of the *9./FschJgRgt.1* and *11./FschJgRgt.1.*

All those thoughts pass through my mind while I can't take my eyes off the Greek and the German dead. They must have parents, brothers, or even wives and children somewhere waiting for them to return one day. I was about to cry.

A fellow soldier shouted: 'More Germans are dropping. On them boys,' and he started firing. A young lieutenant from another company that had just arrived said: 'On them boys. Shoot them without mercy. They are invaders while we are defending our country' [...] While this lieutenant was speaking, I thought that he had read my thoughts when I felt mercy for the dead Germans and he was looking at me [...] Yes, I was now recovered for good. My duty at this crucial moment was to fight with all of my strength.

The place where a paratrooper had landed was easy to spot by the big parachute canopy. In a vineyard we counted seven parachutes, hence there must have been seven Germans somewhere around. The vineyards in Crete all have hedges around them made of stones. We surrounded the vineyard and started shooting into it. When we spotted them, they were all dead in a few minutes.

A bit further away there was an isolated parachute. We all were searching to find the owner. The first to see the German was my friend Ioannis Papadopoulos from Rigio. The German was wounded in the leg. As soon as he saw the Greek soldier he raised his hands and threw away his pistol in order to show his intention to surrender. The moment Papadopoulos bent over to pick the pistol up, the German shot him with another pistol. Fortunately he missed but then Papadopoulos shot the German in the chest and killed him. We all rushed there and when we went near the German we saw the big injury on his leg.

After a while the dark began to fall. The officer in charge told us to move and occupy the nearby hill before the Germans do so. It was already dark when we climbed onto the hill and sentries were put about 20 steps in front of our positions. We were told that the code word was 'Kriti' (Crete) and the reply was 'Korakas' (crow). If there was any other response we had to shoot immediately.

A group of civilians approached our positions and they said: 'Hello soldiers. Hit the bastards and we will all help you. All the people of Heraklion and all the people from the villages are coming in a while.' Two or three of them were holding guns but no one asked where they had found them. The rest were armed with axes, sticks and the traditional Cretan knives with the white grip. With black moustaches, wearing Cretan traditional clothes and boots and with blazing eyes they were saying while twisting their moustaches: 'This is Crete and anyone who dares to invade will pay for that and never return home alive.'

Every time they met a dead German they said: 'Go to hell bastard. What are you doing here in our Crete?' And they hit the corpse. A Greek soldier told them to stop. He said: 'These aren't nice things that you are doing. They are dead. Leave them.' And the Cretans replied: 'Let us express our anger.' [...]

The English were very well organised and with many AA guns they did great damage to the Germans. Those AA guns were firing at the Junkers that carried the paratroopers. Many aircraft were shot down around Heraklion but most of them on the east side near the airfield. Many crashed after they dropped the paratroopers while others were in flames while still loaded with the fully armed paratroopers who were falling like candle sticks. The men who were trying to jump from the burning planes, they were burning as well, falling and hitting the ground with some of them descending without arms, legs or heads that had been cut by the explosions of the AA shells.

Corpses in this condition were found in our area west of the town as well. The shattered bodies of two Germans had landed in a small creek. The water became red from their blood. Others were caught with the parachute on the branches of trees where they were shot many times even if they were already dead.

> Two German planes were circling flashing their lights but nobody knew what they wanted. A Greek officer ordered some soldiers to wear German uniforms and make signals with torches. They made a *swastika* on the ground by using a white parachute. That was it. The trick was a success. The two planes, believing that they were German soldiers, dropped their load to them. At the beginning we thought that it was dropped to the Germans but then when our soldiers started cheering, we understood what had happened.
>
> We rushed there and what we saw was our soldiers dragging the containers under the olive-trees. There were five or six containers and we opened all of them. Two contained 15 rifles each, brand new, while the others had machine-guns and ammunition.[47]

Among the armed civilians who participated in the battle against the paratroopers in Mastabas was Manolis Badouvas, who later became one of the leaders of the Resistance in Crete. Badouvas and his men attacked a group of 15 paratroopers outside the cemetery of Agios Konstantinos – killing six of them and taking the rest prisoner. Through this action, Badouvas managed to release the Greek soldiers that were earlier taken prisoner by the Germans and held in the cemetery.

Next to the church of Panagitsa (Holy Mary) in Mastabas was the *gendarmerie* (police) station,[48] with a strength of six men,[49] under Sergeant Emmanuel Pyrovolakis. The station was in the middle of the drop zone of the *9./FschJgRgt.1* and the *gendarmerie* men assumed battle positions in the building. G. Kavroulakis managed to kill the first paratrooper, who was just outside the church.

Manolis Badouvas – one of the leaders of the Resistance in Crete – pictured here (front row, second from right) with his men. (Author's archive)

47 Roussopoulos, pp.79-102.
48 At that time in Greece, police duties in rural areas were actually the responsibility of *gendarmerie* units – hence in this book when *gendarmerie* or police are mentioned, they are actually one and the same.
49 Those were: G. Apladianakis, M. Petralis, K. Kagaiampakis, G. Kavroulakis and G. Spyridakis.

The building in Mastabas where Manolis Badouvas' stables were, near the cemetery of Agios Konstantinos, as it is today. This building was the stronghold of Badouvas and his group during the battle. (Author's collection)

The church of Panagitsa today. (Courtesy of Menelaos Pratikakis)

M. Pytikakis describes what he saw:

> [...] G. Kavroulakis saw a paratrooper outside the church, moving very cautiously and holding his sub-machine-gun. Without any hesitation and without permission from his commander, Kavroulakis shot the paratrooper. The paratrooper fell to the ground and tried crawling to reach the corner of the church but Kavroulakis shot him four or five more times. The paratrooper didn't manage to use his gun, meaning that he was seriously wounded already from the first shot. He was later found dead a few metres away from the place where he fell.[50]

The paratroopers attacked the *gendarmerie* station, but the Greeks held their positions. When the paratroopers left for another area, the *gendarmerie* men left the building as well and moved towards the Agios Konstantinos Cemetery, from where the noise of the battle was coming. At the cemetery, a fierce battle was taking place between the men of the 3rd Greek Infantry Regiment and the Germans, while a short distance away, the British of the 2nd Battalion of the York & Lancaster Regiment were fighting. When the British saw the grey-green uniforms that the *gendarmerie* men wore, they mistook them for Germans and shot at them without hitting anyone.

During the battle – in the surrounding vineyards next to the road to Mesampelies and Knossos – *gendarmerie* men Kavroulakis, Apladianakis and Petralis were wounded (the latter more severely). The men found cover in a small gorge south-east of the cemetery where, after a British medic had dressed their wounds, they tried to return to the cemetery. While they were attempting to cross the road with quick jumps, Kavroulakis was mistaken for a paratrooper and the British shot him in the back and the leg. Kagiampakis stayed next to the unconscious Kavroulakis to keep the Germans at a distance, but when Pyrovolakis jumped over the wall, he took a hit and fell dead on the ground. Pyrovolakis was buried at the cemetery the next day.

M. Pytikakis, the *gendarmerie* CO in Heraklion during the bombing raids and just before the invasion, was in the officers' club at the Heraklion Guard HQ with Major Tzoulakis. Pytikakis described what happened:

> The bombing lasted for a long time with very short breaks. Till noon when we used to gather at the officers' mess for lunch, the noise of the explosions and the AA firing from the airfield is continuous. I'm sitting at the same table with Major (Inf.) M.Tzoulakis.[51] Cheerful and talkative as ever he always finds a new joke for the cooks in the kitchen. All the tables are full of officers since most of the officers of the Heraklion Guard have gathered here.
>
> Suddenly the building is shaking from an explosion and the glass on the windows makes a big noise. 'I think that those devils [the Germans] have gone too far today, what do you think?' Tzoulakis said. Actually it was the first time that the bombing was so intense during lunch-time.
>
> I thought that what we did was probably not so clever, gathering in the officers' club, since it would be an easy target for the German planes if they had spotted the place! It seems that the other officers had the same thought and right after lunch they left.[52]

In the Heraklion Guard HQ, at the corner of Vasileos Georgiou (today Dikaiosynis) and Evans Streets, only the Guard commander – Major Emmanuel Tsagkarakis – and 2nd Lieutenant

50 M.I. Pytikakis, *Storm Over Crete*, p.70.
51 Major M. Tzoulakis was killed the next day during the street fights in the area of the officers' club.
52 Pytikakis, p.60.

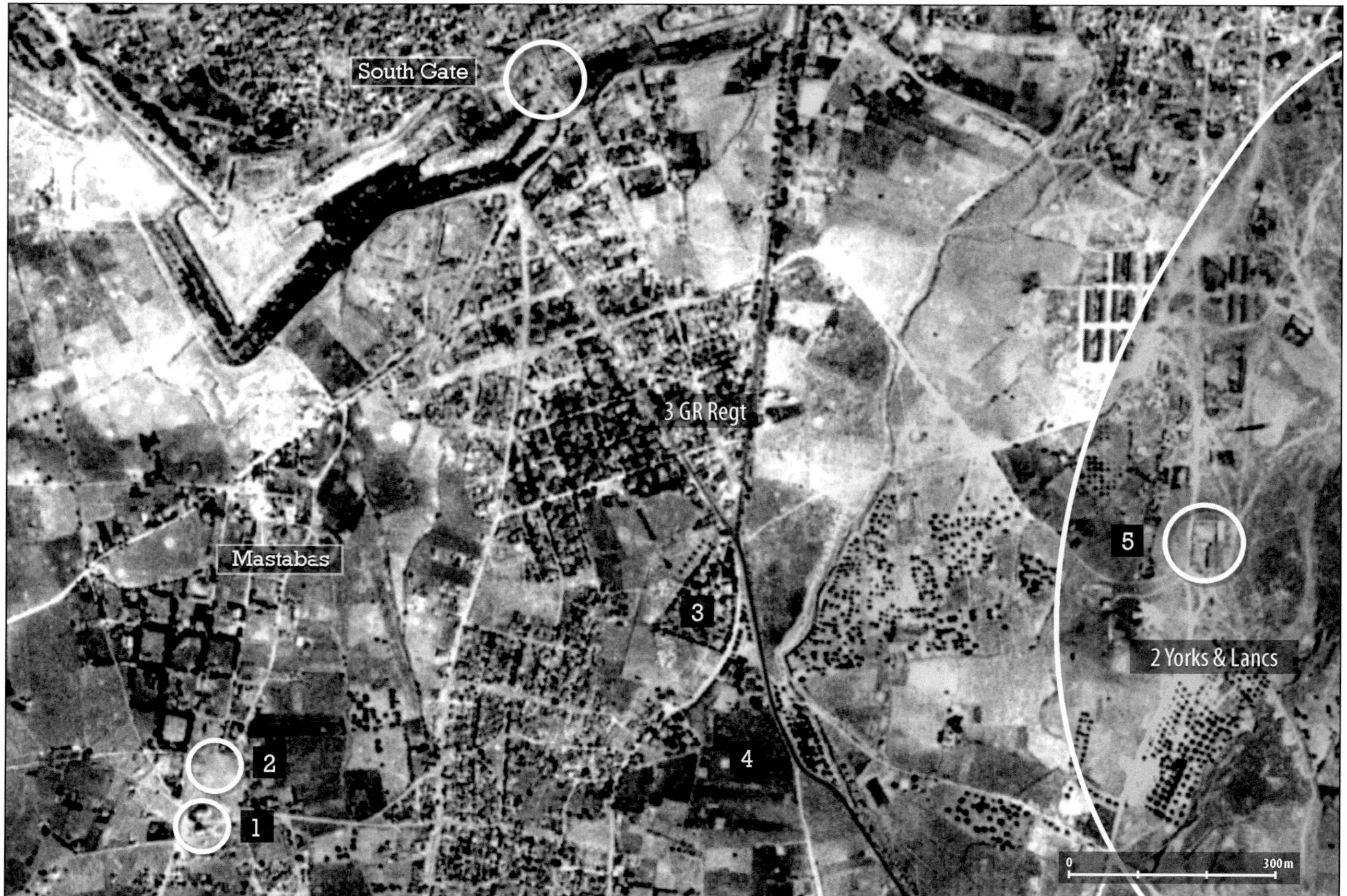


Map 2.6 The battle area in Mastabas, south of the town. The line between the 3rd Greek Regiment and the 2nd Bn, York & Lancaster areas of responsibility was the north-south road to Mesampelies, just east of the cemetery. (1) The church of Panagitsa, (2) the police/*gendarmerie* station, (3) Agios Konstantinos Cemetery, (4) vineyards, (5) Badouvas' stables. (N. Valasiadis, 2015)

The building where the Heraklion Guard HQ was established during the battle, at the corner of Dikaiosynis and Evans Streets. (Author's collection)

The Dialynas building, located opposite the Heraklion Guard HQ. It was the HQ of the Military Command's Heraklion-Lasithi sector. (Courtesy of Nikos Valasiadis)

Major General Michael Linardakis, commander of the Greek forces in the Heraklion-Lasithi sector. (C.E. Mamalakis' archive)

Major Emmanuel Tsagkarakis (1879-1977) was born in Malia, Heraklion. During the battle, he was the commander of the Heraklion Guard. It is said that when the Germans asked him to surrender the town, he answered: "The towns of Crete do not surrender. They fall." He retired after the war as a lieutenant colonel. (C.E. Mamalakis' archive) Note: Heraklion is famous for having endured the longest siege in history. The Turks tried for 21 years to occupy the town, between 1648 and 1669. The Cretan and the Venetian defenders finally surrendered because of exhaustion after all those years.

Eleftherios Malagardis were left when the invasion began. The other officers had gone to their posts according to their respective duties, such as the gathering and transportation of additional beds to the hospital, the collection and the burial of the dead, and the supply of food to the troops.

When the attack began, Colonel Charalampos Papathanasopoulos and Major General Michael Linardakis – commander of the Heraklion-Lasithi Military Command – settled into the Dialynas building right opposite the Guard HQ and tried to co-ordinate the defence of the town. An imminent threat seemed to appear from the south – coming from the Mastabas area.

The paratroopers who landed north of Mastabas, near the walls, tried very quickly to exploit the opportunity given by the general confusion and surprise that prevailed among the defenders. They attempted to enter the town through the South Gate called 'Kenourgia Porta' ('New Gate'). The men at the fire station next to the South Gate were desperately phoning the Guard HQ and the central *gendarmerie* station for help. The paratroopers were about to enter the town and the situation was very dangerous for the defenders at that point.

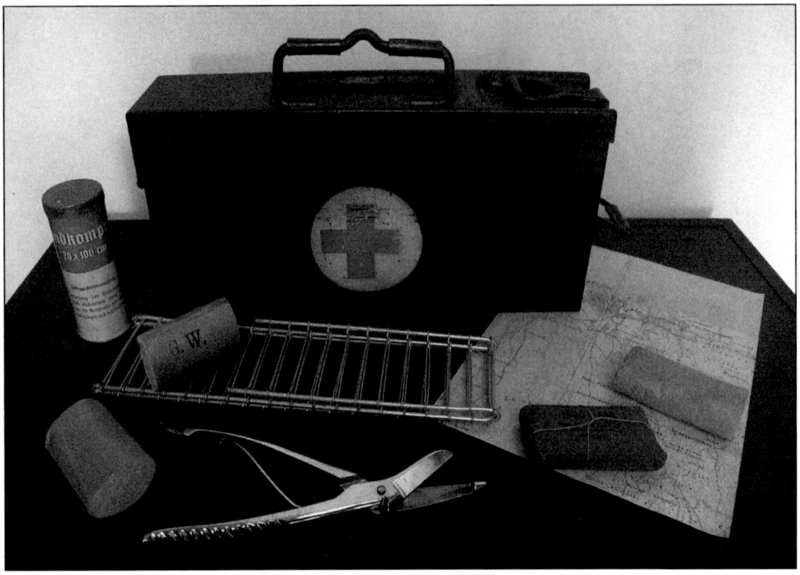


A first aid tin with contents, found near the South Gate of the Heraklion walls. It most probably belonged to *Oberarzt* Möller's medical group that dropped with the *9./FschJgRgt.1*. (Courtesy of C.E. Mamalakis)

The noise of the battle very quickly attracted many armed civilians and mixed groups consisting of civilians and *gendarmerie* men, under Sergeant Emanouel Sifakis and Antonios Galanakis,[53] to the South Gate. In addition, at the South Gate, a British machine gun platoon was positioned; this unit reinforced the defenders and played a key role in the effort to repel the Germans. In the end, the Germans failed in their attack and the few survivors retreated southwards to Mastabas and Atsalenio. The losses of the *9./FschJgRgt.1* were so devastating that this company was no longer a threat to the town for the remainder of the battle (please refer to the Colour Section for a Special Presentation of Fritz Weller of the *9./FschJgRgt.1*).

M. Pytikakis described the action:

> After taking the defenders by surprise, the paratroopers managed to approach the walls and the south gate, moving very decisively. They were no less brave and decisive than we were. It seemed that they intended to enter the city at any cost but the British machine-gun fire was so heavy that they didn't have any luck and were almost totally eliminated. The German mortars were firing on our positions and their sub-machine-guns were firing continuously as well. Those paratroopers who came close to the gate immediately dropped dead before they managed to throw their hand-grenades. The German planes were machine-gunning our positions but in vain. The defence had been stabilised.[54]

2nd Lieutenant Malagardis, who had stayed in the Guard HQ, explained his role:

> [...] When the telephone rang, it was the signaller of the Military Command and he reported that the paratroopers had advanced just outside the south gate and that it was imperative to send reinforcements to the defenders, in order to prevent the Germans from entering the city.

53 In those groups were also D. Kaffetzakis, G. Arkalakis, N. Sarris, E. Vlachothanasis, N. Moraitakis, K. Kyriakakis, E. Dermitzakis and many other *gendarmerie* men (Pytikakis, p.83).

54 Pytikakis, p.84.

The view that the men of the *III./FschJgRgt.1* had during their jump west of Heraklion, with the town and the walls on the left, exactly as described by Dr Eiben. The walls surrounding the city dominate the landscape in the area where *Major* Schulz and his men jumped. At the time of the battle, the town was confined within the walls, while the area outside the walls was mainly fields, vineyards and farms. (Author's archive)

> At that time there weren't any men available so we (the CO of the Guard and I) decided to go at the area of the battle in order to have a better understanding of the situation and better coordinate the forces fighting there. We took the staff car and with our guns in hand we set out for the south gate. After passing many obstacles, we finally arrived at the battle area, but we were a bit late since the paratroopers who had managed to infiltrate the city had already been killed by the units that guarded this place. They had been helped by the policemen and the civilians who rushed there just in time.
>
> In order to have a close look at the battle situation as it had evolved, we moved towards Mastabas but outside the Academy building we found ourselves in the middle of cross-fire between the Greeks on the walls and the Germans on the other side, hence we returned and drove to Chanioporta [West Gate] where bitter fighting was in progress.[55]

In the meantime, the next waves of the paratroopers were coming. When *Major* Schulz's Ju-52 approached the coast, north of the city of Heraklion, heavy AA fire started – indicating that the paratroopers could not count on the element of surprise anymore. *Major* Schulz was the first to jump out of the plane, followed by Dr Eiben and then his adjutant, *Leutnant* Wilhelm Proff. The fact that Schulz jumped first saved his life, since of the men on this aircraft, only Schulz and Dr Eiben, who had jumped right after him, survived the jump. All the rest, including *Leutnant* Proff, were killed. The tragic irony of this incident is that Proff had asked Eiben to change their order of jump so that he (Proff) could be next to his commander, but Eiben refused and said that one must not play with one's luck in a situation like that.

Dr Eiben described what occurred:

> Even before reaching the coast, we received heavy fire. In a short time, I counted 12 to 13 holes in my vicinity in the fuselage that were not there before. A frantic exchange ensued

55 C.E. Mamalakis' archive.

**Special Presentation 8: Karl Lothar Schulz**

Karl Lothar Schulz (30 April 1907-26 September 1972) was born in Königsberg and was the son of a teacher. He was an early paratroop officer – assuming the duties of company commander in the *FschJgRgt.1* in April 1938.

In 1940, he took part in the operations in Holland as the CO of the *III./FschJgRgt.1* – occupying the Waalhaven Airport. For his actions in Holland, he was awarded the Knight's Cross and was promoted to *major.*

During the Battle of Crete in May 1941, he was the CO of the *III./FschJgRgt.1*; after Crete, he fought on the Eastern Front and Italy – adding Oak Leaves (May 1944) and Swords (November 1944) to his Knight's Cross. He reached the rank of *generalmajor* and was captured in May 1945 by the Western Allies in Italy. He was kept in captivity until 1947.

Karl Lothar Schulz. (BDF e.v. Archiv, Freiburg/Breisgau)

> between the commander and the pilot because being to left [east] of the formation, we were drifting too near the town [just outside the walls]. 'Further right!' shouted the commander but it was too late by then. When I jumped I saw two other planes already streaming smoke.[56]

During their jump west of the city, the paratroopers were descending among burning and exploding Ju-52s, with some of the planes crashing to the ground just next to the walls. The noise from the ground of the AA guns and the small arms of the defenders could be heard, and many paratroopers were hit while still in the air; parachutes of others were torn by enemy fire. In many cases, the paratroopers were spread in an area much wider than originally planned – leaving them to cope with a hellish situation. Also, the drop of the supplies and ammo containers further delayed this unit's jump.

After an agonising drop into enemy fire, Schulz himself landed in a field in the Therissos area, just a few metres away from the walls and far from his men. The remaining men from his plane weren't so lucky and landed south-south-east, right on the positions of the 7th and 3rd Greek Infantry Regiments in Therissos and Mastabas. After quickly releasing his parachute harness, *Major* Schulz took cover in a cornfield and tried in vain to spot and join his men. Trying to move away from the walls under heavy fire, he met *Oberleutnant Graf* von der Schulenburg's group and escaped from the enemy with them.

The men of *II./FschJgRgt.2*, under *Hauptmann* Schirmer (which had been dropped earlier in the Gazi-Tsalikaki area), were watching the dramatic drop of the *III./FschJgRgt.1* west of the city. Paratrooper Adolf Strauch describes the spectacle: 'I shall never forget [...] We were watching the transport planes burning and crashing and our comrades jumping from the planes with burning parachutes. Our thoughts were with them and we knew that that day many comrades had been lost'.[57]

56 R. Kershaw, *Sky Men. Always Expect the Unexpected. The Real Story of the Paras*, pp.120-121.
57 A. Strauch, BDF e.v. Archiv, Freiburg/Breisgau.

### Special Presentation 9: Dr Eberhard Boerger

Eberhard Boerger, pictured here as a *leutnant.* (Courtesy of Dr Eberhard Boerger)

Dr Eberhard Boerger (7 October 1916-15 January 2016) joined the *Fallschirmjäger 1st Battalion* on 2 November 1937 in Stendal, where he went through his basic paratrooper training and qualified as a paratrooper. He also trained as a pilot – and in 1939, he was promoted to *leutnant.*

Boerger participated in operations during the Polish campaign and in May 1941, he fought in the Battle of Crete. He was a platoon leader in *II./FschJgRgt.1*, which dropped on Heraklion, where he was seriously injured after being shot in the stomach.

In October 1941, he saw action in Leningrad, where he was injured in one of his legs; in 1942, he was transferred to the *Fallschirmjäger* Training Regiment and in 1943, he was posted to North Africa with the *2./FschJgRgt 'Barenthin'*. He was decorated with the German Cross in Gold and the Golden Wound Badge for serious injuries suffered during the North Africa campaign.

In 1944, he fought in Normandy as a battalion commander of the *FschJgRgt.9*, where he was also wounded by a bullet in the thigh during the Battle of St Lo. He was then promoted to *major* in *FschJgRgt.*5 and in September 1944, he was taken prisoner by the British and held in captivity until February 1946.

From 1948 until 1952, he studied Law and later founded the company E. Boerger KG, Tankbehälter.

*Leutnant* Eberhard Boerger with his platoon (*III. ZUG 11*) in a picture taken a few months before the battle. (Courtesy of Dr Eberhard Boerger)

The *11./FschJgRgt.1*, under *Oberleutnant* Becker, landed right outside the walls. *Leutnant* Boerger's platoon landed in front of Chanioporta (West Gate), with most of the paratroopers killed immediately by the Greeks on the walls and at the Chanioporta barricades. *Leutnant* Boerger was wounded, but with three other paratroopers, managed to get into the small Municipal Customs (Dimotikos Foros) building and found cover there – exactly 90 metres away from Chanioporta and at the point where the statue of Michael Korakas is today.

*Gefreiter* Hans Schmickl was killed immediately after he jumped, while still in the air. His battlefield grave is seen in a photograph in Chapter 5. (Courtesy of Dr Eberhard Boerger)

Dr Eberhard Boerger recalls:

> After the operations in Holland and Norway, the *Fallschirmjäger* faced their biggest test: The airborne assault on the island of Crete. I was a 2nd lieutenant [*leutnant*] and a platoon leader in the 11th Company of the 1st *Fallschirmjäger* Regiment at that time and jumped with my men west of the town of Heraklion.
>
> The unspeakably scary picture of the mass jump into enemy fire will remain to the last breath as an unforgettable impression in my memory.
>
> I jumped first from my plane. The jump-master was obviously panicky and pressed the horn [jump signal] too early but I was lucky since I realised his error and waited a few seconds clasping desperately at the door-handles; otherwise I would have drowned in the sea. I landed unharmed, just 250 m from the sea on a harvested cornfield.
>
> My faithful comrade Hans Schmickl from Vienna was already mortally wounded in the air. After a short fight I reached first the so-called 'West Gate' [Chanioporta] of Heraklion. After my leap over the crossroads [today Mahis Kritis and 62 Martyron Avenue] the only man who had followed me was Buchen who was from my home-town. He was the son of Police Chief Buchen from Altenhundem while I was from the neighbouring area of Elspe (Lennestadt). We faced the Scottish Highlanders[58] who were positioned on the medieval walls of the town.
>
> While I was trying to find cover behind a small stone-building[59] Buchen was heavily wounded. He was completely immobilized and kept crying: 'Help me!' I made an attempt to pull the large man into cover and there a bullet scratched my chest and I started bleeding quite a lot.
>
> I tried to stop the bleeding using my field-dressing. Then help arrived in the form of a machine-gun squad under *Gefreiter* Weckert, a dashing daredevil. Immediately they started shooting with the machine-gun. With Weckert I grabbed the moaning Buchen and moved him into cover. Buchen couldn't move his legs anymore and asked for water. While I was unscrewing the canteen cup, I got a shot in my belly. Weckert was later shot in the head and

58 Eberhard Boerger had the impression that he was confronting Scottish troops, but in that area, there were only Greek troops and civilians, along with a few soldiers form the 2nd Battalion of the York & Lancasters.

59 It was the Municipal Customs (Dimotikos Foros) building, which was a distance of about 100m from the West Gate.

killed. In the evening, Buchen also closed his eyes forever. As though this was not enough, suddenly: '*Essch peep*!' Another small shell exploded between us where we were lying in the blood and I was hit by a fingernail-sized piece of shrapnel on the left knee (it is still in my thighbone today) and on the liver (also still in the liver).

The heavy blood-loss had made me fall asleep, and I regained consciousness later in the evening when my comrade *Oberleutnant* Fritze Merkordt cried: 'Hey guys, Boerger is still alive.' They transported me in unspeakable pain to a village behind the River Pofiros [Giofyros]. Next to me was lying *Oberleutnant* Glawe from the 10th Company who had been also shot in the belly. Glawe was a great-grandchild of Bismarck, as the daughter of Herbert von Bismarck had married professor Glawe. He was always cheerful, even on our bed of straw in the cowshed. Since we were not allowed to drink because of our belly shots, in 40 degree heat we went through indescribable thirst torments. We then both vowed to pay 100 Reichmarks for the first glass of lager beer at home. I fulfilled my vows in August 1941 on the trip from Fürth to my home in Elspein, Frankfurt. Glawe could not enjoy the joy of a cool glass of beer any more. He died in the military hospital in Athens.

From my straw-bed I witnessed also the death of our battalion adjutant, *Oberleutnant* Schramme. He was an SA group leader (*SA- Obergruppenführer*) in Dortmund/Westphalia and was rather high ranked in the [Nazi] party. He had been shot in the belly as well. The doctors tried to operate on him on an old wooden door but his heart couldn't stand the operation. When I was transferred to the hospital in Athens after the fighting on Crete, I wrote a letter to my parents in Elspe (Sauerland). There I also mentioned that *Leutnant* Schramme, an *SA - Obergruppenführer* from Dortmund had fallen, so the news of his death came quickly to the party authorities, faster than the official message sent by the battalion commander, *Major* Schulz. I fought death with a high fever for a long time in hospital in Fürth.[60]

Many paratroopers were killed within just a few metres of Chanioporta. The same fate met the paratroopers who landed in the Venetian ditch surrounding the walls, at the place where the Eleftherias Stadium is today. Barricades had been built in Chanioporta, where men of the Heraklion Regimental Depot Battalion had been deployed, while civilians were on the walls and at the barricades as well. Among the Greek forces were 20 men under Captain Manolesakis and some more from the HQ Company, under Lieutenant K. Gounalakis.

The soldiers and the armed civilians were positioned on the walls – killing all the paratroopers who landed in this area. To escape from the devastating bombing of the city, many people had sheltered in the tunnels under the walls, like the one opposite the Pananion Hospital.

2nd Lieutenant E. Malagardis recalled the scene:

The whole city was literally hell. The nerves of the people were broken over the last few days. Women and children were running all over without any specific reason. Cries and shouts were coming from everywhere.

On the road we stopped outside an old Venetian tunnel opposite the Pananion Hospital. The crowd had broken the door down and were taking the weapons stored there by the British. We were trying to restore order and stop the fights for guns among the civilians when suddenly I heard somebody calling me: 'Hello dear Lefteris. All together, with it or on it.'[61]

60 Dr E. Boerger, *Errinerungen eines Alten Fallschirmjägers*, pp.31-35.

61 An ancient Spartan mother said these words to her son leaving for the war – meaning: 'Come back victorious holding your shield or dead on it, but do not dare to come back without it, as only a coward leaves his shield behind in order to run and escape from the enemy'.

The area outside the West Gate, where *Leutnant* Boerger's platoon landed. The points marked with numbers are the places where his men were killed: A. Müller (1), Labitzki (2), Keller (3), Dr Lutz (4), Binnebesel (5) and Buchen (6). The Municipal Customs building (marked 7) can be seen on the left. (Courtesy of Dr Eberhard Boerger/Mike Smythe)

The early graves of paratroopers W. Buchen, A. Muller, G. Labitzki, W. Majewski, W. Keller, Dr Lutz, H. Binnebesel, H. Ristau, H. Weckert and K. Alte close to Chanioporta (West Gate). (Courtesy of Dr Eberhard Boerger)

*Obergefreiter* Walter Buchen (first on the right) in his Ju-52 on the way to Crete. The picture was taken less than two hours before he was killed. (Courtesy of Dr Eberhard Boerger)

> I turned and saw my friend Vicar Fotios Theodosakis holding a long-barrel rifle, raising it high and shaking it as if he were waving, then running onto the walls. I never saw him again. When the incident with the guns was over we moved on and arrived at the Chanioporta. [...]
>
> In the middle of the gate, barricades had been built just like at the other city gates. They were made of big stones, and were about 1.5 metres high, so that anybody who tried to enter or leave the city had to pass through the narrow zig-zag passage between the barricades.
>
> Sheltering behind those barricades, our fighters were keeping the enemy away. The Germans occupied the small Customs building right opposite the Chanioporta where today the statue of Michael Korakas stands.
>
> On our arrival there civilians and soldiers immediately surrounded us, as well as two Australians who were holding the only machine-gun there and asking for instructions about what to do with the Germans in the Customs House.[62] The commander of the Guard, influenced by the crowd and the two Australians, agreed to attack the Germans and then I said that it was not very wise for this crowd to charge virtually unarmed against the machine-gun fire of the Germans, since this would be a slaughter without a reason.
>
> While we were arguing a burst of machine-gun fire[63] followed by mortars fell on our positions. Mortar shrapnel tore apart the jaw of one of the Australians while the other who left his cover trying to shoot, took a hit in the chest and dropped dead [...]
>
> In the heavily bombed trenches and next to the corpses of the dead, among them the body of Captain Manolesakis, we were fighting against the Germans in the Customs building and the surrounding houses and buildings. Many paratroopers were hiding in the vineyards and they were shooting and shelling us with mortars while at the same time the very low-flying German planes were machine-gunning our positions.[64]

The paratroopers' drop right in front of the Venetian walls took the Greek Military Command of Heraklion by surprise, since the defence plans were mainly orientated to confronting paratroopers on the outskirts of the city at the predicted drop zones, which were well away from the walls.

The defensive perimeter was much broader than the perimeter of the walls – and in many cases, the paratroopers landed in the area between the walls and the defensive lines. Here, only small and reserve units were left, as was the case near the area west of the city and the Chanioporta. Only a few men defended this area and they barely managed to hold the paratroopers outside the city. The main Greek forces were deployed quite a distance west of the walls – thus leaving enough space for the paratroopers to move and attack the city. In the area south of the city (and especially in Mastabas) the paratroopers' drop between the walls and the defensive perimeter caused them to be trapped in a narrow space – leading to their total elimination. This explains the devastating losses of the *9./FschJgRgt.1* on the first day of the battle.

Despite the resistance of the Greek forces – consisting of army and police/*gendarmerie* units, as well as civilians – the paratroopers who dropped in Giofyros and Kaminia gradually managed to advance eastwards near Chanioporta. They established strongholds at the Kitriki juice factory in the Talos area and at the Tzoulakis warehouse in present-day Mahis Kritis Street, just 300 metres away from Chanioporta.

The *III./FschJgRgt.1* was supported by a platoon of the *13./FschJgRgt.1* – the heavy weapons unit (mortars and machine guns) – and was dropped far to the west of the town.

Paratrooper Ernst H. Simon from the *13./FschJgRgt.1* described his experiences:

62 Eberhard Boerger and his men were in the Municipal Customs building.

63 *Gefreiter* Weckert and his machine gun, as mentioned by Boerger.

64 C.E. Mamalakis' archive.

The inner side of Chanioporta, on the west wall of the town, photographed in 1941 soon after the battle; note the barricades built for the defence of the city. (G. Müller & F. Scheuering, *Sprung über Kreta*)

Chanioporta photographed in 2013. Bullet holes can still be seen today on the stonework of the gate – an indication of the fierce battles that took place here in May 1941. (Author's collection)

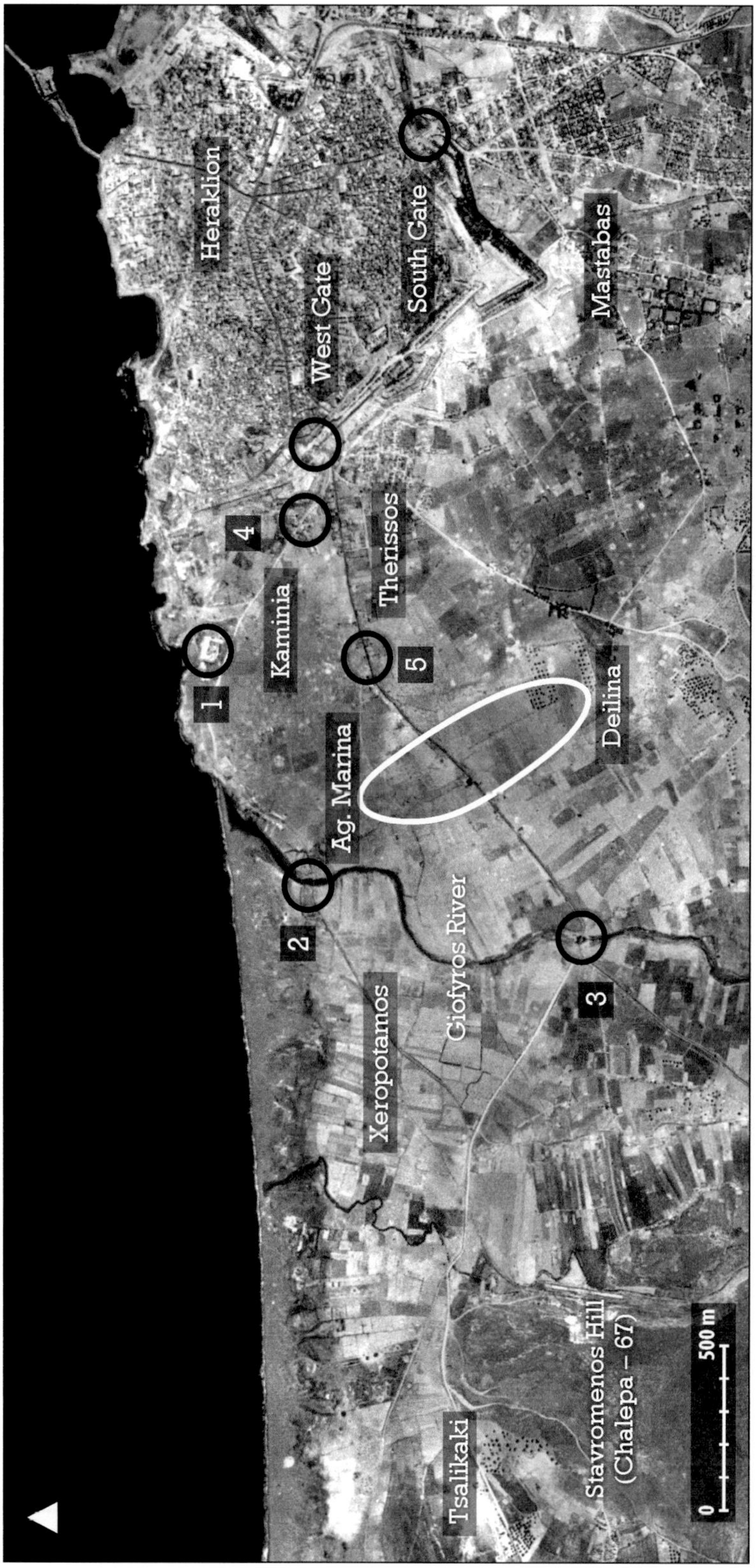


Map 2.7 The area west of Heraklion outside the walls: (1) Kitriki juice factory, (2) iron bridge of Giofyros River, (3) main bridge of Giofyros River, (4) Tzoulakis warehouse and (5) Piraeus Bank (today). (N. Valasiadis, 2015)

The bus station area at the western entrance to Heraklion, outside the walls. Chanioporta lies far to the right. This is the crossroads where *Leutnant* Boerger and his platoon landed. (Courtesy of Nikos Valasiadis)

The Kitriki juice factory, in the Talos area. (Author's archive)

The remains of the factories today, in the area where Kitriki was. (Author's collection)

In the Ju-52 on the way to Crete, *Oberjäger* Luders sits without his helmet, his bone-sack [jump-smock] and his machine-gun. The truck on which he had deposited his kit left during the refuelling of the plane. We fly over the sea at about 20 to 50 m height. In front of us and behind us there are Ju's as far as you can see. There isn't any sign of the Me-110s which were supposed to support and cover our drop. I drink water and empty the radio operator's canteen without him noticing me.

When the first peaks of Crete appear in the horizon, we hear the command, 'Get ready!' Immediately we secure the hooks of the static lines. I'm No. 13, the last man and the worst position if the plane is hit. Through the window, we see other Ju's amid anti-aircraft fire and some of them are going down in flames. Just before the coast, our pilot pulls the plane up to a height of 250 m. Now comes the signal 'Ready to go!' We are gathered in front of the door. Rifle and machine-gun fire is heard. The horn sounds and in a moment we are out hanging from the parachutes.

The Ju's turn away steeply while we try to orient ourselves just a few seconds before the landing and spot the weapons containers which have been dropped by the radio operator of the plane. About five feet away from me descends our gunner, Adam Drescher. A burning Ju-52 approaches in flames and crashes on the ground. I myself saw eight planes shot down that day. In most of cases, five to eight of the 13 paratroopers manage to jump out of the damaged planes while the rest of the men and the crew had no chance. A Ju-52 makes a crash landing on the beach and it is surrounded by snipers. The paratroopers in the plane fight back for two days until they are all dead. The most effective weapons are obviously the British 40 mm Bofors guns, but also the machine-guns and the rifles cause many casualties in the planes or during the jump. Surprisingly there is no protection from escort fighters which were supposed to protect us [...]

Our platoon lands in a vineyard and we quickly find our weapon containers. Only the floor plates of our mortars were separated from the harness of the parachute and landed after a free fall from a height of 250 m. It takes a lot of time to find them but finally they are all found undamaged thanks to the soft ground. We have been dropped too far to the west – as we understood later we were lucky to be dropped there – and we march towards the town. Sometimes we hear isolated rifle shots in our area but nothing else happens. It is already dark and we spend the night wrapped in our tents.[65]

A traditional German wooden skier toy, which was found by Odysseas Vamvoukakis in the cockpit of the crash-landed Ju-52, west of the town. Vamvoukakis was among the armed civilians who were fighting around the downed plane. (Courtesy of C.E. Mamalakis)

65 E.H. Simon, BDF e.v. Archiv, Freiburg/Breisgau.

Georgios Paleakis, a soldier of the Heraklion Regimental Depot Battalion, recalled:

> Although I was on leave after my serious injury on the Albanian front, I couldn't stay out of action so I went to Heraklion and found an old machine-gun in my company in Chanioporta [...] At the Agia Marina west of Kaminia I put the machine-gun in front of a small cave [...]
>
> The Germans[66] were dropped in the area from Xeropotamos to Giofyros. At that time there weren't many houses or buildings west of Chanioporta and the ground was mostly fields and farms. I was firing with my machine-gun for the whole night without stop[ping]. We didn't leave anyone moving. We killed all of them within the firing range of my machine-gun. We counted many dead Germans and we buried them near Giofyros River at the place where the Anastasakis wood factory is today.
>
> We were fighting with whatever we could find available. After some time I decided to move and establish my post on a hill. There at the old iron bridge I argued with my platoon leader since he wanted to move down the slope to lower ground, something that I didn't like at all.
>
> Finally we moved eastwards to Kaminia and arrived at Chanioporta. The Germans advanced and started shelling our positions on the walls (where the bus station is today) with mortars. Bitter fighting started and suddenly I fell off the walls completely unarmed but fortunately I found an old single-shot rifle and I managed to climb on the walls again.
>
> There I saw Major Beteinakis[67] coming with many more troops and we all advanced to Kainourgia Porta [South Gate] where four Germans were shooting at us, but finally we killed them all.
>
> The top of Chanioporta was hit by mortars, opening a big hole. I met two officers[68] there who were later killed and buried outside the church of Agios Titos.
>
> [...] Some time later I left Beteinakis' group and moved to Kaminia via the present 62 Martyron Avenue at the exact place where the Piraeus Bank is today. A German was hanging with his parachute caught on an electricity pole. I shot and killed him.

The exact spot where the paratrooper mentioned by Georgios Paleakis was seen hanging from his parachute on an electricity pole. (Author's collection)

66 The men of *10./FschJgRgt.1.*

67 He means Lieutenant Colonel Antonios Beteinakis.

68 He means Major Tzoulakis and Lieutenant Marinelis who were killed on 21 May during the street fighting in Heraklion.

**Special Presentation 10: Georgios Paleakis**

Georgios Paleakis was born on 5 May 1918 in the village of Rogdia, near Heraklion. He enlisted in the 43rd Infantry Regiment on 18 October 1939. On 21 November 1940, he was transferred by ship to Piraeus and then to the Albanian Front.

He fought in the Battles of Kleisoura and Trembesina, where he was seriously injured by mortar fire. He was transferred to a hospital in Athens, where he stayed until the German invasion and the collapse of the front. He finally managed to travel to Crete and reached his village on 19 April 1941.

Private Georgios Paleakis at the age of 20 as a soldier of the Greek Army (Courtesy of Korina Kafetzopoulou)

Paleakis at the age of 93 – showing the scar from the wound on the head that he received during the Battle for Heraklion. (Courtesy of Korina Kafetzopoulou)

Right after that I fell unconscious, having been hit by machine-gun fire. I took a hit by a bullet on my head. Luckily I was wearing a brand new helmet and this was what actually saved my life.[69]

[...] At the hospital there was a shortage of everything. They were cutting sheets in order to dress my wounds. I stayed 22 days in the hospital and when my mother visited me there she met the German wife of Dr Chasapes.[70]

The men of the *III./FschJgRgt.1* suffered heavy losses without succeeding in entering the city. They were involved in local fights and remained in the area south and west of the town – spreading from Mastabas and Therissos to Kaminia, Deilina, Gyofyros and Stavromenos. The largest group, under *Major* Schulz, and the *II./FschJgRgt.2*, under *Hauptmann* Schirmer, established themselves in the area of Gazi on Stavromenos Hill (Hill 67), where the command post and a field hospital were organised. German casualties in the area west of the town were quite significant during the first two days of the battle. The dead paratroopers were buried near the Giofyros River on the field where the Anastasakis wood factory stood later.

69 The 21 year old soldier was transferred to the Pananion Hospital. Although the doctors believed that he had no chance of survival and he was left alone, he suddenly opened his eyes and the doctors treated his wounds. Dr Nicolaos Chasapes (Director of the Hospital) operated on Paleakis and removed the bullet from his head.

70 G. Paleakis interview with Korina Kafetzopoulou, 2011.

A *Luftwaffe* aerial image of the Giofyros River area in 1941 – depicting the drop zone of the *10./FschJgRgt.1.* The white spots visible on the fields are actually the parachutes, while the note marked with the number '1' at the top-right of the picture indicates the position of the Greek forces – exactly at the place where Paleakis had placed his machine gun. (Fritz Dahm & Hans-Georg Schnitzer, *Kreta – Sieg der Kühnsten*)

The estuary of the Giofyros River, west of the town. The sandy beach and the fields, with low vegetation and vineyards, were the landscape of the *10./FschJgRgt.1* drop zone in this area. (Courtesy of Dimitris Skartsilakis)

Because of the presence of Greek soldiers and armed civilians, many groups of paratroopers remained isolated from their companies, despite their efforts to move and join their units under the cover of darkness. The first day of the invasion passed without any substantial progress by the paratroopers, who were trying to recover from their losses and reorganise in order to achieve their objectives. The night was a good opportunity for each side to prepare for the crucial second day of the battle, as the first day had been a confusing shambles for both the defenders and the attackers; for both sides, the second day was looking to be decisive.

The grave of *Gefreiter* Fritz Grüdelbach and the common graves of *Oberjäger* Otto Kiebach and *Gefreiter* Walter Hoppe from the *11./FschJgRgt.1*, who were killed on 20 May in the area west of the town. (Courtesy of Dimitris Skartsilakis)

Otto Kiebach (first on the right) with his comrades from *11./FschJgRgt.1* in a picture taken on 7 January 1941 in Kleinwalsertal. Also seen here (from right to left): Fleischhauer, Horst Weber (KIA 20.05.1941), Böse, Knoll, Hänsel and Otto Wagner (KIA 20.05.1941). (Courtesy of Dr Eberhard Boerger)

*Gefreiter* Walter Hoppe (first on the right) posing on the camera during leave in Athens, just a few days before the invasion; note the absence of paratrooper badges on the uniforms. Also seen here are *Gefreiter* Hermann Wollenzien (middle – KIA 20.05.1941) and Gottwald. (Courtesy of Dr Eberhard Boerger)

# 3

# The Drops on Gournes and the Battle at Kopsas Hill

*I./FschJgRgt.1* and the regiment's HQ were dropped in the Gournes area, some nine kilometres east of the airfield. The *3./FschJgRgt.1* was the only company that dropped according to the schedule, as this company flew to Crete aboard the planes of *K.G.z.b.V.107* (*Hauptmann* Wendorf), which took off from Tanagra. The *I./FschJgRgt.1* HQ, under *Major* Walther – with *1./FschJgRgt.1* and *2./FschJgRgt.1* – followed after a three-hour delay. They were transported by *K.G.z.b.V.60* (*Major* Hammer) from Topolia, where the backlog was quite significant. The *2./FschJgRgt.1* was supposed to jump two kilometres west of Gournes and occupy the radio station, but was dropped seven kilometres too far to the east and joined the rest of the battalion later that evening. The paratroopers who landed in Gournes occupied the radio station, which was in the area where after the war, an American base was established. The *4./FschJgRgt.1* was not dropped on Crete that day due to the lack of aircraft, and was later used in the Maleme sector with *Gruppe West*.

The radio station in Gournes; in the background can be seen Kopsas Hill, which dominates the landscape in the area. (G. Müller & F. Scheuering, *Sprung über Kreta*)

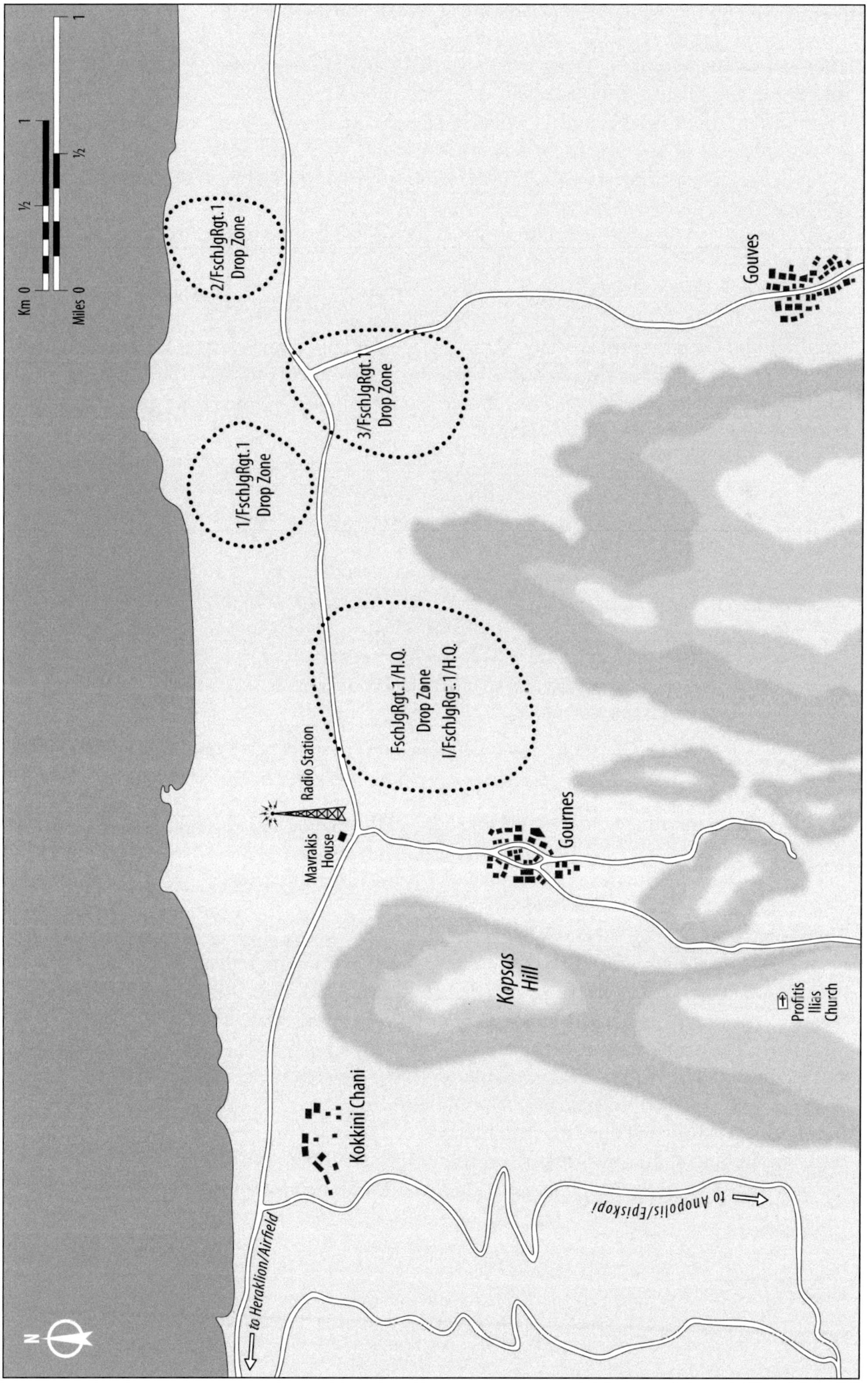


Map 3.1 The drop zones in the Gournes area, east of the airfield. (N. Panos, 2016)

The dispatch and the drop of the *I./FschJgRgt.1* was organised as follows:

- The staff of the battalion, along with a signals platoon (seven officers and 56 NCOs and soldiers) in five planes, without losses
- *1./FschJgRgt.1* (four officers and 113 NCOs and soldiers) in 10 planes instead of the planned 12, with the loss of one aircraft, which made an emergency landing on the island of Milos
- *2./FschJgRgt.1* (four officers and 127 NCOs and soldiers) in 10 planes instead of 12, without losses
- *3./FschJgRgt.1* (four officers and 116 NCOs and soldiers) in nine planes instead of 12, without losses
- *4./FschJgRgt.1* did not drop that day, since only seven planes of the 12 needed were available

The terrain in the Gournes area is rocky in some places and not really suitable for paratroop landings; as a result, 15 men were injured during the jump – six of them seriously. During the drop and the initial assembly, the *I./FschJgRgt.1* encountered only minor resistance from *gendarmerie* units and armed civilians from the nearby villages.

The dead on the first day were:

*1./FschJgRgt.1*
*Objg* Julius Bosse, 5 October 1919-20 May 1941

*2./FschJgRgt.1*
*Gefr* Kurt Kittendorf, 9 September 1921-20 May 1941
*Gefr* Kurt Martin, 18 November 1918-20 May 1941
*Jäger* Wilfried Timm, 4 November 1921-20 May 1941
*Feldw* Karl Traub, 24 September 1914-20 May 1941

*3./FschJgRgt.1*
*Oblt* Otto Friedrich, 26 March 1916-20 May 1941
*Objg* Heinz Gottschalk,[1] 9 October 1919-20 May 1941 (missing)

Paratrooper Gerhard Broder from the *2./FschJgRgt.1* described the drop:

> The second wave started from the airfield between 15 and 16 hours. Between 16 and 17 hours we board our Ju-52. *Graf* von Blücher is the officer in command and he jumps first. I'm the fourth man. The *Hauptfeldwebel*, who keeps the company together, jumps as the last man. The planes that carry the company fly together in tight formation. From the window I observe tensely each plane and focus on every noise. My mouth is dry and the strong coffee only worsens the thirst and increases the heartbeat. We are not used to such a dose of caffeine. For the first time not all the weapons are dropped separately. The sub-machine-guns are fastened around our chests.
>
> I see the Acropolis and draw it to the attention of a comrade but he waves it away and only swears something to himself. At sea the ships are already on the way to Crete but in fact they never managed to reach the island.[2] It is already late and we are approaching our objective.

1 Heinz Gottschalk fell during the Battle of Crete, but his remains were not recovered. According to the BDF Archives, he fell into the sea. His name is recorded at the war cemetery in Maleme.

2 He refers to the convoys of boats loaded with German troops, which were intercepted and destroyed by the British fleet.

Gerhard Broder (left), with his fellow paratrooper Rudolf Jacobs, before boarding the Ju-52 for Crete. (Courtesy of Adrian Nisbett) Note: This was also the plane that Wolfgang *Graf* von Blücher travelled in.

The formation flies at very low altitude over the water. There, Crete emerges! I see the small island just before the coast. We fly eastwards over it, thus we are not going to jump at the originally planned spot. Now everything evolves very fast. 'Get Ready!' We check each other's gear and we are ready for the jump. *Graf* Blücher is positioned at the door already. He looks tense. We fly over the coast then a honking signal sounds and Blücher forces himself away. We jump in very fast succession behind him.

My parachute is deployed and I hear the rattling of machine-guns and the shooting of snipers. No flak fire. Under me I see vineyards, olive trees and the coastal road. After only a few swings of the parachute I end up gently in the ditch of the coastal road, with the help of the evening upwind of the summer days. While still lying down I release the buckles of the harness and I see the weapons container approximately 30 metres away from me. The terrain is rocky and landing was dangerous. The planes make a wide turn and fly back to Greece without any losses. They have fulfilled their mission.

[...] *Hauptfeldwebel* Hermann Vogler, who should have jumped as the last man from the plane, did not and he has returned to Greece with the Ju-52. It is a unique case. It is said that his parachute was damaged but nobody can confirm this. He went through a court-martial and he was expelled from the paratroopers. Vogler was a sensitive man and a career soldier who always worked responsibly and behaved with dignity towards his subordinates. He was a really respected man.[3]

3 G. Broder, *Guerre Mondiale Contre Moi*, pp.85-95.

The drop of the HQ Company in the Gournes area, east of the airfield. The pictures were taken by Dr Günther Müller, who was an NCO in a medical unit of the *FschJgRgt.1*. The drop container shown in the picture belonged to Müller's medical unit; the drop was conducted east of Kopsas Hill. (G. Müller & F. Scheuering, *Sprung über Kreta*)

Resistance by the Greeks grew stronger as time passed. Nikos Patatanes, from the village of Episkopi, described how the fighting began:

> [...] The bombing and the blitz continued for the whole morning of 20 May until the time that the paratroopers began dropping. Along with my family I was in Episkopi where we heard that the paratroopers were falling in the Karteros valley, at the Kako Oros, at Kokkini Chani, Anopoli and Gouves. The master sergeant of the local Gendarmerie force in Episkopi addressed the crowd in the central square of the village [Agios Minas Square] and after a short patriotic speech he asked anyone who wanted to fight to follow him to Anopolis, where the battle against the Germans was underway.
>
> We formed a group with Master Sergeant Antonios Fragakis in the lead along with Sergeant Vardis, and the civilians, Dimitrios Tsatsadakis, Panagiotis Mylonakis, Konstantinos Fouskokolakis, Nikolaos Papadakis and many others. We were virtually unarmed. We had only two old single-shot rifles, I had a knife and Fouskokolakis just a stick. We began for Anopolis but the master sergeant ordered us to pass by the English camp in Agios Romanos first, in order to ask for weapons. When we were approaching the camp, the English started shooting at us, why I never understood. Finally we arrived at the camp where an English sergeant told us to ask for guns from the Greek Army units which were deployed and fighting the Germans in the Karteros area. A villager from Elia warned us not to go to Karteros because the area was occupied by strong German forces, so we decided to go to Anopolis. When we arrived there it was already dark and the village was empty. There we met an old man and he told us that the Greeks had established themselves near the cemetery. After a while we joined them. There were two decimated platoons under 2nd Lieutenant Vasilios Galenianos and a sergeant. They were very happy to see us there. 'We do not have any spare weapons to give you but we can take some from the Germans,' they told us. This was what exactly happened the next morning when dozens of German troop-carriers arrived and started dropping paratroopers and supplies in Kokkini Chani. The paratroopers were using mortars and machine-guns and bitter fighting began at Kopsas Hill. More paratroopers dropped in the area and with their machine-guns they were shooting at everything that was moving. They were caught by surprise because they didn't expect such a resistance. The battle was even and lethal. Emmanuel Kokkinakis from Anopolis was killed when he rushed the Germans, crying 'AERAA![4] On them! We got them!'
>
> The losses were heavy on both sides. About 70[5] German and 17 Greeks were killed while many others were wounded or captured. When things calmed down, I moved a bit further to find cigarettes and I saw a wounded paratrooper trying to dress his wounds, holding one edge of the field dressing with his teeth. I felt sorry for him and I went close to help him. When he saw me he kicked me and tried to reach his gun while pressing his arm on my throat trying to strangle me. We started wrestling and then I stabbed him a few times with my knife. I then took his gear and threw it into the bushes. I was afraid of reprisals and during the night I took the gear and hid it very carefully. The next day I reported the incident to the 2nd lieutenant and he admonished me, saying that if I had been killed nobody could have known what had happened to me.

4 The war-cry used by the Greeks during the Second World War.

5 The number of German losses are probably a personal estimation by Mr Patatanes and cannot be confirmed. The total German losses in this area were 20-25 dead and many more wounded or taken prisoner, which is in agreement with the German records and the official Greek accounts.

> The fight went on and we were all shooting together. The area was full of corpses when we handed over the prisoners to the Greek authorities in Episkopi for interrogation. After the battle, the Germans retreated eastwards, to Gouves. The news about the German losses raised our spirits and the villagers from the nearby villages supported the fighters by supplying food and water.[6]

*Oberst* Bräuer arrived in Gournes with the *FschJgRgt.1* HQ at around 1840.[7] Immediately after his landing, about 800 metres east of the radio station, Bräuer was briefed about the situation by *Major* Walther. Bräuer decided to move westwards to the airfield without having contact with the rest of the units, which had been dropped around the airfield and west of the city. The main priority at that time was to get in contact with *Hauptmann* Burckhardt's *II./FschJgRgt.1*, which had been dropped around the airfield.

A dead paratrooper in the area west of Kopsas Hill, where Nikos Patatanes described the action. (Author's archive)

The same location today, with Kopsas in the background. (Author's collection)

6 M. Liapaki-Antonaki, 'Chronicle of the Battle of Kopsas, 24 May in Anopolis Pediados', Heraklion, *PATRIS* newspaper, 24 May 2003; available online at <http://www.patris.gr/articles/9028?PHPSESSID=#.VWwlh8-qqko>

7 German time.

## Special Presentation 11: Bruno Bräuer

Bruno Bräuer was a First World War veteran, a career officer and one of the pioneers of the German paratroopers. He was tough and decisive, and had proved his skills and bravery in battle, so winning the respect and admiration of his men.

Two years after the battle – and now a *general* – Bräuer assumed duties as the commander of Fortress Crete. After the war, he was convicted and sentenced to death by a Greek court for war crimes committed during the German occupation of the island. He was executed along with *General* Müller (also a former commander of Crete) ironically on 20 May 1947: the sixth anniversary of the invasion. As such, he was the last victim of the Battle of Crete and was buried along with his comrades. His grave today is at the German war cemetery in Maleme.

*Oberst* Bruno Bräuer in a wartime postcard. (Author's collection)

Bräuer sitting on a vehicle and patiently awaiting his turn to board the Ju-52 for Crete with his adjutant, *Hauptmann* Rau. (G. Müller & F. Scheuering, *Sprung über Kreta*)

*Oberst* Bräuer in the Ju-52 on the way to Crete. (G. Müller & F. Scheuering, *Sprung über Kreta*)

Der königliche Kommissar des speziellen Gerichtes für Kriegsverbrechen teilt mit:

Heute am 20. Mai 1947, Dienstag, um 5 Uhr morgens, fand am Platz der Infanteriekasernen von Xaidari die Vollstreckung der Todesstrafe an den Verurteilten

1. Friedrich Wilhelm Müller,
2. Bruno Oswald Bräuer,

auf Grund des Beschlusses Nr. 3 vom 9. Dezember 1946 des speziellen Gerichtes für Kriegsverbrechen statt, nachdem ihre Gnadengesuche abgelehnt worden waren.

The announcement of the execution of Bräuer and Müller at the Greek military camp in Chaidary on 20 May 1947. (Courtesy of *DDF*)

Bräuer's grave (No.851) in Maleme at the famous Hill 107, next to the airfield. (Author's collection)

Kurt Student laying a wreath in 1957 in memory of Bräuer and the other fallen *fallschirmjäger*. (Courtesy of *DDF*)

Mrs Bräuer (on the right) at a veterans' gathering in Bochum in 1957. (Courtesy of *DDF*)

Dr Günther Müller described the moment of his jump:

> [...] At last I feel that I'm ready and through the noise of the engines which sound like a hammer in my head, I hear a voice call 'Rush to the enemy! Rush to the enemy!' We were probably in flight for two hours before we saw Crete. The rocky coast of the island can be barely seen, blurred in the distance. We bypass the small island of Dia on purpose since we suspect that there are AA guns there. We hear a voice from the cockpit shout 'GET READY!' and everything comes to life in the plane. We take off the life-vests, and hook the static lines on the wire, checking each other's gear and parachutes.
>
> Tension and absolute silence prevails! I see tough and decisive faces. 'GET READY FOR THE JUMP.' That was it! With these thoughts in my mind I stand in front of the door. The waves are splashing on the rocks below and then we are over a vineyard. This is very good since we can find cover there if needed. I can't see anything else. The air brings tears to my eyes and pushes me hard. I bend over like a cat and I'm pressed onto the left side of the door. Because of the noise of the engines I can't hear the signal to jump but suddenly I feel a push on the side from my comrade behind me and I already see the plane moving away. Damn it! This time the parachute deployment was delayed for too long, I'm thinking while I'm falling. Then a 'giant hand' grabs me and pulls me up. The harness holds me tight as I'm hanging from the parachute.
>
> Everywhere I see comrades descending under their parachutes. I'm heading towards a shed in a vineyard and I have a grenade ready to use, holding the porcelain ball in my hand. The noise of an explosion comes through my body as I see my commander. I'm thinking that he will have already cleared and secured the area. When one jumps by parachute into battle one goes into the unknown and uncertainty, but all the paratroopers are in the same position, from the general to the corporal. I land very hard next to the shed into the vineyard. I learned later that the explosion came from a drop-container that crashed violently to the ground because the parachute had failed. This day hundreds of comrades jumped from the aircraft. The *Fallschirmjäger* attacked Crete![8]

Since 19 May, Lieutenant Theodoros E. Kallinos (Greek Army) – leading a force of approximately 150 men – had been established on Kako Oros Hill, between Kopsas and the airfield. At the beginning of the drops on Gournes, Kallinos realised that it would be better to occupy the top of Kopsas, right next to the drop zone in Gournes – so putting the paratroopers within range of his weapons. Moreover, the hard and rocky surface of the Kako Oros didn't allow his men to dig in and prepare appropriate defensive positions.

During the afternoon of 20 May, Kallinos and 70 of his men moved very quickly and occupied the top of Kopsas, where they posed a serious threat to the Germans on their drop zone. Kallinos' men established their defensive positions with the front towards Gournes and to the coast. Their only machine gun was an old 1915 model, and quite soon it was jammed – rendering it useless. Without the support of a machine gun, the Greek soldiers could only rely on their rifles and hand grenades in order to fight an enemy with vastly superior firepower.

The steep and rocky slopes of Kopsas actually compensated for the Greeks' lack of firepower: a platoon of the *1./FschJgRgt.1*, under *Leutnant* Boris Lindenberg, was assigned the task of protecting the paratroopers' left (southern) flank from the Greek forces in Kopsas and the hills south of Gournes. At around 0530 on 21 May, the paratroopers took advantage of the darkness and advanced to the foothills of Kopsas – and there they took up their start positions for an assault.

8 G. Müller & F. Scheuering, *Sprung über Kreta*, pp.47-51.

*Oberst* Bräuer, immediately after his landing in Gournes, conferring with *Major* Walther (centre) and the adjutant of *I./FschJgRgt.1*, *Leutnant* Schulz (right). This photo was taken by Dr Günther Müller – the author of the book *Sprung über Kreta*. (G. Müller & F. Scheuering, *Sprung über Kreta*)

The same area today. In the background is the hill east of Kopsas – providing good evidence for the exact drop zone of the *I./FschJgRgt.1* and the HQ Company. (Author's collection)

**Special Presentation 12: Erich Walther**

Erich Walther in a late-war photograph. (Courtesy of Wolf Walther)

Erich Walther (5 August 1903-26 December 1947) joined the Berlin Police in 1924. After serving in the '*General Göring*' Regiment, he was promoted to *hauptmann* and transferred to the *fallschirmjäger* – following the same path as many of the German paratrooper pioneers. He participated in the operations in Holland and Norway with *FschJgRgt.1*, where he distinguished himself by his decisiveness in action, and was awarded the Knight's Cross. Subsequently, he was promoted to *major* on 19 June 1940.

In May 1941, he fought in the Battle of Crete – in the area east of Heraklion – as the CO of the *I./FschJgRgt.1*. After the battle, he served on the Eastern Front in the Leningrad area, where he was awarded the German Cross in Gold. In August 1942, Walther was promoted to *oberst* and in September, he assumed command of the *FschJgRgt.4*. He participated in the fighting on Sicily and at Monte Cassino.

In the Battles of Nijmegen and Arnhem, during the famous Allied Operation 'Market Garden', he was the CO of the 'Walther' Battle Group. Later, he assumed command of the paratrooper units belonging to the 2nd Armoured Brigade, '*Hermann Göring*' in Eastern Prussia – and on 30 January 1945, he was promoted to *generalmajor*.

On 8 May 1945, he was captured by the Soviets and died in captivity in the POW camp at Buchenwald on 26 December 1947. Walther had been awarded the following decorations: Iron Cross (2nd Class 18 April 1940 and 1st Class 26 April 1940), Knight's Cross (24 May 1940), German Cross in Gold (31 March 1942), the 411th Oak Leaves (2 March 1944) and the 131st Swords to the Knight's Cross (1 February 1945).

*Major* Walther with *Oberst* Bräuer in Gournes, standing in front of Kopsas Hill. (Courtesy of *DDF*)

Under the cover of a machine gun barrage, they attacked both from the north and the east; in fact, they took the defenders on the east of Kopsas by surprise, as they had never expected an attack up such a steep slope. The paratroopers followed an old track that was used by the local shepherds – managing to reach the top of Kopsas from the east and then suddenly appearing right in the middle of the Greek defensive positions. Chief petty officer Nikolaos Koukovinos' platoon, which was positioned lower on the northern slope, was very quickly surrounded and captured by the Germans. Having been totally surprised by the unexpected attack from the east, the remaining Greeks were forced to retreat to the south towards the church of Prophitis Elias. Realising that this was a turning point in the battle, Kallinos took a chance and, leading his men with his revolver in hand, attacked the Germans just 50 metres in front of his position. The Germans did not expect this counter-attack and they found themselves in a very difficult position – being outnumbered and isolated between the cliff and the attacking Greeks. Moving rapidly to the right of Kallinos, a Greek sergeant from Dodecanese started throwing hand grenades at the paratroopers' most forward positions; they were forced to retreat – leaving guns and ammunition behind – and releasing the Greek prisoners. The unexpected success of this counter-attack raised the spirit of the Greeks, who immediately charged the paratroopers and ended up in close combat with them. About 10 Germans were killed,[9] while the rest were taken prisoner. The Greeks only had one seriously (Dimitrios Liakakis) and another slightly wounded (Private Ioannis Chatzis).

When the fight was finally over, Kallinos noticed that some signal flares were coming from a small building on the road east of Kopsas. This was Andreas Mavrakis' house, which was located on the main road to the east and not far from the radio station. A group of paratroopers had been trapped there and were trying to indicate their position and call for reinforcements. Kallinos ordered Sergeant Orestis Andreadakis and a group of soldiers to advance downhill to the east slope of Kopsas and wait there for further instructions. Along with the soldiers, many armed civilians had gathered and were participating in the fight. Contrary to his orders, Andreadakis decided to attack immediately, but his assault failed, as the paratroopers were very well protected in the small house. During the conflict, Andreadakis himself was killed, as were Emmanuel Kokkinakis and Ioannis Charitakis. When Kallinos was informed of the loss of his men, he decided to take revenge at any cost. He moved covertly along the west side of Kopsas and positioned a captured German machine gun approximately 300 metres away from the house. During this move, the machine gunner was shot at and injured by the Germans, but he remained at his post. Kallinos ordered his machine gunner to fire short bursts successively at the two windows and the door of the house. Twenty minutes later, a white flag appeared in one of the windows and thick smoke was seen coming from the building. The tracer rounds had ignited sacks filled with sulphur, which had been stored in the building for use in the vineyards. Seventeen paratroopers emerged from the house and surrendered – thus avoiding suffocation from the thick smoke.

Nikos Patatanes remembered:

> We were ordered to move downhill very carefully and we established ourselves at the area where later the American base was built right next to the radio station. There we realised that some of the Germans had moved eastwards and occupied the house of Andreas Mavrakis [with nickname 'Katsikis'] where sacks with sulphur for the vineyards were stored. We moved forward very carefully and we surrounded the house which was built of bricks. The house was surrounded by vineyards and we couldn't find any good cover. The fight lasted for quite

9 According to the German archives, the remains of 17 paratroopers were collected from the area of Kopsas after the war and were transferred to the Maleme Cemetery. This number also includes the paratroopers killed during the drop.

The area east of Kopsas, with the house where the paratroopers were trapped, right next to the road and the vineyards. (Author's archive)

The view to the east from the top of Kopsas. The paratroopers managed to cross the plateau unnoticed under the cover of darkness and then climbed the steep slope – taking Kallinos' men by surprise. (Courtesy of C.E. Mamalakis)

some time but we couldn't reach the house because of the heavy gunfire coming from inside. We thought that this would be a long fight but suddenly at around 6:00 pm the door opened and a white flag appeared. We rushed to the house and the Germans started coming out almost blinded by the smoke, while some of them were injured and were asking for medical treatment. We transferred them to the hospital in Episkopi where the doctors treated their wounds. In this fight Yannis Chatzis from Anopolis was seriously wounded, while two of our comrades, Spyridakis and Aretakis from Gouves were killed. I also remember that Antonios Liapakis from Anopolis fought in this battle. We then returned to Prophitis Elias and we were really hungry and thirsty. The sergeant went to the monastery of Agios Ioannis where

> the monks provided him with food. The next morning we moved southwards to regroup and continue our struggle and resistance.[10]

As a result of this action, by the evening of 21 May, there were no German strongholds left in the Gournes area.

According to the German after-action report,[11] *Major* Walther received the order (at approximately 2340 on 20 May) to pull together his scattered battalion and march in the direction of the airport. Communicating this order at night to companies spread out to the east and the south took a long time. A platoon of the 1st Company, under *Leutnant* Lindenberg, could not be found. Lindenberg – in contravention of his orders – had advanced into the mountains to the south of Gournes and, as was discovered later, was attacked by Greek troops. Many of Lindenberg's men were killed, while the rest were taken prisoner. Lindenberg had been severely wounded and was transferred by the Greeks to Episkopi, where a Greek nurse treated his wounds; however, he died on 23 May and was buried in the local cemetery. The people of Episkopi, near Gournes, still remember this incident and describe Lindenberg as a very tall and strong man. During the next day of the battle, villagers from Anopolis and Episkopi buried the dead paratroopers in makeshift graves.

Evangelos Vardakis from Episkopi recalled:

> In my village, Episkopi, the English had established a field hospital. They were providing treatment to the wounded, both Allied and German. After treatment, the wounded were transferred to the Archangel Michael Church to recover. A *gendarmerie* sergeant named Vardis was carrying the wounded on his back – having also two machine guns hanging from his shoulders and a Luger pistol in his belt. At one point, he carried a wounded German officer[12] who was a tall man with his body full of buckshot.[13] He was shot with a shotgun or a hunting gun. The German was put on a bed in Emmanouel Antonakakis' house [Antonakakis was a teacher]. A couple of days later, the German was transferred to the church, where he died. He was buried at the local cemetery by Antonakakis and Noikokirakis, with the help of Hatziioannou and Katergianakis. Zacharias Roditakis, a carpenter, made a wooden cross and placed it on the grave, while a nurse named Mourmouri wrote the name of the German on the cross. Some days later, a German truck – escorted by two motorcycles with side cars – arrived at the cemetery. After questioning the villagers, the Germans had lunch at the house of Antonakakis and then they recovered the bodies of the paratroopers.[14]

On 29 May, when the battle was over and the Germans were investigating what had happened to Lindenberg's men, the villagers led the investigators to the graves, where they recovered the bodies.

---

10 Liapaki-Antonaki, *PATRIS* newspaper, 24 May 2003.

11 *XI Fliegerkorps, Gefechtsbericht 'Einsatz KRETA'*, p.7.

12 *Leutnant* Boris Lindenberg.

13 Lindenberg, while leading the attack against the men of Kallinos at the top of Kopsas, was most probably injured by the shrapnel from the grenades that the Greeks threw at the paratroopers. As a result, Lindenberg's body was riddled with shrapnel, which could have been mistaken for buckshot by the people who carried him.

14 Interview with C.E. Mamalakis in Heraklion, 10 December 2015.

The grave of *Leutnant* Lindenberg at the Episkopi cemetery, next to Agioi Apostoloi Church. (Courtesy of Steffen Rhode)

The same place today, with a corner of the church visible in the background. (Courtesy of C.E. Mamalakis)

Paratrooper Gerhard Broder from the *2./FschJgRgt.1* observed:

> A platoon is ordered to take retaliatory action against civilians for the murder of the wounded. A lorry departs full of heavily-armed soldiers with *Oberleutnant* Otto in command. The destination is a mountainous village called 'Gournes'. This place has a reputation of being a nest of partisans. I do not know who gave the order and what exactly their instructions are, but I can imagine what is possible when revenge and punishment become legal military actions. I'm glad that I do not participate in this mission. After some hours the platoon returns and I sit with my comrades. I ask them what happened. Amazed and relieved I hear: 'Nothing!' After a long conversation with the local authorities in the village of Gournes we realised that there weren't any partisans or murderers there. *Oberleutnant* Otto decided not to take any action against the population of this village.[15]

At the top of Kopsas, there is a big cross – placed there by the Americans in the 1960s. According to some accounts, the cross was erected by the German wife of an American officer from the Gournes base. At the base of the cross, there was a plaque with the names of the dead Germans.

15 Broder, p.99.

The cross at the top of Kopsas, which was placed by Americans from the military base in Gournes in the 1960s. (Author's archive)

According to the German archives, the losses of the *1./FschJgRgt.1* on 21 May (most of them killed on Kopsas) were the following:

*Objg* Egon Bartel, 28 September 1920-21 May 1941
*Jäger* Hans Joachim *Graf* von Blücher, 23 October 1923-21 May 1941 (killed at Karteros, near the airfield)
*Gefr* Heinz Bock, 16 March 1914-21 May 1941
*Gefr* Kurt Kilgus, 20 April 1920-21 May 1941
*Ltn* Boris Lindenberg, 20 January 1918-21 May 1941
*Jäger* Hans Meyer, 3 April 1921-21 May 1941 (killed at Karteros, near the airfield)
*Gefr* Friedrich Robitzeck, 10 October 1920-21 May 1941
*Obgfr* Wilhelm Skrandis, 26 July 1913-21 May 1941
*Gefr* Hans Scheps, 23 September 1918-21 May 1941 (killed at Karteros, near the airfield)
*Objg* Hermann Veit, 20 June 1919-21 May 1941
*Oblt* Albert Wittmann, 8 October 1915-21 May 1941 (killed at Karteros, near the airfield)
*Gefr* Hans Ziesing, 5 March 1921-21 May 1941(most probably killed at Karteros, near the airfield)

Bock and Skrandis are buried in the same grave (No.961), along with *Gefr* Arthur Amenda from *3./FschJgRgt.1.* Bartel, Veit and Robitzeck are also buried in the same grave (No.964); these are the men that were killed in Kopsas and buried by the Greeks.

# 4

# The Battle at the Airfield and Blücher

Bräuer moved very fast along the coast during the night hours of 20 May and approached the airfield from the east. He was unaware of the especially difficult position that *II./FschJgRgt.1* was in, since no communication had been established with them by that stage. Assuming that Burckhardt and his men would have attacked and probably occupied the airfield according to the plan, Bräuer decided to order a small group to advance further to the west in order to establish contact with Burckhardt and gather more information about the situation at the airfield. This task was assigned to *Oberleutnant* Wolfgang *Graf* von Blücher and his platoon of approximately 30 men. They moved forward towards the airfield as a vanguard. Approaching the East Hill in Karteros, Bräuer established his command post on the small hill of Amnissos.

Gerhard Broder from the *2./FschJgRgt.1* continues his narration:

> But now something unusual happens. We are left only with low-rank leadership. *Oberfeldwebel* Möller from Schleswig Holstein, a very tall man whom we call 'Baby Möller' as a joke because of his height, collects our men in order to secure our positions to the east. *Graf* Blücher, our platoon leader, has simply disappeared along with the rest of the platoon and he already marches towards Heraklion airfield since here there isn't any contact with the enemy.[1]

At the east edge of the airfield, Agios Ioannis Hill (or East Hill) stands as an obstacle on the way from Amnissos to Heraklion. East Hill can be clearly seen from Amnissos during daylight, but it was not possible for Blücher to have a clear view because of the darkness. On his way to the airfield, he had to move straight onto the hill and attack the British positions at the north edge, opposite the airfield. Following the main road from Amnissos and crossing the 'Rattling Bridge,'[2] they reached the point where the road meets East Hill. At that specific point, accessibility to the top of the hill is relatively easy, while the defensive positions were not very strong. That spot was chosen by Blücher's men as their starting point to climb the hill.

In the darkness – and using the 'jackrabbit' tactic (rapid jumps from place to place) – the paratroopers managed to reach the top of the hill and advanced towards the mouth of the gorge, next to the east edge of the airfield. The darkness not only provided cover for the paratroopers, but also for the British defensive positions. The result was that Blücher's platoon penetrated the British defensive perimeter, while unknowingly placing themselves in a fatally exposed position.

1 G. Broder, *Guerre Mondiale Contre Moi*, p.87.

2 The bridge over Karteros River.

Bräuer, with his adjutant – *Hauptmann* Rau – planning their next move on the map before they started to move towards the airfield. (G. Müller & F. Scheuering, *Sprung über Kreta*)

*Leutnant* Wolfgang *Graf* von Blücher (on the right) during training exercises, with his regimental commander – *Oberst* Bruno Bräuer – on the left. (Courtesy of Adrian Nisbett)

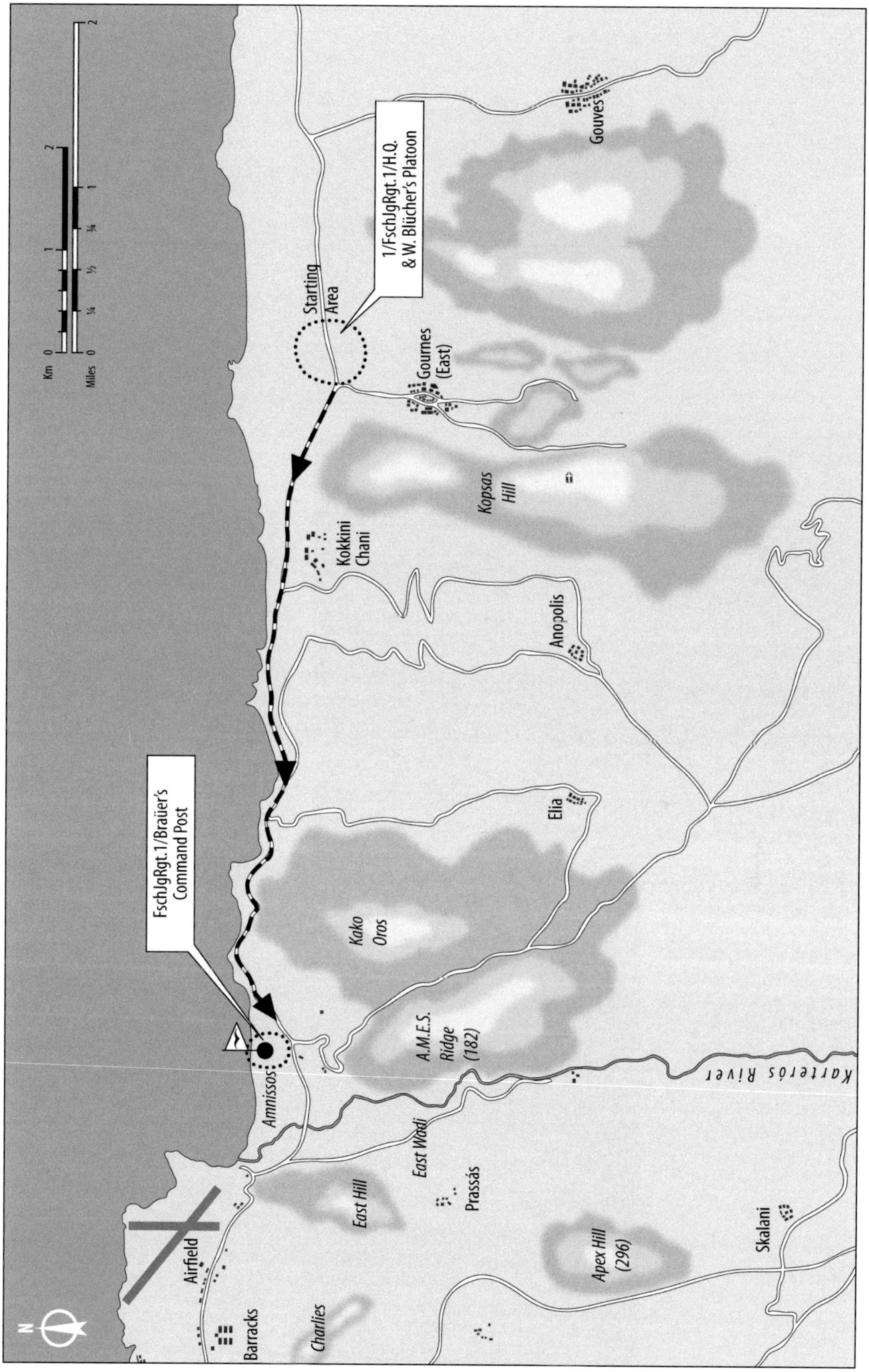


Map 4.1 The route followed by Bräuer along the coast during the night of 20/21 May. (N. Panos, 2016)

The 'Rattling Bridge', as it is today. In the background, East Hill can be seen. (Author's collection)

The access point used by Blücher's men in order to climb East Hill in a picture taken during the battle, and the same area today. (Author's collection)

Wolfgang *Graf* von Blücher with his platoon during training, soon after the operation in Holland. The tall NCO marching immediately behind Blücher (first row on the right) is *Obergefreiter* Hollweck, who was the same age as – and a friend of – Blücher's, while the tall paratrooper on the left is *Oberfeldwebel* Möller. Hollweck and Möller, seen here marching side by side, are also buried next to each other, in graves 649 and 650 at the Maleme War Cemetery. *Leutnant* Spang can also be seen to the left. (Author's collection)

East Hill was the main stronghold for the defence of the airfield from the east. The Scottish soldiers of the 2nd Battalion, Black Watch – and before them the Australians – had had enough time to dig and prepare their defensive positions, and had placed three companies on the hill. Since 9 May, the Black Watch command post had been established on the east slope, with the HQ Coy – under Lieutenant Gerald Barry – a little lower on the east foothill; a platoon from 'A' Coy was on the right of the HQ Coy; another 'A' Coy platoon was at the south edge; a reserve platoon was west of the south edge. 'B' Coy formed a reserve in the gorge on the west slope; a platoon from 'D' Coy was at the east end of the runway, opposite the north edge of the hill; and one more platoon from 'D' Coy was positioned at the east end of the gorge, where the road from Karteros passes near the church of Agios Ioannis (St John). A mortar platoon was positioned in trenches at the top of the hill on the south and north edge – and many fighting trenches and machine gun posts had also been constructed. Four Bren Carriers were placed near the south foothill, and one more Bren Carrier was assigned to 'D' Coy. Immediately after the attack – at 1842 – a platoon from 'B' Coy was positioned at the north edge of the hill, between 'D' and HQ Coys.

All along the road, next to East Hill, the Scots had placed a triple row of barbed wire. Lieutenant Gerald Barry of the HQ Coy described the preparations of the defensive position on East Hill:

> At dawn this morning [19 May], I took out a wiring party into the big vineyard on the other side of the road to put up a third fence across our front. We had not been going long when I heard the whistle blow from Coy HQ which denoted the air alarm. We went on wiring and about five minutes later, the valley was full of *Messerschmitts* flying only a few feet above the vines. Everyone took what cover they could under a vine, which is poor protection at any time. Fortunately we were not discovered, otherwise I think they would have turned on us and machine-gunned us. They flew so low that I could almost have lobbed a cricket ball into them had their cockpits been open![3]

3 C.E. Mamalakis, Ian Powys Archive.

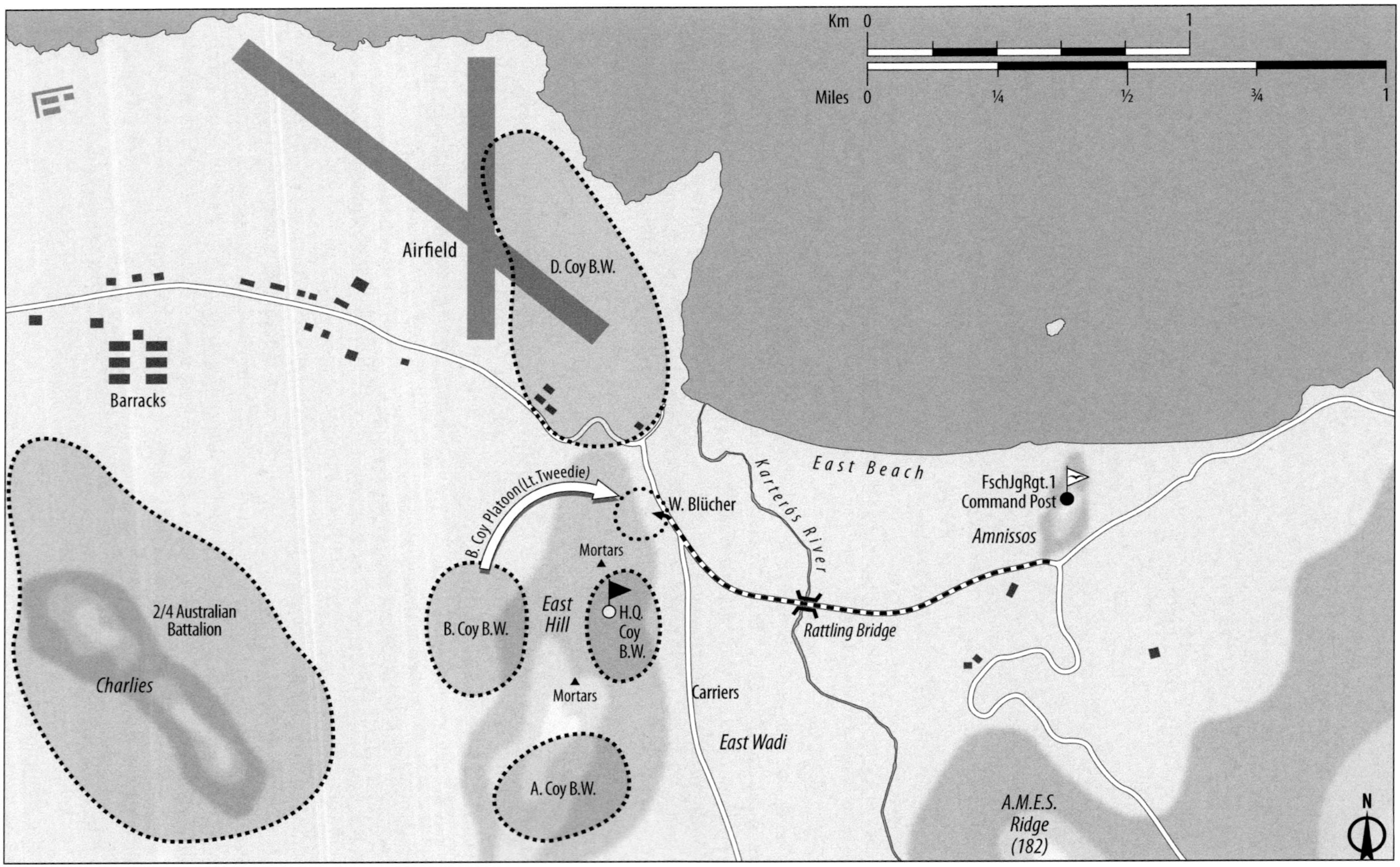


Map 4.2 The positions of the 2nd Bn, BW on East Hill and the route followed by Blücher's men (and the spot where they were surrounded and trapped opposite the east edge of the airfield). (N. Panos, 2016)

The area next to the road where the barbed wire was placed, as described by Gerald Barry. (Author's collection)

That night (20/21 May), when the paratroopers became aware of the presence of soldiers on East Hill, they assumed that they would be Burckhardt's men, and so were totally surprised when the dark figures on the hill responded to their calls by opening fire. For the whole night, the paratroopers near the airfield listened to the sound of bagpipes being played by piper Bill Lark from the Black Watch, who played his pipes at night-time to encourage his comrades and intimidate the enemy.

Dawn found Blücher's men trapped among the Black Watch defensive positions, at the north edge of East Hill. The paratroopers were at a great disadvantage, since the ground was rocky – hence impossible to dig into and so flat that it provided no cover at all, while the British crossfire on the field below forbade any attempt to retreat. In addition, the Scots were well protected in trenches and carefully prepared positions – even using 40mm anti-aircraft guns both from the airfield and the hill.

No matter the difficulty of the situation, the fact that the paratroopers had managed to reach the edge of the airfield presented a great opportunity for the Germans to create a stronghold on the hill; the occupation of the airfield would then be just a matter of hours, as had occurred in Maleme at Hill 107. Bräuer understood the unique opportunity that he had, and ordered the rest of *I./FschJgRgt.1* to move fast and reinforce Blücher's position. Bräuer himself moved eastwards and sent a dispatch rider back to the companies that were marching along the coast from the drop zone in Gournes – urging them to advance as quickly as possible. The men of *I./FschJgRgt.1* (loaded with heavy gear, ammunition and weapons) had been attacked during their march by Greek forces and civilians occupying the hills along the coast – thus they were spread out along the route and delayed in an advance which required them to cover a distance of 12 kilometres.

The spot where Blücher's men were surrounded; in the distance can be seen the east edge of the runway, where 'D' Coy of the Black Watch was positioned – firing 40mm guns at the paratroopers. (Author's collection)

Bill Lark (third from the left) with his bagpipes in Heraklion, just before the battle. (Courtesy of C.E. Mamalakis)

Gerhard Broder from *2./FschJgRgt.1* described the situation from his perspective:

> At dawn we follow Blücher's men on our own initiative. Twelve men who were injured during the jump remain with a medic. Those wounded were bestially murdered by Greek civilians during the night and their corpses were buried somewhere. Now murder has become a part of the war?
>
> Totally exhausted we march towards Heraklion airfield trying to protect our advance at the same time. A donkey carries the heavy ammo-boxes and the machine-guns for some kilometres. With the first rays of daybreak we reach a height and the airfield is now visible. Before the airfield lies a field with vineyards. Small-arms fire already dominates the area. At this

moment some green flares are fired followed by the cry, 'Tanks from the front!' Our forward units are equipped with a 3.7 cm anti-tank gun which is rather ineffective. We understand that the airfield is not yet occupied by the paratroopers. We are fired at from very well camouflaged positions protected by sand-bags; they are manned by Englishmen who are definitely not demoralised by any means, despite our expectations. Our regiment's staff establishes its command post on a hill north of the coastal road.

I hear the cry of my company commander, Gröschke, 'SMGs with me!' and then he positions them on a height south of the coastal road. *Oberleutnant* Blücher and his platoon crossed the vineyard during the darkness and penetrated the English positions. There isn't any contact with him and his men are under heavy fire from the British. They are trying to take cover on a flat rocky area, exposed both to the enemy and friendly fire since they are so close to the British positions.

On the hill a young *Leutnant* from the staff tells me that my company is to mount a frontal attack. The British tank has probably retreated. Our anti-tank weapons can't do any damage to the Mark IV tank. Now I must attack the airfield but I must first descend the slope without any cover and then cross the vineyards. Each position there can be seen by the enemy. Then I must climb the opposite slope. I shoot with my rifle and run, reaching the vineyards, but then I fall to the ground and take cover because I simply cannot continue anymore. The stone walls provide some cover from the enemy. The sun comes up. We haven't slept at all for a long time and my tongue sticks to my dry mouth. The sun is amazingly hot and there is no shade anywhere. My heart beats quickly because of the strong and disgusting bean coffee.[4]

Despite Bräuer's efforts, he was unable to mount the attack before dawn. Bräuer's intention was to unleash a co-ordinated assault under cover of the night of the 20th/21st, both from the west (towards the town) and from the east (to the airfield). He sent an order via radio to *Major* Schulz to attack during the night. *III./FschJgRgt.1*, under *Major* Schulz (along with the 7th and 8th Companies of the *II/2 Battalion*, under *Hauptmann* Schirmer), had established positions west of the city in the area of Therissos-Kaminia-Deilina-Giofyros-Tsalikaki-Gazi.

In the end, the co-ordination of the attack was a total failure, since the units to the west had never received the relevant orders, while the units to the east could not reach the airfield before dawn. At around 0445 (German time), the first groups of men from *1./FschJgRgt.1* began approaching the regimental command post in Amnissos from the east. *Oberst* Bräuer personally ordered *Oberleutnant* Wittmann (and later, *Leutnant* Hubner as well) to move forward in support of *Oberleutnant* von Blücher.

The attack started early in the morning, with the men of *I./FschJgRgt.1* moving along the coast and through the Karteros Valley to come up against the Black Watch on the East Hill, the remainder of *II./FschJgRgt.1* attacked south – starting from Hill 182 (Koprena) – towards the southern edge of East Hill. The co-ordination of the paratroopers at that stage was extremely poor – resulting in actions by small, separated groups under the command of the platoon leaders (including *Oberleutnant* Otto, *Leutnant* Spang and *Oberleutnant* Zuber – all from *2./FschJgRgt.1* and all of whom were desperate to help their comrades fighting close to the airfield). The strong Scottish defensive positions on East Hill were very well prepared – reinforced with concrete in some areas – and their superior firepower gave the Germans little chance of success. The paratroopers in this attack were actually operating more like light infantry, as they were without the support of the *4./FschJgRgt.1*[5] (heavy weapons company); *Luftwaffe* support proved inadequate.

4 Broder, pp.87-88.
5 As mentioned previously, because of the lack of planes, *4./FschJgRgt.1* did not drop at Heraklion.

Bräuer at his command post, speaking on the radio. (G. Müller & F. Scheuering, *Sprung über Kreta*)

The same spot today, on the hill where Bräuer had his command post. (Author's collection)

*Oberst* Bräuer (right) explaining the attack plan to *Major* Walther (left). The officer in the middle is *Leutnant* Schulz – the adjutant of *I./FschJgRgt.1.* (G. Müller & F. Scheuering, *Sprung über Kreta*)

A recent search of the German positions in Karteros – and at the location of the *FschJgRgt.1* command post – revealed much shrapnel from heavy artillery shells. (Author's collection)

Occupying the high ground, the Scots on East Hill had a strong advantage, as the Germans had to attack from a distance of 1.5km in front of the British positions, through a valley of flat and cleared ground, with vineyards and cornfields providing no effective cover. The airfield defenders were shelling the German positions in the Karteros Valley with captured[6] 75mm Italian guns, along with various other guns and mortars, so making any attempted attack by the paratroopers extremely difficult.

In the morning, the Scots realised that Blücher's group comprised just a few men – hence they started securing and tightening the encirclement of the paratroopers (trapping them on the hill and isolating them from their comrades). With the support of the 40mm Bofors guns firing directly onto Blücher's position, the Scottish troops managed to close up to a distance of less than 50 metres from the paratroopers. Despite their efforts, the paratroopers could not destroy the British guns, as they were protected by sandbags. The men of 'B' Company of the Black Watch, under Lieutenant John Tweedie, advanced to the north edge of the hill and took their positions in trenches and on the roofs of the few buildings in the area. With their Lee-Enfield .303-inch rifles – equipped with telescopic sights – the Scots were picking off Blücher's men as they tried to find cover on the flat ground.

Blücher sent paratrooper S.[7] to Bräuer's command post (about 1,500 metres to the east) in order to ask for immediate reinforcements. Against all odds, the messenger twice came through a hail of fire, managed to accomplish his mission and reported to Blücher that reinforcements were coming soon and that Bräuer had ordered him to hold his position.

Despite the intense enemy fire, the men of *I./FschJgRgt.1* and *II./FschJgRgt.1* unleashed their attack through the valley, but they suffered heavy losses. The paratroopers managed to reach and occupy the bridge over the Karteros River ('Rattling Bridge') and then advanced even further, but they found it extremely difficult to accomplish their main task of joining and reinforcing Blücher's platoon in order to attack and occupy the airfield. Moving to the left (south) of the German attack, a platoon under *Oberleutnant* Kissling from *3./FschJgRgt.1* managed to approach East Hill early in the morning and advance quite close to the Black Watch positions – remaining unnoticed by the Scots for more than two hours. This platoon finally drew the attention and fire of the defenders on the hill, and as a result, relieved the pressure on the Germans' right (north) flank. The attack was

6 These field guns were war trophies from the battles against the Italians in North Africa.

7 The full name is not mentioned in *Sprung über Kreta*, but could possibly be Bruno Schlenski, since he was next to Blücher when he was killed. This cannot be confirmed.

The point closest to the airfield that Blücher's men managed to reach was also the location of the grave of *Oberjäger* Karl Wanke. The reserve platoons of 'A' Coy and 'B' Coy of the Black Watch were positioned in the gorge west of East Hill. In the background (behind the modern buildings), the southern hill of the Two Charlies can be seen, where the Australians of the 2/4 Battalion were positioned. (Author's collection)

The area to the east of East Hill, as seen from Blücher's position. The messenger had to cross this area twice – under heavy fire from machine guns and rifles from the British positions – in order to reach the regimental command post at the small hill in Amnissos, and then return to his platoon. (Author's collection)

The grave of *Obergefreiter* Wuchenauer, near the south edge of East Hill. He was a machine gunner from *3./FschJgRgt.1* and one of *Oberleutnant* Kissling's men. (Author's collection)

supported by only five machine guns, that were later co-ordinated more effectively by *Hauptmann* Gröschke. The most forward German units managed to reach a position about 150 metres from the British defensive perimeter, where those who had survived the assault were forced to halt because of the overwhelming enemy fire. The *I./FschJgRgt.1* command post was established in a small house next to the coastal road, and especially close to the German forward positions.

Fritz Scheuering[8] described the attack:

> We must carry a radio to the forward positions of the battalion in order to establish communication with the regimental command post. It is impossible to move forward even for only a few steps. The enemy machine-gun fire is very heavy despite us being 1200 to 1500 m away from the enemy positions. The 'Tommies' obviously occupy an excellent observation post. We are trapped in a real 'mouse-trap'. We manage to advance with extreme difficulty, using every vine for cover.
>
> In the fields of oats which lie in front of us, the English spot us and we really do not have anywhere to take cover. Machine-gun bursts sweep the field. We are now on open rocky ground without any cover. Lungs cough and salty sweat soaks the ground. 'Medics! Medics!' is heard from many places around us. Until now I hadn't realised that the reason many comrades had fallen to the ground was that they had been hit by bullets. 'Are you all right there?' 'Yes! Everything is OK,' the response is heard from behind.
>
> Now a terrible situation begins. I crawl to the open field in front, pulling the heavy radio at the same time. The fact that I'm short and not very strong doesn't help me at all. The bullets whizz all around me as do shrapnel and dust. Damn it! Machine-gun fire comes from the side.

8 The co-author of *Sprung über Kreta*.

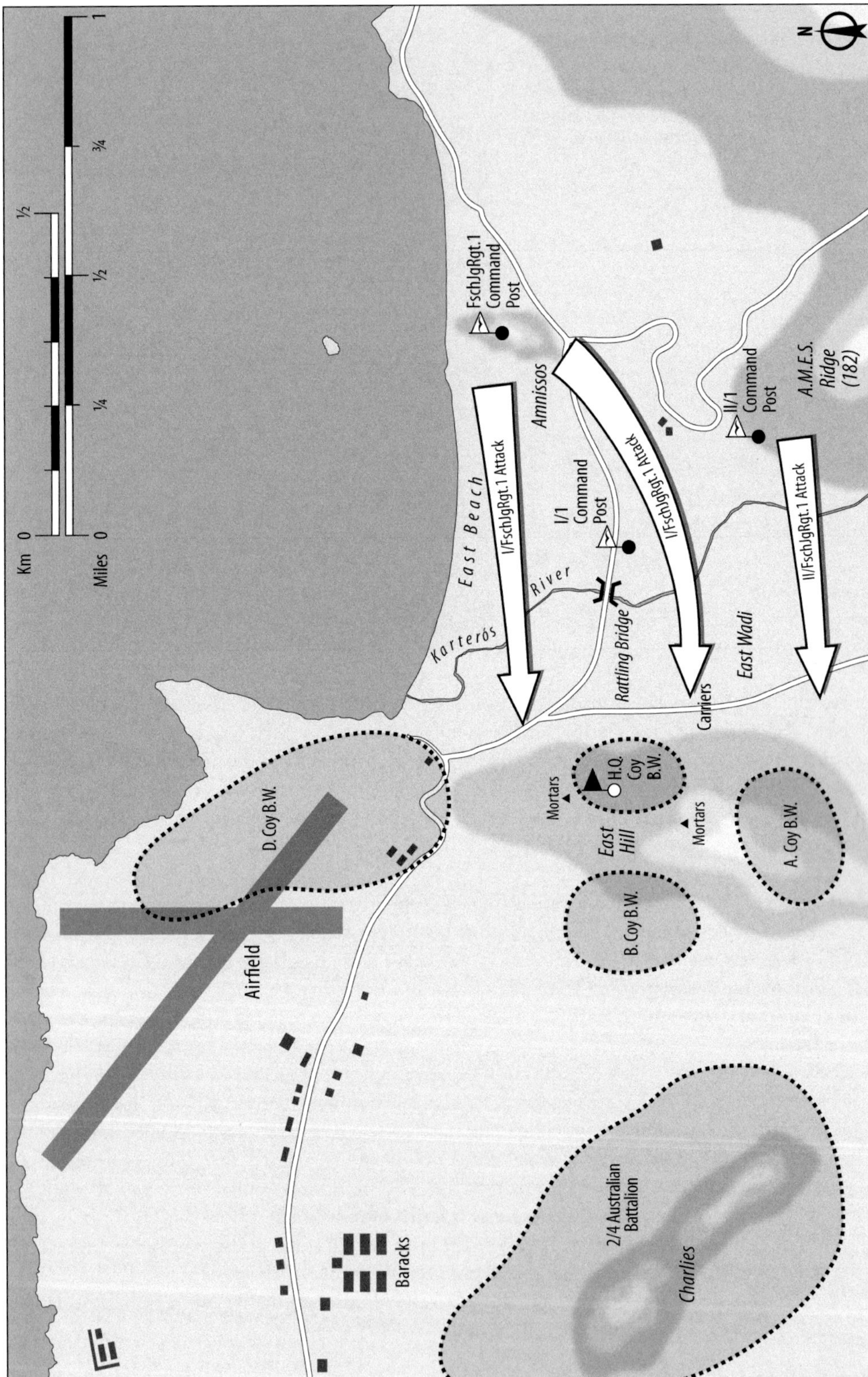


Map 4.3 The main axis of the German attack in the Karteros Valley. (N. Panos, 2016)

Very quickly I realise that it is pointless to stay lying on the ground because they are going to hit me sooner or later. I jump up and rush forward and I do not care for anything else but to escape from this wasp-nest! Fortunately I find a small ditch and there I take cover.

My comrades have also realised that it is pointless to crawl, so they follow me with short and fast jumps. My trousers are ripped and covered with blood at the knees but I don't feel anything. My heart punches like a hammer and there is only one thing in my mind: to move forward and deliver the radio to the battalion [...] it seems that there are no good opportunities to move forward any further and we are still 400 m away from the battalion command post, which has been established in a deserted house next to the road... Along with *Major* Walther's few men we manage to reach a point 150 m away from the enemy positions but we are under heavy fire from the defenders, coming from three different sides.

Poor Blücher, we won't manage to reach your position. Each step forward results in pointless bloodshed. The enemy firepower is so overwhelming. Blücher's men must be in a desperate situation and I can understand how difficult it must be for the battalion commander to leave them to their fate. It's noon on 21 May and the men prepare their defensive positions waiting for the enemy counter-attack.[9]

Gerhard Broder from the *2./FschJgRgt.1* described his part in the attack:

It is 21 May. Without leadership we attack separately in isolated small groups. With fast jumps I manage to move further into the vineyards and try to identify our objectives on the hill. Just a few metres in front of me I see an English sergeant and I take him prisoner. He has already thrown away his weapons. We lie behind a stone wall while the bullets whistle in the air and ricochet around us. We start a conversation and smoke a cigarette. I ask him how strong our enemy is and he just says: 'So many!' [...] As a precaution I ask him to empty his pockets and turn them inside out. He has a small Bible with him. I explain to him how to move back to our positions and tell him that he must make himself easily recognisable as a prisoner otherwise he is in a great danger. After the end of the battle, he recognised me and waved to me from a truck carrying prisoners.

I leave my cover and start running. At daybreak a British fleet appears on the far horizon which makes me think that we have been cut off here. I also think of the effect that a naval bombardment could have in this open field with vineyards, but the ships turn away in order to avoid an attack from the *Luftwaffe*. These are the advantages that the good weather offers to the *Luftwaffe*. I now reach a well near the road which is under heavy bombardment. I cannot resist any more and I jump behind the well and take a bucket with a rope, fill it with water and put my head in it. I drink feverishly, risking my life as I am exposed to enemy fire. I move further along the coastal road, towards the airfield. To the left I see *Gefreiter* Hans Schem from the MG-34 platoon. Another man runs behind him, carrying the ammunition and indicating the targets.

I see a Knight's Cross inside his jump-smock. It is our battalion commander, *Major* Walther. I begin to realise that we will not be able to occupy the hill in front of us. I jump into an abandoned English foxhole; it is deep and provides cover and shade. Immediately another soldier jumps in almost on my head. It is my friend Mathes Schäfer, a carpenter from Kruft Andernach! He has two water bottles with him. Projectiles whistle over the foxhole. I ask: 'Mathes do you have anything to drink?' and he says, 'Yes!' and gives me the bottle. I drink the liquid which is as thick as glue in my mouth and I try to spit it out. Mathes has found an

9 G. Müller & F. Scheuering, *Sprung über Kreta*, pp.61-66.

*Oberst* Bräuer watching the attack in the Karteros Valley, while standing next to a rock at his command post. (G. Müller & F. Scheuering, *Sprung über Kreta*)

The same spot today, with the distinctive rock. (Author's collection)

Paratroopers Rudolf Jacobs (left, with the MG-34) and Mathes Schäfer from *2./FschJgRgt.1.* (Courtesy of Adrian Nisbett)

*Major* Walther, with *Oberst* Bräuer and *Hauptmann* Rau, during the Battle for Heraklion. Walther wears his Knight's Cross inside his jump-smock. (Courtesy of Wolf Walther)

The grave of *Oberleutnant* Albert Wittmann in the vineyard, very close to the Scottish positions. (Courtesy of C.E. Mamalakis)

The same place today, in the Karteros Valley. (Author's collection)

English canteen in a building on his way here. He took cover there and as he also discovered some shorts he took off his long jump trousers. Having almost lost his mind because of the thirst and tiredness he asks me: 'I wonder if someone pees in their trousers whether it is going to cool him at all.' I give no answer to this question and after a while he says: 'This is even warmer!'

We continue to move separately and I meet *Oberleutnant* Zeiler who is now the adjutant of the battalion. He gathers a few men in order to go around and outflank the English positions. We rush to the south and turn towards the enemy, achieving some of our objectives. During our attack we manage to reach a summerhouse near the centre of the hill and there we find some of our comrades, most of them wounded. Under these conditions it is not possible to occupy the enemy positions. We remain lying down. The attack against Heraklion airfield failed.

*Oberleutnant* Otto, a nice and sympathetic officer who is a teacher, gathers the remains of the platoon and we return for the night to our positions north of the road. Rudolf Jacobs and I dig a shallow foxhole where we put our MG-34. He takes a blanket from a house and we wrap ourselves in it as protection from the cold night and fall into a deep sleep.[10]

*Oberleutnant* Albert Wittmann, with his platoon from *1./FschJgRgt.1*, tried to reach Blücher's position without any success. Some paratroopers managed to approach a building close to the slope of the hill, right in front of the Scottish defensive positions, but they were killed by fire from the 40mm AA guns. *Oberleutnant* Wittmann himself and many of his men were also killed during their attack, while *Oberleutnant* Tyska was seriously wounded. Wittmann, who was Hans Joachim von Blücher's platoon leader, managed to reach a point about 200 metres away from Wolfgang *Graf* von Blücher's men, but the intense enemy fire gave his enterprise no chance of success. At this most forward spot, he was buried in a vineyard.

The Scots on East Hill were struggling to cover the gaps in their defence, and they soon realised the significance of Blücher's advance to their left flank at the north edge of the hill. When the German attack started, it was difficult for the men of the Black Watch to hold their positions, since the Germans were using machine gun fire in an attempt to suppress the Scottish fire.

Lieutenant Gerald Barry from the HQ Coy of the Black Watch was among the defenders:

I was very worried over my left flank, where there was a large gap [he means the passage where the church of Agios Ioannis is today, on the northern slope of East Hill] between us and D Coy, and sent an urgent message requesting some assistance in that quarter as Sgt MacDonald had reported the Germans getting round his left flank. But no troops could be spared. During this day we were left alone by aircraft, only a few German recce planes came over, and by evening the attack had died down. Our positions, however, were kept under a heavy fire from machine-guns, and being on the forward slope of this hill, no one can get out of their trenches until dark. These two days were frightfully tiring and I imagine the Germans must have been very tired too. But I managed to get some hot tea and hot M &V [meat and vegetable stew] for the men, cooked in the big house after dark, which revived us all a lot.[11]

At this point, according to some accounts – and as described in the book *Sprung über Kreta* – a rider suddenly appeared; he was loaded with ammunition cans and furiously encouraging his horse. He managed to approach close to Blücher's position before he fell dead – shot down by the

10 Broder, pp.90-91.
11 C.E. Mamalakis, Ian Powys Archive.

British. Risking his own life, a paratrooper managed to reach the dead man and recognised Hans Joachim von Blücher, Wolfgang's youngest brother.

The story of Hans Joachim's death cannot be confirmed exactly as described above. There is another description by an unnamed paratrooper:

> Since Jochen's [Hans Joachim's] platoon leader especially valued his reliability and his soldierly conduct, he appointed him as his combat messenger. During the attack, Jochen received a serious lung shot as he stood next to his *Leutnant*. He collapsed immediately yet still attempted to say something. Twice he began: "*Leutnant*, sir..." and then just: "Sir, *Leutn*..." A stream of blood, he turned pale as ash and was being carried back. Half an hour later he was gone.'[12]

After learning of his brother's death, Wolfgang gritted his teeth and kept observing the enemy positions with his binoculars. Suddenly, a Matilda tank appeared – going down the road from the gorge at the east end of the airfield and moving towards the paratroopers. Paratrooper E.,[13] taking with him a bag of explosives, left his cover and, under a hail of British fire, went down the slope and threw the explosives at the tank – forcing it to retreat. The paratrooper returned to his position – covered in blood from wounds caused by shrapnel from the Bofors shells.

Blücher's men were soon running out of ammunition and Wolfgang himself found – and used – a sub-machine gun and ammunition taken from a dead British soldier. Only 18 men were left, and 11 of these were wounded. The paratroopers realised that they had few options left and they began to consider surrender. It was at this point that Blücher was shot in the head and fell dead. At the same time, a shell exploded next to *Obergefreiter* Hollweck, who was next to Wolfgang, and he was also killed. Hollweck was a friend of Wolfgang and they were buried next to each other. *Oberfeldwebel* Schneider tied a white handkerchief to the barrel of his sub-machine gun and pushed it up into the air – thus surrendering the whole platoon. The time was approximately 1530 and the battle was all over for these paratroopers. A tragic irony is that Lt John Tweedie, the Black Watch platoon leader who had fought against and captured Blücher's men, was also killed just two hours later.

Gerhard Broder from *2./FschJgRgt.1* was in the Karteros Valley – a few hundred metres away from Blücher's position – and described what he saw:

> With my binoculars I watch *Oberleutnant Graf* Blücher's platoon surrender. They go to captivity. The Englishmen have prepared each position very carefully so that it is almost impossible for us to make any movement or to defeat them with just our infantry weapons. The enemy approached Blücher's men to within a hand-grenade throwing distance and it was not possible for the paratroopers to hold their positions any longer. *Graf* Blücher doesn't put his hands up. He keeps his hands by his body as protection and he stands out with his white-blond hair. He immediately gets a deadly shot in the head. On the day before, his two younger brothers, also paratroopers, were killed. *Oberfeldwebel* Baby Möller, who tried to reach Blücher's position, was also killed.[14]

12 Adrian Nisbett, *Heroes in Death*, p.141.
13 Only the initial is mentioned in *Sprung über Kreta.*
14 Broder, pp.91-92.

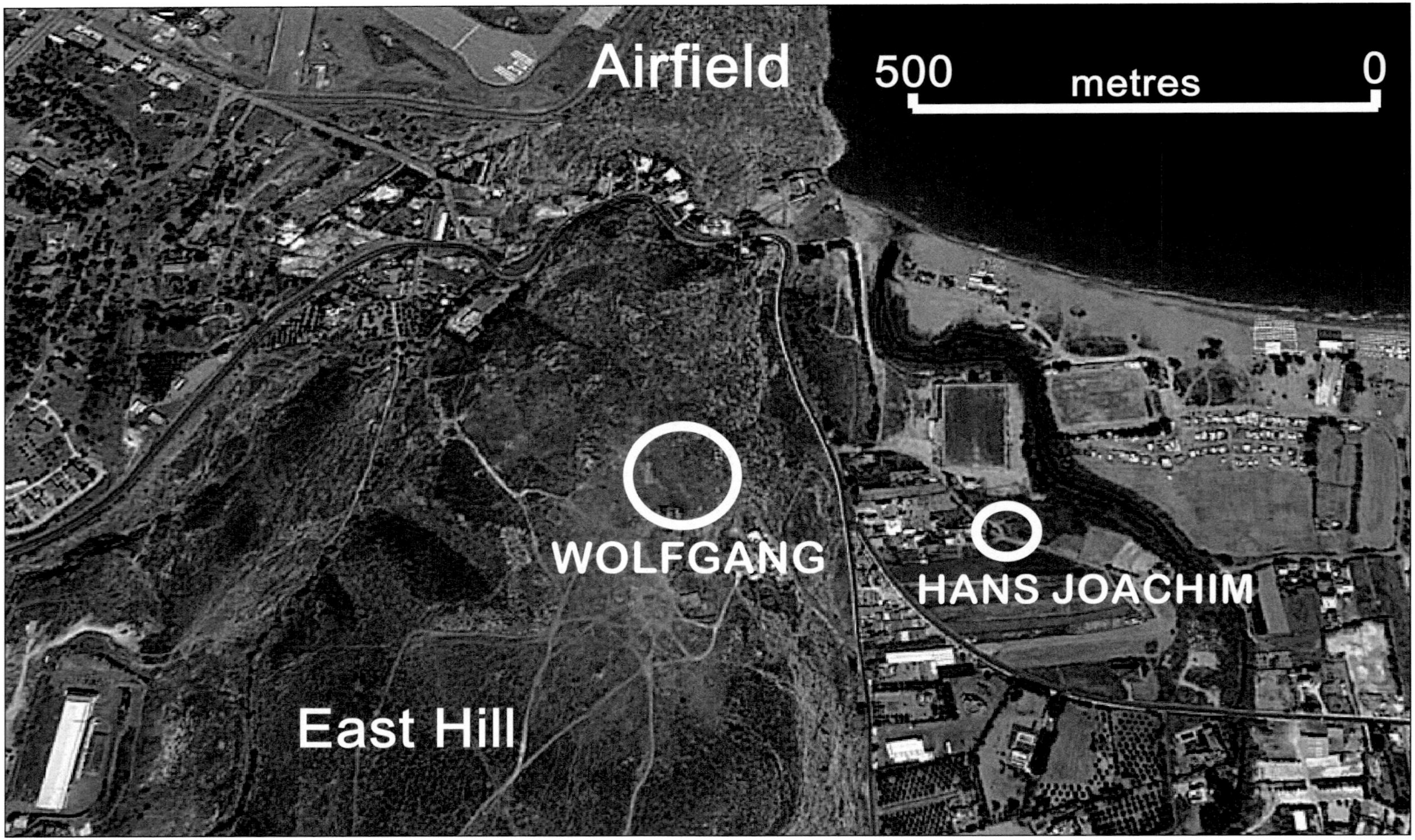


Map 4.4 The exact spot where Hans Joachim von Blücher was killed – a distance of about 300 metres away from Wolfgang *Graf* von Blücher's position and fewer than 200 metres from the rearmost men of the platoon down on the foothill. At this place, on the side of the small path, Hans Joachim was buried in a makeshift grave. (Author's collection)

Hans Joachim's temporary grave, at the location where he was killed beside the small path, in a period picture. (Courtesy of Adrian Nisbett)

The same spot today; the old path, seen in the wartime picture, is still present today – helping to identify the exact location. In the background is Hill 182 (Koprena): the assembly point of the *I./FschJgRgt.1* and *II./FschJgRgt.1*. (Author's collection)

The place where Hans Joachim was killed (marked with an arrow), as seen from Wolfgang's position. (Author's collection)

The Matilda tank that attacked Blücher's men, which was destroyed after the battle on the beach next to the mouth of the gorge, east of the airfield. (G. Müller & F. Scheuering, *Sprung über Kreta*)

The same spot today, at the rocks next to the beach. (Author's collection)

A shell found next to the place where Wolfgang *Graf* von Blücher was killed. (Author's collection)

The war diary of the 2nd Battalion of the Black Watch recorded the incidents relating to Blücher's platoon as follows:

- 21/5/41 – 00.40 One German shot near Commanding Officer's OP [at this time, Blücher's platoon was approaching East Hill].
- 10.52 … Enemy trying to get across to East end of aerodrome ….
- 11.30 "I" tank [Matilda] moving down gorge [the gorge between the airfield and the East Hill. It is the tank that attacked Blücher's men].
- 12.15 Orders to one tank to move to East Wadi [Karteros Valley].
- 14.35 HQ Coy reports enemy in front to be withdrawing [this was the withdrawal of the *I/ FschJgRgt.1* after their failure to reach Blücher's positions].
- 15.10 Orders to B Coy to destroy post established by enemy at north end of East Hill. Believed to be a small party with LMGs.[15]
- 15.16 B Coy ask for mortar support for their attack on enemy post in RAF Sangar at north end of East Hill. Inform us that two sections already surrounding it and using EY [enemy] rifle.
- 15.40[16] B Coy capture enemy MG post above Gorge taking 20 prisoners [they were the survivors from Blücher's platoon].

The exact spot where Wolfgang *Graf* von Blücher was killed is located at the north edge of the East Hill – and here he was buried in a makeshift grave. Soon after, East Hill was re-named 'Blüchersberg' by the Germans. Günther Müller writes: 'The whole day was devoted to burying comrades at the Blüchersberg and the spot where the *Oberleutnant* was killed also became his grave and a big cross was placed'.

*Oberfeldwebel* Schneider, a platoon member, told the story of Blücher's platoon during the evening of 29 May, when the battle was over and the paratroopers were gathered at the Greek barracks – relating their experiences and stories from the battle. Many years later, another platoon member – Bruno Schlenski – told the whole story. Schlenski wept as he described the events, and he also confirmed that Wolfgang *Graf* von Blücher was shot in the head while he and his men were surrendering.

15 Light machine guns.

16 The same time is also confirmed by *Major* Walther in his after-action report, designated as 1430 German time, which was 1530 for the British.

The original grave of *Oberleutnant* von Blücher and *Obergefreiter* Hollweck, with two crosses made from ammunition boxes. This was probably a Scottish defensive position – judging by the sandbags on the left side of the grave and the British helmet on the top. (Courtesy of Shaun Winkler)

The remains of the grave on the battlefield – 73 years after the exhumation of the bodies and their burial at the Heraklion War Cemetery. It is even possible for some of the stones to be identified as having been on the original grave. (Author's collection)

Another picture of Wolfgang *Graf* von Blücher's grave. A few days after the battle, the two crosses were replaced by one large cross. All the graves in the area were marked with crosses; note that on the cross, 'Hollweck' appears to be written incorrectly (which was often the case in battlefield graves) as 'Hollmed'. (Courtesy of Dimitris Skartsilakis)

The Heraklion Airfield immediately after the battle. The sandbags indicate the position of the guns at the east end of the runway. In the background, damaged Allied aircraft can be seen among the German ones. (Courtesy of Mike Smythe)

Paratroopers from *I./FschJgRgt.1* at the Greek barracks – resting after the battle and exchanging their experiences. (Courtesy of Shaun Winkler)

**Special Presentation 13: Bruno Schlenski**

Bruno Schlenski was born in Allenstein, East Prussia and joined the *Luftwaffe* in 1938. He volunteered for the paratroopers and participated in the Battle of Crete. He was right next to Wolfgang *Graf* von Blücher when he was killed. Schlenski was then taken prisoner by the British and finally released when they evacuated the island. He also participated in the Russian and Italian campaigns (Monte Cassino, Po River), where he was finally captured by the Americans.

Schlenski treasured his memories from the battle – and especially the story of his platoon leader, *Oberleutnant* von Blücher, until the end of his life.

Bruno Schlenski in a wartime photo. (Courtesy of G.W. Cone)

According to Schlenski, after they had been captured, the paratroopers were transferred and held at the Agios Konstantinos Cemetery south of the city, on the road to Knossos. When this area was bombed by *Stukas*, they formed a *swastika* on the ground with their bodies in order to display their nationality to the German pilots. The wounded paratroopers were transferred to the British field hospital in Villa Ariadne, next to Knossos.

Bruno Schlenski (first on the left), with other veterans. (Courtesy of G.W. Cone)

After the battle was over, five surviving paratroopers from Blücher's platoon were found in a small house in no man's land. Three of them were wounded and they had waited eight days for their comrades to rescue them. (Courtesy of Stephan Janzyk)

A small hamlet in the Karteros area, located just to the east of Agios Ioannis Hill (seen here on the left). It was in buildings like this that the paratroopers tried to find cover. Many of them remained trapped for days in what had become a no man's land. (Author's collection)

Wolfgang *Graf* von Blücher and his men during training after the operation in Holland. The paratrooper seen here (standing fourth behind Wolfgang) is the same paratrooper who is seen injured in the photo where he waited eight days for his comrades to rescue him. (Author's collection)

The Scottish defensive positions, as they are today, on East Hill. These were the positions that Blücher had to capture in order to approach the airfield – a task that was finally accomplished under the cover of darkness. According to the account of a local shepherd, in the 1980s, a German veteran was seen at these positions – weeping and remembering his comrades who had fallen there during the battle. (Author's collection)

The positions of the 2nd Bn, BW on East Hill – bombed by *Stukas* during the battle. (G. Müller & F. Scheuering, *Sprung über Kreta*)

The same area today. The whole area on and around East Hill still holds many relics from the battle, such as bomb and shell shrapnel, barbed wire and cartridges. (Author's collection)

Relics from the battle found in the same area where Blücher's platoon was surrounded. (Author's collection)

Lieutenant Gerald Barry from the HQ Company of the Black Watch witnessed the German assault:

> At dawn, they had organised themselves more or less, and tried to attack our position from in front. This we beat off, killing a good many again. A number had survived on the hill behind us [Blücher's men, at the north edge of the hill], and a platoon of B Coy was sent out to deal with them. Unfortunately they met with a lot of fire and suffered heavy casualties, about ten killed, I heard, with Tweedie missing.[17]

Most of the dead from *2./FschJgRgt.1* belonged to Wolfgang *Graf* von Blücher's platoon, and were the following:

*Oblt* Wolfgang *Graf* von Blücher – 21 May 1941
*Obfw* Ernst Möller – 21 May 1941
*Gefr* Kurt Martin – 20 May 1941 (unidentified)[18]
*Objg* Karl Wanke – 21 May 1941
*Obgfr* Walter Hollweck – 21 May 1941
*Gefr* Heinz Vosshage – 21 May 1941
*Jäger* Hans Meyer – 21 May 1941
*Gefr* Julius Kleber – 21 May 1941
*Gefr* Kurt Kittendorf – 21 May 1941
*Obgfr* Fritz Bohnstedt – 21 May 1941
*Objg* Günthner – 20 May 1941
*Gefr* Mathes – 20 May 1941
*Gefr* Karl Bauer – 21 May 1941
*Obgfr* Willi Röhl – 21 May 1941

As was the custom, the fallen paratroopers were buried on the battlefield exactly where they were killed.

The expected British counter-attack never came. After the elimination of Blücher's platoon, the Matilda tank which was positioned at the east edge of the airfield moved along the road towards the paratroopers and into the valley in order to investigate the situation, and make a reconnaissance of the German positions; however, it was soon forced to return because of German anti-tank fire. A fierce battle began between the tank and a light anti-tank gun, which had been placed in a forward position next to the road. The paratroopers immediately replaced a severely wounded member of the gun crew and kept firing at the tank. With successful shots onto the tank's tracks, the Germans forced the tank to retreat, but failed in their attempts to destroy it. The wounded member of the anti-tank gun crew was *Oberjäger* Hans Erning from the 14th Company. His comrades transferred Erning to the field hospital, which was in a tavern next to the regimental command post.

17 C.E. Mamalakis, Ian Powys Archive.
18 Unidentified despite the fact that he was buried in a marked grave on the battlefield, with his name written on the cross.

The grave of *Oberjäger* Karl Wanke was the nearest to the airfield and some 50 metres away from the grave of Wolfgang *Graf* von Blücher. (Courtesy of Stephan Janzyk

The remains of a grave, which most probably belonged to Karl Wanke, as it is today. (Author's collection)

The grave of *Gefreiter* Heinz Vosshage. East Hill is seen in the background. (Courtesy of Stephan Janzyk)

The position of *Gefreiter* Heinz Vosshage's grave, as it is today. (Author's Collection)

*Gefreiter* Heinz Vosshage loading a drop container onto a Ju-52 during preparations for the invasion on 20 May 1941. (Courtesy of Stephan Janzyk)

**Theodoros E. Kallinos:** "The Battle of Crete could have been won. Right after the defeat of the Italians by the Greek Army, the V Division 'Crete' should have been returned to Crete. The defence of the island should have been prepared in each possible amphibious or airborne landing zone. The people of Crete were ready to defend their island – something that was really proved during the battle. Everlasting glory and honour to those who gave their lives for Crete; those who are not afraid to die, they live forever."

**David Hutton:** "The Battle for Crete was a short period in my life, but one that has had such a profound impact. The battle itself, I will always remember for the German paratroopers dropping in such large numbers they turned the sky black – landing all-round the Black Watch positions. We had very few automatic weapons, but we made them tell – causing huge casualties on those that came down within reach. I am sure if the battle elsewhere had gone better, the Black Watch would have been able to hold."

**Dr Eberhard Boerger:** "At the time of the Battle of Crete, I was a 2nd lieutenant and a platoon leader in the 11th Company of the 1st Fallschirmjäger Regiment and jumped off with my men west of the town of Heraklion. The unspeakably scary picture of the mass jump into enemy fire will remain for me as an unforgettable impression in my memory until my last breath."

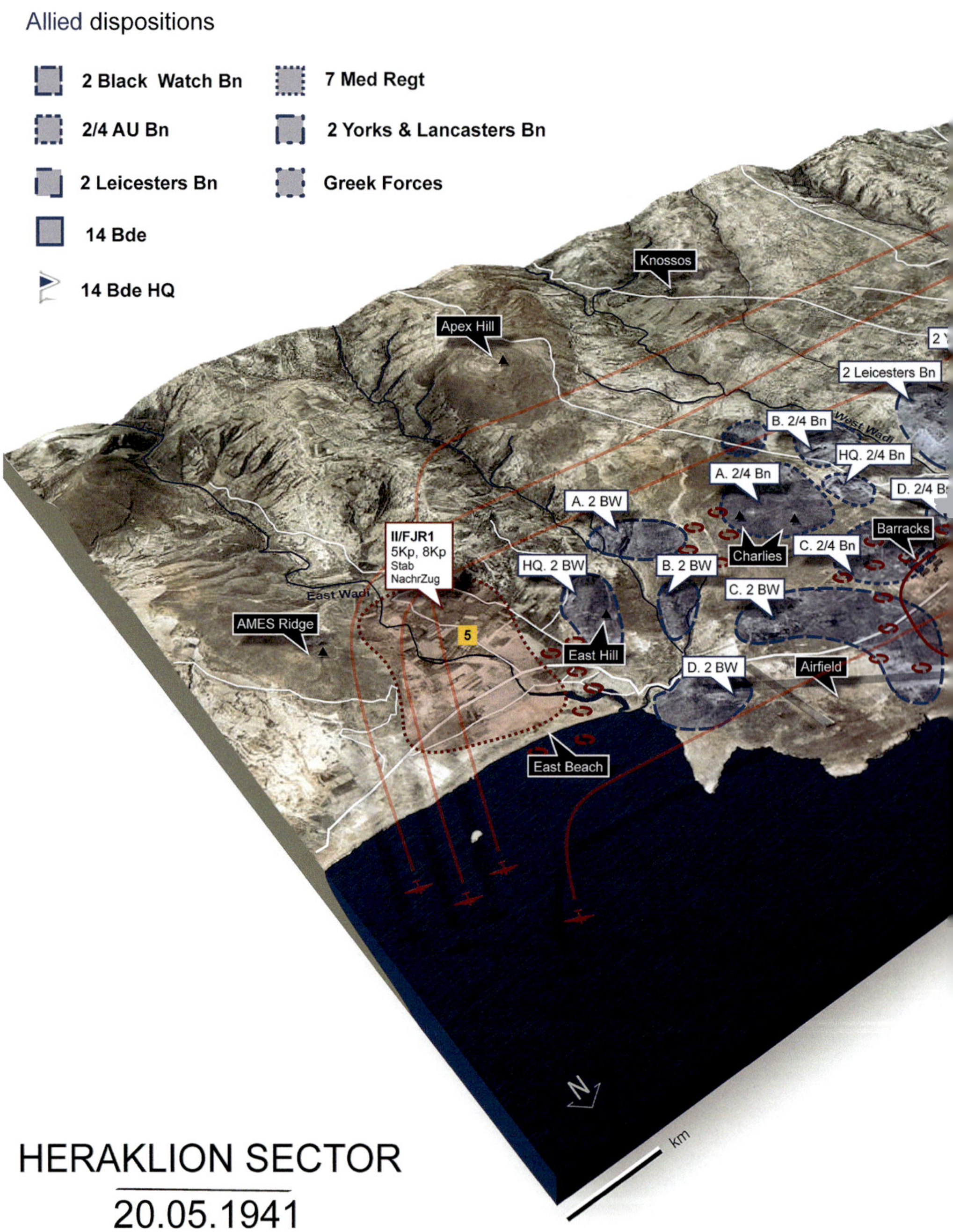


Map 2.2 Heraklion sector, 20 May 1941. (N. Valasiadis, 2015)

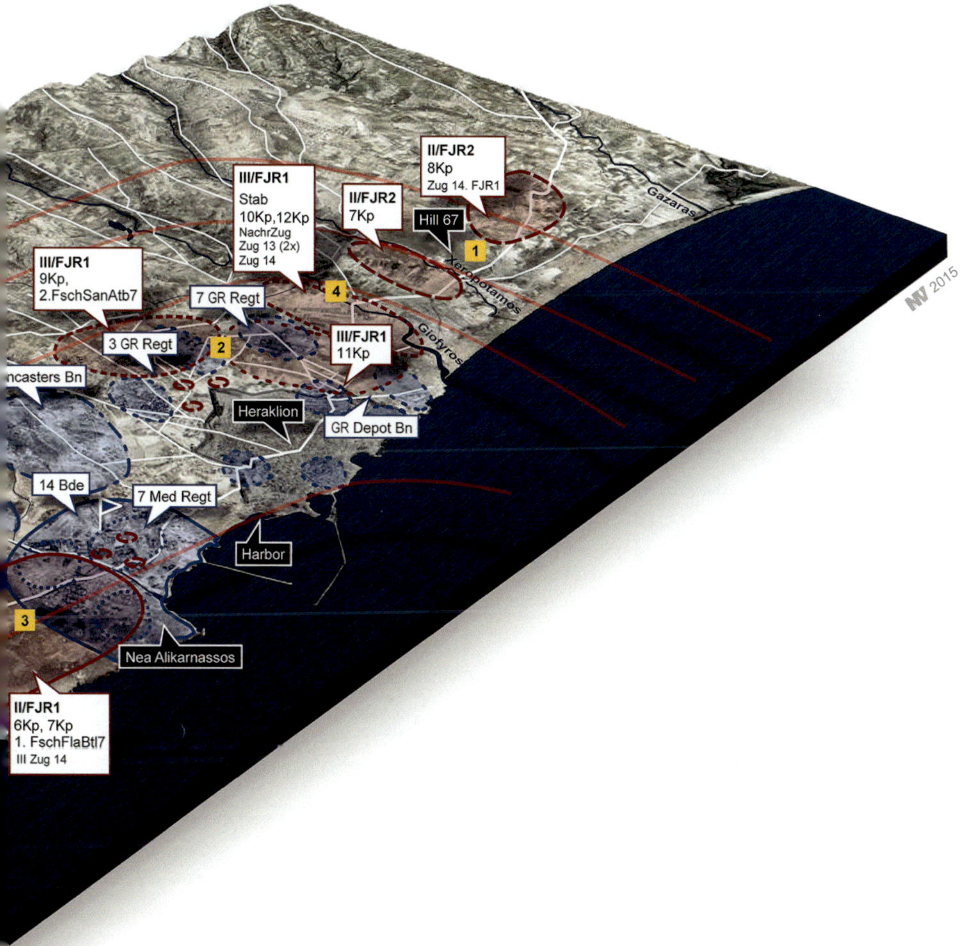


German attack

**II/FJR1**
5Kp, 8Kp
Stab
NachrZug

**III/FJR1**
9Kp, 11Kp
2.FschSanAtb7

**II/FJR2**
7Kp, 8Kp
Zug 14. FJR1

**II/FJR1**
6Kp, 7Kp
1. FschFlaBtl7

**III/FJR1**
10Kp, Stab
NachrZug
Zug 13, Zug 13
Zug 14

**Ju 52**
flight
paths

**Scattered**

1 16:30 -17:00
2 17:30 - 18:00
3 17:35 - 19:17
4 17:50 - 18:25
5 18:10 - 18:40

## Special Presentation 7: Fritz Weller

Fritz Weller was killed in Mastabas, south of Heraklion, on 20 May 1941. He fought and fell next to *Obgfr* Paul Scholz and *Gefr* Günther Klingberg from *9./FschJgRgt.1*. The grave numbers of these three paratroopers (302, 303, 305) indicate that they were killed very close to the walls and they had probably tried to enter the town via the South Gate.

Paratrooper Fritz Weller, *9./FschJgRgt.1*. (Courtesy of Shawn Winkler)

Fallschirmschützenschein

Nr. 117 / III

für Obgefr. Fritz Weller

(Dienstgrad, Vor- und Zuname)

geboren: 20. 4. 1916

Diensteintritt: 20. 10. 1936

Truppenteil: 9/F. J. Rgt. 1

Inhaber ist befördert:

am:

zum

am:

zum:

am:

zum:

III./F.J. Rgt. 1

(Ausstellende Dienststelle)

(Eigenhändige Unterschrift, Vor- u. Zuname)

Gardelegen, den 13. 7. 1939

(Ort) (Datum)

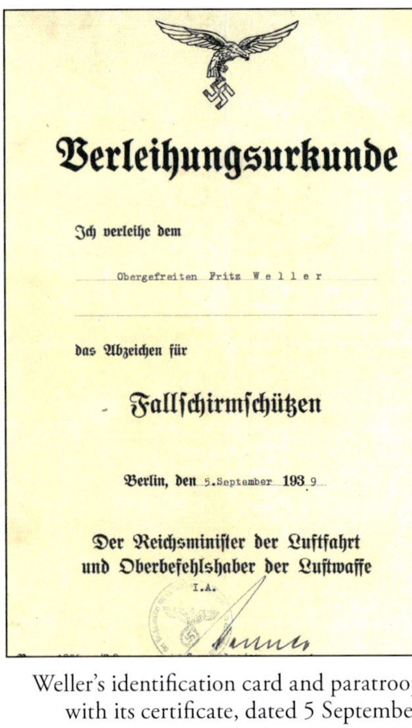

Verleihungsurkunde

Ich verleihe dem

Obergefreiten Fritz Weller

das Abzeichen für

Fallschirmschützen

Berlin, den 5.September 1939

Der Reichsminister der Luftfahrt
und Oberbefehlshaber der Luftwaffe

I.A.

Weller's identification card and paratrooper's badge (*fallschirmschützen-abzeichen*), together with its certificate, dated 5 September 1939. His grave can be found in Maleme War Cemetery, Block 1, No.305. (Courtesy of the Shaun Winkler Collection)

Lieutenant Hope-Morley's images were digitally combined into one for this reconstruction of the 1941 landscape. The same place was photographed from approximately the same angle in May 2008, in the Katsabas area. The rock formation, where Chappel's HQ was located, has undergone some major changes since 1941, but still stands. (Courtesy of Nikos Valasiadis)

The remains of a paratrooper's grave at the drop zone of the *8./FschJgRgt.1* – today, very close to the positions of the Black Watch. (Author's collection)

Some of the Black Watch HQ Company trenches, as they are today. (Author's collection)

A wide-angle view of the Karteros Valley (East Wadi), as seen from the positions of the Black Watch HQ Company. (Author's collection)

The remains of Wolfgang *Graf* von Blücher's grave on the battlefield – 73 years after the exhumation of the bodies and their burial at the Heraklion War Cemetery. It is even possible for some of the stones to be identified as having been on the original grave. (Author's collection)

Sfakianakis Metohi at the south-west edge of Height 67. (Courtesy of C.E. Mamalakis)

Bill Lark's tam o'shanter and pocket knife. (C.E. Mamalakis' archive)

The York & Lancaster Regiment's Regimental Colours, which were found after the battle at the HQ of the 2nd Battalion. The evacuation was so sudden and rushed that many items were forgotten by the British troops. This banner was found by the Germans after the battle and later kept by a Cretan. It was finally discovered in an old military trunk in a deserted house. All the regiment's battles and the campaigns before the Battle of Crete are recorded on the flag. (C.E. Mamalakis' archive)

The graves of *Obgfr* Willi Röhl and *Gefr* Kurt Martin in the Karteros Valley, and the grave of *Gefr* Karl Bauer on the east slope of East Hill. (Author's collection) Note: Marked on the grave as '*oberjäger*', but according to the German archives, his rank was *gefreiter*.

The grave of *Gefr* Julius Kleber and *Jäger* Hans Meyer on the east slope of East Hill. (Author's collection)

The same spot today. (Author's collection)

Even today, the remains of paratroopers' makeshift graves are identifiable on the battlefield. (Author's collection)

The place where Hans Erning was initially buried on the battlefield in Amnissos, next to the regimental command post. He was the only *oberjäger* buried next to the field hospital that day. (Courtesy of Stelios Tripalitakis)

Dr Günther Müller was there:

> Eventually an *Oberjäger* is brought in [*Oberjäger* Hans Erning]. He gasps jerkily, and a hole the size of a big fist shows on his chest. The doctor examines him carefully while he is unconscious. The eyes of the senior physician darken and with a silent gesture, we know that he cannot do anything more to help him. His comrades carry him out without saying a word. They stay silent next to his stretcher… after two hours he died.
>
> The men haven't slept since the jump and were then attacked and came under heavy fire. They have already had a very long day with the glowering sun burning over their heads. But they do not abandon their dead comrade. With their hands and spades they dig a grave in the rocky ground of the coastal road. The dead comrade is buried there under the light of the artillery bombardment.[19]

By carefully studying the accounts of the battle, and the pictures of the graves in the area east of the airfield, it is possible to identify the exact spots where the paratroopers were killed, and then to use these points to trace the exact route of the attack and the evolution of the battle.

19 Müller & Scheuering, pp.73-74.

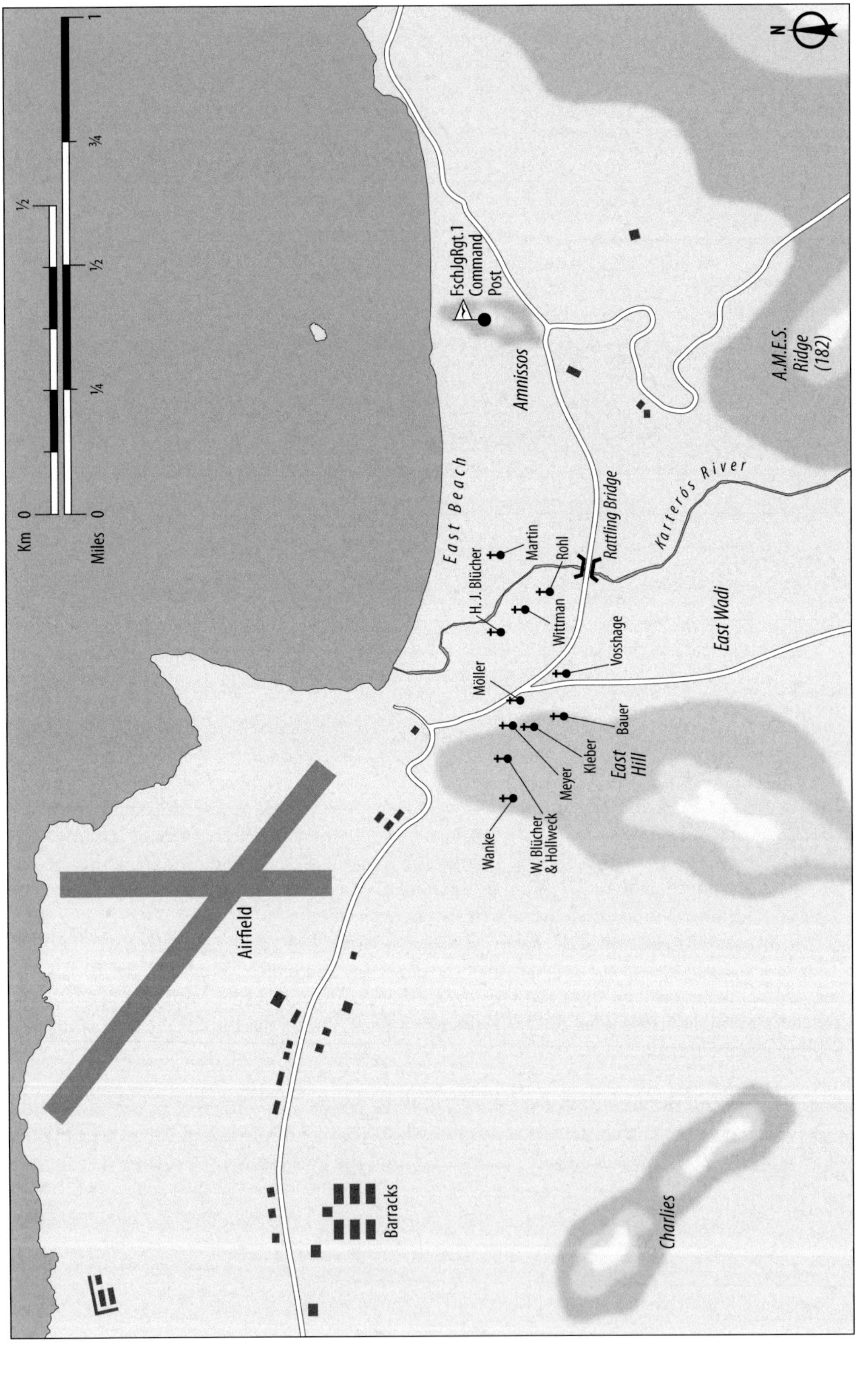


Map 4.5 The positions where the men of *1./FschJgRgt.1* and *2./FschJgRgt.1* were killed during the attack of 20/21 May, east of the airfield. (N. Panos, 2016)

The story of the rider who tried to bring ammunition to Wolfgang's men, but who was shot and killed – and later identified as Hans Joachim von Blücher – was told by *Oberfeldwebel* Schneider and is described in the book *Sprung über Kreta*. There are some problems with this story, since no other eyewitness has confirmed it; furthermore, the place where Hans Joachim was killed – about 300 metres away from Wolfgang – is not consistent with this specific description. The position of Hans Joachim's death 300 metres away from Wolfgang was also confirmed by *Oberst* Bräuer (see Nisbett, p.127). In fact, this story appears to conform exactly with what happened to *Oberfeldwebel* Ernst ('Baby') Möller. According to Gerhard Broder (see Broder, p.87 and p.92), Möller was left behind at the drop zone in Gournes – trying to gather the men of *2./FschJgRgt.1* – while Wolfgang and his men were already advancing to the airfield. Later, when Möller arrived in the Karteros area, he rushed to join and help Wolfgang's men, but he was killed at the foot of East Hill, very close to Wolfgang's position. The place where Möller was killed is next to the Karteros Road – and it was here that a paratrooper ran downhill and reached the dead man whom he recognised as Hans Joachim; it is likely that the dead man was, in fact, Ernst Möller. The story was changed either by misinterpretation of various accounts, or on purpose in order to describe the battle in a more dramatic way. Considering that *Sprung über Kreta* was published in 1944, when the German war news was rarely positive, the story's value as propaganda cannot be discounted.

The grave of *Oberfeldwebel* Ernst ('Baby') Möller. (Author's collection)

Lebrecht *Graf* von Blücher, Wolfgang's middle brother, was also killed near the Heraklion Airfield, but his body was never found. Mystery overshadows the fate of Lebrecht *Graf* von Blücher: he belonged to the 7th Company of the *II/1 Battalion* that dropped on 20 May, west of the airfield. The 7th and 6th Companies jumped over the same drop zone and they were probably the unluckiest, since they were almost annihilated.

For some years, it was thought that Lebrecht was initially buried next to a man named Mickileit from the 5th Company, but that later, Lebrecht's remains were lost, since there was no grave bearing his name in the Heraklion War Cemetery that was built in 1942. The fact that there was a grave for Mickileit in the cemetery makes the whole story even more complicated, and it is not easy to explain how the remains of Lebrecht were lost. According to the German archives, the remains of *Gefreiter* Herbert Mickileit were exhumed from the Amnissos area where Hans Joachim was killed – and well away from Lebrecht's drop zone. I believe, based on the available evidence, that the grave with the inscription '*Gefr Graf Blücher II. Batt. Fallsch Jg Rgt 1 - ..... Mikoleit 5. Fallschirm Jäger Rgt 1*' probably belonged to Hans Joachim von Blücher – not to Lebrecht. Some aircraft carrying paratroopers crashed into the sea. Additionally, in the area west of the airfield, there were so many bodies scattered around that the British buried them in rough and unmarked mass graves in order to avoid the smell of the rotting bodies and the danger of disease. One of these fates most probably explains what happened to Lebrecht. Human remains are occasionally discovered in this area even today – more than 70 years after the battle.

In the letter sent from Athens to his mother on 19 May, Wolfgang *Graf* von Blücher wrote:

> … I have been appointed transport commander. I have to command my 2nd company and half of the 1st company. That includes Jochen, too. It is so good to have him with me! Yesterday he paid me a visit in my compartment. He really presents himself excellently. If you say something to him he immediately understands. Both he and Lebs will soon jump for their first time and they will do so in the face of the enemy....

By the time the letter was in their mother's hands, all three brothers were dead and they had made their jump into history.

On 21 May, the paratroopers in the eastern sector took offensive action not only in the Karteros area, but also in the area south of the airfield and the town. In Prassas, the paratroopers were surrounded and trapped, while in Chani Babali – and on the road to Knossos – they met strong resistance from the men of the 2/4 Australian Battalion and the 2nd Battalion of the York & Lancaster Regiment. As a result, they did not make any substantial progress in their efforts to achieve their objectives.

At around 1700, reinforcements were dropped in the area of Karteros-Kako Oros, near the *FschJgRgt.1* command post, and activity from both sides to the east of the airfield died down during the evening of 21 May.

A paratrooper's grave in front of the north gate of the Greek barracks. Despite only unconfirmed information that this was Lebrecht's grave, it is definitely the area where he was killed. (Courtesy of Shaun Winkler)

Es starben den Heldentod auf Kreta
unsere geliebten Söhne Brüder Enkel
und Neffen

der Ritterkreuzträger

**Wolfgang Graf von Blücher**
Oberleutnant in einem Fallschirmjägerregiment
im Alter von 24 Jahren

**Leberecht Graf von Blücher**
Gefreiter in einem Fallschirmjägerregiment
im Alter von 19 Jahren

**Hans=Joachim Graf von Blücher**
Jäger in einem Fallschirmjägerregiment
im Alter von 17 Jahren

Darze, Post Stuer, in Mecklenburg
Posen und Altengottern, den 23. Juni 1941

Gertrud v. Nordheim, geb. Freiin Marschall
verw. Gräfin Blücher
Ludwig v. Nordheim, Gaulandwirt im
Luftgau II
Elisabeth Gräfin v. Blücher
Adolf Graf v. Blucher, Leutnant zur See
Gertrud Gräfin v. Blücher
Richenza v. Nordheim
Wilhelmine Freifrau Marschall,
geb. Gräfin Rittberg
Charlotte Freiin Marschall

The announcement of the three brothers' deaths on the family remembrance card (left) and the grave of two of the brothers (Nos.457-458) in the Maleme War Cemetery (right). (Courtesy of the von Blücher family)

The three brothers: Wolfgang (left), Lebrecht (middle) and Hans Joachim (right). (Courtesy of the von Blücher family)

## Special Presentation 14: The regimental command post and field hospital

Bräuer and his staff established the regimental command post on Amnissos Hill. The paratroopers called the hill the '*Regimentsberg*'.

Amnissos Hill ('*Regimentsberg*') during the battle, in a picture taken from the east. (G. Müller & F. Scheuering, *Sprung über Kreta*)

The same hill today, as seen from the east. (Author's collection)

Bruno Bräuer, with his staff, watching the battle from his command post. Radio antennas can also be seen in the picture. The paratroopers use parachute canopies as tents to protect them from the sun and the unbearable heat. (G. Müller & F. Scheuering, *Sprung über Kreta*)

The same spot today, on the east slope of Amnissos Hill, where the command post was protected from enemy fire and observation. In the previous picture, Bräuer and his staff watch what was probably a parachute supply drop. (Author's collection)

For the protection of the command post, a PAK 3.7cm anti-tank gun and an MG-34 machine gun were positioned on the southern slope of the hill.

The machine gun at the south edge of the hilltop. (G. Müller & F. Scheuering, *Sprung über Kreta*)

The machine gun position today. (Author's collection)

The anti-tank gun which was positioned alongside the Karteros Road. It was this road that the Matilda used to reach and attack the command post. (G. Müller & F. Scheuering, *Sprung über Kreta*)

The same place today, in a picture taken from the exact position of the anti-tank gun. The big rock on the lower right corner is also seen in the period picture. (Author's collection)

Shrapnel, probably from the duel with the Matilda, found at the spot where the anti-tank gun was positioned. Also found was a cartridge case with the date 1936 (the most common date found on cartridge cases from the battle around Heraklion) lying in the position of the machine gun. (Author's collection)

Bruno Bräuer (sitting on a drop container) discussing the operation with *Oberleutnant* Harry Herrmann – commander of the 5th Company, who had suffered a head injury and was temporarily blinded. Totally exhausted by the continuous fighting, paratroopers have found an opportunity to rest under the shadow of the small bridge. (G. Müller & F. Scheuering, *Sprung über Kreta*)

The bridge is located approximately 100 metres from Amnissos Hill and still exists today; however, it is clogged with debris which has been washed downstream by the creek, as can be seen in the picture. (Author's collection)

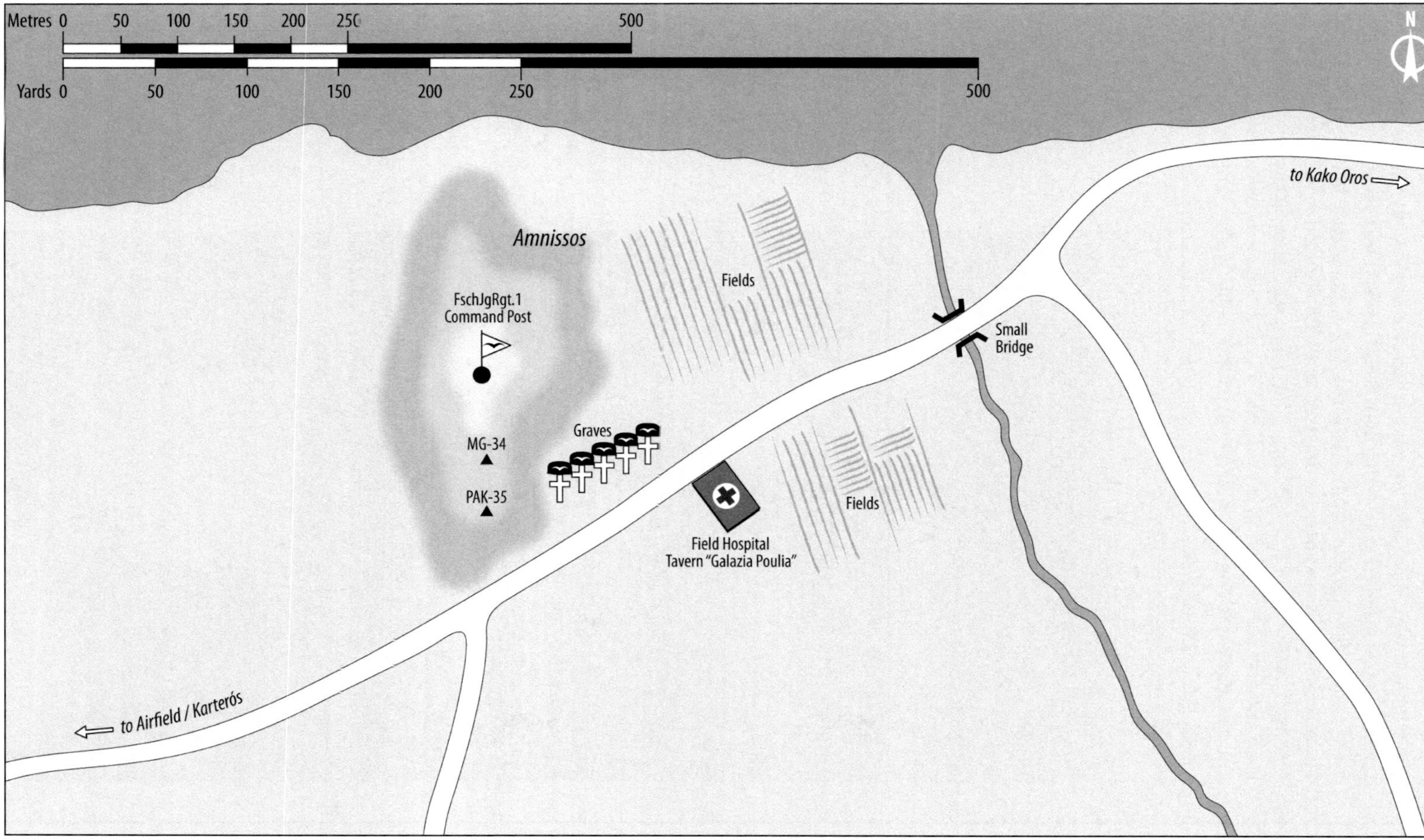


The exact positions of the command post, the small bridge nearby, the guns and the tavern (where the field hospital was situated). (N. Panos, 2016)

The command post included communication facilities, as well as a medical treatment detachment. The field hospital (*truppenverbandsplatz*) was established in the tavern '*TA GALAZIA POULIA*' ('The Blue Birds'), which was located on the Karteros Road, just a few metres from Amnissos Hill. The tavern belonged to Georgios Tyrakis and was a landmark in the area until 2005, when it was demolished and a residence was built on the same site. The tavern was easily accessible because of the road and was surrounded by a yard with a vine arbour – providing shade during the hot days of May. It was also near a well with drinking water – thus providing an ideal refuge for the wounded.

The area south-east of the command post, as seen from the top of the hill, in a picture taken during the battle. (G. Müller & F. Scheuering, *Sprung über Kreta*)

The same area today. The arrow on the picture indicates the tavern, which housed the field hospital. (Author's collection)

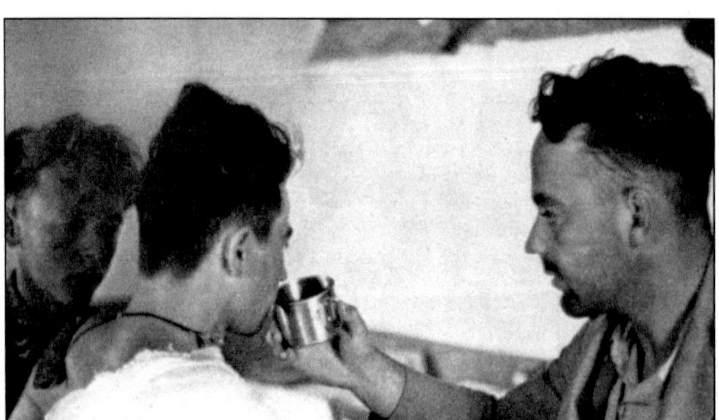

Dr Breuer and his medics did their best to help the wounded. (G. Müller & F. Scheuering, *Sprung über Kreta*)

Dr Günther Müller recorded the scene at the field hospital:

> There are so many wounded men that they have to lie in the congested summer-house and in the garden next to it. The arrival of wounded never ends. Troops arrive continuously carrying more wounded paratroopers.
>
> In a surgeon's jacket that was once white, *Oberarzt* Dr. B. [Dr Breuer from Hamburg] operates on a severely wounded man under the light of candles and flashlights. Medics with instruments and bandages stand nearby. "Tweezers! Tetanus syringe!" ... "Bandages!"... The helpers noiselessly hand the required items to the physician. In the next room silence prevails, sometimes interrupted by the moans of the wounded. Nearly all the severely wounded who leave the operating theatre have a big smile on their faces. The inconspicuous, colourless morphine relieves them from the pain for hours [...]
>
> The field hospital is not only a place for treating the wounded but also a place for rest and shelter for other comrades. With caring foresight, the regimental staff physician Dr. M. boils tea, and everyone who arrives receives food and drink. This all sounds so simple, but a lightly wounded man tells me: "The two doctors have worked continuously since early in the morning. There is nothing that can bring calm and peace here now. Sometimes the artillery fire was so strong that we had to carry away the wounded. All now lie in ditches behind rocks and they are well protected from fire."[1]

Photos of the field hospital. (G. Müller & F. Scheuering, *Sprung über Kreta*)

1 Müller & Scheuering, pp.76-77.

Supplies dropped on Amnissos, close to the command post and the field hospital. (G. Müller & F. Scheuering, *Sprung über Kreta*)

Field dressing found in Karteros, in a drop container. The container was found by a local farmer after it had been dropped well into the valley, instead of on the beach. (C.E. Mamalakis' archive)

The photographs of the command post and the field hospital during the battle were taken by medical NCO Dr Günther Müller. He dropped on Gournes – on 20 May – with the staff of *FschJgRgt.1*.

Dr Günther Müller standing at the entrance of the tavern '*TA GALAZIA POULIA*' with one of his comrades. Müller wears a British pith helmet – a common sight during the battle – since British tropical uniforms and gear were very popular among the Germans on Crete. (G. Müller & F. Scheuering, *Sprung über Kreta*)

Dr Günther Müller standing at the *FschJgRgt.1* command post on Amnissos Hill. (Author's collection)

The severely wounded who died at the field hospital were buried on the opposite side of the street, near the southern slope of Amnissos Hill, next to the command post.

The graves of *Oberjäger* Karl Frohlich (*I/1 Battalion* staff), *Obergefreiter* Willy Hahn (*I/1 Battalion* staff), *Oberjäger* Alfons Menter (regiment staff), *Oberfeldwebel* Reinhold Krüger and *Oberjäger* Hans Erning (14th Company and killed by the Matilda on the 21st) on Amnissos Hill. (Author's collection)

The site of the graves today. (Author's collection)

*Oberjäger* Alfons Menter (regiment staff) – 30 July 1917-24 May 1941. (Courtesy of David Lenk)

Today, these paratroopers are buried at the war cemetery in Maleme, in the same relative positions as they were buried on the battlefield. (Author's collection)

# 5

# The Attack on the Town

*Major* Schulz of *III./FschJgRgt.1* had never received Bräuer's message to attack the town during the night; however, he heard – by chance – a *Luftwaffe* radio message saying that the town of Heraklion was about to be bombed during the morning of 21 May between 0900 and 1000 (0800-0900 German time). Schulz decided to act rapidly and take the town's defenders by surprise by attacking in the morning, in order to take advantage of the confusion that the bombing would have caused. A meeting of Schulz's company commanders was held in an olive grove, where he was briefed first about the overall situation and the losses that his units had suffered up to that time; he then said that the battalion's mission was to occupy the town – hence they were to attack and to try to enter the town from the west. *Oberleutnants* Becker and Kerfin pointed out the difficulty of the enterprise on account of the strong defensive positions and the size of the Venetian walls around the town – a problem that Schulz himself was well aware of, since he had landed very close to the walls.

The primary goal of the *III./FschJgRgt.1* was to occupy the town, secure the port, advance eastwards in order to join the units that had been dropped in the east sector and make contact with *Oberst* Bräuer. This would result in the airfield being surrounded. Communication with regimental HQ and with *I./FschJgRgt.1* and *II./FschJgRgt.1* remained a major problem, yet to be solved. *Oberleutnant* Kappel, the signals officer, was assigned the vitally important task of finding the missing radios and establishing communications with the other units.

Two main groups were assembled for the attack: the first – consisting of *11./FschJgRgt.1*, under *Oberleutnant* Becker – would attempt to enter the town by advancing along the coast from a point next to the coast called 'Gyali Kiosk', or 'Kommeno Bedeni' ('Broken Walls'), where the walls had been demolished. This group was to advance on and secure the port. The other group consisted mainly of men of the *10./FschJgRgt.1*, under *Oberleutnant* Egger, and would attempt to enter the town through Chanioporta (West Gate) and advance eastwards to the town centre. In addition – to obtain proper medical treatment for the wounded – the second group was to occupy the Pananion Hospital, which was located just a few hundred metres from the West Gate. The *III./FschJgRgt.1* was also supported by two platoons from the 13th Company: the mortar and machine gun unit.

The plan was for *Oberleutnant* Becker's group to attack first – moving along the coast as a distraction to the defenders of the town; simultaneously, *Oberleutnant* Egger's group with *Major* Schulz, *Hauptmann Graf* von der Schulenburg and *Oberleutnant* Kerfin would attack at the West Gate. Forming-up time for the units was set for very early in the morning (before dawn), since the paratroopers had to cover a distance of approximately 3.2km through an area occupied by the enemy. After the attack plan and its details were set, Schulz returned to his command post, where he paid a visit to the wounded at the field hospital and was briefed by Dr Alfred Eiben regarding the losses and the condition of the wounded.

The Venetian walls around the town of Heraklion were a strong defensive structure and a reminder of battles in medieval times. (Author's collection)

The same area as above, between Chanioporta and Gyali Kiosk, with graves of paratroopers from *II./FschJgRgt.1* next to the Venetian walls. The location of this photo can be determined – and these are the graves of *Gefr* Hans Schmickl (931), *Gefr* Gerhard Lemke (932), *Obgfr* Wilhelm Dietrich (933), *Jäger* Karl Frede (934), *Jäger* Heinz Friedrich (935) and *Gefr* Herbert Böttcher (936). (Courtesy of Mike Smythe)

*Gefr* Herbert Böttcher (right) with his platoon leader, *Ltn* Eberhard Boerger, in a picture taken in Greece just a few days before the battle. (Courtesy of Eberhard Boerger)

Gyali Kiosk, where the walls had been demolished, was the entry point into the town for the *11./FschJgRgt.1*. The paratroopers moved along the coastal road to enter the town. (Author's collection)

Chanioporta (West Gate) – the focus of the attack of *10./FschJgRgt.1* on the morning of 21 May. (Author's collection)

Only a small force from Schirmer's *II./FschJgRgt.2* joined the attack groups, while the rest of the battalion remained at the command post on Hill 67 in Gazi. They were to secure the area and provide cover from the west. More specifically, for the attack, the *II./FschJgRgt.2 Battalion* provided a platoon from the 7th Company (under *Oberleutnant* Schrader) and one more platoon from the HQ Company (under *Leutnant* Krückeberg). In addition to the *II./FschJgRgt.2* units, during the previous evening, the 1st Platoon (*I. Zug 14*) of the 14th Company (anti-tank guns) had also joined the *III./FschJgRgt.1* for the attack. The *II./FschJgRgt.2* men who joined the assault groups were attached to *11./FscJgRgt.1*, since this company had suffered the heaviest casualties during the first day – losing 44 dead – while the *10./FschJgRgt.1* had only 14 killed.

*Hauptmann Graf* von der Schulenburg belonged to the staff of *III./FschJgRgt.1* and provided exemplary support to *Major* Schulz. He was killed in action three years later (15 July 1944) in St. Lô (Normandy). (Courtesy of *DDF*)

During the street fighting that followed in the town, *Leutnant* Krückeberg was killed, but his body was never identified. A study of the casualty lists of the units that participated in the street fighting during 21 May reveals that some bodies were never found or identified after the battle. Wounded paratroopers who were captured in the town were transferred by the Greeks to the Pananion Hospital, where they were treated by Greek doctors. Some of the wounded died at the hospital and they were buried in two large common graves, along with bodies of Italian prisoners of war, Greek soldiers and civilians. When the Germans arrived at the hospital eight days later, it was not possible to identify all of the buried corpses. This was most probably the case with Krückeberg, since his date of death was 23 May. In addition, dead paratroopers whose bodies were left in the town were buried by the Greeks.

A not uncommon incident took place near the port – not far from the town centre – more than 50 years after the battle: during roadworks, an old man approached the workers and told them not to dig at a specific point because he had buried there a paratrooper whom he had killed during the battle. The workers paid no attention to the old man and kept digging, but uncovered the remains of the paratrooper soon after.

*Leutnant* Krückeberg is pictured here (sitting behind *Oberleutnant* Thiel) with the men of the *5./FschJgRgt.2*. The picture was taken in Plowdiv (Bulgaria) in 1941, just a few days before the battle. Thiel was the company commander of *5./FschJgRgt.2* and was also killed on Crete. (Courtesy of Jose Ramon Artaza Ivañez)

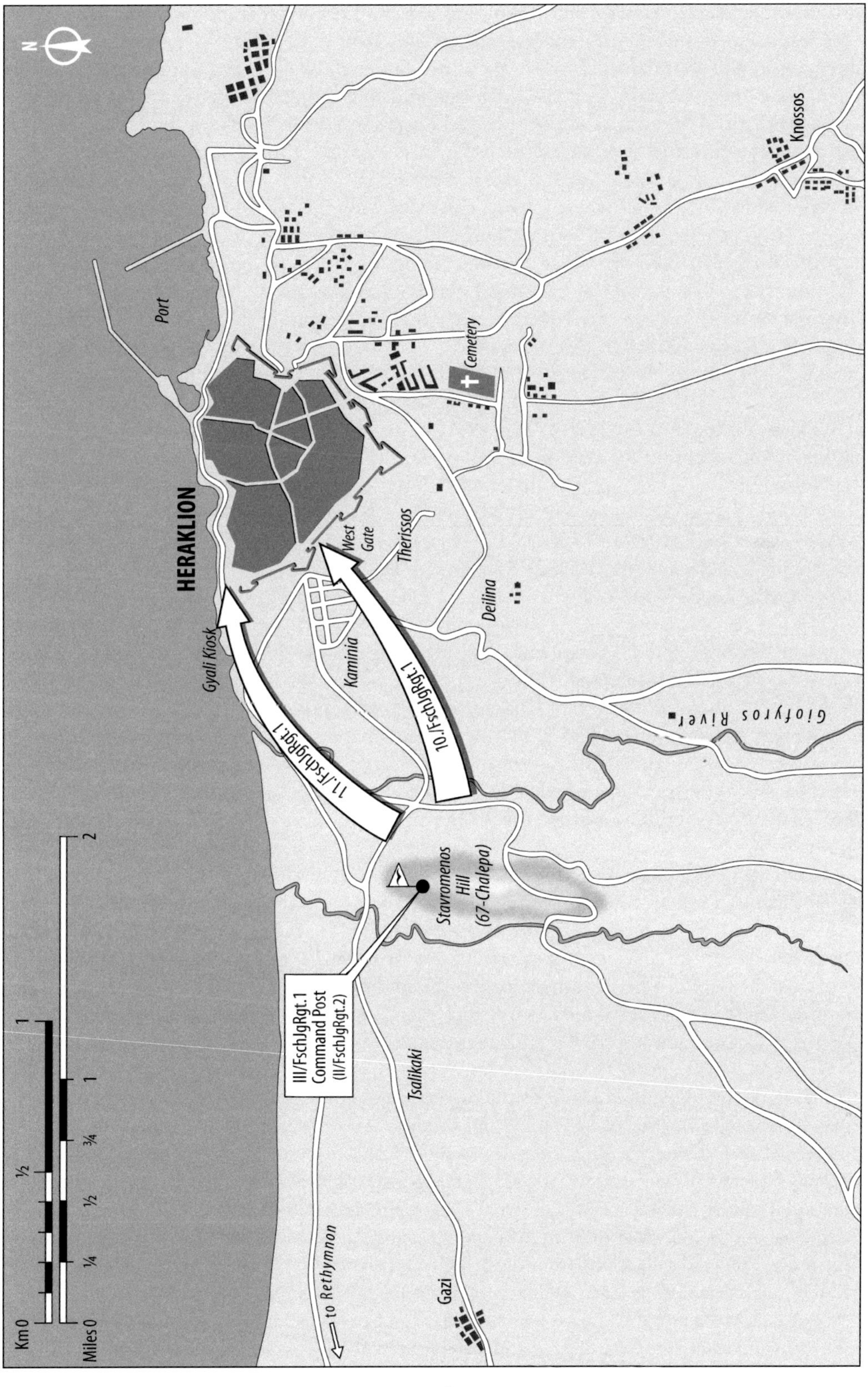


Map 5.1 The plan of attack from the west, on the morning of 21 May. (N. Panos, 2016)

During their advance to the town, the paratroopers faced resistance from the Greek forces (army units, *gendarmerie* and civilians) deployed west of the town, in the area of Giofyros, Deilina and Kaminia, where the Germans split into two groups. At dawn, two mixed groups of Greek soldiers and civilians – under Captain Alejakis and Lieutenant K. Kounalakis respectively – conducted a reconnaissance patrol in the area of Therissos and Kaminia as far as Giofyros; they collected information about the movements of the Germans and also captured some prisoners.

A group under *Gendarmerie* Sergeant Voutirakis advanced to Kaminia. Taking advantage of the cover provided by the tall wheat in the fields, they took a group of paratroopers by surprise, who were firing at Chanioporta with an anti-tank gun (the paratroopers from the 1st Platoon (*I. Zug 14*) of the *14./FschJgRgt.1* that was supporting the attack of the *III./FschJgRgt.1*). During the fighting that followed, Voutirakis himself managed to kill two of the paratroopers, while the remaining members of the gun crew surrendered – leaving the gun in the hands of the Greeks. An armed civilian was also killed in this incident.

There were six paratroopers from the *14./FschJgRgt.1* killed in action that day:

> *Objg* Hans Erning (29 May 1917-21 May 1941) – Grave 636 (he was killed by a Matilda tank at the command post of the *FschJgRgt.1*, east of the airfield)
> *Objg* Ewald Kissel (14 December 1910-21 May 1941) – Grave 866
> *Gefr* Alfons Krause (21 August 1919-21 May 1941) – Grave 486
> *Obgfr* Gustav Orth (10 April 1919-21 May 1941) – Grave 868
> *Gefr* Willi Schäuble (18 May 1920-21 May 1941) – Grave 862
> *Obgfr* Oskar Zappe (7 December 1919-21 May 1941) – Grave 864

Kissel, Orth, Schäuble and Zappe are buried in adjoining graves – indicating that they were killed very close to each other in the area west of the town. Schäuble and Zappe were killed between 0630 and 0700 – about 500m west of Chanioporta – and they were the crew of the anti-tank gun that Voutirakis attacked. Kissel had been killed earlier that morning (0600), just 5m behind the bridge to Agios Myron, while Orth was also killed west of the town at around 0645 – and he is among the losses of the gun crew which are mentioned by paratrooper Ernst H. Simon later in this chapter. *Gefr* Alfons Krause was killed east of the airfield in the area of Skalani, next to the road to Amnissos.

The fact that the Germans had been attacked by armed civilians from the first moment of the battle led them to arrest any civilians found possessing guns, or even anyone from the areas where they were attacked. Some of the civilians who were arrested – among them women and children – were gathered near the coast west of the town, not far from the West Gate and Gyali Kiosk; as a result of this, the Greek military authorities and the soldiers and fighters in the town believed that the Germans were using women and unarmed civilians as a shield in order to advance.

Lieutenant Colonel Antonios Beteinakis reported on the action:

> When the Germans realised that it would be very difficult to approach the gates of the town they did the following: by using women and children as cover during their attack they finally succeeded in reaching the gates since we stopped firing in order to avoid killing innocent people. After their success they gathered a strong force right outside the gates and with the support of Stukas they entered the town – approximately 400 of them. As soon as I was informed of this and while I was in my command post in Mastabas just 500 metres south of the town, I ordered a company from the 3rd Greek Infantry Regiment to enter the town via Kainourgia Porta [South Gate] and stop the advance of the Germans. This manoeuvre was indeed a success and the Germans were forced to find cover in various buildings where they were surrounded by the Greek forces under the command of Colonel Papathanasopoulos and

A photo of civilians arrested and held by the paratroopers near Chanioporta (West Gate). (Courtesy of Mike Smythe)

> the Commander of the Guard, Major Emmanuel Tsagkarakis. After bitter street fighting that lasted for a few hours, all the Germans were forced to retreat to their initial positions outside the town, while many of them were killed or captured.[1]

The *11./FschJgRgt.1*, under *Oberleutnant* Becker, managed to enter the town from the north-west by moving along the coast, according to the plan. After a short fight with the Greeks and the British Guard at Gyali Kiosk, the paratroopers established themselves in the Akratou raisin factory and in the Raisin Co-operatives Union of Crete factory, just a few metres away from their entry point – thus they were able to control and secure this gate, and provide a clear path to retreat and exit the town if needed. After leaving guards in those two buildings, the paratroopers advanced further east to the port. On their way, they occupied the Heraklion electricity power station – killing the director, the chief engineer and two clerks, who had resisted the Germans.

*Oberleutnant* Becker. (Author's archive)

Despite the efforts of the Greek troops (under Lieutenant Lelos), the armed civilians and the group led by Antonis Grigorakis (also known as 'Satanas', or 'the Satan'), they did not, in the end, manage to stop the paratroopers, who were supported in their attack by machine guns and mortars. When the news spread that the Germans had entered the town, many civilians rushed to help the town's defenders. A *gendarmerie* force under Sergeant Georgios Papadoulakis (including civilians) rushed to Gyali Kiosk – managing only to slow down the advance of the paratroopers. The Heraklion Military Command sent a combined force of *gendarmerie* and Greek troops – at that moment, the only reserve available. The task of this force[2] was to occupy

1 Lt Col A. Beteinakis, *After Action Report about the battle in Heraklion, 20-29 May 1941*, p.6.
2 The force had the strength of a company, as reported above by Lt Col Beteinakis.

The Bodosakion School in 1941. (Author's archive)

The Bodosakion School today, near the coast of Heraklion. In the background can be seen the electricity power station. (Author's collection)

the main streets from the coast to the town centre, and to prevent the paratroopers from moving into the town by keeping them on the coast.

The Germans were fighting in a very difficult and complex urban environment – a mission that actually required a far bigger force than they had available. Since they had to move along the road next to the coast, it was necessary to secure their right flank; this was actually the town – an area full of narrow, labyrinth-like streets where the paratroopers could be very easily trapped or surrounded after a counter-attack. In addition, they had to safeguard an exit route from the town in case the attack failed.

2nd Lieutenant E. Malagardis:

> After leaving some men at the places where the Germans had been surrounded, I informed the Guard HQ about the situation as it had evolved in the town to that time. With the rest of my men I moved through Michelidakis Square to the Bodosakion school, right opposite the power station where we positioned ourselves in order to prevent the Germans from moving into the town.[3]

3 C.E. Mamalakis' archive.

Evangelos I. Dedeletakis recalled:

> On the day after they dropped the Germans moved into the electricity power station. Kostis Mamounis was at the arch opposite the station, which was the Venetian gate leading to the small harbour.
>
> He was there,[4] just a 15-16 year old boy, holding a very old single-shot gun and when the Germans came out of the power station he opened fire on them, but without success. The Germans fired back and killed him! After that, the paratroopers moved further, towards Koules.[5] The group of Germans who tried to occupy Koules was literally annihilated so Koules remained in Greek hands.[6]

The *10./FschJgRgt.1* split from *Oberleutnant* Fischer's group near Kaminia and moved slightly south on the right flank (towards Therissos), while the remainder of the group advanced directly to the West Gate. As the paratroopers approached the West Gate, firing was heard coming from the direction of the coast – signifying that the attack by the other group had begun. Almost immediately, the defenders started shooting from the top of the gate and the paratroopers responded with mortar fire. A mortar shell exploded on the top of Chanioporta – opening a large hole in it. The Greeks were shooting from the windows of the old barracks on top of the gate and from the barricades that were placed in the middle of the road.

With a continuous barrage (and supported by mortars), the German machine gunners managed to suppress the enemy fire and keep the defenders covered – preventing them from returning fire. The paratroopers took advantage of this situation, and with quick leaps, reached the gate and the barricades on the road, where they found cover from the enemy fire. Using smoke grenades for cover, the paratroopers entered the gate, passed through the barricades and climbed on top of the walls via the internal slope. A group with machine guns occupied the top of the walls and the old barracks there establishing a post with excellent observation and fire lanes into the city.

Paratrooper Ernst H. Simon from the *13./FschJgRgt.1* described this event:

> West of the town, the night of 20 to 21 May passed quietly and we are all afraid that we have missed all the fun which of course later proved a very unjustified worry! At dawn we finally move to the front [towards the town]. The *III./FschJgRgt.1* is divided into groups in the suburbs on the western outskirts of the town. The fighting is fierce but we only have rifles, sub-machine-guns and 5 and 8 cm mortars. Our third mortar (*Objg* Stöwe) is already in the suburbs and battles the enemy at very short range – a very difficult task. We place our guns on a hillside position south of the road to Rethymnon with our observation post on the edge of the slope, just a few hundred metres away from the town. From here we cover the suburbs with fire, first with high explosive and then with smoke shells, in order to support the attacking companies.
>
> [...] Since observation is almost impossible, we take a mortar with us and follow the companies on their attack into the town. On the main road next to the walls there is still heavy gunfire. Having spent most of our ammunition, we only have 24 shells per mortar and we are ordered to attack as an infantry unit. We leave the mortar behind and move towards the town walls. On the road lie many dead paratroopers. We are heading to the town-gate which is the only one on this side of the 10 metre high walls. The gate is blocked by a barricade

4 It is the old Venetian Dermatas Gate, right next to the coast.
5 The big Venetian fortress at the port.
6 Interview with C.E. Mamalakis.

The Dermatas Gate, where Kostis Mamounis was killed, according to Evangelos I. Dedeletakis' account. In the background can be seen the old Heraklion electricity power station, also known as 'Electriki'. The Greeks occupied this whole area – so forcing the Germans into a continuous fight during their advance. (Author's collection)

A view of the old power station, where the Natural History Museum is today. (Author's collection)

The same building in a photo from the era of the battle. (Author's archive)

*Oberleutnant* Egger. (Author's archive)

The old barracks on the top of Chanioporta, where the Greeks were positioned to defend the town. (G. Müller & F. Scheuering, *Sprung über Kreta*)

The barricades placed in the middle of Chanioporta during the battle. (Courtesy of Dimitris Skartsilakis)

The internal slope of the walls. (Author's collection)

*Oberleutnant* Adolf Wehner (standing in the middle) – the CO of *13./FschJgRgt.1* – pictured here in 1940 after the operation in Holland, among men from *11./FschJgRgt.1.* Also seen here (standing left to right): Harmuth, Nows, Himmel, W. Zimmerman, Brüns, Kiebach; and (seated left to right) Unknown, Homberg and Röder. (Courtesy of Jose Ramon Artaza Ivañez)

> made of big rocks. A 3.7 Pak[7] arrives and fires on the barricade, forcing the Greek soldiers and the Cretan civilians to retreat. Some of the civilians are armed with English military rifles while many others have hunting rifles. We finally manage to overpower the barricade and pass through the gate into the town. In other places, paratroopers climb the walls like monkeys. The companies are split and mixed groups are formed, fighting from house to house into the town. The groups consist of men from the 10th, 11th, 13th and 14th Companies.
>
> My platoon leader, *Leutnant* Görse, has fallen in front of the town walls while as I learn much later, our company commander, *Oberleutnant* Wehner, was killed during the jump with a shot in his heart that went right through his Iron Cross 1st Class medal.[8]

*Major* Schulz left a group as a guard at the gate – thus securing his rear and keeping a safe exit from the town if needed. This group was established at the nearby Konstantinidis Brothers raisin factory, while the rest advanced towards the town centre, along the main street of Heraklion (called Platia Strata[9] at that time). Schulz himself, with a group of approximately 80 men, moved via Valestra Street towards the coast in order to join with – and reinforce – the *11./FschJgRgt.1.* This occurred after a short march, near the power station, without meeting any strong resistance on the way.

7 An anti-tank gun from *14./FschJgRgt.1.*
8 E.H. Simon, BDF e.v. Archiv, Freiburg/Breisgau.
9 Today called Kalokairinou Street.

Valestra Street leads from Chanioporta to the coast, near the power station. (Author's collection)

G. Kanavakis was killed by paratroopers right in front of his house, at the corner of Valestra and Bosporou Street. (Courtesy of C.E. Mamalakis)

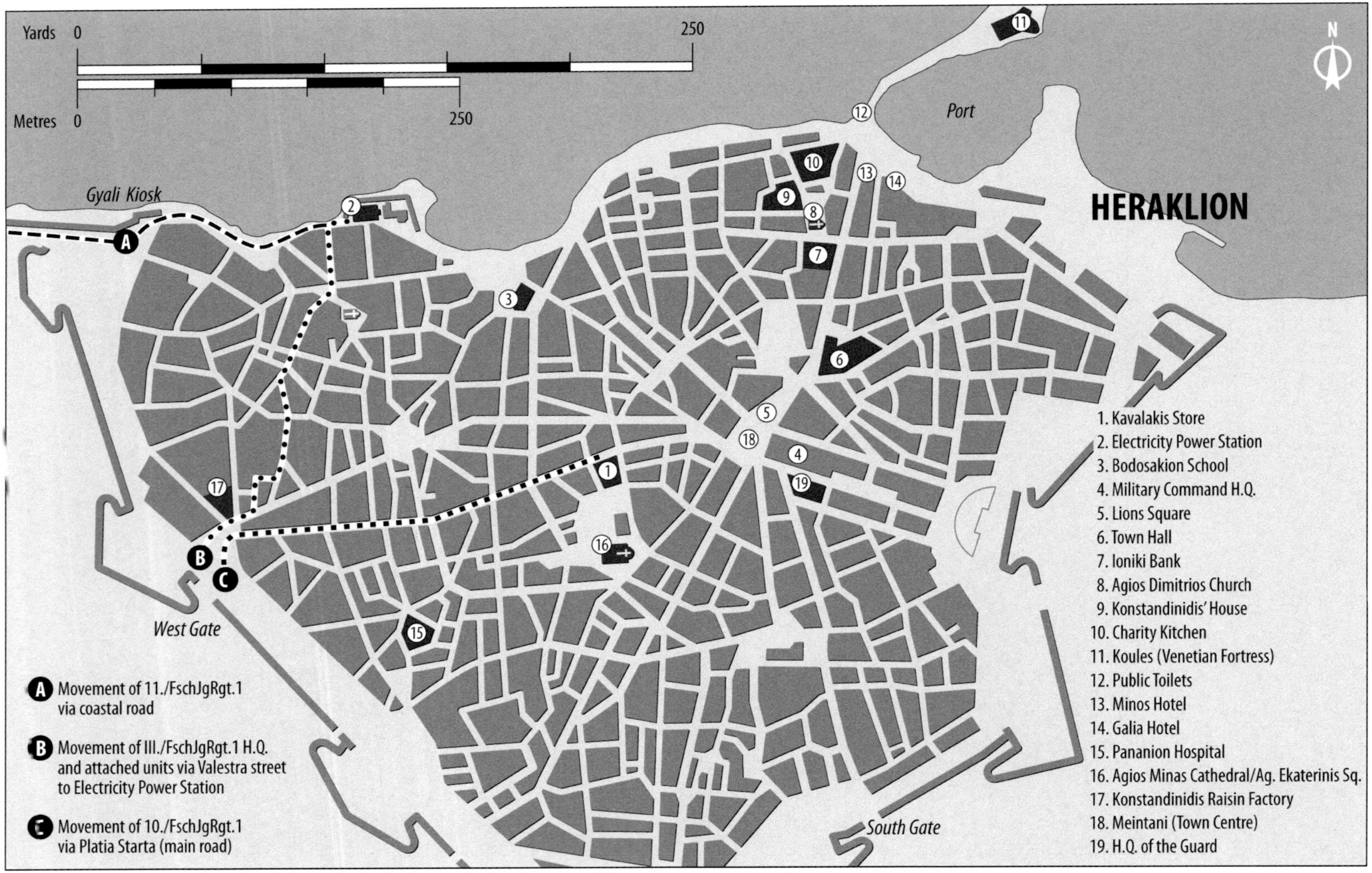


Map 5.2 The routes followed by the paratroopers into the town. (N. Panos, 2016)

Despite the exhaustion resulting from almost 24 hours of fighting, the paratroopers had to make a last major breakthrough in order to occupy the town and the port. They had to act immediately, since there were no reserves or supplies available for long-term fighting. Schulz's plan was as follows: a group under *Hauptmann Graf* von der Schulenburg was to occupy the port and the large Venetian fortress of Koules; another group, under *Oberleutnant* Becker, was to occupy the Town Hall, which was opposite the Agios Titos Church; a third group, under *Oberleutnant* Kerfin, was tasked with securing the South Gate (Kainourgia Porta); and a fourth group, under *Oberleutnant* Lassauer, was assigned to occupy the East Gate at the Eleftherias (Freedom) Square. Schulz ordered *Oberleutnant* Kappel to send a radio message asking for supplies. Even before the message was sent, shooting was heard coming from the direction of the Town Hall. After a while, *Oberleutnant* Becker arrived – reporting that his group had met strong resistance and had halted. At the same time, firing was also heard coming from the direction of the port – meaning that *Hauptmann Graf* von der Schulenburg's men were also involved in combat.

After their entry through the West Gate, the group under *Oberleutnant* Egger advanced along the main street of Heraklion – managing to reach the area of the Agios Minas Cathedral in the town centre, near Meintani Square. On their way, the paratroopers engaged in a short fight and occupied a two-storey building, in which a group of British soldiers had established a machine gun post. In the centre of town, in today's Dikaiosynis Street,[10] was the HQ of the Heraklion Guard. Around the HQ, strong *gendarmerie* forces were deployed, along with men from the 7th Greek Infantry Regiment and armed civilians. With a Bren light machine gun placed on the roof of a tall building opposite the HQ – and operated by Sergeant Stromathias – the men of the *gendarmerie* controlled the main street of Heraklion (Platia Strata). Right in front of the HQ, barricades were built and manned by armed civilians. In the window of the ground floor, a captured MG-34 was placed, while on the first floor of the HQ were a handful of officers and men from the staff.

The window of the HQ's ground floor, where the MG-34 had been placed to cover the whole main street of the town. (Author's collection)

10 '*Vasileos Geogiou A*' ('King George I') in 1941.

### Special Presentation 15: Georgios Kouromichelakis

Georgios Kouromichelakis (1910-1942).
(C.E. Mamalakis' archive)

Georgios Kouromichelakis, a *gendarmerie* corporal, played a key role in the fight for the town of Heraklion. He was at the van of the attack against the paratroopers who had infiltrated the city during the second day of the battle. According to official accounts, Kouromichelakis never returned to his duties in the *gendarmerie* after the battle. He was hiding from the Germans, who were aware of his actions during the battle, and were seeking to arrest him.

At the beginning of June 1942, he decided to take the bus to his village, Nippos Apokoronou, in Chania. The bus stopped at a checkpoint, where Kouromichelakis was arrested and later imprisoned. He was executed on 14 June 1942 in Gazi, west of Heraklion, along with 49 other members of the Cretan Resistance.

Yannis Kouromihelakis, the uncle of Georgios Kouromichelakis, had been killed in August 1921 during the war against the Turks in the Greek Asia Minor campaign. Lieutenant Kouromichelakis and his men were surrounded by the Turks on 8 August 1921 and as he was running out of ammunition and had no opportunity to escape, he preferred to commit suicide rather than surrender to the enemy – thus honouring the heroic history of his family.

*Gendarmerie* Sergeant Voutirakis and Corporal Kouromichelakis – leading a *gendarmerie* unit and many armed civilians – ambushed the Germans near Kavalakis store by moving parallel to the main street. When the paratroopers approached that area, they were caught totally by surprise and they retreated under heavy fire – leaving a dead paratrooper[11] lying on the road. The Germans found cover in the Kounalakis, Kapnistou and Georgantas stores on the main street, while others found refuge behind a barricade of sandbags placed outside the Kavalakis store. Major Michael Tzoulakis led an attack against these men. A veteran of the First World War, Tzoulakis was a very experienced fighter who had also served in the Greek Army campaign in Asia Minor during the war with the Turks,[12] where he had proved his bravery and fighting spirit. Despite warnings from his comrades to take cover, Tzoulakis attacked holding only his revolver; he was shot and fell down dead at the corner of today's Kalokairinou and Psaromiligon Streets.

11 According to some other accounts, there were two paratroopers killed in that incident.

12 This was the case with many senior officers of the Greek Army and many civilians in their forties who had participated in the campaign, and in the war against the Turks. They were very experienced fighters and did not hesitate to join the battle. This explains why the paratroopers found such strong resistance: they were fighting against civilians who were actually experienced fighters with military training.

The spot where Major Tzoulakis was killed. The Kavalakis store and the other buildings where the paratroopers found cover can be seen in the background. (Author's collection)

The place where Tzoulakis was killed, in a period picture taken from the roof of the Guard HQ in 1942. This was the most forward point that the paratroopers managed to reach via the main street before they retreated. The picture shows the fire lanes provided to the machine guns that were placed on the roofs of the nearby buildings – making this part of the main street a deadly area for the paratroopers. (Author's archive)

## Special Presentation 16: Michael Tzoulakis

Michael Tzoulakis was born on 1 July 1896 in Agios Myron, near Heraklion. In October 1916, he joined the army – and after graduating from the academy for junior officers, he managed to rise in the ranks.

He fought at the Macedonian Front during the First World War and in the campaign in Asia Minor. He was wounded in battle several times and was awarded the Golden Merit of Bravery (1925), two War Crosses (1918) and the Medal of the First World War Allies.

Tzoulakis was buried outside the Agios Titos Church in the centre of the town, along with Lieutenant Marinelis, who was killed on the same day. After the war, his family transferred his remains to the village of Agios Myron. Still later, he was buried at the Battle of Crete Memorial, along with others who had been killed during the battle.

Major Michael Tzoulakis. (Author's archive)

Tzoulakis (second from the left) seen here wounded during the campaign in Asia Minor. (Author's archive)

The Agios Titos Church today. (Author's collection)

E. Malagardis recorded:

> The fever of the battle was at its peak when suddenly through the noise of the shooting I heard cries, 'On them!' and the war cry, 'Aera!'[13] I went downstairs immediately and rushed to the area of the fighting where I saw Major Tzoulakis lying on the ground covered with blood. A huge paratrooper[14] was lying dead as well on the opposite pavement, while the rest of the Germans had retreated [...]
>
> [...] The dead body of Major Tzoulakis had been placed on a stretcher and covered with a blanket so that only his boots could be seen, right in front of the small door at the side of Agios Titos Church. I went close, uncovered him and saw for the last time the face of a really brave, honest and good friend of mine.
>
> [...] A few days later when the battle was over, I passed by the church of Agios Titos. There was not much damage to the church from the bombing, except that the steeple had been demolished. In a narrow space between the wall of the church and the road there was a grave with a cross and a candle with flowers. I went close and read 'Major Michael Tzoulakis 21.5.1941'. Then I continued on my way.[15]

After Tzoulakis' death, the Greek forces – with *gendarmerie* units and civilians – managed to force the paratroopers to retreat from the town centre and move towards the West Gate. During their retreat, the paratroopers were under constant fire from the Greeks, who occupied the buildings along the main street. Although most of the Germans exited the city, some of them found cover in a bedding factory in Agias Ekaterinis Square, opposite the cathedral; others occupied the Konstantinidis Brothers raisin factory next to the West Gate in order to keep the Chanioporta under German control. The paratroopers in those buildings refused to surrender and kept fighting, despite the fact that they were surrounded. Using cans of petrol, the Greeks set the buildings on fire and left the paratroopers no option but to surrender or face certain death – thus both of those German strongholds were destroyed.

E. Malagardis continues his narration:

> I moved via Kalokairinou Street with the soldiers and the armed civilians towards Chanioporta, following the retreating Germans on their way out the town. A group of paratroopers had entered the Linardakis bedding factory and the nearby Neratzoulis shoe-shop where they found and killed the owner.
>
> From the window of the 1st floor they were able to control both the small road that was parallel to the main street and the other road that leads to Agias Ekaterinis Square. When I made an attempt to cross the road in order to surround them, I found myself in a hail of fire, and I was forced to turn back [...]
>
> [...] In the meantime, the CO of the Guard, Major Tsagkarakis had gathered a small group of soldiers, some of them carrying tins of petrol. I followed them and we arrived at the bedding factory where with the help of an interpreter we asked the Germans to surrender.
>
> Their response was a hail of bullets which killed and injured some of our men. We immediately threw the petrol tins into and around the building and set it on fire. As a result the Germans were forced to exit the building with their hands up; one of them was seriously wounded. After this incident the road was clear and we moved to Chanioporta.

13 'Aera' was the war cry of the Greeks during the Second World War.
14 Quite possibly Objg Heinrich Schröder from *10./FschJgRgt.1.*
15 C.E. Mamalakis' archive.

The Konstantinidis Brothers raisin factory (the first building on the left), as seen from Chanioporta. This was the building in which the paratroopers were surrounded during their retreat and exit from the city. The men Schulz had left to guard the gate were positioned in the same building. The factory has been demolished since the war. (Author's collection) Note: Among the guards of the raisin factory were also *Feldw* Lothar Nickolaus and *Gefr* Hugo Ristau – both from *11./FschJgRgt.1* – and reported KIA on 21 May at approximately 1500 at the West Gate.

The road that leads to Agias Ekaterinis Square. In the background, the Agios Minas Cathedral can be seen in a picture taken on 29 May 1941. The paratroopers were surrounded in these buildings and bitter street fighting took place in this area during the second day of the battle. (G. Müller & F. Scheuering, *Sprung über Kreta*)

The mole in a period picture taken from Koules: 1 – The furthest point on the mole that the paratroopers managed to reach; 2 – The public toilets where the surviving paratroopers sheltered during their retreat from the mole; 3 – Hotel Gallia. (Author's collection)

> Instead of exiting the town[16] some of the retreating Germans entered the Konstantinidis Brothers raisin factory which controlled the gate (West Gate). We again set fire to the building and forced the Germans to exit, but some of them were probably trapped inside and burned with the building. So the centre of the town had been cleared of the paratroopers who had entered the town that morning.[17]

The *11./FschJgRgt.1*, under *Oberleutnant* Becker, had established itself in the power station and soon the battalion staff, with Schulz, Schulenburg and Kerfin – and a little later the *10./FschJgRgt.1*, under *Oberleutnant* Egger – joined them. After their failure to occupy the centre of the town, the Germans formed a large unified group centred on the coast and the port; this group attempted to move eastwards in order to reach the port and gradually to advance south to the town centre. A group under *Hauptmann Graf* von der Schulenburg advanced via the mole towards the old Venetian fortress of Koules, but was forced to retreat under heavy crossfire both from Koules and the buildings next to the port. The officer in charge in Koules, Captain Georgios Logiades, was asking desperately via telephone for reinforcements from the HQ of the Guard. He had had only a handful of men in the fortress and they were insufficient to hold off the paratroopers for long. Colonel Papathanasopoulos of the Heraklion Military Command had already ordered the reserve company of the 3rd Greek Infantry Regiment to enter the town and reinforce the Greek units that were fighting the paratroopers. The Greeks – moving through the narrow streets that they knew very well – entered the Gallia (France) Hotel from the staff door on Fragkoklisias Street and started shooting at the paratroopers, who were exposed during their advance on the mole directly opposite to the hotel. The paratroopers on the mole were fully exposed to crossfire, with nowhere to take cover apart from behind the bodies of their dead comrades. The Germans retreated from the mole and tried to find cover in the nearby buildings. Some of them entered the public toilets at the start of the mole, where they were surrounded and trapped.

16 It is quite possible that these paratroopers were the men who were left by Schulz to guard the Chanioporta when the Germans entered the town.

17 C.E. Mamalakis' archive.

After the Germans' retreat, the defenders of Koules exited the fortress and joined the Greek forces that were fighting in that area. A group under Lieutenant Marinelis attacked first and Marinelis was shot and killed by the paratroopers, who were in the public toilets. The Greek soldiers threw hand grenades through the narrow windows at the top of the building and rushed in – killing all the Germans inside. Outside the public toilets were mortars – indicating that the paratroopers inside were men from the *13./FschJgRgt.1.*

The route that the paratroopers followed on the mole. Koules is seen in the background. (Author's collection)

The public toilets building, preserved today almost exactly as it was during the battle, with the only difference being that the road was elevated after the war. The Greeks threw hand grenades through the narrow windows shown in the picture. (Author's collection)

According to other accounts,[18] Lieutenant Marinelis approached the toilets and asked the paratroopers to surrender. Their response was a shot that killed Marinelis. The furious Greeks, who had witnessed the scene, then rushed into the building using grenades and executed all the paratroopers who were still alive.

The paratroopers in the area around the port were involved in bitter street fighting. The Greeks had the advantage in this battle, since they knew the area's complex urban environment very well. Using hand grenades, they were pressing the paratroopers – and the distance between the enemies was often just a few metres. The Germans began to face the problem of a shortage of ammunition and supplies without having succeeded in any of the key goals of their attack. Many dead and injured paratroopers were lying on the road along the coast, while others were surrounded in buildings near the port with only one way out: to the west, but without the ammunition and supplies required to continue the fight.

The dead bodies of paratroopers in a picture taken in Heraklion. These men were probably killed as a result of the incident in the public toilets, as there is no record of similar occurrences in Heraklion. The interior of the building also matches the inside of the public toilets in this picture, which was taken from outside the window. (Courtesy of Dimitris Skartsilakis)

The public toilets window, which today is sealed with glass. (Author's collection)

18 M.I. Pytikakis, *Storm Over Crete*, p.103.

Lt Ioannis Marinelis on the day of his wedding, with his wife, Evangelia. Marinellis was born on 11 February 1896 on the island of Lesvos and volunteered for the Greek Army on 14 January 1913. He participated in the Balkan Wars (1912-1913) and he served at the front during the First World War. He then took part in the Greek campaign to Asia Minor during 1919-1922. In 1940, he fought against the Italians on the Albanian Front, where he was injured and transferred to Crete for recovery. He had been injured many times during his long military career and received various Greek and Allied commemorative and campaign medals – the most exceptional being the War Cross and the Medal for Gallantry in Silver. (Courtesy of John Marinelis

None of the groups that Schulz sent to occupy the Town Hall and the gates managed to advance into the town. The first group was attacked by the Greeks and snipers on the roofs of nearby buildings. They were forced to stop before finally finding cover in the small church of Agios Dimitrios. Some of the paratroopers sheltered in Konstantinidis' house (opposite the church of Agios Dimitrios and only a few metres away from the charity kitchen building, parallel to 25th of August Street), while the main German force remained in the charity kitchen[19] building. Since the church was a very small building surrounded by much taller buildings, it was not a suitable place for defence, so the paratroopers left the church and entered Konstantinidis' house and the charity kitchen building. The Greeks on the roof of the Ioniki (Ionian) Bank building had the advantage of height and kept firing on the Germans – allowing them no opportunity to move on the road. At the same time, armed civilians and soldiers had blocked the surrounding streets that led to the town centre.

A group of soldiers with a captured German machine gun moved from the Hotel Gallia to the roof of the neighbouring Hotel Minos. This was the highest building in the area and provided an excellent field of fire and observation points. Another group, under Sergeant Chatzakis, remained at the Hotel Gallia to prevent any attempt by the Germans to repeat their attack on the port and Koules.

19 The exact name of the building in Greek is 'Laika Sysitia', which is translated as 'Public Meals', or better as 'Charity Kitchen'. It is most probable that Schulz and his staff were among the paratroopers in this building.

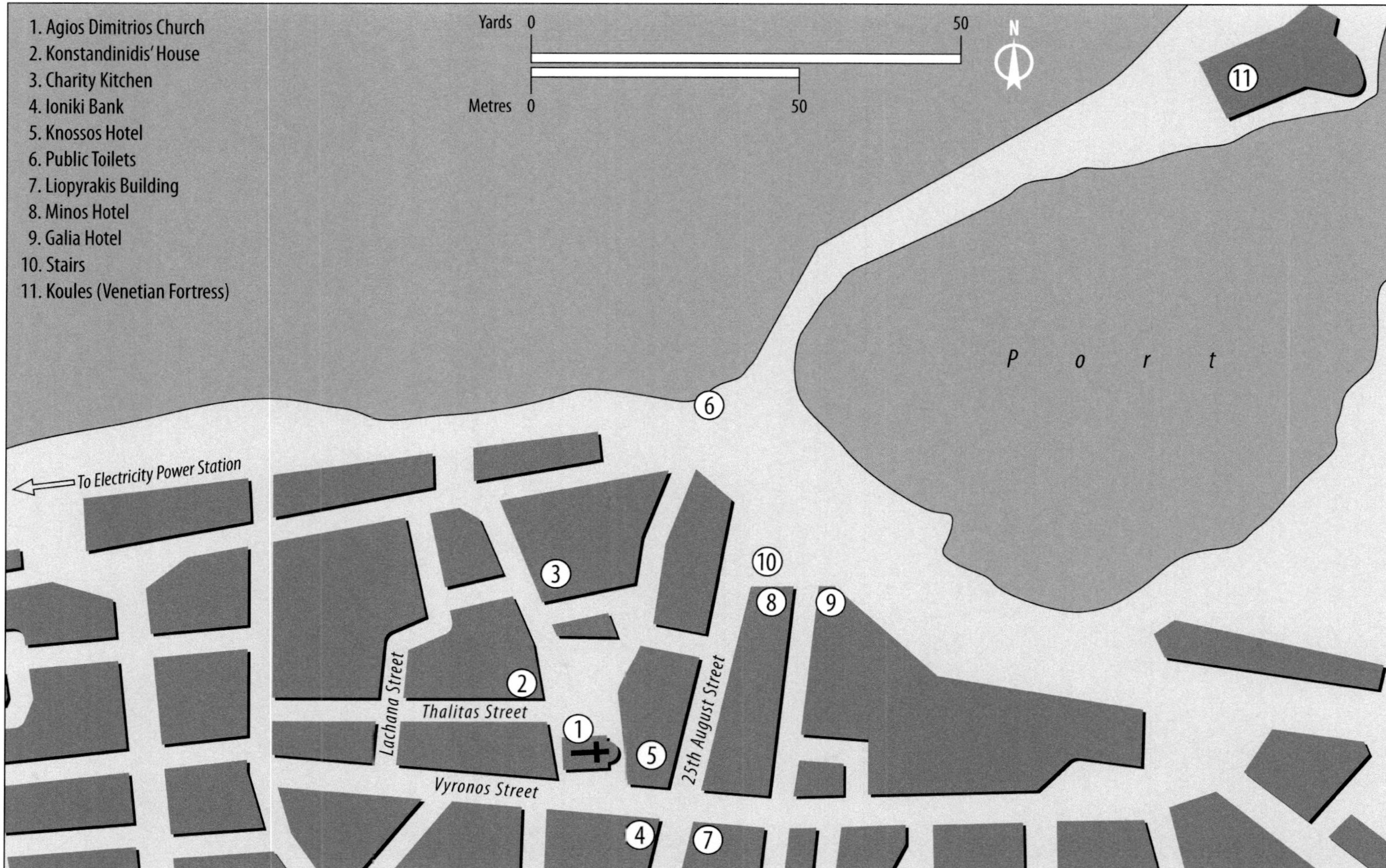


Map 5.3 The area near the port where the street fighting took place on 21 May. (N. Panos, 2016)

The church of Agios Dimitrios and next to it (on the left), Konstantinidis' house in a picture taken in the 1940s. In 1952, the church was restored and modified to its present shape. (Author's collection)

1 – The church of Agios Dimitrios today; 2 – The modern tall building on the left is exactly at the spot where Konstantinidis' house was in 1941; 3 – Opposite the modern building and behind the church is the charity kitchen. (Author's collection)

The Minos and Gallia Hotels were landmarks at the port of Heraklion. They stood at the start of 25th of August Street. (Author's collection)

The Hotel Minos building – ruined and abandoned. The neighboring Hotel Gallia has been demolished since the war. (Author's collection)

In the Ioniki Bank building was a group of armed civilians, under Antonis Grigorakis ('Satanas'[20]), from the village of Krousonas. Grigorakis was a retired *gendarmerie* officer and a leading member of the group that John Pendlebury had formed. Just like the other villages in the foothill of Psilorites Mountain, Krousonas had a great martial tradition and a strong fighting spirit.

Pendlebury's residence was a few metres away from the bank, in the Knossos Hotel. The Germans in Konstantinidis' house and the charity kitchen were enduring a hail of gunfire and hand grenades. *Oberleutnant* Egger and his men tried to join the paratroopers who were trapped in Konstantinidis' house and help them to escape, but he was forced to retreat because of heavy

20 The nickname 'Satanas' actually means 'Satan' and has the connotation of a very energetic, clever and powerful man.

fire from the Greeks. Schulz, along with his staff and the men in the charity kitchen, were under constant pressure from the Greeks. Because of the shortage of ammunition and supplies, they were forced to leave the building and started moving westwards – retreating along the coast. The men in Konstantinidis' house remained trapped. The Town Guard commander, Major Tsagkarakis – via a German prisoner, along with the German-speaking officer Grigoris Chatzidakis – demanded that the paratroopers inside the house surrender, since they were the only German force remaining in the city. The Germans initially refused to surrender, but after the Greeks threatened to burn the house, they finally agreed on the condition that they would surrender only to British troops, not to Greeks. The presence of armed civilians among the Greek fighters made the Germans suspicious and they asked for the presence of the British in order to avoid any act of retaliation by the Greeks. A force of less than a platoon from the 2nd Battalion of the York & Lancaster Regiment arrived at the port from the east and took responsibility for the German prisoners. This was the only British contribution to the defence of the town that day, since Greek forces were responsible for the town and the west sector.

Antonis Grigorakis – 'Satanas'. (Author's archive)

2nd Lieutenant E. Malagardis described the fighting in this area:

> Along with my men (around 15), I went out into Vyronos Street. I turned right on Lachanas Street where at the corner of Thalita Street I met some armed civilians waiting there without knowing exactly what to do. I told them to stay there and wait for me and I continued on my way until the end of Lachanas Street, where I found myself right in front of the big iron-gate at the main entrance of the charity kitchen. Using rocks we managed to build a makeshift machine-gun post from where Sergeant Stromathias started firing at the walls of the charity kitchen. This is how we managed to surround the Germans.
>
> I then returned to Thalita Street and along with four soldiers I got into the backyard of Konstantinidis's house which was built right in the middle of a garden. We moved with our backs against the walls and tried to figure out the positions and the strength of the enemy.
>
> As soon as I reached the north side of the house, we were fired on by the Germans who were in the building opposite the charity kitchen. We returned and took cover immediately with one of my soldiers injured in the leg. I rushed to Stromathias's post and told him to fire continuously with the others at the charity kitchen.
>
> I took with me two soldiers and some hand-grenades and returned very cautiously to Konstantinidis's house. Under the balcony of the 1st floor in the backyard there was an upside-down wooden chicken coop which was just one metre shorter than the height of the balcony. The door to the balcony was left open and I immediately understood that this would have been the way the paratroopers gained entry to the house. I told my soldiers that we were going to enter the house the same way and throw hand-grenades into the rooms.
>
> We helped one soldier to climb onto the balcony and while I was trying to climb up the Germans noticed our presence there and shot at us with sub-machine-guns from the windows of the 2nd floor. I felt like my left arm was hit with a brick and I dropped down with my face

> on the ground and right against the wall in order to take cover. The soldier next to me was hit by a burst of bullets while I was hit by only one bullet. The other soldier on the balcony was stranded on the wall and I told him to throw the grenade into the house and wait there. The grenade explosion shook the whole building and at that moment I took the opportunity to escape with three big jumps and under a hail of fire and fell right next to the fence. I crawled into a nearby warehouse where I cried out to the men there and explained the situation at the house, telling them to keep shooting at the windows and the doors to stop the Germans from coming out. That way we would be able to help the soldier on the balcony escape and recover the wounded soldier left right in front of the house. This was exactly what finally happened.[21]

Sifis Migadis, one of the armed civilians who participated in the street fighting, described his role:

> The bombing of the Venetian walls started very early in the morning. When it stopped we realised that the Germans had entered the town via Chanioporta and the power station on the coast.
>
> We outflanked them while they were moving along the Platia Strata [the main road] in the area of the Kounalakis, Kapnistos and Georgantas stores. It was there that the heroic Major Tzoulakis and a German were killed. Immediately after the German had been killed, the rest of the paratroopers retreated towards the Kavalakis store.
>
> After a while the Germans reached the port. I went there and I dared to climb the stairs where I could fire on the Germans who were in the charity kitchen. My single-shot rifle with its big bullets was very effective at a distance of 35-40 metres but I had to wait for the barrel to cool after five or six shots.

2nd Lieutenant E. Malagardis. (C.E. Mamalakis' archive)

Sifis Migadis continues:

> The Germans entered the charity kitchen and were throwing hand-grenades from there. I was injured by shrapnel, fortunately nothing too serious, so I decided to climb onto the roof of the Liopyrakis building which was one of the tallest buildings in the area. There I could take care of my wounds and have some rest.
>
> As soon as I got onto the roof, I saw that someone was trying to open the door of the laundry-room on the roof of Konstantinidis's residence right opposite the building I was in. I rested my rifle on the railing of the roof and aimed at the door of the laundry-room. After two or three seconds a German tried to exit the door but I got him and he turned back immediately, holding his belly.
>
> After a while the shooting died down. Neither the Germans nor we tried to do anything until some Greek officers arrived along with a German prisoner and managed to convince the Germans to surrender.
>
> During the battle that lasted for three or four hours, I didn't see many soldiers apart from a group of 11 Englishmen[22] who arrived marching as if on parade and the Greek 2nd Lieutenant G. Iniotakis who threw hand-grenades into the backyard of Ag. Dimitrios Church.

21 C.E. Mamalakis' archive.

22 These were the men from 2nd Bn, York & Lancasters, who went there at the request of the German

The stairs at the beginning of the 25th of August Street, next to the port, in a war era photograph. Hotel Minos can be seen on the left. (Author's archive)

A contemporary picture of the stairs, immediately in front of the Hotels Gallia and Minos (the demolished building at the top-left of the stairs) and opposite the public toilets and the mole that leads to Koules. (Author's collection)

During the Germans' surrender I went down to the front of the Ioniki Bank building, looking towards the charity kitchen. When I counted the prisoners and understood that they were quite numerous (I counted 42), I realised how lucky we were.

Among the seven dead Germans in the house, I found the one who was shot in the belly. We had had two dead comrades: a 2nd lieutenant and the son of 'Captain' Vardas. The 2nd lieutenant, a handsome young man, was lying on the pavement right in front of Konstantinidis's house wearing an expression of pain on his face. His left hand was raised with his fist clenched. It seemed that he had had an agonising death. Quite the opposite was the son of 'Captain' Vardas, a sixteen year old boy – I knew him well – who was lying on his back in a trench in the Ag. Dimitrios Church yard without any expression on his face. When I went close I saw a big blood stain on the back of his head and then I realized that the bullet had gone through his right eye without leaving a large entry wound.

The Germans had placed their dead comrades side by side in a room and had lit candles on the floor.[23]

Paratrooper Ernst H. Simon from the *13./FschJgRgt.1* recorded his experience:

The Greeks and the Tommies[24] shoot from every window and corner. We have to jump without cover from corner to corner. My sub-machine-gun is jammed because of dirt and sand in the magazines. We have long ago thrown away all of our equipment except for weapons and the ammunition. I even put some grenades into my bread bag. All of us shout with joy when we finally make it to the sea and find the mole and the port just 300 metres in front of us. We believe that we are almost there. Our thirst is unbearable and there is no water but our medic, Willi Stöveken, has managed to find a few bottles of lemonade and some fruit which are priceless at this moment.

We attack along the coastal road toward the port. Fierce rifle and machine-gun fire prevails along with the explosions of grenades. We move further forward but with heavy losses. *Major* Schulz, our battalion commander, is also with us, holding his P08 pistol in his right hand and his grey suede gloves in his left. The machine-gunners fire on the move, placing the machine-gun on the shoulder of their helper, but it is difficult to reach the top windows of the tall buildings. A 3.7 Pak of the *14./1 Company* is at the front of our advance and supports us with direct shots on the enemy from close range. Its crew consists only of an *Oberfeldwebel* who loads and shoots and a Greek soldier who is forced, very much against his will, to help in moving the cannon. The rest of the Pak crew have already fallen to enemy fire that passed under the gun's shield. We take cover in the rear corner[25] of a house. I stay there along with *Oberfeldwebel* Brückmann, *Feldwebel* Weide, Priester, and Fieser. Brückmann is a huge man and he jumps first, falling after two metres, shot right in the heart. Then Weide follows and manages to reach the ditch. I jump next and get shot in the shoulder. I move close to *Feldwebel* Weide who is lying in the ditch in front of me and then I return to the corner with Fieser. I'm lucky that the enemy missed my head by just 10 cm and also only flesh is hit. Ischinski also arrives and I sit with him in the next building which is a guest house.[26] We have breakfast there. We sit in the corner which is a blind spot and provides cover, although quite often bullets fly in through the window. In the same house is a woman who has been shot

prisoners.

23 Hatjipateras & Fafalios, pp.245-246.

24 The slang word used by the Germans to describe British soldiers.

25 Quite possibly the corner of Monis Agarathou and Zotou Streets.

26 The charity kitchen building.

The Liopyrakis building on 25th of August Street. (Author's collection)

From the roofs of these buildings, the Greeks were shooting at the Germans in the buildings opposite and in Konstantinidis' house. Being in much higher positions than the Germans, the Greeks had the advantage and did not allow the paratroopers to advance any further into the town. Scars and bullet holes from the battle are still present on the old buildings. (Author's collection)

> three times and behind the corner there are many wounded comrades. At his request I give one of them who has no weapons with him, my private pistol, a small 6.35 FN.
>
> Meanwhile it is evening and the order comes, 'All out of the town!' After eight hours of urban warfare we are running out of ammunition and we do not have enough men to occupy the town. The enemy has closed up behind us again and our attack-groups are trying to break through. We move back to the sea-shore almost into the water and we retreat through the town walls and outside the town.
>
> The battalion's losses during this attack were very high and we hear that only 100 men managed to return. We walk into the vineyards outside the town, totally exhausted. The remaining ammunition is shared equally. Fifteen cartridges are left for each rifle and half a box (150 rounds) for each machine-gun. An MG-34 machine-gun can therefore shoot for about nine seconds. The food supplies were left in the town and we are hungry.[27]

Inside Konstantinidis' house, the Greeks found two radios, four machine guns and many other weapons and ammunition. After the paratroopers' surrender, there were no other German strongholds left in the town. According to the Greek accounts, approximately 40 to 50 paratroopers were captured around Agios Dimitrios. The prisoners were gathered at Evropis Street, very close to the scene of the fighting.

Reg Spurr from the 2nd Battalion of the York & Lancasters witnessed this:

> We heard a lot of activity in the area of the harbour. Then someone brought a message that half our platoon was to make towards the harbour and join up with a platoon of ours and a platoon of the Leicesters, who were engaged in trying to dislodge some Germans who had taken the harbour.[28] I joined the group to go there. It didn't take us long to defeat the enemy there, who withdrew via the West Gate, leaving behind about 20 or so prisoners.[29] I was left with the other half of my platoon to deal with the prisoners who looked terrified of us. We didn't know what to do with them, as we had no prison compound.
>
> All the prisoners were lined up against a wall while we tried to decide what to do with them. Then two men from the Black Watch came with about 15 more. We told them we didn't want them [the Germans], as we didn't know what to do with them. As we stood arguing about it, I saw someone at the top of the street taking photos. I pointed him out to the other chaps. I don't remember whether it was me or someone else who went to see who he was and what he was doing there. It turned out he was a Greek newspaper photographer, though there were no papers being printed of course. He was trying to get a scoop. Someone said: 'Leave him alone, if he gets killed it will be his own stupid fault.'
>
> A little while, maybe about 10 minutes after that, a group of about 20 or 30 Cretans, armed with all kinds of weapons, a lot of them German, came round the corner clambering over piles of rubble that a day or two before had been buildings. I believe it was me that suggested we hand the Germans over to them. This we did, explaining that after all, it was their country that the Germans had invaded. They [the Germans] seemed all the more terrified. As far as I can remember, they were herding the Germans none too gently towards the old Venetian Fort. Later on we noticed dive bombers seemed to be intent on bombing it.[30]

27 E.H. Simon, BDF e.v. Archiv, Freiburg/Breisgau.

28 According to Greek accounts, there were only a few British soldiers as machine gun and AA gun crew at the South Gate, and at Gyali Kiosk. When the British reinforcements arrived in the town, the fight was over.

29 The number of prisoners was almost double this according to other accounts, and confirmed by the photo referred to in Spurr's account, in which at least 30 paratroopers can be counted.

30 R. Spurr, *To Have and to Lose – Testimonies 1*, pp.226-228.

German prisoners of war in Heraklion. The single-colour jump-smock without camouflage indicates that they are men of the units that dropped in the west sector. These paratroopers were captured during the street fighting and the picture was most probably taken in Evropis Street, not far from the church of Agios Dimitrios. The British guards are the soldiers from 2nd Bn, York & Lancasters, who took responsibility for the prisoners. Among the guards is Private Reg Spurr, who describes this scene exactly as it is seen in this photo. (Author's archive)

The same spot in Evropis Street today. (Courtesy of Nikos Valasiadis)

Paratroopers of the *III./FschJgRgt.1* on 25th of August Street after the battle, between the Liopyrakis building (left) and the Ioniki Bank (right). (Courtesy of Shaun Winkler)

The same spot today, with the buildings from the era of the battle still present. Bullet holes are still visible on the walls of the bank. (Author's collection)

Metal insignia taken from the uniforms that the paratroopers had left on the streets around the church, at the spot where *Oberfeldwebel* Brückmann was killed. The insignia were found by Evangelos Dedeletakis, who was an eyewitness to the fighting. (C.E. Mamalakis' archive)

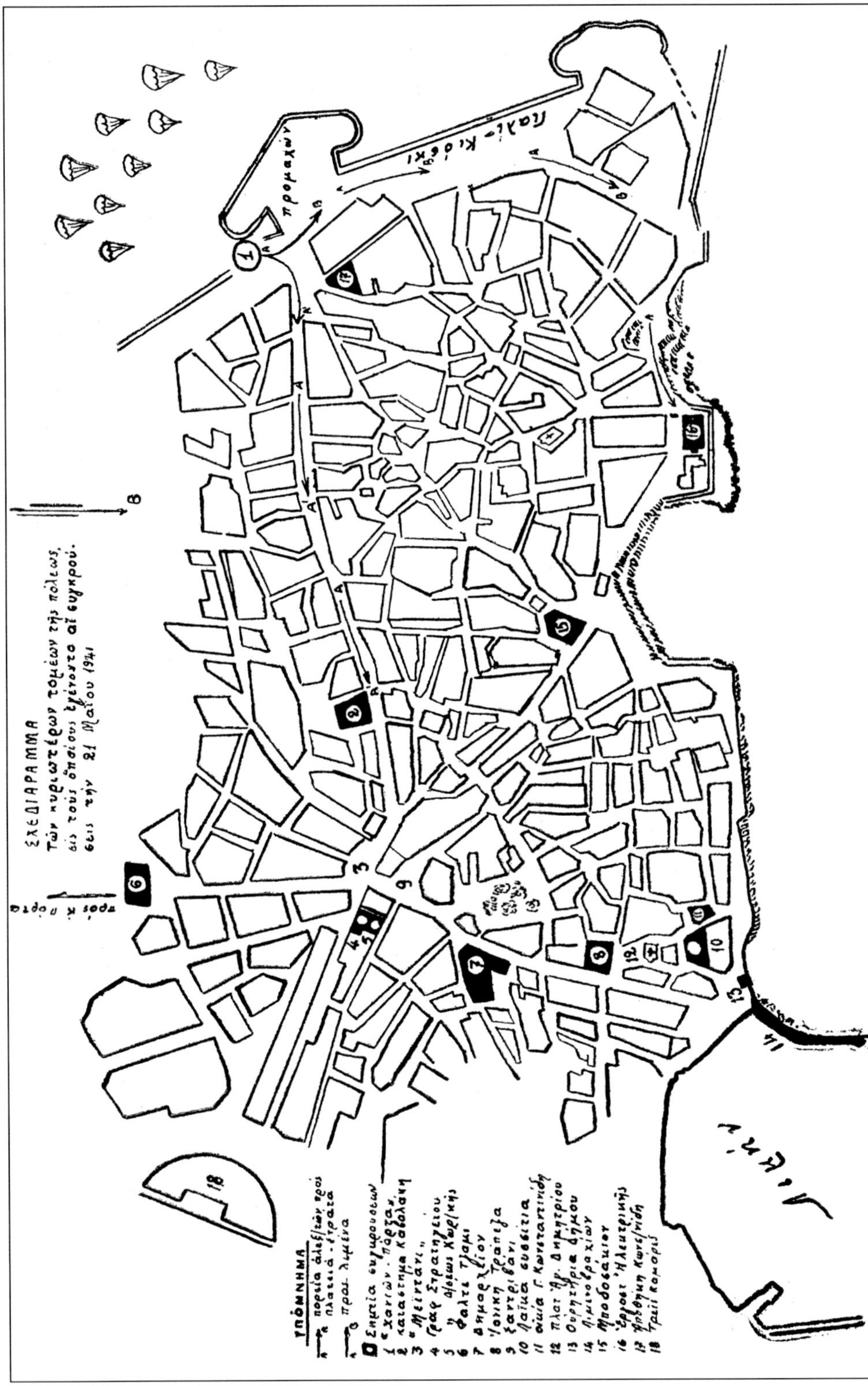

Map 5.4 A map of Heraklion, drawn by M. Pytikakis. The areas marked in black indicate the main areas where street fighting took place. (Courtesy of C.E. Mamalakis)

The main group of paratroopers retreated to the west along the coast – following the railway line that was providing some cover, since it was laid in a ditch two metres deep. This railway was used by the three small locomotives *Minos*, *Theseus* and *Ariadne*, which carried stones from the mines west of the town for the construction of the port.

The railway ditch along the coast as it is today. In the distant background, Koules Fortress can be seen. (Author's collection)

After withdrawing to the west, the paratroopers established themselves in the vicinity of Kaminia, as far as Giofyros and Stavromenos. They left their wounded and the dead in the town, as they were unable to retrieve them. This was despite their efforts to carry them using makeshift stretchers such as doors and whatever else they could find; even the officers helped to carry them. Among the wounded was *Oberleutnant* Fischer, who was found by the Germans on 29 May in Pananion Hospital, along with the other wounded paratroopers. Greek accounts about a German major captured in Konstantinidis' house most likely refer to *Oberleutnant* Fischer, since the only major in this area was *Major* Schulz, who had left the town and returned to his command post.

By noon, order had been restored and only isolated paratroopers were left in the town. Many of the dead and the wounded were scattered around the Venetian walls and in other places. The Greeks were unable to reach them because of German snipers positioned outside the walls, who were firing on anything that was moving in the town.

The outcome of the battle on 21 May had raised the morale of the Greeks, who started to believe in their ultimate victory, since they had managed to keep the Germans out of the town after two days of fighting. The Greeks' armaments and equipment had been vastly improved – mainly due to the use of captured German supplies and weapons. At the Heraklion *gendarmerie* station, such a large quantity of German supplies and gear had been gathered that there were even thoughts of creating a museum after the battle. Such premature ideas were based on the Greeks' belief that the battle had been won.

Cretan irregulars, also known as 'Antartes', fully equipped with German weapons and gear. (Author's archive)

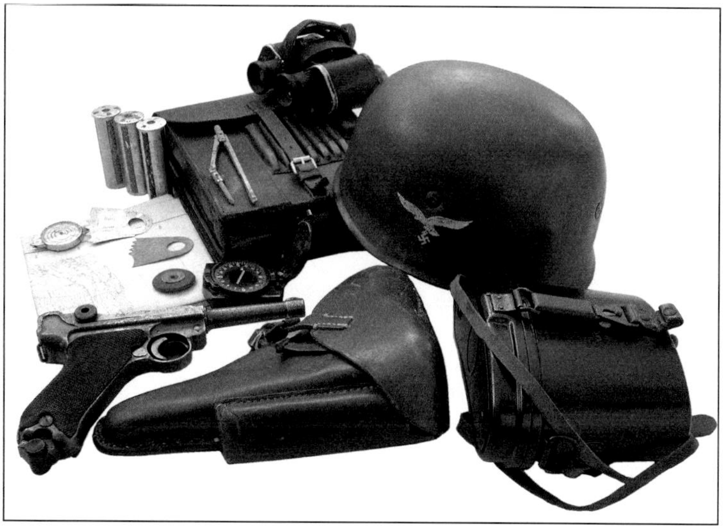

Typical gear carried by the paratroopers during the battle. (Author's collection)

M. Pytikakis describes what had been assembled:

> Every time the men of Gendarmerie returned after a fight they brought with them new souvenirs taken from the paratroopers: different types of leather cases; marvellous pistols; binoculars; cameras; folding shovels; tools whose purpose was unknown; helmets and many other things.
>
> In some cases I found maps more detailed than those available to either the British or our own staff. Other maps were made from combined aerial photographs which provided a three-dimensional representation of the whole island. By examining those maps I realised that the battlefield was no more familiar to us than it was to the Germans. Some other marks drew our attention. Do they mark their main targets and goals that way? Nobody knows what those red arrows on the maps mean!

M. Pytikakis continues:

> The idea of a museum excites the men and they promise to bring even more things with them. The display windows of the nearby shop are full of captured German supplies and gear. There were automatic knives[31] whose steel blades are hidden in the grip and spring out with the press of a button, making a lethal weapon. There are all sorts of pastilles whose purpose is unknown to us; white and coloured parachutes, some with blood-stains, a sign that their owners had not survived; a field-telephone and a radio were also added to our collection.[32]

The official after-action report of the *XI Fliegerkorps*[33] reported that on 21 May at around 1600 (German time), a Greek major offered the surrender of the town, but later – under pressure from

31 The '*kappmesser*', also known as the 'gravity knife', was standard issue to paratroopers and other flying personnel.

32 Pytikakis, pp.130-131.

33 *XI Fliegerkorps, Gefechtsbericht 'Einsatz KRETA'*, p.9.

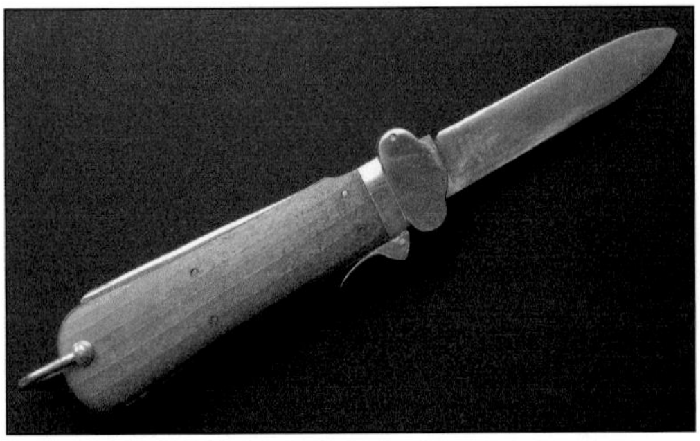

A gravity knife which was found during the battle in the Karteros Valley, east of the airfield near the drop zone of the *8./FschJgRgt.1.* The blade comes out from the grip with the press of the release button – exactly as described by M. Pytikakis. (C.E. Mamalakis' collection)

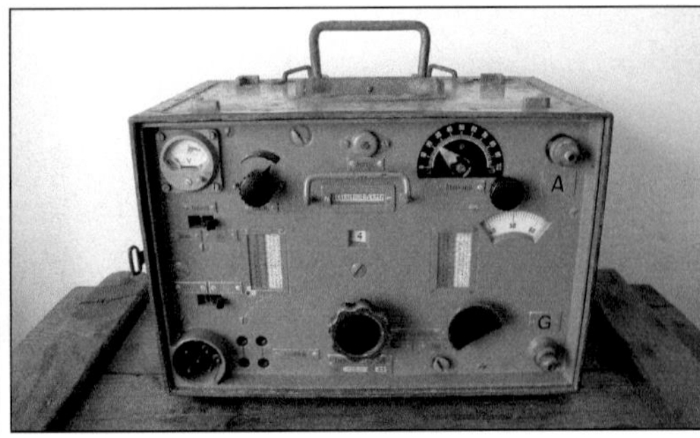

A radio, which was also found in the Karteros area – suggesting that it belonged to a unit from *II./FschJgRgt.1.* (C.E. Mamalakis' collection)

the British – the Greeks were forced to continue fighting. The biography[34] of Karl Lothar Schulz also mentions that the commander of the Guard and the prefect had offered the town to the Germans. More specifically, it reported that while Schulz was in the town, three men and a woman suddenly appeared – one of whom was a Greek officer. *Feldwebel* Ahrens reported that the Greek officer was the commander of the Guard – hence it would have been Major Tsagkarakis – and that he offered the surrender of the town. The woman, who spoke German fluently, said she was German and had accompanied her husband, a doctor named Lagotos, to Crete.

This story is not entirely accurate and should be clarified: first of all, the name 'Lagotos' most probably refers to the Greek doctor Michael Logiades, who took care of many German wounded during the battle – hence his name was well known to the Germans and mentioned in the German reports. There is confusion about the German woman: it is well known that Doctor Chasapes's wife was German and it is possible that she was the woman reported in the German sources. Doctor Nicolaos Chasapes (1873-1970) was the director of Pananion Hospital and he was caring for the wounded during the battle. One of the civilians, who was wearing a suit and a white hat according to the Germans, was the prefect of Heraklion (Mr Ieronymakis) and he was the one who discussed the terms of the surrender. *Oberleutnant* Kerfin kept the minutes of the meeting and drew up the terms and the official document of the surrender.

The offer to surrender the town on 21 May is not reported in any of the many Greek reports and accounts. All of the photographs of the meeting mentioned in the previous paragraph were taken on 29 May. This can be concluded from the location of the pictures and the people appearing in them. The following picture from the German book *Kreta – Sieg der Kühnsten* (published in 1942) shows paratroopers talking with the prefect in 'Liontaria' Square, at the town centre. The picture was taken on 29 May according to its caption.

At this point, there are two more issues to resolve: the first is that the Greek officer in the pictures is not the commander of the Guard, Major Tsagkarakis, but rather another officer, Major Filippakis; the second is that the German woman, who on 21 May was at the Pananion Hospital helping her husband, met the paratroopers there on 29 May and went with them as an interpreter. This account was given by Dr Eiben in his statement.

34 F. Kurowski, *Generalmajor Karl Lothar Schulz*, p.83.

*Major* Schulz, with *Oberleutnant* Kerfin (killed in 1943 on the Eastern Front), talking with the prefect on 29 May. (Fritz Dahm & Hans-Georg Schnitzer, *Kreta – Sieg der Kühnsten*)

Paratroopers led by *Major* Schulz, along with the prefect (Mr Ieronymakis), moving from Liontaria Square towards the Town Hall. (Fritz Dahm & Hans-Georg Schnitzer, *Kreta – Sieg der Kühnsten*)

The same spot today in Liontaria Square. The wartime era buildings are still standing. (Author's collection)

Major Filippakis in a post-war picture. He is the Greek officer pictured in the photos negotiating with the Germans. Filippakis fought in the Battle for Heraklion and took part in the Greek attack on Hill 296 (Ai Lias), south of the airfield. (Courtesy of C.E. Mamalakis)

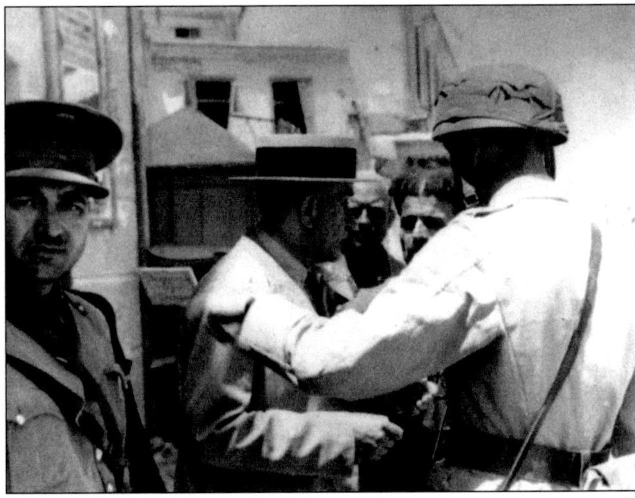

Major Filippakis, the prefect (Mr Ieronymakis) and *Major* Schulz. (Author's archive)

*Major* Schulz (sitting on the chair); at the extreme left of the picture (barely visible) is the German woman who was the interpreter. The same picture also shows Major Filippakis, Mr Ieronymakis, *Oberleutnant* Kerfin and *Hauptmann* Schirmer. The presence of Schirmer confirms that the picture was taken after the battle on 29 May. (Author's archive)

The same spot today, as the picture at the top right (next to the Guard HQ), at the corner of Dikaiosynis and Evans Streets. (Author's collection)

All the pictures above were taken around and near the Guard HQ in the town centre – a place that the Germans never managed to reach on 21 May. Additionally, it is clear that the paratroopers were not carrying their weapons with them – meaning that the battle was over when the photos were taken. The details above provide conclusive evidence that all the quoted accounts about the offer to surrender the town refer to 29 May. What is written in the German reports about this issue is not completely wrong – rather it is a misunderstanding about the intentions of both the Greek and the German sides.

There are other incidents that support this explanation: the first is that many different accounts from Greeks who took part in the street fighting around Konstantinidis' house mention that among the Germans, there was a major. That is true, and the only major in that area was Schulz. According to the Greek accounts again, Major Tsagkarakis (the commander of the Guard) was the Greek officer who asked the surrounded Germans to surrender – hence his rank and duties were known to the Germans. What then occurred was that before Schulz and the main group of Germans retreated, they made contact with the Greek authorities, whereby a misunderstanding obviously arose: the Greeks were asking the Germans to surrender, while the Germans – seeing the white flag and communicating through interpreters – believed that it was the Greeks who were surrendering. When the Greeks continued fighting, the Germans believed that under pressure from the British, they had later changed their minds. To understand what really happened, this episode must be seen in the context of the pressure and the stress of the battle. In the end, the Greeks did not surrender, nor did the Germans manage to occupy the town. The reported involvement of the prefect, Mr Ieronymakis, is also confused with the negotiations that took place during the last day of the battle on 29 May.

In this regard, Mrs Pari G. Kavou stated:

> On 30 or 29 May 1941 I was on a hill at Kanli Kasteli (Prophitis Ilias) village. I was there with the Prefect, Georgios Ieronymakis, the so-called 'Togkos'. Suddenly two Greeks arrived and told him that the Germans were asking him to surrender the town. Ieronymakis took his walking-stick and followed them.[35]

The second incident is described in an account written by E. Malagardis:

> The German prisoners [on the evening of 21 May] reported to Colonel Papathanasopoulos[36] that they had been informed before the attack that if they failed to occupy the town the Luftwaffe would bomb and destroy the town, so they asked Papathanasopoulos to surrender the town to the Germans in order to avoid the town's destruction.
>
> Papathanasopoulos immediately informed Major General Linardakis as well as the Greek authorities. They all refused to discuss surrender any further with the Germans.
>
> Before that there was one more attempt by the Germans to negotiate with the Greeks. They sent Greek prisoners to propose surrender but nobody paid attention to them.[37]

On the morning of 21 May – when the paratroopers entered the town – they took prisoner the staff of the Agrotiki Bank, which was very close to Gyali Kiosk and to the Raisin Co-operatives Union of Crete factory. Sheltering in the bank were the manager of the branch, Sotiris Papapolychroniou,

35 Interview with C.E. Mamalakis – Heraklion, 2013.
36 Second-in-command of the 2nd Military Command of Crete.
37 C.E. Mamalakis' archive.

from Krestena; Kostas Katsaros, from Trikala; and Apostolos Moschonas, from Rethymnon. The Germans took them out of the building and later they joined the rest of the paratroopers who had entered the town from the West Gate. There, Papapolychroniou spoke to the Germans in French and asked for their release, since they weren't soldiers, but civilians. The German officer in charge told them that the town should be surrendered, or else it would be considered a fortress and destroyed by bombing. Papapolychroniou asked if the German officer had informed the commander of the Guard about this and the German responded that Papapolychroniou should go and tell the Greek authorities himself, so the three Greeks went together to the town authorities and informed them of the Germans' intentions.

The above-mentioned accounts indicate that there was not an official offer from the Greek side to surrender the town, despite the opposite impression created in the Germans' minds. In the end, the Germans abandoned the town and retreated west, where they regrouped, as their forces had not proven strong enough to occupy the town at that stage of the battle. The attack group had consisted of just two companies with inadequate supplies for long-term fighting in the complicated and man-consuming urban environment.

The fact that Schirmer's battalion did not contribute more forces to the attack, but rather remained out of action at that point, was assessed as a serious mistake in the attack planning, as is clearly stated in the report of the *XI FliegerKorps* of the *Luftwaffe*.

It is also interesting to read an Australian assessment of this decision:

> ... the German commanders under-estimated the strength of the defenders at Heraklion. Nevertheless, even if the German attacks had been coordinated, it is unlikely that the result would have been different. The Black Watch was unshaken by the ill-organised probing in which Bräuer spent his already-weakened force; and, even if a Greek officer had surrendered in Heraklion, it is doubtful whether his men would have ceased fighting; and, if they had, the town and harbour would still have been under fire from the York and Lancasters and the 7th Medium on the slopes to the east. In addition Brigadier Chappel had a reserve – the Leicesters – who far outnumbered the Germans in the town...[38]

It is very doubtful that the outcome would have been any different had Schulz and Schirmer joined their forces for the attack on the town. Before making any judgement about decision-making and planning, we have to consider the general situation of the battle and the information available to the commanders and their staff at that time. Obviously, Schulz and Schirmer were concerned about an organised attack from the west, which in the end, did not happen that day, but two days later, the men of the Argyll & Sutherland Highlanders moved from Agioi Deka and carried out a surprise attack on Schulz's command post west of the town. On 21 May, it was not possible for Schulz to know the precise British order of battle, so he had to be very cautious and secure his rear during the attack. That threat was not realised on 21 May, but had the Argylls attacked on the morning of the 21st, the result would have been total disaster and annihilation for the *III./FschJgRgt.1* and *II./FschJgRgt.2*.

The paratroopers killed in action from the units that took part in the attack on 21 May were:

Staff/*III./FschJgRgt.1*
*Gefr* Hubert Hiemann – 3 May 1920-21 May 1941

38 G. Long, *Australia in the War of 1939-1945*, p.286.

*10./FschJgRgt.1*
*Jäger* Gerhard Melcher – 15 April 1921-21 May 1941 (grave 730)
*Objg* Heinrich Schröder – 15 July 1915-21 May 1941 (grave 304)
*Obgfr* Willi Stark – 14 October 1919-21 May 1941 (missing/unidentified)
*Obgfr* Ernst Tost – 29 December 1919-21 May 1941 (grave 732)
*Obgfr* Arthur Winkelmann – 23 August 1918-21 May 1941 (grave 769)

*11./FschJgRgt.1*
*Feldw* Lothar Nickolaus – 30 December 1917-21 May 1941 (grave 414)
*Gefr* Hugo Ristau – 27 October 1921-21 May 1941 (grave 462)

Staff/*II./FschJgRgt.2*
*Ltn* Roland Krückeberg – 11 August 1918-23 May 1941(missing/unidentified: he was attached to the staff of *II/2 Battalion* from his own unit, the 5th Company, and dropped on Maleme)
*Gefr* Johan Litz – 8 September 1920-21 May 1941 (killed at around 0900 in Heraklion; missing/unidentified)
*Gefr* Erich Schlüter wasn't killed near Heraklion, while *Gefr* Fritz Esdorn jumped and was killed in Rethymnon

*7./FschJgRgt.2*
*Gefr* Rudolf Kretschmar – 9 December 1920-21 May 1941 (killed 40m east of the bridge to Agios Myron, near the command post of *II./FschJgRgt.2*, west of Heraklion)

The *13./FschJgRgt.1* had 13 dead on 21 May:

*Jäger* Rudolf Böhm – 30 March 1922-21 May 1941 (grave 497)
*Jäger* Hans Bräunlich – 16 April 1921-21 May 1941 (grave 972)
*Obfw* Karl Heinz Brückmann – 25 September 1917-21 May 1941 (grave 413)
*Gefr* Hans Franzke – 12 December 1919-21 May 1941 (grave 497)
*Ltn* Otto Görse – 28 June 1912-21 May 1941 (grave 301)
*Gefr* Kurt Hüber – 17 February 1920-21 May 1941 (grave 501)
*Gefr* Heinz Lange – 19 February 1922-21 May 1941 (grave 824)
*Gefr* Gustav Lexmaul – 14 April 1920-21 May 1941 (grave 419)
*Jäger* Karl Pamme – 18 April 1920-21 May 1941 (grave 499)
*Gefr* Fritz Riemer – 15 December 1920-21 May 1941 (grave 500)
*Gefr* Herbert Schneider – 9 January 1923-21 May 1941 (grave 411)
*Gefr* Richard Tauber – 2 October 1920-21 May 1941 (grave 838)
*Objg* Otto Tessenow – 14 August 1917-21 May 1941 (grave 460)

It is not possible to identify which of the dead belonged to the two platoons of *13./FschJgRgt.1* that were supporting the *III/1 Battalion*, or to the platoon that was attached to the *II/1 Battalion*, but we can draw some conclusions by studying the available information: it is known that Bruckmann was killed during the street fighting in the area of Agios Dimitrios, close to the port – hence we can conclude that Lexmaul and Schneider from *13./FschJgRgt.1*, who are buried very close to him, were also killed in the same area (and quite possibly in the action at the public toilets). Pamme and Riemer[39] were killed east of the airfield, and we can assume the same for Hüber, Franzke and Böhm,

39 Riemer was killed in the Gournes area, near the radio station.

who are buried in adjoining graves. *Leutnant* Görse was killed right outside the town, in front of the walls, at the beginning of the attack on 21 May. *Objg* Heinrich Schröder from *10./FschJgRgt.1*, who is buried in grave 304, was therefore also killed either close by, or even in the town. Schröder is buried among men of *9./FschJgRgt.1* who had been killed close to the South Gate – hence he must be the paratrooper who was killed in the town centre, in the incident in which Major Tzoulakis was also killed. *Objg* Otto Tessenow from *13./FschJgRgt.1*, *Gefr* Hugo Ristau from *11./FschJgRgt.1* and *Feldw* Lothar Nickolaus from *11./FschJgRgt.1* were killed outside Chanioporta. *Jäger* Gerhard Melcher and *Obgfr* Ernst Tost from *10./FschJgRgt.1* were killed west of the town.

**Special Presentation 17: John Pendlebury**

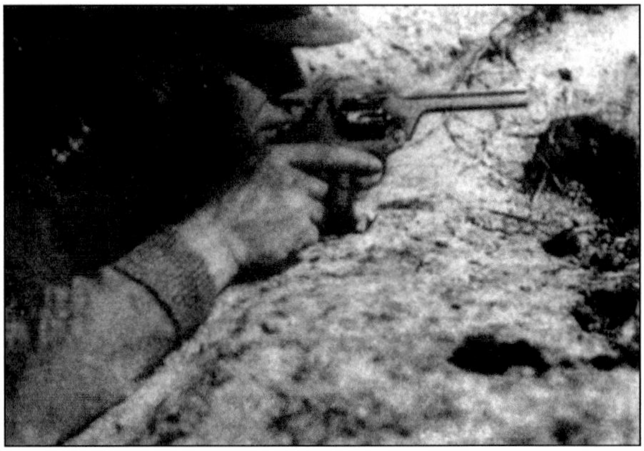

John Pendlebury. After finishing his studies in Archaeology at Cambridge, he joined the British Archaeological School in Athens and participated in the excavations at the Minoan Palace of Knossos. He spoke Greek and the Cretan dialect fluently. In 1940, he was sent to Crete as a member of SOE (Special Operations Executive), with the task of organising local groups of fighters who would be able to take up arms against the Germans, or act in a Resistance and spy network if needed. Pendlebury would leave his glass eye on his office desk as a sign that he was out of the office for some time. (C.E. Mamalakis' archive)

Among those who took part in the fighting in Chanioporta, as well as in the street fighting in the town, was John Pendlebury – a British SOE officer. Despite being aware of the presence of German paratroopers in the area west of the town, on the evening of 21 May, he drove his car through Chanioporta and headed west in order to make contact with the locals in the villages around the south-east foot-hill of Mount Psiloretis. Pendlebury had arrived on Crete long before the battle. He had organised groups of local fighters who were ready to join the Resistance and the fight against the Germans in the event of the expected invasion – and possible occupation – of the island. One of the leaders of these groups was Antonis Grigorakis ('Satanas') from the village of Krousonas.

Pendlebury drove via today's Machis Kritis Street in the Kaminia[1] area, where he came up against a force of paratroopers and was seriously injured in the ensuing battle. The road where the fighting took place is now named Pendlebury Street as a tribute to him.

According to some accounts, Pendlebury was transferred to the house of his friend, Georgios Drosoulakis, where he was treated by two women: Aristea Drosoulaki and Theonymphi Manousaki. One story says that the next day, he was discovered by a group of paratroopers and was executed, as he was in civilian

1 A suburb of Heraklion, west of the town.

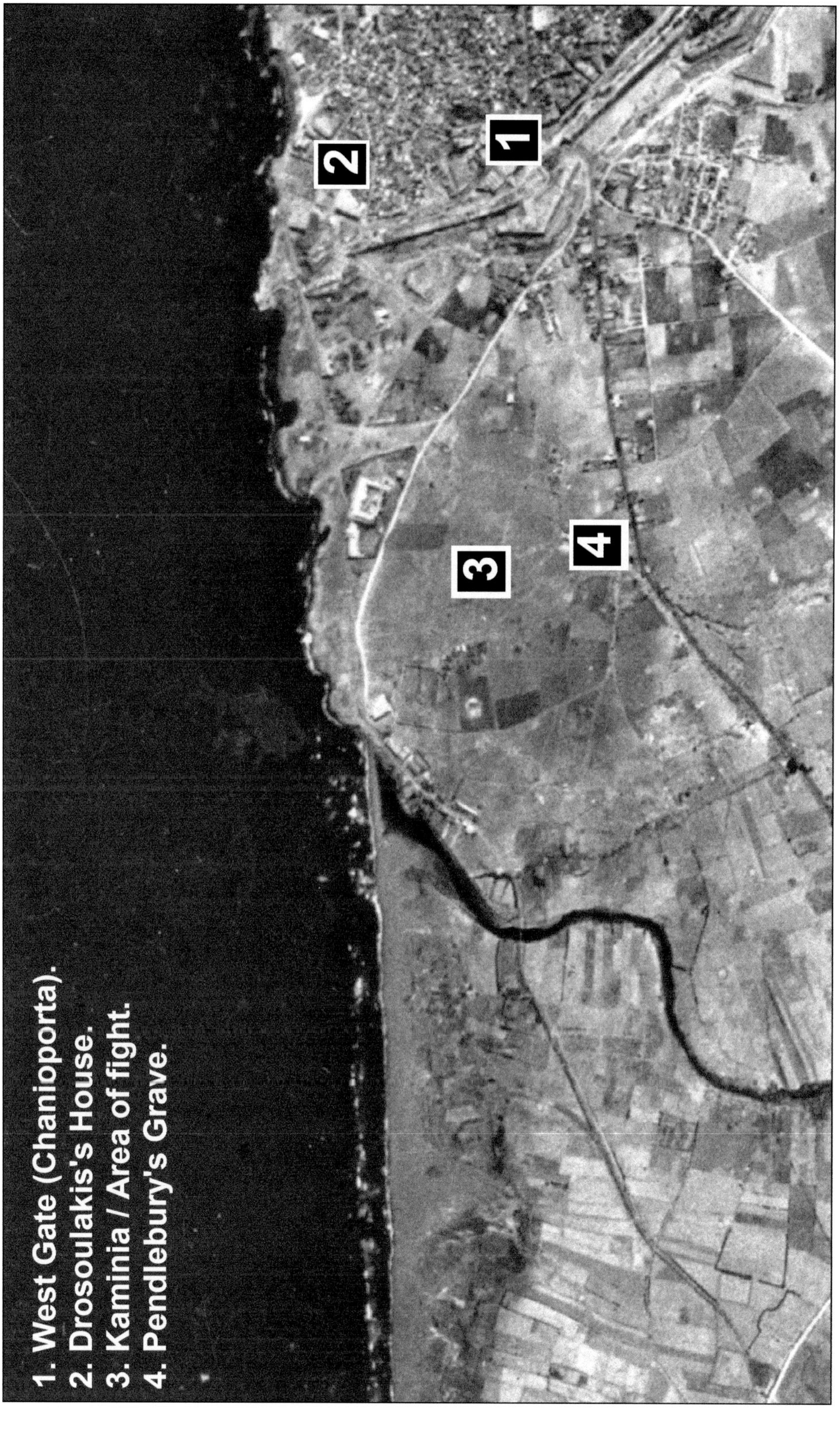


The area of the fight and the location where Pendlebury was killed and buried. (Author's collection)

clothes and therefore considered an irregular combatant. According to another account, Pendlebury eventually died of his injuries. If it is true that Pendlebury was transferred to Georgios Drosoulakis' house, then it is very unlikely that he would have been spotted by the Germans. This house was in Daimonakidon Street in the Agia Triada area, inside the town walls, where there were no Germans on 22 May.

Pendlebury was initially buried near the spot where he was killed and a wooden cross bearing his name was placed on the grave. There was also the inscription: '*Britischer Hauptmann*' ('British Captain'). Later, the Germans transferred his remains about half a mile west of Chanioporta to a small vineyard in Kaminia, next to the road to Rethymnon, where the Agricultural Co-operative Union of Heraklion stands today. Pendlebury's grave became a symbol of resistance for the Cretans, who frequently left flowers on the grave during the occupation without being spotted by the Germans.

After the war, Pendlebury was not forgotten by the Cretans. In addition to the naming of a street in his honour, memorial services were held for many years at the place where he was killed in Kaminia.

The Knossos Hotel – deserted today – at the corner of 25th of August and Lord Byron Streets, where John Pendlebury lived during the battle. (Author's collection)

John Pendlebury's grave at the Allied war cemetery in Souda, with the inscription: 'CAPTAIN J. D. S. PENDLEBURY – GENERAL LIST – 22ND MAY 1941 AGE 36'. (Author's collection)

# 6

# The Battle Continues

Having an overwhelming superiority – and thus retaining the initiative in the Mediterranean – the Royal Navy had literally isolated the island by sea. Operating mainly from Alexandria, the British fleet's tactic was to deploy its units north of Crete during the night – planning their time on task so that the ships were able to sail to the south of Crete during daylight, so avoiding *Luftwaffe* attacks. This tactic very effectively blocked any German attempt at amphibious landing operations, since it was not possible for a flotilla loaded with troops to cover the distance from Athens to Crete before darkness. In addition, when the situation dictated, British ships did remain north of Crete in daylight – prepared to pay the price of this risk.

Particularly early on 22 May, Force C[1] – under Admiral King – turned north after sweeping the north coast of Crete from the Kasos Strait, looking for a convoy of caiques.[2] The convoy comprised some 30 small steamers and caiques and had sailed the previous day from Piraeus (Athens) under the escort of the small Italian destroyer *Sagittario*, commanded by Lieutenant Guiseppe Cigala Fulgosi. This was the second[3] and larger convoy of the Heraklion-bound invasion forces. While still close to Piraeus, *Sagittario* was accidentally attacked by German bombers, but was not damaged. The convoy proceeded towards its destination, but was eventually spotted by the British fleet at 0909 – approximately 40 kilometres south of Milos. It was only at 0930 that morning that Fulgosi had received orders to reverse course to the northward because of the presence of the British fleet to the south, but by that time, it was too late, as the British had already spotted the convoy. As soon as Fulgosi detected the presence of the enemy ships, he ordered the convoy to pull away as fast as possible, while *Sagittario* began laying a smokescreen. The British cruisers opened fire at a range of about 11,000 metres, but the visibility of the targets was very poor because of the smoke. *Sagittario* fought exceptionally bravely and returned fire by launching torpedoes at about 7,000 metres, but without success.

Meanwhile – at 0930 – *Hauptmann* Cuno Hoffmann and his squadron[4] (*I/LG 1*) had taken off from Eleusis, near Athens, and his Ju-88s soon started attacking the British ships. The non-stop heavy attacks by the German aircraft resulted in a high consumption of AA ammunition by the ships, which had become dispersed during the pursuit of the convoy and were not in the standard formation for air defence. Admiral King soon ordered his ships to abandon the pursuit of the fleeing convoy and to withdraw to the westward, since it seemed only a matter of time before the British fleet suffered great damage and losses. The outcome of this action was that the convoy never reached Heraklion. There were to be no more attempts to reach Crete by sea, as the first convoy heading for Maleme had already been destroyed by the British during the previous night. The action was now focused on land – and especially the area around the town.

---

1 Comprised of the light cruiser *Naiad* and the Australian light cruiser *Perth*, with destroyers *Kandahar*, *Nubian*, *Kingston*, and *Juno*.

2 Large fishing boats.

3 The first one destined for Maleme had set out 24 hours earlier.

4 *I Gruppe*, *Lehrgeschwader 1*. (*Gruppe* – Group comprised of three squadrons. *Lehrgeschwader* – advanced training and experimental tactics wing).

A Greek caique loaded with troops and supplies en route to Heraklion, under attack from the Australian light cruiser *Perth*. (AWM Archive)

Lieutenant Guiseppe Cigala Fulgosi – the commanding officer of *Sagittario*. He fought bravely, despite the overwhelming superiority of the British fleet. (Courtesy of the Italian Navy)

The Italian small destroyer *Sagittario*, which was the escort for the Heraklion convoy. (Courtesy of the Italian Navy)

Early on the morning of 22 May, *Major* Schulz decided to attempt a new attack on the town from the west, with his *III./FschJgRgt.1. Hauptmann* Schirmer allocated four platoons from the *II./FschJgRgt.2* (two from the 7th Company, one machine gun platoon from the 8th Company and one anti-tank platoon from the *14./FschJgRgt.1*) for the attack. The assembly area for the attacking units was located at the Giofyros River. The men of the *II./FschJgRgt.2* moved along the main road[5] leading from Giofyros to the town, but soon realised that the *11./FschJgRgt*, which had advanced as far as the Kaminia area, had been forced to halt because of strong resistance by Greek units in the area. At about 0930 – and following *Major* Schulz's orders – the machine gun platoon from the *8./FschJgRgt.2* moved further east in order to keep Chanioporta and the west walls of the town under constant fire.

On 22 May, there were strong detachments of the 3rd and 7th Greek Infantry Regiments west of the town, as well as the Regimental Depot Battalion, *gendarmerie* units and armed civilians. They had managed to advance to the west as far as the Giofyros River and to the south to Foinikia and Archanes. Early in the morning, two groups under Lieutenant Colonel Evangelos Cheretis and Captain Alexakis – reinforced by *gendarmerie* men under Sergeant Evangelos Chatzidakis and Antonios Galanakis, and accompanied by armed civilians – advanced west of the town. Their task was to take the German strongholds at the Kitriki factory in Talos; at Tzoulakis warehouse, near Chanioporta; and the tanneries next to the estuary of the Giofyros River. Thereafter, they were planning to attack the paratroopers in the Stavromenos and Gazi-Tsalikaki area, where the *III./FschJgRgt.1* and *II./FschJgRgt.2* command post was situated.

The first clashes between the Greek forces and the paratroopers took place in the Kitriki factory and the old cemeteries located in the area, where today the local team (OFI) has its football pitch. After bitter fighting, the paratroopers' advance was halted and they retreated – having lost eight dead, with a further eight paratroopers taken prisoner by the Greeks.[6]

With the support of a captured German mortar – operated by 2nd Lieutenant Fokeas – the Greeks attacked the paratroopers, who were dug in on the west bank of the Giofyros River, near the old iron bridge. The paratroopers were forced to remain west of the river, near the command post at Stavromenos-Agakoy Metohi-Mines. They kept control of the main bridge over the Giofyros River, which was located a little south, on the main road to the town.

Sifis Migadis described his experience during the fighting west of the town on 22 May:

> The previous night I went to my home in Spilia where I ate and slept. I put on clean clothes and at around ten in the morning as I was walking along with some other fighters on the coast towards Giofyros, I saw two wounded Germans sitting on the side of the road having their wounds dressed. Just before we arrived at the river I saw a cylinder[7] which contained guns and ammunition and I thought that it would be better to leave my old *Gras*[8] rifle for a new German one.
>
> I remember that I then thought that it might not be a good idea to leave my lucky gun. And it wasn't indeed since after I crossed the river and while I was shooting with my new German rifle, I was hit by shrapnel in the leg right above the ankle, suffering one big and six smaller wounds. Using the rifle as a walking-stick I managed to return to the river and my comrades took me to the Pananion Hospital.[9]

5 What is today 62 Martyron Avenue.
6 The number of dead and prisoners according to Greek sources.
7 A drop container.
8 A very old and outdated single-shot rifle – especially common in Crete at that time. This was the most commonly used rifle by civilians during the Battle of Crete.
9 C. Hatjipateras & M. Fafalios, *Kriti 1941 Martyries*, p.246.

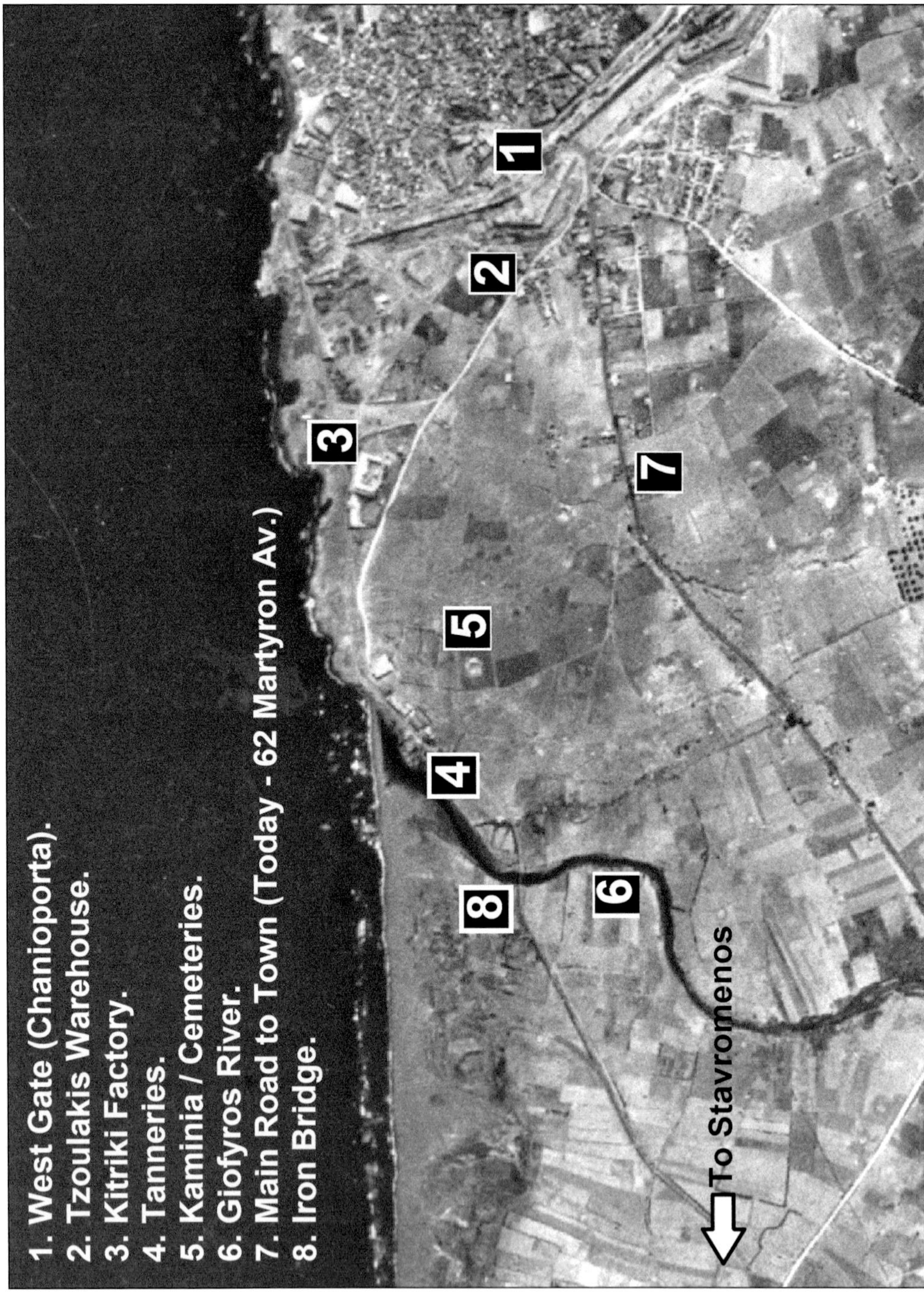


Map 6.1 The area of the battle, west of the town, on an aerial picture taken in 1944. (Author's collection)

The remains of the tanneries, as they are today. (Author's collection)

The iron bridge over the Giofyros River, where the fighting took place on 22 May. The bridge pictured replaced the old one, which collapsed during the floods of 1986. (Author's collection)

The men of *10./FschJgRgt.1*, with *Oberleutnant* Egger in the lead, marching across the iron bridge over the Giofyros River, and the same spot today. (Author's collection)

Major General Linardakis of the 2nd Greek Military Command requested the support of British forces in order to clear the area west of the town, but all he received was a weak artillery barrage which produced no substantial results. The attack was repelled by the paratroopers, with the loss of two NCOs and two soldiers from the *II./FschJgRgt.2.*[10] The paratroopers west of the town spent the rest of the day regrouping and improving their defensive positions, while the *Luftwaffe* strafed and bombed the roads that led to the town.

The paratroopers west of the town arrested many civilians and held them in Tsalikaki, near the *III./FschJgRgt.1* command post. On 22 May, *Major* Schulz ordered the execution of 40 civilians on the grounds that they had been arrested while in possession of German weapons, and that they had participated in attacks against the paratroopers. The number of civilians arrested west of the town had reached a hundred by 23 May.

Some German strongholds remained in the area south and south-west of the town, but these consisted of isolated groups of paratroopers.

Lieutenant Colonel Antonios Beteinakis reported:

> A Greek Army force with a strength of approximately 150 men under my leadership was besieging some 50 Germans who were sheltering in a cottage. After strong resistance and a spirited fight the Germans were finally forced to surrender. They were very well armed and organised and fought very bravely, like heroes, and they surrendered only when they were not in a position to fight any more, since 35 of them had been killed while the rest were wounded.

10 According to German sources.

> I dispatched all those wounded German prisoners via cars to the town hospital[11] for proper medical treatment.
>
> At around noon my nephew Private Antonios Beteinakis (class of 1940) was killed right next to me while he was fighting. He had fought heroically for three days, attacking with his bayonet and killing many paratroopers in close combat and capturing some 10 prisoners. This hero finally met his destiny and found a glorious death while he was attempting to enter via a window a building which was occupied by the Germans.
>
> A little later the same day another one of my soldiers was also killed. Shortly before his death he had wounded a German lieutenant who was operating a machine-gun. He rushed to capture him and the German officer told him in Greek: 'It is true that the people of Crete are really brave fighters,' and he offered his rations and supplies to the Greek soldier. The German had been seriously wounded and passed away shortly afterwards, holding a picture of his children.
>
> From our side, 2nd Lt. E. Zacharioudakis, 2nd Lt. (Medical) I. Anagnostopoulos, 2nd Lt. Dervenis from Kymi, and 2nd Lt. G. Antonelos were killed that day.[12]

On the eastern sector, the Scots of the Black Watch and the Australians of the 2/4 Battalion cleared the area around the airfield of isolated groups of paratroopers and then advanced as far as Knossos to the south. New supply drops were conducted in the Karteros Valley – helping the paratroopers to strengthen their positions in this area and especially on Hill 182 (Koprena), which was directly opposite the Scottish and Australian positions. Brigadier Chappel realised that the Germans were strengthening their positions in Karteros and were resupplying. This situation posed an imminent threat to the airfield and he ordered the Black Watch to launch a counter-attack in order to clear the paratroopers from the Karteros Valley and Hill 182. To reinforce the attack, a force from the Leicester Battalion was attached to the Black Watch.

On the morning of 22 May, a Matilda tank moved from the airfield to the East Beach (the coast of Karteros) and conducted a reconnaissance of the German positions so that the British could make an assessment of the German strength. Reaching the river, the tank turned right and moved along the road towards the *FschJgRgt.1* command post. The positioning of the anti-tank gun on the hill next to the road saved the command post from total destruction. A duel began between the anti-tank gun and the tank; finally, the tank was forced to retreat under constant fire from the anti-tank gun. Paratrooper Wilhelm Eiting from the *2./FschJgRgt.1* was decapitated by one shot from the tank and he was buried next to the Karteros Road.

Paratrooper Gerhard Broder recalled the duel:

> The noise of a tank again: a tank is approaching through the ravine and continues on a rough track. It is firing and stops at a distance of about 20 metres from our position. The vineyard is hiding us from sight but the shallow hole does not protect us physically. I am lying on my back-side and have pulled all my belongings which might attract attention into my shallow hole. From time to time Jacobs looks for the tank to see in which direction its gun-barrel is pointing. *Feldwebel* Eiting, a reservist, married and the father of children, loses his nerve. He leaves his cover and rushes towards a brickwork well, in order to find cover behind it. A shell tears off his head.[13]

11 Pananion Hospital.
12 Lt Col A. Beteinakis, *After-Action Report of the battle in Heraklion, 20-29 May 1941*, p.7.
13 G. Broder, *Guerre Mondiale Contre Moi*, pp.92-93.

## Special Presentation 18: Antonios Beteinakis

Antonios Beteinakis (1886-1943) was born on 7 June 1886 in the village of Archanes, south of Heraklion. In civilian life, he was a teacher. He participated in the Balkan Wars (1912-1913) as an NCO in the Greek Army and he saw active service in all the major and bloodiest battles of this war.

His battalion commander, Major Antonios Papanikolaou, described Beteinakis in his official evaluation report of 31 March 1914 as follows:

Antonios Beteinakis in a pre-war picture, wearing his decorations. (Courtesy of the Hellenic Army General Staff, Army History Directorate Archive)

> He is a very brave, bold, disciplined, decent, humble, energetic, well-educated and clever man. During combat operations as a patrol leader he successfully conducted very dangerous missions and combat patrols [...] during the siege of Bizani, acting as a messenger, he carried an envelope from the King [King of Greece] to the Turkish Commander, Essat Passa. He accomplished his mission with courage and bravery under heavy Turkish fire. They had not realised that he was a messenger. He then provided valuable information and intelligence on the general condition and morale of the Turks in Bizani.

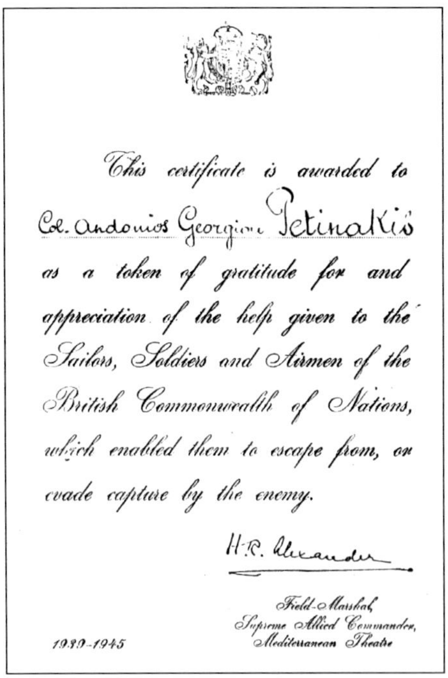

This certificate is awarded to
Col. Andonios Georgiou Petinakis
as a token of gratitude for and appreciation of the help given to the Sailors, Soldiers and Airmen of the British Commonwealth of Nations, which enabled them to escape from, or evade capture by the enemy.

H.R. Alexander

Field-Marshal,
Supreme Allied Commander,
Mediterranean Theatre

1939-1945

The certificate which was awarded to Antonios Beteinakis by Field Marshal Alexander for his assistance to the trapped British and Commonwealth soldiers on Crete. (Courtesy of the Hellenic Army General Staff, Army History Directorate Archive)

Major Antonios Papanikolaou concluded his evaluation by writing: 'Keep this NCO in active service; he will become an excellent officer and I propose awarding him an appropriate decoration'.[1]

Beteinakis also participated in the First World War and was promoted to 2nd lieutenant on 10 May 1918. He continued fighting with the Greek Army during the campaign in Asia Minor against the Turks (1919-1922).

1 Hellenic Army General Staff, Army History Directorate Archive.

At the end of this campaign, Beteinakis had participated in an astonishing 25-plus major battles in his wartime career.

His last battle was that for Crete, where he was recalled to active service at the beginning of May 1941. With the rank of lieutenant colonel, he assumed command of the 3rd Greek Infantry Regiment. He played a key role in the battle and his leadership resulted in the town remaining in Greek hands – thus presenting a major stumbling block to the paratroopers in his sector south and west of the town.

After the battle, he was held in captivity for a few months and finally released on 27 September 1941. Beteinakis became a leading member of the Cretan Resistance during the German occupation, and for this role he was arrested by the Germans and condemned to death. He was executed on 27 October 1943 at the famous prison of Agia (Prison Valley), near Chania. The people of Heraklion honoured Antonios Beteinakis by giving his name to a street in the Mastabas area of Heraklion, where he had fought during the Battle of Crete.

The grave of *Feldwebel* Wilhelm Eiting at the vineyard next to the road, as described by Gerhard Broder. (Author's collection)

The Matilda that attacked the command post on 22 May, here destroyed and abandoned after the battle on the beach east of the airfield. (Author's collection)

The information provided by the Matilda – combined with their general appreciation of the situation in the Karteros Valley – led the Scots to conclude that they did not have sufficient forces available to attack the Germans. Instead, taking advantage of their excellent observation posts overlooking the valley, the Scots unleashed a precisely targeted artillery and mortar barrage on the German positions. The command posts of the *FschJgRgt.1* on Amnissos Hill and the *I./FschJgRgt.1* near Rattling Bridge were under constant shelling from the British artillery. Due to its proximity to the British positions, *I/1 Battalion's* command post was very exposed to enemy fire – and during the night, *Major* Walther decided to move his headquarters to a better-protected place. The new command post was established in the ruins of a semi-demolished house, next to a small cave at the foot of Hill 182, where two MG-34 machine guns were placed for protection. Drinking-water supplies were provided by a well just a few hundred metres away from the command post, though it was possible to reach this only under the cover of darkness.

The command post of *I./FschJgRgt.1* at the deserted house. The radio set seen here was the only one that had arrived intact at the command post. The other set was hit by a bullet while a paratrooper was carrying it on his back. (Courtesy of Mike Smythe)

The area of the command post today. (Author's collection)

When darkness fell, the paratroopers in the Karteros Valley managed to retrieve the supplies dropped earlier in the day and they now had sufficient mortars. *Major* Walther contacted *Oberst* Bräuer via telephone and discussed the repositioning of the *I./FschJgRgt.1* command post, as well as the rearrangement of the available forces, given that the *4./FschJgRgt* would not join them, as it had been dropped in the Maleme (Chania) area. As a result, only three companies remained in the *I./FschJgRgt.1* area of responsibility.

On the morning of 23 May, despite its repositioning, the new command post came under British artillery fire once again. The *2./FschJgRgt.1* received the newly-arrived mortars and its leader, *Hauptmann* Gröschke, deployed his company in positions on Hill 182 that best offered a clear field of fire towards the British positions and the airfield; both were now under mortar fire. This development gave the men of the *2./FschJgRgt.1* the opportunity to avenge the death of their platoon leader, *Oberleutnant* Blücher, and his men. For the rest of the day, there was no substantial action from either side and the adversaries used the lull to bury their dead, except for the bodies of the paratroopers who had fallen in no man's land between East Hill and Rattling Bridge. The bodies of paratroopers who had been killed during the drop remained on East Hill and in the valley below, and were still in the contorted positions in which they landed. Most of them had been killed before they landed. This was an unpleasant and unsettling sight for their comrades, who could see the bodies very clearly, but could not reach them.

The command post's new position offered an excellent view for German snipers, although they were at extreme range from the British positions. Throughout the day, three snipers kept the Scottish positions under close surveillance with binoculars – waiting for the right moment to act; finally, their patience was rewarded. At the south edge of the hill was a small building that was probably the British artillery observation post. When a figure appeared in the distance next to this building, a shot was immediately heard and the figure fell to the ground. From that moment, the Scots would be especially cautious in their movements.

*Hauptmann* Gröschke – the commander of *2./FschJgRgt.1.* (Author's archive)

A German sniper during the battle, using a K-98 rifle with telescopic sight. (Author's archive)

Lieutenant Gerald Barry, of the Black Watch HQ Coy, described their ordeal:

> We are still in the same slit trench. The life we lead is terribly tiring. We are compelled to sit in this narrow, cooped-up place for sixteen hours a day. Since we are situated on the forward slope of the hill behind us, and well above valley level, it is impossible to move outside one's trench at all in daylight, because of the number of machine-guns posted on the other side which immediately open up on one. Our Coy casualties are now about fifteen killed. Yesterday MacLean was hit on the head by a machine-gun [round] and Blair had his legs smashed by a mortar bomb on the aerodrome.[14]

On 23 May, the 2nd Greek Military Command received information that the Germans had arrested many civilians and were holding them west of the town. When *Major* Schulz sent *Leutnant* Schulze to demand the surrender of the town, the Greek authorities refused. Instead, Major General Linardakis replied by sending Major Tsagkarakis to Schulz's command post to ask for the immediate release of the civilians and threatening retaliation against the German prisoners who were held by the Greeks in the town. Major Tsagkarakis – accompanied by the German-speaking director of the Teachers' Academy, S. Mpourlotos (according to other accounts, Tsagkarakis was accompanied by a German medical officer who had been taken prisoner) – went to the *III./FschJgRgt.1* command post in Stavromenos and met *Major* Schulz at the Kera Elias Kamara. Tsagkarakis handed Schulz a letter in which Major General Linardakis requested the Germans' surrender and the immediate release of the arrested civilians.[15] Schulz agreed to release the civilians, but refused to surrender and replied that he was giving the Greeks two hours to surrender the town – otherwise, it would be bombed in the afternoon. According to Schulz, this outcome could be avoided, as the rest of the island had been occupied by the Germans and there was no reason for the Greeks to continue fighting in Heraklion. Of course, Schulz's claim about the occupation of the island was not true and the Greeks rejected his proposal.

Georgios Psarakis recalled:

> Some officers of the Heraklion Guard who were on the top of the Venetian walls at Chanioporta saw a German soldier[16] coming towards the town from the west, holding a white flag. Initially they thought that the white flag meant that the Germans west of the town were about to surrender. Five officers and soldiers with five armed civilians were ordered to move outside the gate and meet the Germans. We had advanced for about 300 metres when suddenly the Germans started shooting and we were forced to dive to the ground. The shooting lasted for about 10 minutes and we stayed on the ground without moving. When the shooting stopped I raised my head and saw the German soldier with the white flag coming towards me. I stood up and then I noticed a dead German officer lying just five metres away from me. Next to him was a leather case.
>
> I took the case in my hands and moved towards the German soldier with the white flag. When I asked him what he wanted he said that he had been sent to give an ultimatum to the British Commander of Heraklion. With this letter the Germans were demanding the

14 C.E. Mamalakis, Ian Powys Archive.

15 Major Tsagkarakis' proposal for the Germans to surrender is confirmed in the after-action report of the *II./FschJgRgt.2*.

16 *Leutnant* Schulze.

Georgios Psarakis in a wartime picture. (Courtesy of C.E. Mamalakis)

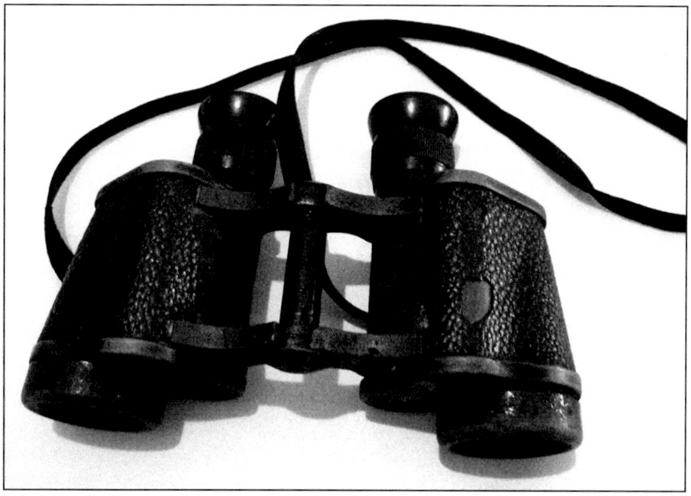

The binoculars that Georgios Psarakis describes in his account. (C.E. Mamalakis' archive)

> unconditional surrender of the town by 4 p.m.; otherwise it would be bombed. The Greeks rejected the ultimatum and at 4 p.m. the bombing began, with devastating effects for the town.
>
> The leather case that I took from the dead German contained a pair of binoculars, a 1:5000 scale map of the area and a notebook. The next day I gave the map and the notebook to Major Tsagkarakis while I kept the binoculars and the case. During the German occupation I buried them in my backyard where they remained for four years until the end of the war. I excavated them in May 1945 when I returned home from the Middle East. The rain and the earth had caused some damage to them.[17]

At 1500, the silhouettes of German bombers appeared on the horizon – approaching the town from the sea; at 1600, the town was bombed – exactly as was promised in the ultimatum. The bombing was merciless – destroying a large part of the town, but without causing many casualties among the civilians, who had either left the town or found shelter in the old Venetian walls and fortifications.

M. Pytikakis described the scene:

> Two soldiers who were in the centre of town in Meintani did not manage to take cover in a trench during this hell and destruction and they panicked. Two policemen took them and led them to the Guard HQ when there was a pause in the bombing.
>
> A bit further to the right, outside the Reginakis store, another civilian also panicked and started running and shouting. Sergeant Papadogiannis took him and led him to the Olympos Hotel.
>
> Right next to the police station, where he was a sentry, shrapnel shredded both Constable Kastanakis's legs. Two other policemen carried him to the Pananion hospital where he died after a time.

17 Letter to C.E. Mamalakis, 15 May 1994.

The bombing of Heraklion in a photo taken by paratroopers west of the town.
(Courtesy of Dimitris Skartsilakis)

> Everywhere in the town tragic and dramatic scenes took place. Sergeant Fountoulis from Mastabas had been wounded and was lying on the operating table when the bombing started. The doctors hurried to the hospital basement and waited for the raid to finish, since they thought that it was just another of the usual bombing raids. A bomb exploded in the operating room and Fountoulis literally disappeared![18]

The raid caused so much damage to the town's infrastructure that supplying Greek units became very difficult – especially as the military bakery and the water supplies were destroyed. As they had been fighting for four days without a rest, the Greek units were exhausted. Because of this situation, the British and the Greek Command decided to move the Greek forces to the south (towards Knossos and Spilia) during the night of 24/25 May. The Greeks now assumed responsibility for the protection of the Heraklion-Knossos Road and the field hospital that had been established in Villa Ariadne, next to Knossos. The defence of the town from the west was then assigned to two companies of the York & Lancaster Regiment that had moved from the Mastabas area.

At noon on 23 May, two Matilda tanks arrived in the eastern sector – having come from Tymbaki on the island's south coast. According to orders issued by CREFORCE,[19] those two tanks – with the only Matilda still in working condition in Heraklion and two 75mm guns – were to be transferred to Souda Bay by sea. On the same day, the 1st Battalion of the Argyll & Sutherland Highlanders moved from Tymbaki to Agioi Deka, with their final destination being Heraklion. This battalion had sailed from Alexandria aboard the troopship HMS *Glengyle* at midnight on 17/18 May and disembarked at Tymbaki at dawn on 19 May.

18 M.I. Pytikakis, *Storm Over Crete*, p.136.
19 The command centre of Allied forces on Crete.

The battalion's mission was threefold:

1. The defence of the Messara Plain and its preparation as an emergency landing ground for the RAF
2. To watch for possible parachute landings on the Nida Plateau, in the hills north-west of Agioi Deka
3. The defence of the beach at Tymbaki, in anticipation of expected landings there of further German reinforcements

HMS *Glengyle* anchored about 500 metres off the coast of Tymbaki at 2330 on 18 May. There were only a few hours before dawn – during which to unload the supplies and the troops. The ship would sail no later than 0400 so as to avoid the *Luftwaffe* during daylight. Because of the short period before dawn, only a portion of the supplies and fuel was unloaded. The failure to send ashore the entire cargo later proved critical for the Argylls. The ship sailed on time, but the landing craft remained at Tymbaki, where they were used for the evacuation of the island after the battle.

The battalion remained concealed from aerial observation throughout the daylight hours of the 19th. The Bren Carriers, under Lieutenant Guy Valentine, moved to Agioi Deka to investigate the suitability of the area as an emergency landing ground. Lieutenant Valentine reported that the area south of Agioi Deka was ideal for this purpose and his unit settled in there. 'A' and 'B' Companies, under Captains E.T. Tidmarsh and George Giles, also moved forward to Agioi Deka, while 'D' Company – under Captain A.T. Bardwell – moved to the village of Moires.

Shortly after the invasion had begun, the Scots identified the main German effort as being focused along the north coast of the island – hence there was no point in the Argylls remaining south in Tymbaki and Agioi Deka. On 23 May, the CO of the battalion – Lieutenant Colonel R.C.B. Anderson, after reconsidering the larger battle situation – decided to advance towards Heraklion and attack the Germans who had become established south-south-west of the town at Cheretis Metohi, on the road from Tymbaki to Heraklion. The aim of this attack was to clear and secure the road to the town in order to allow the reinforcements expected from Egypt to move to the town unhindered.

The assault ship *Glengyle*, which with two other Glen Line ships (*Glenroy* and *Glenearn*), gave invaluable service during the Crete campaign. (IWM, FL 22266)

A knife bearing the badge of the Argyll & Sutherland Highlanders. It was found near the village of Voroi, on the road from Tymbaki to Agioi Deka. (C.E. Mamalakis' archive)

At 0600 on 23 May, the two Matilda tanks set out for Heraklion at the head of the Argylls' advance, followed by the Bren Carriers and the rest of the battalion. These two tanks were to be transferred to Chania, but a shortage of fuel necessitated a refuelling stop in Heraklion before they departed the area.

When the Scots approached Heraklion, the Bren Carriers carried out a reconnaissance patrol around Cheretis Metohi, south of Tsalikaki. At 1000, the patrol reported that it was feasible to drive out the Germans with the support of at least one company. Because of the transport shortage, many men were still in Agioi Deka, so only very limited forces were available at that time. 'A' Coy, under Captain E.T. Tidmarsh, was ordered to attack at 1100. The attack's main objective was to occupy Cheretis Metohi and then to take another position to the north. This was, in fact, the *III./FschJgRgt.1* command post in Stavromenos.

The attack eventually got under way at 1700, with the support of six armoured vehicles (four Bren Carriers and two Matildas), and focused mainly in the area of the *7./FschJgRgt.2*. The paratroopers managed to repel the Bren Carriers, but the Matildas finally managed to break through the German defence and reach the British positions south of the town. The Argylls occupied Cheretis Metohi, but the arrival of about 200 paratroopers forced 'A' Coy to return to its starting position. Night found the Scots in the area of Gournes[20] – occupying the hills west of the Agioi Deka-Heraklion Road and awaiting reinforcements. Among the 'A' Coy casualties were Lieutenant J.R. Large, who was killed in action, and Lieutenant A.J. Aldridge, who was wounded.

During the night of the 23rd, a strong Argylls patrol tried to pass through the *8./FschJgRgt.2* positions in order to reach the British defensive perimeter from the south. This attempt was a failure, as the Germans detected the Scots' movement and defended their positions very effectively. *Leutnant* Rada and his men unleashed a counter-attack – forcing the Argylls' patrol to retreat (having left three dead on the battlefield). The Germans had only one loss: *Obergefreiter* Kurt Schöpper (6 March 1920-23 May 1941) from the *7./FschJgRgt.2*.

20 This is the Gournes west of Heraklion and should not be confused with the Gournes in the east, near Kopsas. In most books about the campaign, there is a misunderstanding on this point – incorrectly referring to the Gournes east of the airfield.

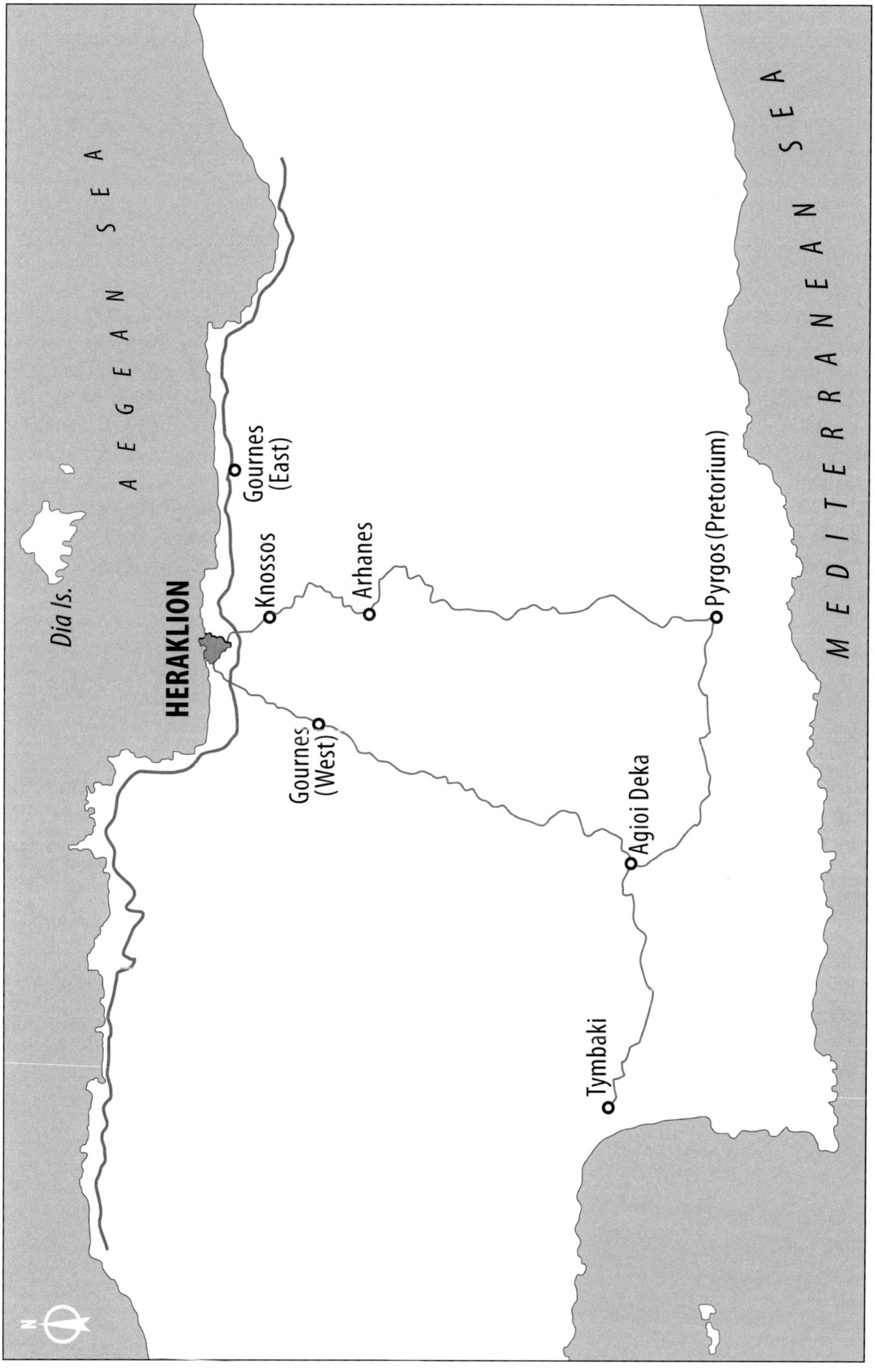


Map 6.2 The central part of the island. (N. Panos, 2016)

Earlier – during the afternoon of the 23rd – a formation of six Hurricanes appeared over Heraklion Airfield. They were mistakenly identified as enemy fighters and the AA guns around the airfield opened fire on them – shooting down two aircraft, while another was forced to land on the airfield due to severe damage. The remaining three planes returned to Egypt. Later in the evening, six more Hurricanes appeared – and after a dogfight with German planes, they eventually landed on the airfield. Four of these aircraft sustained damage to their tail sections and one more was destroyed on the ground by the *Luftwaffe.* The Hurricanes on the airfield were very soon under mortar fire from *Hauptmann* Gröschke's *2./FschJgRgt.1*, which had been established on Hill 182 and had an excellent field of fire to the airfield. After a short stay at the airfield, two Hurricanes took off and, after machine gunning the paratroopers' positions, they returned to Egypt. Late in the evening, formations of Ju-88s bombed the town and the airfield.

A platoon from the 2/4 Australian Battalion, under Lieutenant K.L. Kesteven, moved south of the airfield to Ai Lias Hill (Hill 296, or 'Apex Hill'), which offered an excellent view of the entire area around the airfield and east of the town. The Australians established an observation post there to monitor the paratroopers' movements as they tried to surround the airfield by moving both from the east and the west. Using a flashing light for signals, Lieutenant Kesteven's men kept the commander of the 2/4 Australian Battalion, Colonel Dougherty, informed of the enemy's movements.

When night fell, the paratroopers in Karteros Valley managed to approach the British positions and no man's land, and were able to evacuate the wounded who had been left on the battlefield. *Oberleutnant* Harry Herrmann of the *5./FschJgRgt.1*, who had suffered a serious head injury from a bullet during the jump and had been blinded, was finally transferred to the field hospital located in a tavern next to the regimental command post. Despite his severe injuries, *Oberleutnant* Herrmann had led his men, along with the men of the *8./FschJgRgt.1* (under *Oberleutnant* Dietrich Platow), in an attack on the airfield immediately after they landed on 20 May. They had suffered heavy casualties when many men dropped on top of British positions and they were forced to retreat – leaving many dead and wounded behind.

In recognition of his heroic actions during the battle, *Oberleutnant* Herrmann was awarded the Knight's Cross. An article about the battle appeared in the magazine *Der Adler* – a wartime *Luftwaffe* publication.

Hill 296, or 'Apex Hill', south of the airfield – overlooking the area around it. The mountain in the background is Mount Jouhtas. (Author's collection)

Harry Herrmann in a photo taken after the battle (and now a *hauptmann*) wearing the Knight's Cross. (Author's archive)

*Oberleutnant* Herrmann lying wounded in the field hospital in the Galazia Poulia Tavern in Karteros. (G. Müller & F. Scheuering, *Sprung über Kreta*)

The evacuation of a wounded paratrooper to the field hospital in the Galazia Poulia Tavern in Karteros. (G. Müller & F. Scheuering, *Sprung über Kreta*)

# DER BLINDE HELD VON HERAKLION

ZUM 1. JAHRESTAG DES KRETA-EINSATZES

Die beispiellose Tat eines Kompanieführers der Fallschirmjäger

Gezeichnet von Kriegsberichter Wilhelm Baitz

In diesen Tagen ist es gerade ein Jahr her, seit Kreta besetzt wurde. Wenn wir später einmal die Geschichte dieses Krieges schreiben werden, wird unter den Ruhmesblättern deutschen Heldentums das Blatt der Kreta-Kämpfer mit an erster Stelle stehen. Aus jenen Kampftagen greifen wir eine Episode heraus, die für alle Zeiten festgehalten zu werden verdient. — Mit dem Auftrag, den Flugplatz im Osten der stark befestigten Stadt Heraklion zu stürmen, zu besetzen und zu halten, war Oberleutnant Herrmann in der ersten Welle mit seiner Fallschirmjägerkompanie abgesprungen. Wie mancher seiner Männer wurde auch er in dem schweren feindlichen Abwehrfeuer noch vor der Landung verwundet. Das Geschoß schlug ihm durch den Hals und drang bis zum linken Auge vor. Trotz dieser schweren Verwundung griff er mit wenigen seiner Fallschirmjäger, die sich um ihren Kompanieführer gesammelt hatten, den Flugplatz an. Vorübergehend erblindet, wurde der Oberleutnant im stärksten feindlichen Feuer von seinem Hauptfeldwebel geführt. Der Hauptfeldwebel fiel. Ein anderer Fallschirmjäger sprang sofort an dessen Stelle. Auch er fiel. Doch der Angriff stockte nicht. Und wenn die Männer einmal glaubten, in dieser Hölle aus Sonnenglut und feindlicher Abwehr nicht mehr weiter zu können, dann brauchten sie nur auf ihren blinden Kompanieführer zu sehen

Nach schweren Verlusten mußte der Angriff am Rande des Flugplatzes schließlich abgebrochen werden. Da ein weiterer Vorstoß vorläufig unmöglich geworden war, richteten sich die Reste der Kompanie hier zur Verteidigung ein. Und diese Stellung wurde gehalten. Rücksichtslos gegen sich selbst hatte der Oberleutnant während der ersten kritischen Stunden seinen tapferen Fallschirmjägern ein leuchtendes Beispiel gegeben, hatte sie vorwärts gerissen und so seinem Regiment eine außerordentlich günstige Ausgangsstellung geschaffen. Erst als jede Gefahr, zurückgeschlagen zu werden, behoben war und nur auf ausdrücklichen Befehl des nach vorn geeilten Regimentskommandeurs ließ sich der Oberleutnant endlich zum Verbandsplatz führen. Für seine die weitere Kampfführung entscheidend beeinflussende Tat wurde Oberleutnant Herrmann zum Hauptmann befördert und mit dem Ritterkreuz des Eisernen Kreuzes ausgezeichnet

Nach einem PK-Bericht

The article in *Der Adler* describing Harry Herrmann's actions. (*Der Adler*)

Under the cover of darkness, medics managed to evacuate and save many of their comrades from certain death or captivity; risking being spotted and killed, some paratroopers defied death and managed to pass through the British positions and the minefields. They succeeded in contacting the men of the *II./FschJgRgt.1* and the *III./FschJgRgt.1*, which had been dropped south of the airfield and west of the town respectively.

On the morning of the 24th, the paratroopers watched with relief as an additional battalion and ammunition and food supplies dropped south and west of the town. This was the drop of approximately 400 men under *Hauptmann* Vogel and consisted of two heavy weapons companies and two rifle companies. There was a shortage of everything in the units that had been fighting since the first day. The daily ration per man was just a slice of bread and two cigarettes, since the priority in air supply was ammunition, with food a poor second. The paratroopers knew that the British defensive positions were very strong and that there was no point in attempting an attack without appropriate support and reinforcements – thus they did not move from their positions in the Karteros area east of the airfield for the whole day of the 24th. Despite these difficulties, the paratroopers' morale remained high – based on their belief that strong air support from the *Luftwaffe* would eventually prove decisive and allow them to win the battle.

The men of the Argyll & Sutherland Highlanders – positioned south-west of the town – were planning to attack at dawn on 24 May. On the afternoon of the 23rd, the units stationed at Agioi Deka were ordered by Brigadier Chappel to send a force of no fewer than three companies to advance along the Agioi Deka-Heraklion Road and clear it of Germans by no later than 0500 on the morning of the 24th. Because of poor communications, 'A' Coy was unaware of the new orders issued to the units in Agioi Deka. As a result, they mounted their attack during the afternoon of 23 May without waiting for reinforcements to arrive. Despite the lack of transport – and after a march that lasted for the whole night – the Scots managed to gather two more companies, reconnaissance units, the Battalion Command Group and the Bren Carriers at the 'A' Coy positions and ready to attack at 0445. They had only 15 minutes to clear the way and complete their mission.

At 0500, the attack began, with 'B' Coy – under Captain George Giles – in the lead moving east, and 'D' Coy (under Captain A.T. Bardwell) aiming west. The attack should have been completed before 0730 – the usual time for the appearance of the *Luftwaffe* over the battlefield; however, events did not turn out as planned. The four Bren Carriers were forced to retreat under heavy fire from the German anti-tank guns. The paratroopers of the *8./FschJgRgt.2*, under *Leutnant* Kursten, unleashed a strong barrage of machine gun and mortar fire – forcing the Scots to halt. They suffered 27 dead and were still far from their objectives. According to the after-action report of the *II./FschJgRgt.2*, even the men of the medical units from the field hospital – under Dr Langemeier – participated in this battle.

At 0730, when the *Luftwaffe* appeared in the sky over the battlefield, the situation deteriorated for the Scots and a message was immediately sent to Agioi Deka urging 'C' Coy and the mortar platoon to advance as soon as possible, since the battle was far from won. Lacking a clear knowledge of the enemy order of battle, the Germans never realised that they were confronting the men of the Argyll & Sutherland Highlanders – instead believing that they were units of the Black Watch.

Paratrooper Ernst H. Simon from the *13./FschJgRgt.1* recorded his experience:

> It is 22 May and the remains of my platoon are positioned on a ridge[21] which stretches from north to the south. At midnight we are ordered to move and take positions on the so called

21 Hill 67.

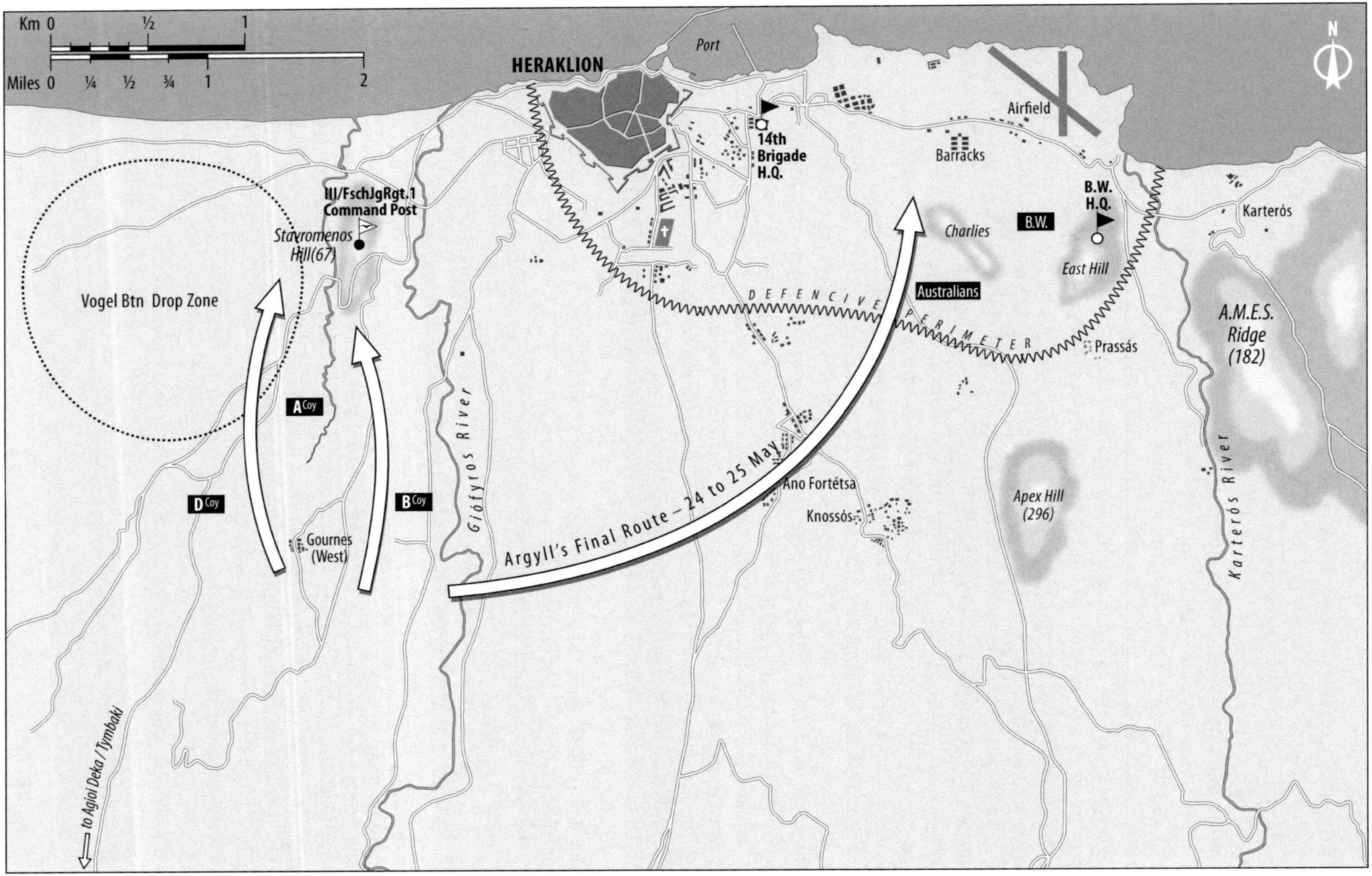


Map 6.3 The battle west of Heraklion on 24 May. (N. Panos, 2016)

Dr Langemeier addressing his men in a picture taken in March 1941. (Courtesy of Jose Ramon Artaza Ivañez)

'*Flohburg*'[22] which is a relatively well-built farm[23] at the southwest edge of the hill, in order to reinforce the positions of the 7./2 Company. Because of heavy rifle fire we have to cover most of the distance over the open and flat ground by crawling on our bellies. At the '*Flohburg*' snipers are shooting at us and we manage to capture two of them. In the evening we have some bread with goat cheese for dinner. We haven't received any supplies yet, but on the other hand, during the day we watched our Ju-52s dropping supplies on the Tommies where they had placed the swastika flags which were the recognition signal for the pilots. They have received a lot of supplies during the two previous days.

The next morning [24 May] six British armoured vehicles [a Mark IIA Matilda, a medium tank and four Bren Carriers] try to break through from the south and enter the town. Our only remaining 3.7 cm Pak [anti-tank gun] has no more armour-piercing shells. Although our anti-tank rifles and our infantry rifles can do no harm to the tanks, the Bren carriers finally retreat to the south under our heavy fire. The other two tanks have managed to break through our lines but without any serious effect on us since their 4 cm gun is pretty harmless against infantry. We are positioned with our front to the right of the '*Flohburg*' and have a good view of the battle. A very unpleasant incident was a low-level bombing attack on our farm by a Do -17 despite the fact that we had the roof properly marked with a swastika flag. In our forward position we didn't receive the message that the *Luftwaffe* would attack every site marked with a swastika flag because the enemy was making more use of it than we were. We now have to use white scarves as signals to indicate our position. Luckily the bomb falls outside the fence of the yard and on the second approach the pilots realised that the fiercely waving figures on the ground were German paratroopers. The pilot wobbles his wings and turns away.[24]

22 'Flea Castle'.
23 It is Sfakianakis' farm.
24 E.H. Simon, BDF e.v. Archiv, Freiburg/Breisgau.

Sfakianakis Metochi at the south-west edge of Hill 67. (Courtesy of C.E. Mamalakis)

At around 0830 – and while the attack was still proceeding – *Hauptmann* Vogel's men were dropped west of the town, right in the middle of the battle. This battalion was actually formed by men and units which had remained in Greece or Germany – and for various reasons, such as the lack of aircraft, they had not been dropped during the first days of the battle. A whole platoon of the *13./FschJgRgt.1*, which had stayed in Greece, finally arrived that day. A company under *Oberleutnant* Jung dropped south of the advanced positions of 'D' Coy – cutting them off from the rest of the battalion and forcing 31 of the Scots to surrender. 'D' Coy's commander, Captain A.T. Bardwell, was among the wounded. The Scots were attacked from three sides and were also under fire from German aircraft; every man ended up fighting for his own survival.

At 1000, the last platoon of 'D' Coy arrived after a night march from Agioi Deka. The remaining men who had been sent from Agioi Deka were delayed on the way due to *Luftwaffe* attacks, so the only available reserve at that time consisted of the 17 men from 'D' Coy who had managed to escape and return to the Scottish lines. 'A' and 'B' Coys had not suffered heavy casualties, but 'D' Coy had been completely destroyed. The attack finally failed and the Scots were forced to return to their initial positions.

*Luftwaffe* pilot Franz Lankenau described this specific drop:

> Saturday, 24 May. We woke up at 04:00. Take-off was planned for 05:00. We took off right on time along with nine other planes from our squadron. Two more squadrons had taken off a little earlier. When the day broke it was still raining. Initially our course was towards the open sea and we then turned southwards to Crete. We will drop the paratroopers near the town of Heraklion. On Friday evening I had a discussion with a paratrooper. It was Karl Loch from my village. He will be aboard another of our squadron's planes. I promised to relay his greetings to his parents. How small the world is!

> We fly over the sea for more than an hour. The darkness has gone and the rain stopped. Having the wind blowing with us, we arrive at the drop zone early and we are circling over the coast. Then we are heading to our target area. The troops on the ground are making signals to mark the drop zones. Here is the road![25] I sound the horn and the paratroopers jump. As soon as they all have left, I turn my plane with its nose to the ground and then to the right and I fly over the sea at a very low altitude. The formation assembled again over the sea. Some of the planes were hit. My plane hasn't been hit but we will be sure about that only after we have landed after a 1½ hour flight [...] At night we received a message via the radio, saying that the Schönicke company (which we carried in the morning) had been dropped very well. All this happened about one km south of the coast of Heraklion[26] and Karl Loch from the town of Uesen was one of the men who participated in this operation.[27]

Early in the afternoon, Major Richard Fleming of the 14th Brigade Staff (who had heard the noise of the battle) rushed to the area in order to have a closer look at the situation. Fleming arrived at the Argylls' command post and delivered Brigadier Chappel's orders – according to which the attack was to be halted and the battalion placed under the guidance of locals, who would lead it during the night towards Knossos to the east and from there to the north and the British defensive perimeter.

The remainder of 24 May passed with the men of the Argylls waiting for darkness to come in the Gournes area on the Agioi Deka-Heraklion Road. When night fell, the Scots set out without their CO (Lieutenant Colonel Anderson), who had been wounded in the legs and could not follow. Anderson was a very capable and active officer, but he did not like to delegate responsibility. This style of command resulted in disorganisation within the battalion when he was absent. The second-in-command of the battalion, Major J.H. Carmichael, assumed command and put himself at the head of 'A' and 'B' Coys, while Captain B.A. Pearson took control of 'C' and 'D' Coys. The march started at 2200 and should have been completed before 0600 in order to avoid *Luftwaffe* attacks. The local guides led the Scots into the darkness, following narrow and craggy paths. The Argylls were exhausted from the continuous fighting and the long marches of the previous days, and could not keep up the pace. When morning came, they were still well away from the British defensive perimeter; in addition, the two main groups of the battalion had lost contact with each other during the march. The men who had been left behind remained hidden in olive groves – trying to avoid a *Luftwaffe* attack. Captain B.A. Pearson and two soldiers from the second group finally managed to reach the 2nd Bn, York & Lancaster positions, where they met the CO (Lieutenant Colonel Gilroy). Also, there was Major J.H. Carmichael from the first group and the rest of the Argylls. Finally, the battalion reached the York & Lancaster positions – moving onto the hills west of the Tymbaki Knossos-Heraklion Road and digging in within the area south of Alikarnassos-Katsabas. They replaced the men of the Leicesters' 2nd Bn, which was Brigadier Chappel's reserve.

At *General* Student's HQ – on the ground floor of the Grande Bretagne Hotel in Athens – anxiety prevailed due the landing of the Hurricanes at Heraklion Airfield. The potential use of the airfield by the British to land reinforcements would pose a severe threat to the Germans. Moreover, the Maleme Airfield was unable to fulfil the Germans' supply needs due to its small size – hence it was imperative that the paratroopers occupy Heraklion Airfield. For those reasons, Bräuer was ordered to attack and occupy the airfield as soon as possible.

25 Agioi Deka-Heraklion Road.
26 In the area of Stavromenos-Gazi and south.
27 Hatjipateras & Fafalios, p.301.

On the morning of 25 May, the paratroopers attacked the town from the west with *Luftwaffe* support. Two companies of the York & Lancasters and a company of the Leicesters turned back the attack. These units had been assigned to the defence of the town from the west after the Greek forces had withdrawn to Spilia during the night of the 24th.

Paratrooper Ernst H. Simon from the *13./FschJgRgt.1*, recalled:

> On 25 May we are relocated to a new position at the centre of our west front. For the first time we see activity from the British air force. A Hurricane flies over but doesn't spot us. The English artillery, consisting of an ancient 7.5 cm battery, shells around our positions but without any substantial results. The stench of the decaying corpses hangs everywhere. The newly arrived battalion moves along the road to the west and attacks towards the town while we attack further to the south as a distraction. We move ahead and capture some Tommies but the Böhmler [Vogel] battalion manages to reach only as far as the suburbs and then returns, having suffered heavy losses. A proposal [by the British] to us to surrender is rejected by *Major* Schulz with the words, 'Our mission is to occupy Heraklion and this will be accomplished.' At the moment it doesn't look like this is really the case.
>
> In the evening we finally receive supplies, mainly machine-gun ammunition and food. For all these days of the battle we survived eating barley grain, unripe melons and chickens cooked without salt or fat. Just before dusk our air force finally arrives and bombs Heraklion with about 200 bombers flying in tight formation at an altitude of about 2,000 - 3,000 m. There are He-111s, Do-17s, Ju-88s and Ju-87s. They have a really devastating effect on the town but the enemy positions outside the town are virtually intact.[28]

The Greek units in Spilia and Archanes were resupplied and the wounded were transferred to the field hospital that had been established in the Archanes School. The 2nd Greek Military Command Headquarters moved from Spilia to Archanes, where telephone communications existed. The Greek forces were organised into two regiments of 1,000 men each, under Colonel Papathanasopoulos.

Early in the morning, the British east of the airfield attacked the *2./FschJgRgt.1* positions on Hill 182 from the south. Their aim was to destroy the mortars that were shelling the airfield and which posed a serious threat. *Feldwebel* Bobrowski and his men counter-attacked the British from two different sides with the support of machine gun and mortar fire. The British retreated – leaving behind 10 dead, many wounded and prisoners. It was obvious then that the paratroopers had strengthened their positions and had been resupplied with heavy weapons – thus making an attack on their defensive positions extremely difficult.

At dawn on 26 May, the Australians on the top of Ai Lias Hill (Hill 296, or 'Apex Hill') reported that a large group of paratroopers – estimated at about 700 men – were approaching from the west. Since 24 May, there had been some signs that the Germans were moving from the west to the east on the hills south of the Allied defensive perimeter, so as to establish contact between the units led by Schulz, Bräuer and Burckhardt. Early on the morning of 25 May Schulz, having regrouped and reorganised his forces from the *III./FschJgRgt.1*, the *II./FschJgRgt.2* and the Vogel battalion along with the attached platoons of the *13./FschJgRgt.1* and *14./FschJgRgt.1*, began advancing to the east. Moving south of the town, Schulz's aim was to establish contact with Bräuer and surround the defenders from the south, cutting them off from the other Allied forces on the island. The *II./FschJgRgt.2* was reinforced by the *12./FschJgRgt.1* which had been dropped on the

28 E.H. Simon, BDF e.v. Archiv, Freiburg/Breisgau.

morning of 24 May, while the *10./FschJgRgt.1* and *13./FschJgRgt.1* were merged into a single force under *Oberleutnant* Egger.

Since the beginning of the battle, Australian units had conducted intensive patrols around 'Apex Hill'; there were many brief battles between those patrols and German groups that were trying to approach the airfield from the south. On 26 May at around 0700, the paratroopers' force was approaching 'Apex Hill' from the south and the west-north-west. In the lead were the men of the *7./FschJgRgt.2* and *8./FschJgRgt.2* (under *Hauptmann* Schirmer). They attacked from the west and the south, while *Oberleutnant* Egger's men attacked from the north-west. The *12./FschJgRgt.1* remained slightly further to the west – acting as a reserve and covering the rear of the attacking units.

Paratrooper Ernst H. Simon from the *13./FschJgRgt.1* described his unit's role:

> Since May 24, we had received the order: the remains of the *III./FschJgRgt.1* were to join the *I./FschJgRgt.1* which has now moved to the heights near the edge of the airfield. They also have serious casualties but fewer than we do. Our path leads around the British positions. We start marching in absolutely darkness and nobody speaks or makes any noise. We carry with us a weapons container full of 10 cm mortar ammunition – these containers have detachable wheels making them mobile – and we hope that our 2nd and 3rd platoons have the mortar tubes with them. We sneak over dirt roads, through creeks and bush paths. Above us flies an English plane dropping parachute flares but it doesn't spot us. At dawn we reach Knossos. Shortly after and while we are on a hill without cover, we come under machine-gun and mortar fire from the left. Our British prisoners, who have to follow us since it was not possible to leave them behind, are terrified by the heavy fire. The enemy cannot be repelled and we attempt a charge to the right, descending the slope and then climbing the next hill. This hill is also occupied by the Tommies but we run so fast that we overcome them very quickly. We still have just a small distance to cover and then we join the *I./FschJgRgt.1.*[29]

Paratrooper Adolf Strauch from the *II./FschJgRgt.2* also described the attack:

> After we broke the enemy defences during a night attack, we managed to occupy Height [Hill] 296 which was right opposite Heraklion airfield. While totally exhausted from the effort and the fighting we also had to deal with a counter-attack by the British on the morning of 26 May. After we repelled the attack successfully, we then counter-attacked. My friend Hans Christoph[30] also participated in this battle. He was wounded by a bullet in the knee while my other friend, Peter, was killed. Hans Christoph was given first aid and was then left under the shadow of an olive tree because at that time the attack was still going on.
>
> We left him wounded, hoping that the medics would find him. Another wounded comrade was left next to Hans and I bade goodbye to my friend. Many years later I learned the whole story. What those two wounded went through is beyond words. For four days after being injured, without water and medical treatment, they stayed there under the burning sun. The man next to him finally died and Hans Christoph had no other option but to remain, lying in the sun next to the corpse which was being attacked by the flies and worms. We finally managed to occupy Heraklion and by pure luck some English soldiers found my friend as

29 E.H. Simon, BDF e.v. Archiv, Freiburg/Breisgau.
30 Hans Christoph Bender.

Adolf Strauch. (Author's archive)

*Oberleutnant* Egger with his men at the top of 'Apex Hill'. (Author's archive)

> they were retreating. They took Hans Christoph to the southern part of the island where our troops found him. He was transferred by air to Athens where the doctors decided to amputate his wounded leg. For a few weeks my friend was hovering between life and death and the doctors had given up hope. He finally survived. I would like to express my thanks to those who saved his life.[31]

Lieutenant Kesteven of the 2/4 Australian Battalion tried to escape from the top of 'Apex Hill' by leading his men downhill along the steep northern slope. The Australians attempted to break through the weakest German unit, which was approaching from the north. Kesteven's men succeeded, and the platoon – with Lieutenant Sargent's men in the lead – managed to pass through a force of approximately 50 Germans. The Australians had been subjected to a fierce hail of fire, but succeeded in reaching a shallow gorge, where they took cover. By following the dry riverbed, they moved quickly to the Black Watch positions at the airfield. The Australian losses were two men killed and three wounded. Lieutenant Kesteven was among the wounded and he was taken prisoner by the Germans.

Private Selby Dean from 2/4 Australian Battalion recalled:

> I was attached to a Platoon commanded by Lieut. Kestevan [*sic*] and we took up a position on Apex Hill. This hill overlooked the whole of the Heraklion area and was an ideal lookout. I was the signaler and had all ready [*sic*] made contact with headquarters. This was a defensive position so sentries were posted each night but we didn't use booby traps. This particular morning I was up early and went out to my post, looked down the side of the hill and saw Jerry advancing towards us. I gave a yell to the mob and commenced sending a message back to H.Q. The method of signaling was using a very antiquated Lucas Lamp. This is a lamp that comes on and off when sending Morse. One had to lie out in the open to operate it. The Germans soon picked up the flash and opened up with a machine-gun. I could not get out until I had finished sending the message. We were now entirely surrounded and Kestevan [*sic*] gave us the order to "charge". This was the only bayonet charge I was ever involved in and I'm

31 A. Strauch, BDF e.v. Archiv, Freiburg/Breisgau.

The dry riverbed that the Australians used to escape and reach the Black Watch positions. In the background (on the left) can be seen the northern slope of 'Apex Hill'. (Author's collection)

> glad there was only one. We did manage to break through and started back to our unit. We had to go through the Black Watch lines and we pulled up and talked to the "Jocks". One of them pointed to my hat. I took it off and was amazed at what I saw. A bullet had gone through the side of it and gouged a great groove around the rim. It had cut a piece of the chin-strap off and I had never felt a thing! Luck was definitely on my side that day. I wish I had kept that hat as a souvenir as I reckon it would be a lucky charm.[32]

With this attack, the German forces in the west managed to join the forces to the east – closing the gap between them and totally surrounding the Allied positions from the east, the west and the south. The only escape route left for the British was the sea.

Understanding the importance of Hill 296, Colonel Papathanasopoulos ordered the 7th Greek Infantry Regiment to occupy the hill – attacking from the south and starting from Archanes and Spilia. The attack failed because of a lack of supplies, ammunition and heavy weapons. When darkness fell, the Greek forces were withdrawn to Archanes – having suffered serious losses. Among the wounded were the commander of the regiment – Lieutenant Colonel Cheretis – and Captain Chardalakis. Lieutenant N. Fragou, Lieutenant I. Vasiliades, Private G. Tzortzakakis, Private E. Zouridakis and Private K. Koutoulakis were some of the Greek dead. The Greek units were not in a condition to conduct further offensive operations, so they deployed into defensive positions in Archanes and Spilia.

32 C.E. Mamalakis' archive.

## Special Presentation 19: Selby Dean

For his actions during the battle in Heraklion, Selby Dean was awarded the Distinguished Conduct Medal (DCM). He found out about his decoration after the battle, while he was in Palestine.

The citation for the medal reads:

*Award of the DCM to Pte. Selby Dean*

*The above-mentioned soldier during the Crete campaign distinguished himself, by his untiring devotion without thinking of his personal safety.*

*Pte Dean is a signaller in Headquarter Company and during heavy enemy air action continued repairing signalling wires, which had been severed by bombs. He also kept his communication intact with the Battalion while out on an isolated post under command of Lieut. Kesteven "B" Coy, and it was directly due to him staying at his post under enemy fire that a visual message was transmitted to Battalion H.Q., giving the condition of this Platoon and enemy movement. Later it was necessary for the platoon to stage a bayonet charge. Pte Dean distinguished himself as a fighting member of the unit.*

*On two nights after this event he volunteered to go out on a dangerous patrol and his Platoon Commander, having confidence in his courage and high ability as a signaller selected him for these tasks.*

Private Selby Dean in a wartime photo. (Courtesy of C.E. Mamalakis)

The Distinguished Conduct Medal. (Courtesy of C.E. Mamalakis)

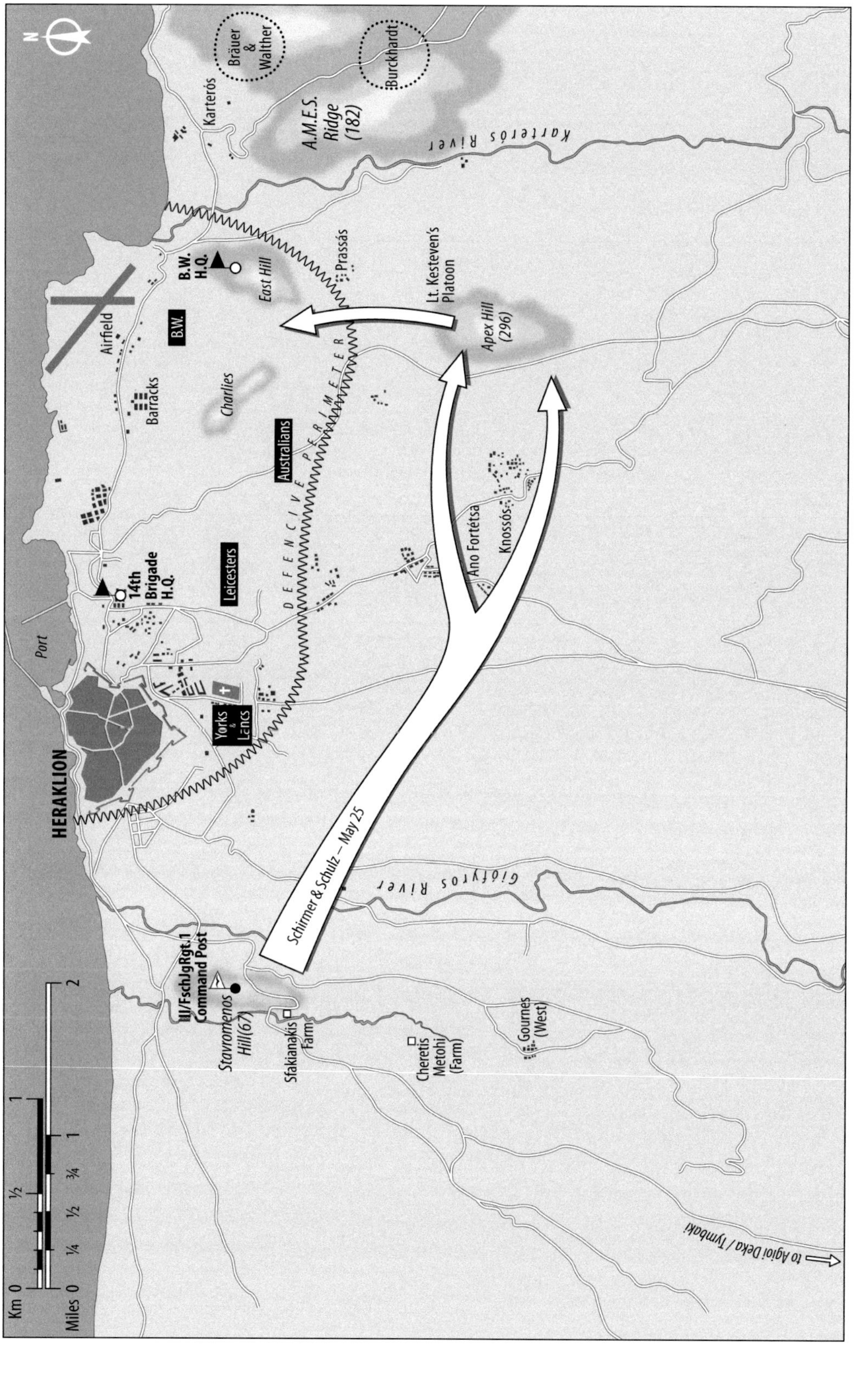


Map 6.4 The German movements and the adversaries' positions during the Battle for 'Apex Hill'. (N. Panos, 2016)

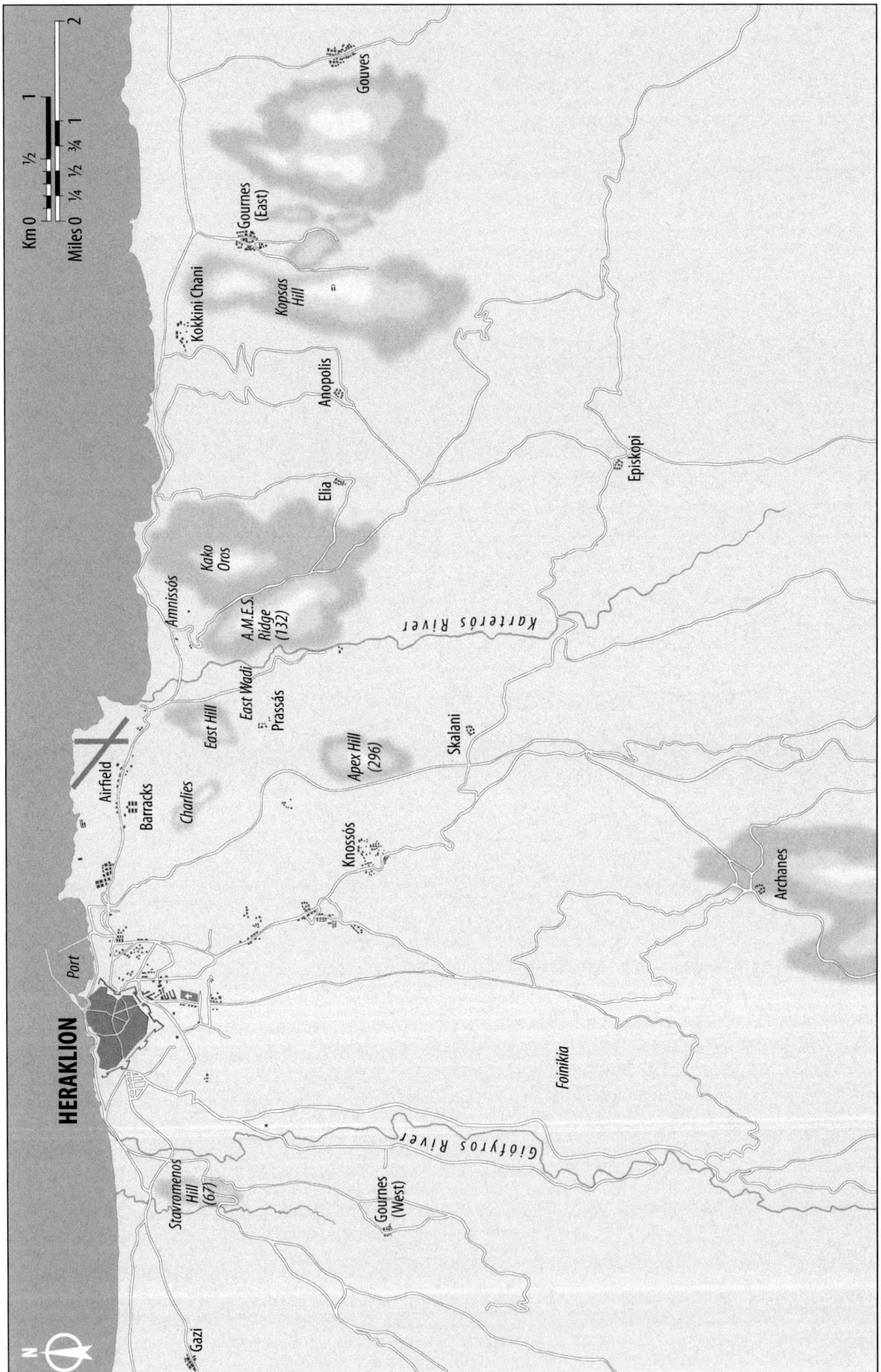


Map 6.5 The area south of the town and the airfield. (N. Panos, 2016)

Schulz with Bräuer immediately after they joined forces at the *FschJgRgt.1* command post in Amnissos, east of the airfield. (Author's archive)

# 7

# The Final Attack and the Evacuation

On the night of 26/27 May, Brigadier Chappel sent a message via Cairo to General Freyberg describing the situation around Heraklion and the airfield. He reported that the Germans had received strong reinforcements and had advanced – surrounding the British defensive perimeter around the airfield and the town, and cutting off links to the south and the west by occupying the roads that led to the town. The Germans had also occupied the hills overlooking the British positions. Chappel requested further instructions as to whether he should attempt a counter-attack to clear the roads and restore communications to the south and the west. General Headquarters in Cairo asked if it was possible to use the port of Heraklion; Chappel replied in the affirmative and then received the order to evacuate the Heraklion area via the port. This order was not relayed to the units in Heraklion in order to prevent any leak of information about the operation to the Germans.

On 27 May, the Germans were preparing very intensively for their final attack on the airfield. More paratroopers were dropped at Gournes (to the east of the airfield) and some Ju-52s attempted to land south of 'Apex Hill' in order to unload supplies and evacuate the wounded. Believing that his units were not yet strong enough, nor properly prepared, Bräuer asked that the attack take place one day later, on the afternoon of the 29th. German Headquarters in Athens accepted Bräuer's request and the day of the attack was set for the 29th.

On the afternoon of 27 May, an operation took place near Heraklion that was similar to the one conducted by *Oberleutnant* Kleye on 21 May at Maleme. At 1400, Ju-52 pilot *Oberleutnant* Franz Lankenau presented himself at the office of *Generalmajor* Gerhard Conrad in Athens. He was ordered to attempt a landing in a Ju-52 on a makeshift landing strip located south of 'Apex Hill'. The mission's main purpose was to find a safer and more efficient way to resupply and reinforce the paratroopers who were preparing for the final attack on the airfield. The crew of another Ju-52, which had conducted a crash-landing in that area, reported that the plateau south of 'Apex Hill' could be used as a landing strip. Franz Lankenau took off from Megara in Ju-52 1Z-AR at 1615 and, after a one and a half hour-long flight, arrived over Heraklion. After flying over the island of Dia, he headed west and south of the town in order to avoid the AA fire and then flew over 'Apex Hill' and attempted a landing by approaching the hill from the east. With the sun in his eyes, he was unable to land, so he circled and approached from the west – eventually landing at the designated area south of the hill. The Scottish and the Australian positions were about two kilometres north of 'Apex Hill', and although they were able to watch the plane's attempted landing, they could not fire directly on it because the hill was providing cover for the aircraft. Lankenau brought his plane to a stop at the end of the 300-metre-long makeshift landing strip. *Hauptmann* Schirmer rushed out and handed the pilot a secret report for *General* Student's staff in Athens.

Without wasting any time, paratroopers unloaded the supplies and put 20 seriously wounded men on board. This occurred despite the pilot's insistence that he could carry no more than 10 persons because of the poor condition and short length of the runway. During take-off, the plane

Paratrooper Arno Reichard took these pictures during the landing of 1Z-AR. In the first photo, the plane approaches the hill from the west, while in the next, the plane has landed south (south-west) of Hill 296 ('Apex Hill'). Next to the wheel tracks on the ground is a drop container that had been left on the strip. During take-off, the plane hit this container. (Courtesy of *DDF*)

*Generalmajor* Gerhard Conrad, who was responsible for the logistical support of operations on Crete. (Fritz Dahm & Hans-Georg Schnitzer, *Kreta – Sieg der Kühnsten*)

hit a drop container left at the side of the strip, but finally managed to lift off – climbing out through AA fire. The aircraft landed in Megara at 2010 and the pilot immediately rode a motorcycle to *General* Student's headquarters in Athens and handed over his report on the flight, along with the other reports he had been given on Crete.

Paratrooper Ernst H. Simon from the *13./FschJgRgt.1* watched the landing of the Ju-52:

> On the ridge south of us large rocks and other obstacles are cleared away and on 27 May a Ju-52 loaded with supplies and ammunition (15 cm rockets) manages to land on this mountain, which was actually a remarkable flying performance by the pilots. Unfortunately, many of the weapons (launcher racks) for this ammunition are dropped into the sea by other aircraft.

> On 28 May another battalion jumps east of the airfield and northeast of our positions. It consists of the last reserve and it has been quickly assembled with men from the parachute training schools in Germany.[1]

On 27 May, Lieutenant Gerald Barry from the HQ Company of the Black Watch wrote in his diary:

> We leave our trench at 9.15 p.m., when it is dark, and a hot meal (tea and M & V) is cooked for the men. They do not get this before 11 o'clock as a rule, then I have to pay visits round the posts, and do not get to bed as a rule before 2 a.m. It is almost impossible to sleep during the day, as one's position is too cramped, and after a bit every bone in one's body aches. The Germans come over every day, usually about 8 a.m., with troop carriers and drop supplies for their men. About 25 men and several large cylinders were dropped up our valley near the village yesterday afternoon, and all our guns opened up on them. At the moment the situation here is peculiar. The Germans are wandering round the perimeter of our defences trying to find an opening to get to the aerodrome - they have attacked west of the town and were driven off, then yesterday they came down from Apex Hill and attacked towards the Charlies, and now today they seem to have moved slightly further east. They have failed completely in their attempt to capture either the town or aerodrome.[2]

On the morning of 28 May, Chappel had a meeting with the unit commanders, minus the Greeks. At this meeting, the details for the evacuation were fixed – including the order of embarkation, routes for leaving forward positions for each unit so as not to alert the Germans, and also details for the destruction of supplies, equipment and vehicles that would be left behind. Explosives with time fuses were placed in the fuel and ammunition stores – and these were set to explode during the morning of the 29th, after the evacuation.

Operational Instruction No.11 – the evacuation order which described in detail the exact routes and time schedule for each unit – was printed (32 copies were produced) and distributed very quickly to the various units.

The key points of the instruction were:

- In the event of an AIR RAID, the following action will be taken:
  a) If unit is on the march, cover will be taken immediately until the aircraft has passed.
  b) If on the Mole or Quay men will lie still faces down [...]
- Explosives will NOT repeat NOT be used.
- Guns and Mortars will be rendered unserviceable by removal of breech mechanism. Fuses will be buried where practicable. Sights must be evacuated.
- Engines will be rendered unserviceable by removing and destroying distributors. Petrol tanks punctured, sand put into the cylinder heads and through the plug holes – plugs then put back.
- Wireless will be broken up.
- Remainder of equipment and stores to be rendered unserviceable by units while keeping quietness and secrecy.
- Tanks will be destroyed by destroying engines, removing gun mechanisms and destroying wireless sets.

1 E.H. Simon, BDF e.v. Archiv, Freiburg/Breisgau.
2 C.E. Mamalakis, Ian Powys Archive.

- Each man will carry one tin of bully, packet of biscuits (emergency rations where available) OR one day's rations. Water bottles will be filled.
- There will be NO SMOKING or lights shown after darkness.
- Quietness is essential. All available means will be taken to prevent rifles and equipment clanking.
- Acknowledge.

SECRET.

HERAKLION SECTOR OPERATION INSTRUCTION No. 11. Copy No. 15

28th. May 1941.

INFORMATION.

1. The garrison of HERAKLION SECTOR will be evacuated on the night of the 28/29 May and must leave not later that 0300 hrs.

METHOD.

2. The evacuation will be carried covered as follows :-

(a). The present out perimeter general line : North Gate - West Gate - South Gate - Rd Junc 4761 - Spur 5158 - Feature 5354 - 2/A. & S.H. near Coy posn 5256 - Gray's Rd at 7152 - Charlies - East Hill - Gorge - will be held up till tactical withdrawals take place, see paras 3 b and Appx. B. They must be prepared to reinforce inner perimeter if necessary.

(b). A second covering line will be held as follows:-

North Gate- West Gate - South Gate - Rd Junc 4761 - Slaughter House - 5162 - West Bank of Opps Wadi - PORUS PT. See para 3 (b) and Appx B & C.

3 (a). Troops not on the outer perimeter or earmarked for the inner perimeter will withdraw to Assembly Positions in Harbour Area as per Appx. A.

(b). Troops holding the actual outer or inner perimeters will move as in Appx B & C. The withdrawal of these troops will be treated as tactical operations.

4. 2 Leicesters will provide :-

(i). A securing party of two officers and thirty men to report to Capt. MacDonald, R.N. at 2230 hrs.

(ii). A picquet of one officer and ten men to report to Capt. Monteith, the Garrison Adjutant at South end of West Mole at 2230 hrs.

(iii). The above parties will embark as in Appx. C.

5. One officer of each party including bn final echelons will be detailed to report to Capt. Monteith as his unit or det passes on to the South end of West Mole. He will report the Serial No., Groups and No. of officers and men of that unit.

6. The C.R.E. will detail det 1017 Docks Coy of one officer and forty four men to report to the S.M.O. at 2100 hrs at Villa Galbia ready to move and to act as a Stretcher Bearing Party. This party with Medical Det and Stretcher cases will move direct to North end of West Mole and lie down.

7. Air Raid.

(i). In the event of an AIR RAID, the following action will

The first page of copy No.15 of Operational Instruction No.11, which was issued by 14th Brigade HQ and outlined the evacuation of the Heraklion sector. (C.E. Mamalakis' archive)

The York & Lancaster Regiment's Regimental Colours, which were found after the battle at the HQ of the 2nd Battalion. The evacuation was so sudden and rushed that many items were forgotten by the British troops. This banner was found by the Germans after the battle and later kept by a Cretan. It was finally discovered in an old military trunk in a deserted house. All the regiment's battles and the campaigns before the Battle of Crete are recorded on the flag. (C.E. Mamalakis' collection)

For the whole day of the 28th, the Germans continued preparing for the attack,[3] while the *Luftwaffe* was bombing Allied positions – concentrating on the Heraklion-Tymbaki Road. *Oberst* Bräuer gave his final orders to the unit commanders and all was finally ready for the attack that was to begin the following morning. In the evening, the Germans noticed the silhouettes of warships on the horizon, but did not realise that the evacuation was to take place that night.

At 0600 on 28 May, a naval force consisting of the cruisers *Orion*, *Ajax* and *Dido*, along with six destroyers, sailed from Alexandria to evacuate the Heraklion garrison. Attacks by the *Luftwaffe* on the naval force began at 1700, while the ships were south-south-east of Crete. At 1920, the *Imperial* – one of the destroyer escorts – was narrowly missed by a bomb (which caused some minor damage), and at 2010, the *Ajax* came even closer to being hit – being damaged above the waterline and sustaining a number of casualties. *Ajax* was ordered to return to Alexandria, since her bomb damage rendered her no longer capable of accomplishing her highly risky mission.

At 2330, *Orion* and *Dido*, with the six destroyers, approached Heraklion Harbour. The cruisers remained off the harbour entrance, while the destroyers entered four at a time – loaded to capacity alongside the pier and then transferred the troops to the cruisers. As the roads were partially blocked by obstacles created by demolished buildings and other bombing raid debris, the troops arrived at the harbour after marching through the town in single file. With characteristic order and discipline, the British soldiers boarded the ships under the direction of Captain MacDonald, who was the naval officer in charge. The last British positions in the Heraklion garrison were abandoned at around 0100 on 29 May.

At 0300, HMS *Kimberley* and HMS *Imperial* were the last ships to leave the harbour – taking with them the entire rearguard. Except for the wounded in hospital near Knossos, who were too ill to move, not one member of the British force was left behind. The Greeks were never informed about the evacuation – and the main reasons for this were that there was not enough space on the ships to carry the Greek troops, and the British Command's fear that the participation of the Greeks would jeopardise the secrecy of the evacuation.

The Scots of the Black Watch were the rearguard during the evacuation. The oath given by Captain Alastair Hamilton that the Black Watch would leave Crete only when the snow on the top

3 Early in the afternoon, four companies of paratroopers – under *Hauptmann* Böhmer – were dropped near Gournes, to the east.

of Psilorites[4] had melted was not to be kept. Hamilton – the 'A' Coy commander – was killed by a mortar shell on East Hill on 28 May, just one day before the evacuation; so in an ironic twist, he upheld his oath, as his body was to remain on Crete. The war diary of the Black Watch recorded: '07:45 A. Coy HQ hit by mortar bomb. Captain J.G.A. Hamilton and One OR wounded… 07:55 Captain Hamilton died of wounds'.

Lieutenant Gerald Barry from the HQ Coy of the Black Watch wrote in his diary:

> In the night of 28 to 29 May, when I arrived at the Observation Post, I found Andy,[5] Keith and Andrew there. I was not prepared in the least for what Andy said. He told me that we were going to evacuate Crete that night, in fact in two and a half hours' time, and gave me some instructions about details of leaving. We were to start thinning our posts at midnight, and at 10 past, everyone was to be clear. We were to take all arms, and as much ammunition as we could, and each man must have two tins of bully beef and two packets of biscuits. I barely had time to get back, and send four platoon commanders to give out my orders when it was almost time to go. It was a quiet night, luckily, no shooting and we sent up the usual number of Verey lights. Bill[6] and I had something to eat that Riddock cooked us, and then I was so filthy dirty that I decided I must change my clothes even if I could not have a bath! The decision to leave Crete is a very distressing one, but apparently things have gone very badly at Souda and Maleme which are now untenable. Therefore we must go from Candia.[7] As a matter of fact, it seems that they have got us here too as they can land as many troops as they like outside our perimeter and choose their point of attack […]
>
> At midnight, I sent Bill on with the first party to RV at the Battalion's HQ cookhouse in A. Coy lines (poor Alastair was killed today by a mortar bomb), and I waited on the road till 12.15 to see the last of HQ. Coy pass. When our listening post was in, I followed on behind until we reached the RV and everybody was reported present. Then down the deep ravine where B. Coy was situated, until we reached the RAF encampment and the main road. The smell of dead bodies was very marked as we went down the ravine, and pools of blood were still lying about. On the main road we turned to the left, and along the aerodrome, hoping that the German machine guns and mortars would not open up on us en route. All was quiet, however, and it looked as if the 'Bosche'[8] had no idea we were going. As we passed the last bit of the aerodrome between the Greek barracks and Alikarnassos, the stench of decaying bodies was awful. This was where David Petherick had run loose with his tanks on the first day of the blitz, and hundreds had been killed. Leaving the aerodrome behind, we went towards Candia, and took a short route down to the beach and mole.
>
> A few Verey lights went up from the West Gate of the town and I was a little apprehensive lest the Germans should send a plane over the harbour and light a flare, which would disclose the warships alongside the Mole, which were to take us off. Luckily, this did not happen, and we found our way to the West Mole, at the end of which four destroyers were waiting for us. We 'crowded' into the *Kimberley*, a beautiful ship and quite new, and Bill and half the Coy went into another one. What a relief it was to get out of the beastly line we were holding, and find ourselves in a place where we could sit on a chair – without machine gun bullets hitting the outside walls, and where lights could be shown. It was 2 a.m. when we arrived, and parties of troops kept on running along the Mole for another three quarters of an hour. I went on the

4 Psilorites is the highest mountain on Crete – its peak covered with snow for the whole year.
5 Refers to the CO of the battalion, Major Pitcairn.
6 Refers to Lieutenant Bill Cochrane, who was the leader of the mortar platoon.
7 Candia was the medieval name for Heraklion.
8 The Germans.

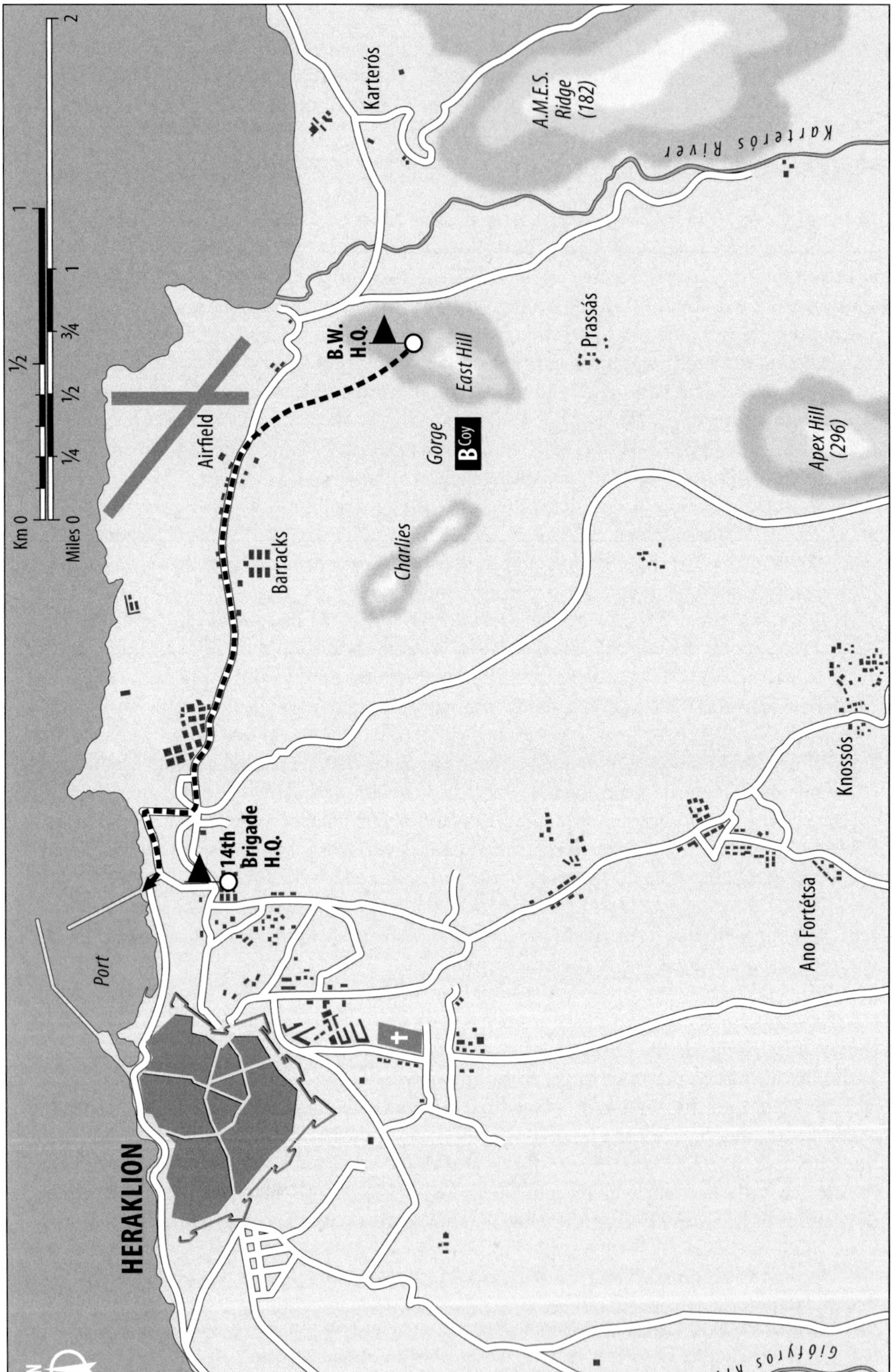


Map 7.1 The route that the HQ Company of the Black Watch followed during the evacuation of the Heraklion sector. (N. Panos, 2016)

> Bridge to advise the Captain when all the troops were on board, but this was impossible, as all sorts of odd people turned up and finally the Brigadier himself. They gave me a cup of hot tea, which after our long walk was very welcome. Finally, we left at 3 a.m., in total darkness, and were the last destroyer to leave.[9]

Patrick Leigh Fermor in a wartime picture. (Author's collection)

The only units that had not managed to escape were those of the Argyll & Sutherland Highlanders, which had remained in Tymbaki and Agioi Deka. A small British detachment was left in the village of Choudetsi, while the wounded in the field hospital in Villa Ariadne (next to Knossos) had also stayed.

One of the lucky ones who avoided captivity – literally at the last moment – was Alan William Delaforce Nicholls, who was an officer of the 2nd Battalion of the Leicestershire Regiment. Nicholls had been wounded during a counter-attack against the paratroopers south of the airfield; one of his men shot a paratrooper in close combat and the bullet passed through the German's body and ended up in Nicholls. He was sent to the field hospital in Villa Ariadne. When the battalion doctor learned about the evacuation, he managed to help Nicholls to escape and board a ship, so avoiding captivity.

Patrick Leigh Fermor was a lieutenant at the HQ of the 14th Infantry Brigade:

> I remember an incident which is very revealing of the character of the Cretans. On the last day of the battle, right after the sunset, the Allied troops began gathering at the port, ready to embark on the warships that were about to arrive at midnight to carry us to Egypt. It was well known that I could speak Greek so an aged Cretan (I'm now sure that he was Captain Satanas from Krousonas – I later knew him very well) with a white beard, wearing boots and having the local traditional hood on his head, approached with some of his men and asked me to be the interpreter in order to speak to the Brigadier. 'My child,' he said, putting his hand on the shoulder of Brigadier Chappel, 'we know very well that you are leaving tonight and we also know that one day you will come back and we all together will win the final battle. In the meantime here on Crete we will continue the struggle for freedom. So please leave us the weapons which are not essential for you.' The Brigadier was deeply moved and he gave the order to gather as many weapons as we could and gave them to the Cretans. That was a very emotional moment and while the ships were sailing into the darkness, I had a bitter feeling and a strong desire to return and help the Cretans in their struggle. As we all now know, the old Cretan was right.[10]

The evacuation nearly ended in disaster, when 45 minutes after leaving Heraklion, the *Imperial's* steering gear broke down as a result of a bomb's near-miss the previous day. The *Imperial* was unable to keep a steady course and could only move in circles, but there was no time to waste

9 C.E. Mamalakis, Ian Powys Archive.
10 From a speech given in the Vikelaia Library in Heraklion on 21 May 1994 – C.E. Mamalakis' archive.

A drawing made by Patrick Leigh Fermor depicting Brigadier Chappel's command post at the 'caves' in Katsabas, during preparations for the evacuation on 28 May. (C.E. Mamalakis' archive)

Crew members helping an officer on the deck of a damaged ship. ('The Mediterranean Fleet. Greece to Tripoli')

The 'caves' in a post-war picture, but in exactly the same condition as they were during the battle. (Courtesy of C.E. Mamalakis)

HMS *Dido* under attack. (AWM Archive)

if they wanted to pass the Kasos Strait under the cover of darkness. Her crew and the troops on board – including the men of Black Watch – re-embarked on HMS *Hotspur*, which rejoined the squadron just after sunrise with 900 men on board. Before joining the other ships, *Hotspur* had sunk *Imperial,* whose steering gear could not be repaired.

Dawn found the ships about one and a half hours behind schedule, and well within the range of the *Luftwaffe* squadrons based nearby at the Scarpanto Airfield. As the ships turned southwards to the Kasos Strait, pandemonium broke out, with continuous attacks by *Stukas* on the ships. At 0625, HMS *Hereward* was hit and fell out of line – unable to maintain the course and speed required to keep up with the formation. Having no other option than to continue with the remaining ships, Admiral Rawlings left *Hereward* to her fate. When last seen, *Hereward* was heading slowly for Crete (five miles away), with every gun in action against attacking aircraft. The majority of the crew and the troops on board survived and were taken prisoner after the ship was sunk.

In order to assist in the anti-aircraft defence of the ships, the troops on board mounted their Bren and Lewis machine guns in every available space on the outer decks. A direct hit on HMS *Decoy* forced the squadron to reduce speed to 25 knots – and later, one more hit on HMS *Orion* further reduced the squadron's speed to 21 knots. HMS *Dido* was hit on the forward turret and then the *Orion* was hit again and set on fire. A Ju-87 dropped a bomb on the 'A' (forward) turret of *Orion*, with the pilot of the *Stuka* making a suicidal attack. The Royal Navy tactic against dive-bombers' attacks was to steer the ship towards the aircraft in order to make its angle of descent steeper and steeper – forcing it to pull out of the dive early, and so spoiling the pilots' aim. In the case of *Orion*, the pilot appeared to be determined to hit his target at any cost – even by a *kamikaze*-like attack. At the last moment, the bomb was released, but the pilot failed to recover from the speed and angle of his descent and the *Stuka* dived into the sea after barely missing the bow of the ship. The bomb exploded with devastating effect upon the 'A' turret.

Captain G.R.B. Back, RN – Admiral Rawlings' flag captain aboard *Orion* – had been mortally wounded by a machine gun bullet at 0735. Just before he passed away, Captain Back regained

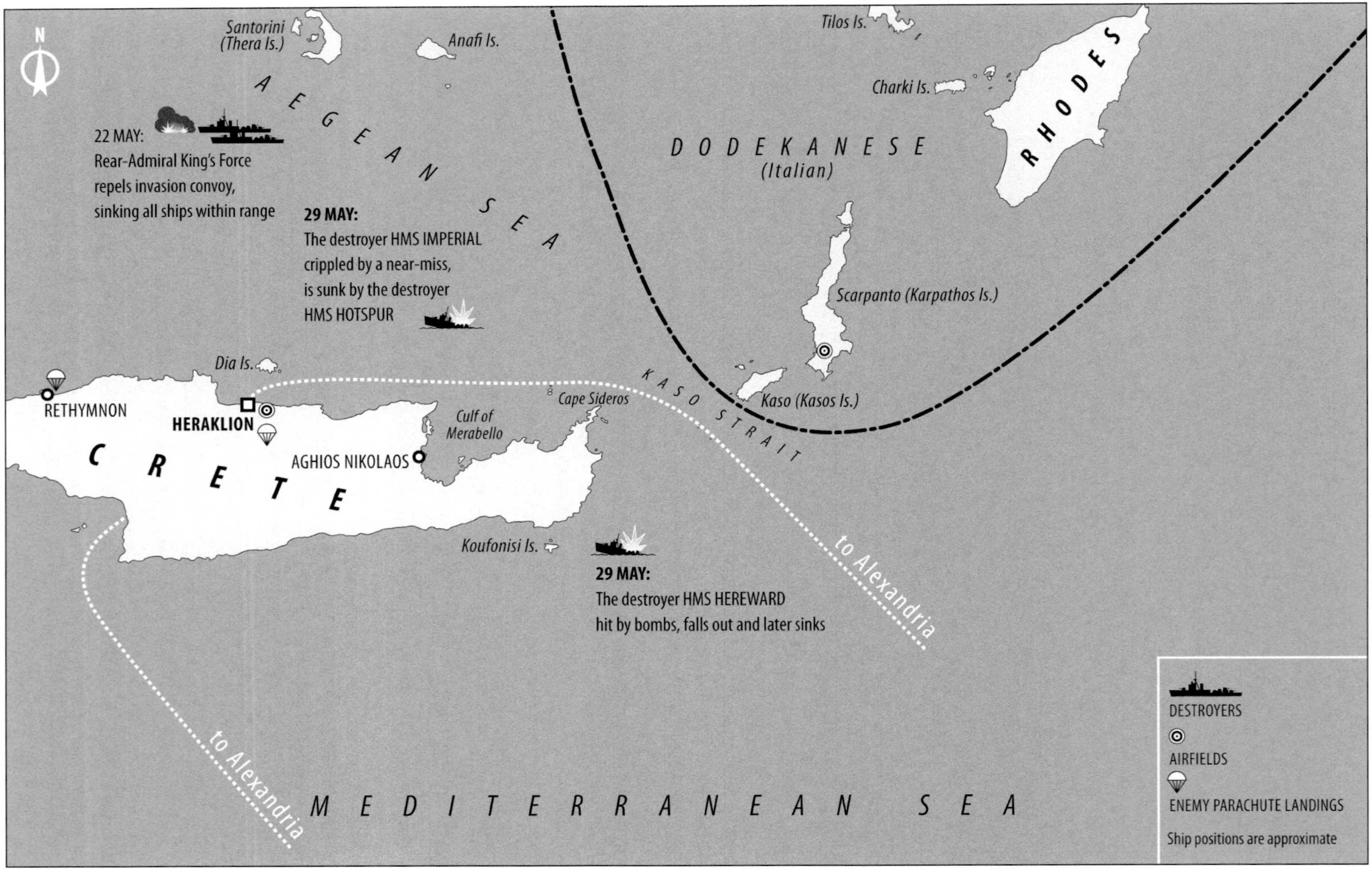


Map 7.2 This map shows the Royal Navy's ship losses during the evacuation of Heraklion on 29 May 1941. ('The Mediterranean Fleet. Greece to Tripoli'.)
Note: 'The Mediterranean Fleet. Greece to Tripoli', The Admiralty Account of Naval Operations April 1941 to January 1943, London. (N. Panos, 2016)

Spent shells piled around a turret on HMS *Perth*. (AWM Archive)

consciousness – and when he saw that his ship was again under attack, he shouted: "Keep steady!" When the attack was over, he said: "It's all right men – that one's over!" before dying. Commander T.C.T. Wynne assumed command of the ship.

A short pause in the attacks, which lasted for about 45 minutes, allowed the fire parties to extinguish the fires and the medical staff to take care of the wounded; then a new series of assaults started, with the Ju-87s attacking in waves. A formation of 11 Ju-87 *Stukas* attacked the *Orion*. One bomb penetrated the bridge and the main deck of the ship and exploded in the stokers' mess deck, which was crowded to capacity, with devastating results. There was a moment of darkness and then the flames began to glow, as all the compartments filled with smoke. Every available man – from both the crew and the troops – participated in the struggle to extinguish fires, transfer and take care of the wounded, remove the dead and restore communications among the various stations and parties on the ship. Since the 1st Lieutenant, who was normally in charge of damage control parties, had been killed, the CO of *Salvia* – Lieutenant Commander Miller[11] – assumed the responsibility of organising the fire parties and the rescuers in this maelstrom of flames and smoke between the decks. Miller kept up the spirits of the men – and thanks to his efforts, many of the wounded were saved.

*Orion* was literally out of control because of the violence of the impact. The compass, engine telegraphs and the steering gear were inoperative, while three of the five engineering officers were dead. The ship was being controlled by the emergency steering wheel in the stern, while orders from the bridge were relayed to the steering compartment by voice, via a long chain of men. Just before noon, the ship took a heavy list to starboard.

11 He was on board *Orion* acting as a pilot at Heraklion.

A destroyer loaded with troops from Crete enters the port of Alexandria.
('The Mediterranean Fleet. Greece to Tripoli')

HMS *Dido* enters the port of Alexandria, with Bill Lark playing his bagpipes on the bridge.
(Painting by Noel Syres; courtesy of the Black Watch Museum)

Commander (E) H.F. Atkins, RN – in charge of the engine room department – wrote:

> Was perhaps the least pleasant moment of a disagreeable day. The heavy list, lack of the light, ship not being under control due to destruction of steering gear, the fires still burning forward, filling the machinery space with smoke, and the fact that only one shaft was turning, tended to cause uneasiness. Every man remained at his post and went on with his job. The steaming registers were properly kept throughout.[12]

Though wounded himself, Admiral Rawlings brought his shattered squadron safely back to Alexandria at 2000. *Orion* had, by then, spent nearly all of her ammunition and fuel, with only two rounds of her main armament ammunition and 10 tonnes of oil fuel remaining.

The heavy cruisers were less agile than the destroyers – and despite their heavy armament, they took the most of the hits. Of the men on board HMS *Orion*, 260 were killed and 280 more were injured, while on HMS *Dido*, more than a hundred were killed. Of those who were killed during the evacuation to Egypt, 103 were men of the 2nd Battalion, Black Watch. When the ships arrived in Alexandria, piper Bill Lark decided to maintain his custom of playing his bagpipes at night, as he had done throughout the Battle for Heraklion, so he climbed onto the bridge of *Dido* and piped the ship into port, under searchlights that had pinpointed him.

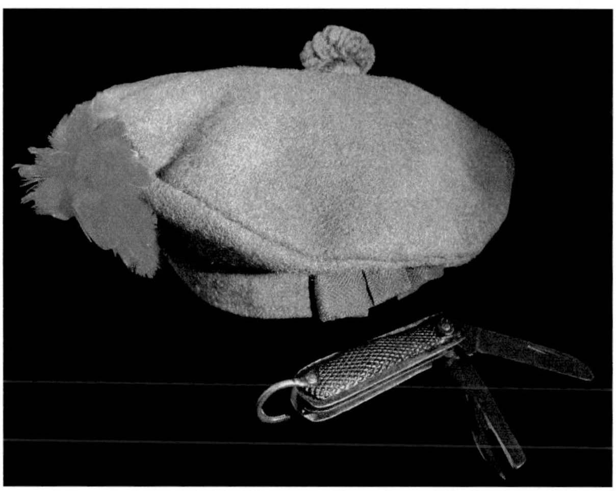

Bill Lark's tam o'shanter and pocket knife. (C.E. Mamalakis' collection)

Bill Lark playing his bagpipes in Heraklion on the sixtieth anniversary of the battle. (Courtesy of C.E. Mamalakis)

12 *The Mediterranean Fleet*, London, His Majesty's Stationery Office, 1944.

Paratroopers entering the Greek barracks (SEAP), south of the airfield. (Fritz Dahm & Hans-Georg Schnitzer, *Kreta – Sieg der Kühnsten*)

A sentry at the south-west gate of the barracks. (Fritz Dahm & Hans-Georg Schnitzer, *Kreta – Sieg der Kühnsten*)

*Oberst* Bruno Bräuer sitting at the entrance to the HQ of the Greek barracks, with *Oberleutnant Graf* von der Schulenburg (sitting on the right corner), *Hauptmann* Schirmer (next to Bräuer) and *Major* Walther (wearing the jump-smock and sitting next to Schirmer). (Author's archive)

The HQ of the Greek barracks (SEAP) and the same spot today, where the above picture was taken. (Courtesy of NikosValasiadis)

Paratroopers from the *10./FschJgRgt.1* – under *Oberleutnant* Egger (first row in the middle) – marching along Kalokairinou Street in the centre of Heraklion. (Fritz Dahm & Hans-Georg Schnitzer, *Kreta – Sieg der Kühnsten*)

The same street today. (Author's collection)

On the morning of 29 May, the paratroopers started moving to their positions for the attack. *Major* Walther's *I./FschJgRgt.1*, with the *II./FschJgRgt.2* (under *Hauptmann* Schirmer) and the remains of the *II./FschJgRgt.1* (under *Hauptmann* Burckhardt) had, as their main objective, the occupation of the airfield and later an attack on the town from the east. Immediately after sunrise, *Oberleutnant* Zimmermann's *7./FschJgRgt.2* advanced north of 'Apex Hill' towards the positions of the 2/4 Australian Battalion and the Black Watch. The paratroopers soon realised that there was no resistance to their advance and that the defenders' positions had been abandoned. The news was immediately reported via telephone to *Major* Walther, who quickly sent reconnaissance patrols to investigate exactly what was going on.

As the paratroopers approached the British positions, they were expecting at any moment the usual heavy gun fire, but nothing happened. Walther ordered a general advance of the battalion, and soon the Germans were walking among deserted defensive positions and trenches, destroyed vehicles and abandoned ammunition and supplies. The *I./FschJgRgt.1* secured the airfield and established itself at the Greek barracks, south of the airfield. A paratrooper stepped on a mine near the airfield – injuring 10 men; these were the last German losses of the Battle for Heraklion. The Germans immediately started the grim task of searching for the wounded left on the battlefield and burying the dead who lay spread all over the area.

Bernd Bosshammer had been wounded on the first day of the battle and was then left in a stable near the British positions, along with other wounded paratroopers. He described the last two days of the battle in his diary:

> 28. May 1941: The night is cold. At 3.40 a.m. a white flare is fired. For a few seconds there is light in our barn. Gulden has gone out to bring water after repairing the hole in the canister. He comes back at 7.00 a.m. (after almost three and a half hours) and brings water along with some field dressings. I think of my brother Willi, and I wonder if he thinks of me also. At 10.00 a.m. everything is dead silent. The whistle of the wind through the boards, the chirping of birds and the buzzing of the fly sounds like sweet music in this wretched war. These cannot bomb or shoot you. This is real life. I must hold even if my strength is abandoning me. I make a makeshift cross and write on it the name "Hans Fiedler *5./ Fallsch. Jg. Rgt. 1*, fallen on 20.5.1941". I am anxious to put the cross next to Fiedler so that his corpse can be identified. On a board I write our names, Bosshammer, Gulden and Rose and I make a cross without writing the date of death on it.
>
> 11.30 a.m. we are alarmed by aircraft engines but we can see nothing. A single plane comes over and drops two bombs on the airfield or in the nearby area. At 16.00 we again hear rifle and cannon fire around the stable. I find a cigarette. Rose is asleep, and I give it to Gulden. We only have 8 matches left and we are very careful with them. We cannot stand this situation for long, since we have all been ill during the last few days. It is likely our stomachs cannot cope with the dirty water that we drink. Between 17.00 and 18.00 we hear heavy bombardment on the northwestern slope and probably on the airfield, but we cannot see anything. German planes bomb the enemy and our stable is shaking and another part of the roof collapses. Everything is shaking. A big piece of wood hits Rose on the head and he moans… Later, it is quiet, the night falls, no one says a word. We get no more water. There are only two cups available for each one of us. I take the water canteen with me and only in an emergency will a gulp be served. I do not sleep at night because Rose is hallucinating incessantly and I'm afraid that he will take the three pistols that I have and he will shoot all of us.
>
> 29.05.1941: In the night we hear English voices, very close to us, probably coming from the defensive positions on the hill slope [the east slope of East Hill]. We expect to be captured any moment but it is still very dark. I hold my gun, and I'm ready to fire, since we do not want to give up so easily. Hopefully we will meet no partisans which is the worst that could happen to

us. We have a cup of water for three men meaning only one big gulp for each one of us. I fall asleep easily and wake up only at Rose's cries. Meanwhile it is dawn. I hear voices and sounds of movement outside.

9.20 a.m. The Rescue: Through a hole, I see two shirtless men coming, holding machine-guns and pistols. I hear their voices but I cannot understand whether they are Germans or English. I take my gun and I give the other one to Gulden. I see on one of the approaching men the Knight's Cross on his bare upper body. I cry, 'Germans here!' but it was actually rather a whisper. I try hard but the words come out so weakly and softly. The men are only five metres away and I cry again, 'Germans here!' The two men approach carefully. I take off a board. They now point the weapons down and come with quick steps. *Oberjäger* Racho from *2Kp./1* and *Oberleutnant* Alfred Schwarzmann from *8Kp./1* come and save us. Some medics then carry us to the field hospital [at the Galazia Poulia Tavern] and lay us on an old table. Meanwhile, it is already 11.00 a.m. and we see a doctor for the first time. *Oberarzt* Bräuer puts me on a stretcher and gives me two injections. He cleans the wound and scrapes out the gangrenous flesh. I also get morphine.

At 12.30 p.m. I'm transferred in a truck to the airfield where I also get an injection for my high fever, and I realize that the battle for Crete is over. The enemy has left the island. We have been saved.

At 17.50 I fly in a Ju-52 to Athens and I'm asleep during the flight. Rose and Gulden are not there. At 19.30 we meet in Olympia Hospital in Athens[...] At 24.20 I get a general anaesthetic, and I realize that they want to cut my left leg off completely. I scream and rage, threatening to shoot them with my pistol, which I still have with me. They put me in a room where a medic takes pity on me. I tell him my story and he puts my leg in a cast and promises to help ensure that I will soon further recover. I still cannot believe it though. I have been stripped of my uniform, washed and lie wrapped in a cloth. I come to a room, with about 20 beds, but I still have my pistol, a Belgian FN which I brought from Holland on 10 May 1940. I hide the pistol in my bed.[13]

The bitter fighting for Heraklion was finally over. Now it was time for all sides to regroup and consider the new circumstances that the battle had brought about.

13 B. Bosshammer's war diary – BDF e.v. Archiv, Freiburg/Breisgau.

# 8

# After the Battle

On 29 May, the paratroopers entered Heraklion at last – accomplishing their mission and bringing to an end the battle in the Heraklion sector. The men who had fought so hard to capture the town were now surrounded by scenes of devastation.

Dr Günther Müller was assigned the task of collecting and evacuating the wounded. He described the route from the airfield to the town and then to Knossos, where a British field hospital full of Allied and German wounded was found:

> [...] For the first time I drive towards the city. The road is full of barricades and obstacles constructed from rocks and sandbags. I manoeuvre between the barricades. The town can be seen from on a hill, far off. The road goes over an old bridge which I cross, fearing its probable collapse, then I continue on the dirt road which climbs steeply up the hill; we see water flowing, most probably coming from the town's broken main water pipe. We see Heraklion very clearly from the hill. High fortress-like walls surround the centre of the town. The gates look as if they were built in the Middle Ages. To the north, the port's long mole extends out to the sea. Through winding, narrow streets we reach a big square. Everything looks devastated. Blocks of houses have been demolished and the debris is stacked in big piles on the road. It is impossible to drive the truck through it all. I manoeuvre and try to find another passage. The same scenes of devastation prevail here as well. Huge bomb craters, demolished buildings, broken electricity poles, beds and furniture – all these create unbelievable mess and confusion. The town looks deserted. Only dogs and cats are wandering around. Each time a plane passes over, they run to take cover. The bombing must have been terrible. Our doctor sees a policeman and stops him. It takes a long time to try unsuccessfully to explain to the policeman what we want and he finally understood only when a medic showed him the red cross on his armband. The policeman then jumped onto the truck and led us to a field hospital which had been the residence of an English lord.[1] It was surrounded by palm and olive trees and other nearby buildings. German, English and Greek wounded are lying in tents and on stretchers.[2]

1 Villa Ariadne, next to Knossos, was the residence of Sir Arthur Evans – a British archaeologist. Evans discovered and excavated the Minoan Palace of Knossos at the beginning of the 20th century. He built his residence near the site of Knossos. Later, this building was associated with other British archaeologists such as John Pendlebury and Tom Dunbabin, who during the war, became officers of the SOE and saw action in Crete. This same building was also the residence of the German commander of Crete during the German occupation of the island. It was nearby to the spot where *General* Kreipe was kidnapped by the Cretan Resistance (under Patrick Leigh Fermor).

2 G. Müller & F. Scheuering, *Sprung über Kreta*, pp.116-120.

Wounded paratroopers lying in a tent at the British field hospital, situated in the yard of Villa Ariadne in Knossos. (G. Müller & F. Scheuering, *Sprung über Kreta*)

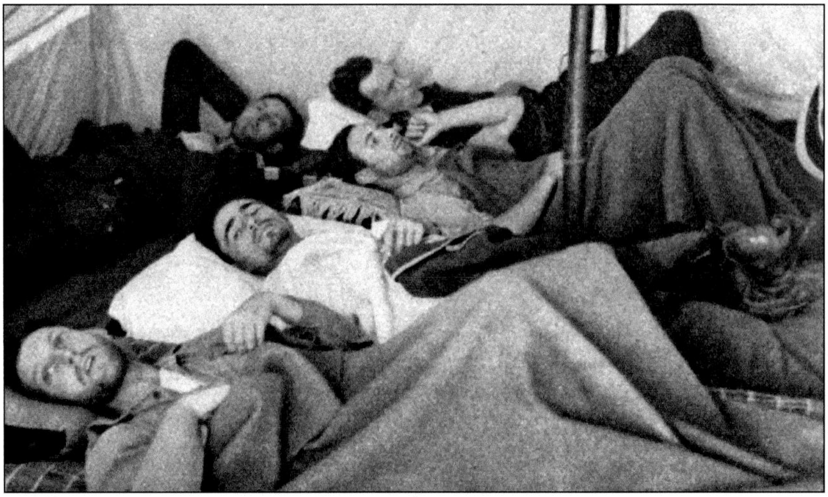

The residence of Sir Arthur Evans, also known as 'Villa Ariadne', as it is today. (Author's collection)

The building which housed the British field hospital in the yard of Villa Ariadne. (Author's collection)

More than 70 years after the battle, remains from the field hospital are still discovered in the yard of Villa Ariadne. (Author's collection)

The condition of the town, as described by Dr Günther Müller, is vividly depicted in the photographs that he took on his journey.

Platia Strata, which was Heraklion's main street (now called Kalokairinou Street), bombed and devastated. (G. Müller & F. Scheuering, *Sprung über Kreta*)

The same place in Kalokairinou Street today. (Author's collection)

Apostolos Zeimbekis, a young resident of Heraklion during the battle, recalled:

During the morning of 29 May, after I left Makasi[3] with a soldier from Chania who had taken off his uniform and was in civilian clothes, we went outside the town walls. We walked along the walls and after walking through the fields we entered Heraklion through Kainourgia Porta [South Gate]. There a bomb had hit the side of the wall and a man had been killed. It was the first time in my life that I had seen a dead man. We reached Valide Tzami through Evans Street and then walked down Market Street to Liontaria [Lion] Square.

From the middle of Market Street and beyond, as far as Meintani,[4] German paratroopers were sitting on the pavements on both sides of the street and resting after the battle. One of the paratroopers called to the soldier who was with me and asked for his sunglasses which the paratrooper took and put on.

As soon as we arrived at the end of Market Street, at the opposite corner right in front of the Grifizas Building, we saw a small group of paratroopers sitting on the pavement. They had a small gun with them, its barrel pointing towards Kalokairinou Street.

We moved further to Katehaki Street where just before the corner of Katehaki and Loukareos Streets was a destroyed shoe shop. We got into the shop and each of us took a very nice pair of shoes. I remember that on the shop this sign was written: '*Saloustros*'.[5]

3 'Makasi' is the term for a gallery in Heraklion's Venetian walls.
4 The centre of the town.
5 C.E. Mamalakis' archive.

The devastation in the centre of the town. (Author's collection)

Paratroopers from the *III./FschJgRgt.1* and *II./FschJgRgt.2* sitting near the corner of 25th of August and Kalokairinou Streets, exactly as A. Zeimbekis describes. Some of the paratroopers wear hats and sunglasses taken from deserted shops in the town centre. (Courtesy of Shaun Winkler)

Soon after the seizure of Heraklion – and exhausted from the continuous fighting – paratroopers rest at the corner of Kalokairinou and 25th of August Streets in the centre of town. At the far left in the background is 'Liontaria' Square, while on the right is an anti-tank gun of the *14./FschJgRgt.1* pointing towards Kalokairinou Street, exactly as described by A. Zeimbekis. (Courtesy of Dimitris Skartsilakis)

The same spot today. (Author's collection)

The same scene, in a picture taken from a rooftop. (Author's collection)

Dr Alfred Eiben, a *stabsartz* from *FschJgRgt.1*, described his entry into the town on 29 May:

> [...] We are heading to the Greek Hospital.[6] It is difficult to find because most of the streets are blocked by debris from the bombing. At the hospital we discover about 40 wounded paratroopers and they are really happy to see us. They have spent some terrible days there. The hospital suffered a lot from the bombing. I found once again *Oberleutnant* Fischer who I was not able to evacuate from the town some days ago.[7] The wounded have been treated extremely well by an old Greek doctor[8] and his German wife. We now can promise our comrades that they will be transferred to a better hospital on the mainland of Greece where they will have the best treatment.[9]

Greek doctor Alexandros Stefanidis, who cared for the wounded in Pananion Hospital during the battle, described the last day of the battle:

> During the night of 28 to 29 May, surprisingly we didn't hear any bombing and a strange calm prevailed in the deserted town. Four doctors, Nicolaos Chasapes with his German wife, Frangisk, Stylianos Miliaras who was the Director of the Hospital, Emmanuel Chatzidakis, and I, felt compassion for the badly wounded, among them many Germans, so we stayed

6 Pananion Hospital, near Chanioporta.

7 *Oberleutnant* Fischer had been left wounded in the town when the paratroopers were forced to withdraw on the evening of 21 May. Fischer was killed two years later on the Eastern Front.

8 Dr Nicolaos Chasapes.

9 C. Hatjipateras & M. Fafalios, *Kriti 1941 Martyries*, p.365.

in the hospital with them despite being unable to do much to help them since the hospital had been devastated by the bombing.

So we spent a relatively calm night. In the morning Director Stylianos Miliaras was informed that the town had been occupied by the Germans. He called us to his office in order to meet the Germans who were coming to see their wounded. As we looked from the windows of the hospital we soon saw that the German flag had been raised on the highest point of the Agios Minas Cathedral, next to the cross.

You can imagine how moved we were to realise that the occupation of our homeland, Crete, had begun despite the resistance of the Cretan people.

After a while German officers appeared holding flowers in their hands and they immediately asked to see the wounded paratroopers whom they embraced and gave flowers. When the wounded men saw their comrades they cheered up and those who could immediately put on their uniforms. Their attitude changed since they were victorious at last; they lost the miserable expressions they had displayed previously, as defeated prisoners.

*Stabsartz* Alfred Eiben. (Author's collection)

A very tall German officer, named Christian, was the senior doctor. He entered the hospital director's office and asked in a rather arrogant manner for the hospital doctors to be presented to him. He then sat in the director's chair and immediately asked the German-speaking Doctor Chasapes to assume the hospital director's duties, as well as the duties of the Medical Director for Heraklion district. He would have [the] German title of *Stadt-Artz*. At the same time he ordered all Heraklion's doctors to be presented to him within the next two days. He then said that he was very satisfied with the treatment that the doctors provided to him and to the rest of the wounded Germans. He asked Chasapes to send a letter to the Greek Ministry, reporting that the doctors in the hospital had done much more than their duty dictated. He shook our hands while maintaining the strict expression of a conqueror and then he left.[10]

It was a miracle that the Agios Minas Cathedral had avoided complete destruction, despite the heavy *Luftwaffe* bombardment.

E. Malagardis described the scene around the cathedral on 2 June 1941 and relates a strange story – the like of which can only occur during a war:

I crossed Kalokairinou Street and reached the Agios Minas Cathedral. This very big church was standing virtually intact with only a few windows broken. A bomb had exploded in the yard, close to the southwest corner of the church, leaving only a small crater. Another very big bomb, unexploded, was lying next to the northwest corner of the church less than a metre from the wall. This would have been a 250 kg or larger bomb.

10 A.G. Stefanidis, 'Memoirs of my Life', Athens, 1992.

The Pananion Hospital before the war. (Author's collection)

The deserted Pananion Hospital today. (Author's collection)

I saw the verger and asked him if the church had suffered serious damage. He answered that Agios Minas [Saint Minas] had performed another miracle and that was why there was almost no damage. I asked him again what he meant exactly and he told me to ask the church-warden, who was standing at the entrance. The church-warden explained that straight after the end of the battle, a German *Luftwaffe* officer had come to the church and was asking about the history of the church and the Saint. When he was asked why he was so interested in such information, he answered that the church was in the sector of the town that he had bombed and that every time he tried to drop his bombs in this area, his hands shook and he couldn't pull the handle and release the bombs at the right moment. This he considered was due to the intervention of the Saint.[11]

11 C.E. Mamalakis' archive.

The area around the cathedral, with buildings devastated by the bombing. (Courtesy of Shaun Winkler)

The north side of the cathedral, next to which the big unexploded bomb had landed. At this exact spot, a model of the bomb has been placed to commemorate the incident and the bombardment of the church. (Author's collection)

Photographs of the town straight after the battle, as well as German accounts, confirm the magnitude of the devastation. Most of the residents fled to the countryside and the nearby villages, while those who stayed in the town sheltered inside the old tunnels of the Venetian walls and fortifications.

On the morning of 29 May, the Greeks realised that the British had evacuated Heraklion. Consequently, Major General Linardakis – lacking men and supplies – decided to negotiate with the Germans and stop fighting. For this reason, Linardakis sent Major Tsagkarakis to Heraklion in order to contact the Germans and end the bombing of the town and the nearby villages. That evening, Tsagkarakis went to the 43rd Greek Infantry Regiment barracks, next to the airfield, where the German HQ had been established. He proposed a truce under the same conditions imposed on the rest of Greece. Bräuer rejected Tsagkarakis' proposal and demanded the unconditional surrender of Greek forces – threatening a continuation of the bombing and an attack on Greek units by German forces, which would be reinforced by units from Rethymnon. Tsagkarakis asked for a halt to the bombing at least, and then returned to Major General Linardakis and briefed him on the outcome of the meeting with the Germans. Linardakis – realising that he had no other option – finally accepted the unconditional surrender and, at 2215, issued the relevant orders to all Military and *Gendarmerie* Commands in Heraklion and Lasithi (East Crete). Only those men guarding Italian prisoners retained their arms and positions until the handover of the Italians to the Germans.

On 31 May, Linardakis signed the surrender document and asked the Germans to assume responsibility for supplying food to the thousand Greek soldiers from mainland Greece who were still on Crete; local troops had already left their units and returned home. In the evening, *Oberst* Wittman's force – accompanied by mountain troops (*gebirgsjägers*) – arrived in Heraklion directly from Rethymnon. They then continued their move towards Ierapetra (east) in order to join the Italians. After being defeated by the Greeks in northern Greece, Italian forces had finally conducted an amphibious landing on Crete, but only after the campaign had been won. They had not been involved in any fighting, but were well prepared for a parade and a celebration.

The end of the fighting now presented the Germans with an unpleasant duty: the collection and identification of their dead comrades, who were scattered all over the drop zones and the battlefield.

Erich Reinhardt from the *7./FschJgRgt.1* described the work:

> On 29 May 1941 we saw the full extent of the tragedy that had occurred around the airfield. Hundreds of dead German paratroopers were strewn around. For the first time in my life I saw the shallow provisional graves dug in a hurry by the British, with the small legend 'Unknown German soldier killed in action.' Our unforgettable company commander, *Oberleutnant* Götte, met his end at the edge of the town.[12] Perhaps he had attempted to form a pocket of resistance there. There was a disgusting stench of decomposition in the heat and for the first time I was made aware of the insanity of war. What is heroism really?[13]

The Germans devoted 30 May entirely to the collection and burial of the dead. Dr Günther Müller described what he witnessed:

> No one was forgotten. A cross in the shape of the Iron Cross along with the helmet of the dead was placed on each grave, which was marked with stones around the small hump of the grave.

12 The area of Katsabas - Nea Alikarnassos.

13 E. Reinhardt, 'Memoirs of a Former German Paratrooper', David Lenk Archive.

To honour all the dead in the area of the fiercest fighting, a hole was drilled in the rock and a cross, made from a ship's mast and 12 metres high, was placed. It looks away over the valley and the hills as far as the sea. Everywhere there are dead comrades. When the sun sets the inscription on the cross shines on the Cretan landscape: '*DEN TOTEN KAMERADEN I FALLSCHIRMJÄGER RGT. 1, 20-29 MAI 1941*'. ('*For the Dead Comrades – I Fallschirmjäger Regiment 1, 20-29 May 1941*'.)[14]

The large cross which was placed on the top of Agios Ioannis Hill (East Hill) as a memorial to the dead of the 1st *Fallschirmjäger* Regiment. (Courtesy of Dimitris Skartsilakis)

The same spot today, with the cross removed. (Author's collection)

14 Müller & Scheuering, p.144.

The foundations of the large cross, with the hole still visible on the ground. (Author's collection)

The initial makeshift grave of *Oberleutnant* Wolfgang *Graf* von Blücher at the exact spot where he was killed, as it was in 1941 (left), and one of the stones that was placed around the grave (right), as it was found at the same spot in 2013 (marked on the original picture with a circle). (Author's collection and archive)

Items found at Wolfgang *Graf* von Blücher's first grave on the battlefield (right). Among them are shards of pottery which were placed at the base of the cross, as are visible in the period picture (left). Another interesting discovery from the grave is a screw, which most probably came from the British wooden ammunition crate that was used to construct the first cross placed on the grave. (Author's collection and archive)

The dead paratroopers remained buried in their makeshift graves on the battlefield for more than a year until the German war cemetery was built in Atsalenios, south of Heraklion. On the southern side of the cemetery, an imposing memorial – decorated with a *fallschirmjäger* eagle – was erected and wreath-laying ceremonies took place there during the period of the German occupation of the island. On each grave was a cross, on which rested a helmet.

*General* Bruno Bräuer, then commandant of the island of Crete, during a wreath-laying ceremony at the memorial in the cemetery in 1943. (Courtesy of Adrian Nisbett)

The graves of Wolfgang and Hans Joachim von Blücher at the cemetery. (Courtesy of Shaun Winkler)

A close-up view of some of the graves at the Heraklion War Cemetery. (Courtesy of Shaun Winkler)

The dead were exhumed during 1959-1960 and the remains collected in plastic boxes. These were stored at the Asy Gonia Monastery, near Rethymnon, before finally being transferred to and buried at the Maleme War Cemetery. The location of the Heraklion War Cemetery is now the local Atsalenios club's football pitch.

Stefanos Kypriotakis, who is a local resident, recalled the old cemetery:

> I remember that I used to climb on this huge memorial, which was made of stone, and there was an eagle depicted on it. This memorial disappeared when the dead were exhumed from the cemetery, but I do not know what exactly happened[15] to it. During the exhumation of the dead, in 1959-1960, I remember that all the personal belongings [of the dead] like cigarette cases, wallets and other items were collected and gathered by the German authorities, while other items were left in the graves. I remember that we found gravity knifes, bayonets, cartridges and lots of other things. The dead were buried exactly as they were found on the battlefield – wearing their uniforms and their field gear – and in many cases, were buried with their weapons. I remember that my uncle had gathered many helmets and weapons in his backyard, and what was really strange was that live ammunition and even hand grenades were found with the dead when they were exhumed 20 years after the battle. Everything that they had been carrying with them when they were killed was left in their pockets and in their gear. Many Luger pistols were also found in the graves. At the entrance to the cemetery was a gate made of stone and there – in a glass bottle – were stored the plans of the cemetery. Using those plans, the Germans were able to identify each grave, since most of the wooden crosses had been destroyed during 20 years since the battle. It was really a pity for those young men, most of them aged 19 or 20, to meet such an end, but that's how war is.[16]

The German war cemetery in the Atsalenios area of Heraklion during the war. (Courtesy of Rolf Marcus: http://www.kreta-wiki.de/wiki/Photos_von_Rolf_Marcus)

15 According to accounts from other residents of the area, the memorial was demolished with explosives one night.

16 Interview with the author in Heraklion, 2014.

The cemetery in Atsalenios in 1960, during the exhumation and transfer of the remains. In the years after the war, the cemetery was not maintained and the wooden crosses gradually disintegrated. Even the stones paving the main avenue were used by the locals for building the surrounding roads. The helmets that were left on the graves were later collected and scrapped or buried. (BDF e.v. Archiv, Freiburg/Breisgau)

Gravity knives (*kappmesser*), cartridges and a K-98 rifle that were found at the cemetery during the exhumation of the remains in 1960. The rocks are also from the cemetery and the memorial. (Author's collection)

As seen in this picture taken in the 1960s, rocks and other construction materials from the cemetery were used by the locals to build fences and other structures. (Author's collection)

The same fence today, where identifiable stones from the cemetery are still present. (Author's collection)

Greek prisoners after the battle, at the barracks of the 43rd Greek Infantry Regiment, next to the airfield. (Courtesy of Shaun Winkler)

On 31 May, the captured Greek units were transferred to Peza, where they remained until 1 July. Two Greek companies were later moved to Heraklion, while the remaining Greek units were transferred to Messara (in the middle of the island). Most of the Greek officers stayed in Peza, from where on 9 June they were transferred by car to POW camps (formerly children's summer camps) in Maleme and Chania. Between June and November, Greek officers and soldiers were gradually discharged and transported to the Greek mainland.

Lieutenant Colonel Antonios Beteinakis wrote in his diary:

> 29/5–8/6/1941: Throughout these days after the armistice we remained in captivity in Archanes, where I had the opportunity to look after my farm and my fields. Two German companies occupied Archanes and settled in at the primary school building and in the nearby houses.
>
> 9/6/41: All 41 officers were transferred by car to Chania. We marched for three hours all the way from Souda to Galatas carrying our belongings on our shoulders, as did the General[17] himself. At around 23:00 on 9-6-41 we arrived at the Children's Summer Camp at the beach near Galatas where we passed the night in a field. Our condition was pitiable.
>
> 10/6/41: We were transferred to the Greek POW camp where we settled into tents. Seven officers were accommodated in the General's tent: General Linardakis, Lt. Colonel Beteinakis, Major Tsagkarakis, Major Doulbiotis, Major Kountakis, Captain Kindylakis, Captain Kisonas. The food was very limited. We received a very small amount of bread and food, just enough to stay alive and survive in this hell-hole of captivity. It would not have been possible to survive had I not brought some bread and cheese with me from my home in Archanes [...]

17 General Linardakis.

> 13-6-41: [...] The German authorities are really angry with the Cretan soldiers and officers, suggesting that we had not acted according to convention in fighting against our country's enemy. Some incidents of mistreatment of Germans by Greeks, had nothing to do with regular army personnel. I know this for sure since no such incident committed by soldiers came to my knowledge. I'm very proud to say that despite the fact that many of my friends and relatives were killed during the battle, both officers and soldiers, and despite incidents of mistreatment of civilians by German soldiers that I saw, I provided medical treatment to the enemy wounded and prisoners. I am confident that I fought with bravery and loyalty for my country, behaving as a civilised human being towards my enemies. Fighting with bravery and respecting the rights of enemy prisoners is characteristic of brave souls [...]
>
> 27-9-41: Today we arrived at Piraeus after a three day trip by ship from Souda. We were transferred to the POW camp at Kokkinia where we were released from captivity. I went to Athens where I received also my salary for September.[18]

Among the prisoners who were transferred to the former summer camps in Chania was Lieutenant Theodoros Kallinos:

> [...] When I arrived at the camp, my main goal was to find a way to escape. I became friendly with a Greek doctor who was going to Chania twice a week and he began taking me with him as an assistant.
>
> In Chania I tried to link up with people who could help me flee from the island, but my efforts were in vain. One day the Germans asked the prisoners to state if they were students. Thinking that fortune aids those who dare, I decided to state that I was a student. Along with my friends, Diamantidis and Giannoudis, we left Souda by ship and after a two-day journey we arrived in Piraeus [Athens] on 16 August 1941. I then went to my family in Tyrnavos and later I was accepted into the Mechanical Engineering Department of the Polytechnic University of Athens. There I was able to join the national Resistance and I abandoned my studies and left for the mountains to fight against the Germans.[19]

The paratroopers also returned to their camps in Germany, where they were welcomed as heroes with parades and celebrations. Most of them took leave in order to rest and visit their families, but the return was not pleasant for all of them.

Gerhard Broder describes:

> We fly back to Greece where *Hauptfeldwebel* Vogler is again in command and we continue to Salonika. After a seven day trip by train we arrive in Stendal. On 25 June 1941 I write to my mother: "We have just arrived a few hours ago by train from Salonika. Unfortunately I couldn't find a post office until now. I will not be at all happy until I have news of Heini (my younger brother who jumped in the Maleme sector). Tonight we will sleep on a bed for the first time in eight weeks. If you find an opportunity to send a letter, write to the following address: R. Jacob, Stendal, Priesterstr. 9."
>
> My worries are confirmed. My only brother jumped over Maleme on the morning of 20 May. Dr. Weitzel informs me that he is dead. He has personally written a letter to inform us

18 A. Beteinakis, *Diary of Antonios Beteinakis in Captivity*, Hellenic Army General Staff, Army History Directorate.

19 Interview with the author, April 2012.

The makeshift grave of *Oberjäger* H. Broder on the battlefield. (Courtesy of Gerhard Broder)

but the news doesn't end with the usual greetings. Besides my great sadness, the fact that my brother was killed right after the jump on 20 May depresses me terribly. I do not believe a word about his death having occurred during an attack on enemy trenches. No, the unit was shot at during landing and never had a chance to fight. They could not even retrieve their weapons. The men were buried exactly where they were killed. On the picture of his grave I see no evidence of digging but only a loose stone cover. He must have bled to death along with many of his comrades. The doctor begins his letter with the words: "Since all officers are dead..." I understand that their participation in the battle was no more than a defenceless parachute descent into an orgy of gunfire. Was that necessary? I'm critical. An analytical and sceptical train of thought runs deep in me.

At home I find my mother in unspeakable misery and abysmal grief. This grief is deepened even more by her son's farewell letter. Full of forebodings of death, he speaks with enthusiasm and devotion for the motherland: "I write this letter with the hope that it will never reach you. If it does then try to be strong and calm because in that way you will honour the dead appropriately...We know that death stands behind us. Be proud of us. I thank you for my wonderful childhood. I had a beautiful life and I had a beautiful death also..."

Only at his signature did I see expressed all the sadness of a young man: "Dear, dear mother! Your Heini."[20]

Paratrooper Ernst H. Simon from the *13./FschJgRgt.1* told of his experiences after the fighting:

The next few days after the battle pass with the digging of graves for fallen comrades of our company and with normal service routine at the airfield, where the Ju-52s bring in supplies and evacuate the wounded. We have the opportunity to post a letter for the first time in two months. *General* Löhr and *General* Jeschonnek come and visit us in their white He-111.

The regiment is fully dressed in English tropical uniforms, a decision dictated by the daytime heat. In the areas vacated by the British and in often hastily destroyed catering stores we find large amounts of pristine supplies. In the ruins of the town we also find thousands of boxes of raisins. However, nobody has the appetite to eat since our stomachs have suffered

20 G. Broder, *Guerre Mondiale Contre Moi*, p.100.

*Oberjäger* Heinrich Broder (27 November 1917, Köln-20 May 1941, Maleme, Crete). (Courtesy of Gerhard Broder)

The return to Germany and the paratroopers' parade. (Courtesy of Jose Ramon Artaza Ivañez)

> quite a lot from the poor quality of the water that we drank during the days of the battle. Many cases of dysentery have already occurred.
>
> On 10 June, the *FjR 1* flies back to the mainland of Greece and the *13./1* Company moves to Tanagra. Almost all of us sleep during the flight. At Tanagra airfield our trucks wait, laden with sacks of mail and parcels [...]
>
> [...] The journey via Vienna, Ostrava, Breslau and Berlin finally ends in Stendal where we arrive at dawn. We are all awarded the Iron Cross 2nd Class but we also begin rehearsals for the big victory parade in the city. Since my shoulder wound is not healed yet, I do not have to participate. Our regimental commander, *Oberst* Bräuer makes his famous address to the regiment: "You are now going on leave. You have recovered from the battle and you should not discuss the operation too fully, which was really shit. I know that myself."
>
> After all this, it is now July and we go home on leave every fortnight. I visit my parents and relatives again in Polaun, Morebenstern and Reichenberg. After returning from leave I'm posted as an instructor under the command of *Leutnant* von Bülow and *Oberfeldwebel* Waide.[21]

Other paratroopers had to spend a long time in hospital recovering from their wounds.

Bernd Bosshammer wrote in his diary:

> On 4 June 1941, at the hospital in Vienna, I found myself in a corridor waiting to be transferred to a room. I saw a nurse helping an *Oberleutnant* with bandages on his head and over his eyes, move towards the stairs. I recognized my company commander, Harry Herrmann. I called him and he answered: "My dear boy, Bosshammer, what has happened to you?" I told him about my condition and he promised to help me. A doctor came and took me to a room right below the room where *Oberleutnant* Herrmann, *Leutnant Freiherr* von Berlepsch and *Leutnant* Fischer were. They gave me a wooden pole with which to hit the ceiling in case I needed something. They put me in a new splint with special bandages. They also put over my left knee a cable hanging on a hook, the other end of which was attached to a weight to pull my leg in the right position. I stayed like that for six and a half months [...]
>
> [...] At the hospital in Vienna Marga Baroness von Suttner visited me. She was the mother of *Gefreiter* von Suttner who jumped from the plane right in front of me but he was found later shot straight through the heart, probably while he was still at the door of the plane [...]
>
> *Stabsartz* Dr Schmidt took a lot of care with my treatment. Just before Christmas I was freed from the splint and received a leg-pelvic plaster covering my body from the foot to the breast. Harry Herrmann, Fischer and von Berlepsch had since been released from the hospital and had returned to service.[22]

Almost 70 years after the battle, David Hutton still had some unfinished business from his wartime service. In 1941, Corporal Hutton's stepmother, Daisy, posted a letter which was dispatched via the Field Post Office in Egypt. Daisy was unaware that David had been wounded and captured by the Germans, and was in hospital with shrapnel peppering his body. He was held as a prisoner of war for four years, in camps in Poland and Czechoslovakia.

21 E.H. Simon, BDF e.v. Archiv, Freiburg/Breisgau.

22 B. Bosshammer's war diary – BDF e.v. Archiv, Freiburg/Breisgau.

David Hutton recalled:

> I was wounded and was in a hospital in Crete, then I was flown to Piraeus where the Germans removed the shrapnel, apart from the biggest piece in my arm. They took me to Germany to a military hospital. They could not have been better to me and the nurses were really nice. We then transferred to *Stalag* 8B and later we ended up in Czechoslovakia. I was a prisoner for four years before the Russians liberated us.[23]

The letter was returned to Daisy – marked 'missing'. She put it, unopened, in a box and forgot about it. It lay there until 2011, when Mr Hutton's sister-in-law found it while rummaging through belongings in the loft of her house in Liff, Angus.

David Hutton continues:

> My brother told me he had a letter for me. It was still sealed, it had a 5d (about 2p) stamp and was initialled by my captain, Jim Ewan. Daisy used to write to me with all the family news and the letter went to Egypt, then was sent back from the Field Post Office there by Captain Ewan. When I made it back home, in 1945, it was never mentioned so I didn't know anything about it. Daisy had all the family news in it and it was good reading it.[24]

When the official capitulation of the town was signed on 30 May, the battle was finally over. Heraklion had surrendered only one other time in its long history, and that was after 21 years of siege; this time, it took a mere 11 days. Once again, the town had not been taken by assault, but had surrendered, just as it had almost 300 years earlier. The fighting spirit of the defenders of the town and its surrounding areas had not been wasted, as they had achieved a military victory which was left unexploited due to the situation that evolved elsewhere on the island.

All sides fought with bravery – a fact confirmed by the high casualty rates. Now, the people of Heraklion were left to resume their lives and rebuild their town under the onus of the occupation.

23 Interview with – and letter to – the author, November 2013.
24 Ibid.

# Epilogue

The battle was finally over and the survivors from all three sides continued with their lives: some by fighting on other battlefields, and others by returning home to their families. The dead soldiers of this battle – most of them aged 18 or 19 – never had the opportunity to have children and enjoy a long and happy life. They remained the beloved sons and brothers who, as time passed, became uncles and distant relatives – and finally, just names and numbers on memorials and casualty lists. The personal stories behind each soldier, fighter or civilian have now been largely forgotten, but these are precisely what will help us to understand the tragedy of war and the immense misery and destruction that it brings upon humanity.

Heraklion today is a modern city – and the battle is a very distant event which has now passed into history. People walk by and live in the places where bitter fighting took place, but very few of them know the history hidden in these surroundings. Buildings with traces of the conflict on them still exist even in the centre of the city, where many lives were lost. Today, no one can imagine the tragic moments of history which occurred in each building or field. Defensive positions and the remains of graves can still be found around the city and, from time to time, human remains or unexploded ammunition are discovered. Some of the planes that were shot down during the battle are still lying at the bottom of the sea near Heraklion. After so many years of research, I was astonished to discover these remains and relics still present around me; I had been totally ignorant of their existence for many years. Veterans kept visiting the battlefield for years afterwards, but many of them were unable to tell the bitter stories of the fighting and the loss of their comrades. Those stories haunted them for the rest of their lives.

Now that most of the veterans have passed away, or are too old to visit Crete, it is our duty to preserve the story of the battle and make every effort to keep alive the memory of such an historic event. I hope that with my work, I have contributed to this story and also that I provide the visitor to Heraklion with a better understanding of the history of what occurred there in May 1941. I hope that I have also assembled both an analysis of the battle and a solid framework of historical data that will be of use to historians and researchers who wish to explore the story more deeply.

# Bibliography


## Manuscripts and Unpublished Accounts

Bosshammer, Bernd, war diary – Bund Deutscher Fallschirmjäger e. V. Archiv, Freiburg/Breisgau.
Reinhardt, E., 'Memoirs of a Former German Paratrooper', Manuscript, David Lenk Archive.
Simon, Ernst H., Bund Deutscher Fallschirmjäger e. V. Archiv, Freiburg/Breisgau.
Stefanidis, Alexandros G., 'Memoirs of my Life', Athens, 1992, Manuscript, C.E. Mamalakis' archive.
Strauch, Adolf, Bund Deutscher Fallschirmjäger e. V. Archiv, Freiburg/Breisgau.

## War Diaries

1st Battalion, Argyll & Sutherland Highlanders war diary, May 1941, The Argyll & Sutherland Highlanders Regimental Museum.
2nd Battalion, Black Watch war diary, May 1941, C.E. Mamalakis' archive.
2/4 Australian Battalion war diary, May-June 1941, Australian War Memorial.

## Official Reports

XI Fliegerkorps, Gefechtsbericht 'Einsatz KRETA', 11.6.1941, Bund Deutscher Fallschirmjäger e. V. Archiv, Freiburg/Breisgau.
I./Fallschirm-Jäger Rgt.1, Gefechtsbericht über den Einsatz Iraklion, 3.6.1941, Bund Deutscher Fallschirmjäger e. V. Archiv, Freiburg/Breisgau.
Gruppe Schirmer, Gefechtsbericht über den Einsatz Iraklion, June 1941, Bund Deutscher Fallschirmjäger e. V. Archiv, Freiburg/Breisgau.
'The Mediterranean Fleet. Greece to Tripoli', The Admiralty Account of Naval Operations April 1941 to January 1943, London, His Majesty's Stationery Office, 1944.
Lt Col A. Beteinakis, After-Action Report about the battle in Heraklion, 20-29 May 1941, Athens, 12 November 1941, Hellenic Army General Staff, Army History Directorate.

## Books

Beevor, Antony, *Crete. The Battle and the Resistance*, London, John Murray, 2005.
Bertke, D.A., Kindell, D. & Smith, G., *World War II Sea War. Volume 3. The Royal Navy is Bloodied in the Mediterranean*, Dayton Ohio, Bertke Publications, 2012.
Boerger, Dr Eberhard, *Erinnerungen eines Alten Fallschirmjägers*, Rottach-Egern, Selbstverlag 2003.
Broder, Gerhard, *Guerre Mondiale Contre Moi*, Amstetten, Dieter Frieß Verlag, 2007.
Buchner, Alex, *Weapons and Equipment of the German Fallschirmtruppe. 1935-1945,* Atglen PA, Schiffer Publishing, 1996.
Gion, Chrestos, *The Battle of Crete. May 1941*, Athens, Hellenic Army General Staff, Army History Directorate, 2000.

Golla, Karl Heinz, *The German Fallschirmtruppe 1936-41. Its Genesis and Employment in the First Campaigns of the Wehrmacht*, Solihull, Helion & Company, 2013.
Hatjipateras, C. & Fafalios, M., *Kriti 1941 Martyries* – Greek edition, Athens, Kedros, 1993.
Kershaw, Robert, *Sky Men. Always Expect the Unexpected. The Real Story of the Paras*, London, Hobber & Stoughton, 2010.
Kühn, Volkmar, *Deutsche Fallschirmjäger im Zweiten Weltkrieg*, Stuttgart, Motorbuch Verlag, 1975.
Kurowski, Franz, *Sprung in die Hölle. Kreta. Fallschirmjäger und Gebirgstruppen erobern eine Insel*, Eggolsheim, Dörfler, 2006.
Kurowski, Franz, *Generalmajor Karl Lothar Schultz* ,Würzburg, Flechsig, 2008.
Linklater, Eric & Andro, *The Black Watch. The History of the Royal Highland Regiment*, London, Barrie & Jenkins, 1977.
Long, Gavin, *Australia in the War of 1939–1945*. Series 1 – Army, Volume II – Greece - Crete and Syria, Canberra, Australian War Memorial, 1st edition – 1953.
Lucas, James, *Battle Group! German Kampfgruppen Action of World War Two*, London, Arms and Armour Press, 1993.
Mastorakos, Manos, *German Paratroopers. 1936-1945. Vol.1*, Athens, Epikoinonies, 2003.
Müller, Günther & Scheuering, Fritz, *Sprung über Kreta*, Oldenburg, Stalling Verlag, 1944.
Nasse, Jean Yves, *1941. Fallschirmjäger in Crete*, Paris, Histoire & Collections, 2002.
Nisbett, Adrian, *Heroes in Death – The Von Blücher Brothers in the Fallshirmjäger – Crete May 1941*, Atglen PA, Schiffer, 2014.
Pytikakis, M.I., *Storm Over Crete (Thyella stin Kriti)*, Salonika, Special Edition of *Driros* journal, 1947.
Roussopoulos, Christos, *The Battle of Crete - Testimonies 5*, Heraklion, Society of Cretan Historical Studies, 2014.
Shores, C., Cull, B. & Malizia, N., *Air War for Yugoslavia, Greece and Crete 1940-41*, London, Grub Street, 1987.
Spurr, Reg, *To Have and to Lose – Testimonies 1*, Heraklion, Society of Cretan Historical Studies, 2007.
Thomas, David, *Nazi Victory – Crete 1941*, New York, Stein and Day, 1973.
Tsorvas, Giorgos, *The Green Devils. The History of the German Paratroopers*, Athens, War History, 2003.

## Magazines and Articles

Anderson DSO MC, Brigadier R.C.B., 'Ten Days in Crete, 1941', *The Thin Red Line, The Argyll and Sutherland Highlanders Regimental Magazine*, January/May/September 1949.
Brown MBE, Lt Col A.W., 'Crete 18th – 29th May 1941', *The Thin Red Line, The Argyll and Sutherland Highlanders Regimental Magazine*, autumn 2001.
*Cretan Panorama* magazine, March-May 2011.
*Der Deutsche Fallschirmjäger* (*DDF*), 1957 issue.

# Index

## INDEX OF PEOPLE


Alzinger, *Jäger* Alois (also mentioned as 'Atzinger'), 43, 46
Apladianakis, G., 72, 74

Badouvas, Manolis, 72-73, 75
Bardwell, Captain A.T., 223, 229, 232
Barry, Lieutenant Gerald, 56, 117, 119, 130, 142, 220, 244, 247
Bauer, *Gefreiter* Karl, 142, 145
Becker, *Oberleutnant*, 82, 161, 167, 175, 181
Bender, Hans Christoph, 235-236
von Berlepsch, *Leutnant* Freiherr, 51, 284
Beteinakis, Lieutenant Colonel Antonios, 69-70, 90, 166-167, 214-217, 280-281, 287
Biewendt, *Unteroffizier* Helmut, 38, 46
von Blücher, *Jäger* Hans Joachim *Graf*, v-vi, 24, 26, 112, 130-133, 149-151, 276
von Blücher, Lebrecht *Graf*, 24, 26, 150-151
von Blücher, *Oberleutnant* Wolfgang *Graf*, v-vi, 24-26, 33, 96-97, 113-114, 116-121, 123-124, 127, 130-134-143, 149-151, 219, 274-276
Boerger, Dr Eberhard, vi, 23, 81-85, 88, 93, 162, 287
Bohlander, *Oberjäger* Erwin, 43, 46
Bosshammer, Bernd, 29, 51-52, 55, 259-260, 284, 287
Bräuer, *Oberst* Bruno, xi, 27, 30, 100-102, 104-105, 113-115, 119, 121-123, 128-129, 149, 152, 154, 161, 204, 219, 233-234, 241-242, 246, 257, 260, 272, 275, 284
Breuer, Dr, 156-157
Broder, Gerhard, vi, 22, 31, 96-97, 111, 113, 120, 127, 131, 149, 215, 217, 281-283
Broder, *Oberjäger* Heinrich, 282-283
Brückmann, *Oberfeldwebel* Karl Heinz, 191, 195, 205
Brüns, *Oberjäger* Johann, 23, 172
Burckhardt, *Hauptmann*, 37, 54, 56, 58-59, 100, 113, 119, 234, 259

Chappel, Brigadier B.H., x, 34, 37-39, 204, 215, 229, 233, 242, 244, 249-250
Chasapes, Dr Nicolaos, 91, 200, 268-269
Chatzis, Private Ioannis (Yannis), 106, 107
Cheretis, Lieutenant Colonel Evangelos, 65, 69, 211, 237
Conrad, *Generalmajor* Gerhard, x-xi, 242-243

Dean, Private Selby, 48, 236, 238
Dedeletakis, Evangelos I., 169-170, 195
Drosoulakis, Georgios, 206, 208

Egger, *Oberleutnant*, 161, 171, 175, 181, 187, 214, 235-236, 258
Eiben, Dr Alfred, 79, 161, 200, 268-269
Eiting, *Feldwebel* Wilhelm, 215, 217
Erning, *Oberjäger* Hans, 142, 147, 159, 166

Fermor, Patrick Leigh, 69, 249-250, 261
Fiedler, *Obergefreiter* Eberhard, 52, 62
Filippakis, Major, 200, 202
Fischer, *Oberleutnant*, 169, 198, 268, 284
Freyberg, General, ix, 34, 242
Fulgosi, Lieutenant Guiseppe Cigala, 209-210

Galanakis, Antonios, 78, 211
Giles, Captain George, 223, 229
Görse, *Leutnant* Otto, 172, 205-206
Götte, *Oberleutnant*, 41, 272
Grigorakis, Antonis 'Satanas', 167, 187-188, 206, 249
Gröschke, *Hauptmann*, 26, 31, 121, 125, 219, 226

Hamilton, Captain J.G.A., 246-247
Herrmann, *Oberleutnant* Harry, 154, 226-228, 284
Hollweck, *Obergefreiter* Walter, 117, 131, 136-137, 142
Hope-Morley, Lieutenant Gordon, 38-40, 43, 46
Hoppe, *Gefreiter* Walter, 23, 93
Hutton, Corporal David, vi, 19, 53, 55, 284-285

Ieronymakis, Mr Georgios, 200-203

Jacobs, Rudolf, 33, 97, 128, 130

Kallinos, Lieutenant Theodoros E., vi, 13-15, 103, 106-108, 281
Kappel, *Oberleutnant*, 161, 175

Kasimatis, Major Demetrios, 14, 69
Kavroulakis, G., 72, 74
Kennedy, Alex, 48-49
Kerfin, *Oberleutnant*, 161, 175, 181, 200-202
Kesteven, Lieutenant K.L., 226, 236, 238
Kiebach, *Oberjäger*, 93, 172
Kissling, *Oberleutnant*, 123, 125
Kittendorf, *Gefreiter* Kurt, 96, 142
Kleber, *Gefreiter* Julius, 142, 146
Kokkinakis, Emmanuel, 99, 106
Korakas, Michael, 82, 85
Kounalakis, Lieutenant K., 166, 176, 189
Krause, *Gefreiter* Wilhelm, 43, 46
Krückeberg, *Leutnant* Roland, 164, 205

Ladas, Lysimachos, 61-62
Langemeier, Dr, 229, 231
Lankenau, *Oberleutnant* Franz, 232, 242
Lark, Bill, 119-120, 254-255
Linardakis, Major General Michael, 77, 203, 214, 220, 272, 280
Lindenberg, *Leutnant* Boris, 103, 108, 111-112
Loch, Karl, 232-233
Löhr, *General* Alexander, x, 282
Loop, *Gefreiter* Otto, 23, 33
Lutter, *Obergefreiter* Willi, 43, 46

Malagardis, 2nd Lieutenant Eleftherios, 77-78, 83, 168, 179, 188-189, 203, 269
Mamounis, Kostis, 169-170
Manolesakis, Captain, 83, 85
Marinelis, Lieutenant Ioannis, 90, 178, 182-184
Martin, *Gefreiter* Kurt, 96, 142, 145
Melcher, *Jäger* Gerhard, 205-206
Meyer, *Jäger* Hans, 112, 142, 146
Migadis, Sifis, 189, 211
Miliaras, Stylianos, 268-269
Möller, *Oberfeldwebel* Ernst 'Baby', 113, 117, 131, 142
Müller, Dr Günther, 20-21, 45, 59, 86, 94, 98, 101-104, 114, 122, 127-128, 134-135, 141, 147, 152-154, 156-158, 171, 180, 227, 261-262, 264, 272-273, 288
Mussolini, Benito ix, 69

Nickolaus, *Feldwebel* Lothar, 180, 205-206

Otto, *Oberleutnant*, 111, 121, 130

Paleakis, Georgios, 90-92
Papapolychroniou, Sotiris, 203-204
Papathanasopoulos, Colonel Charalampos, 77, 166, 181, 203, 234, 237
Patatanes, Nikos, 99-100, 106
Pendlebury, John, 62, 187, 206, 208, 261
Petralis, M., 72, 74
Pitcairn, Major, 55, 247
Platow, *Leutnant* Dietrich, 50, 226
Psarakis, Georgios, 220-221
Pyrovolakis, Sergeant Emmanuel, 72, 74
Pytikakis, M., 74, 78, 183, 196, 199-200, 221-221, 288

Rau, *Hauptmann*, 101, 114, 129
Rawlings, Admiral, 251, 255
Reinhardt, Erich, 41, 59, 272
Ringel, *Generalleutnant* Julius, xi, 27
Ristau, *Gefreiter* Hugo, 84, 180, 205-206
Röhl, *Obergefreiter* Willi, 142, 145
Rösch, *Gefreiter* Paul, 43, 46
Rother, *Gefreiter* Rudi, 43, 47
Roussopoulos, Private Christos, 16-17, 31, 70

Schäfer, Mathes, 127-128
Schamberger, *Leutnant* Otto, 43, 45
Scheuering, Fritz, 20-21, 45, 59, 86, 94, 98, 101-104, 114, 122, 125, 127-128, 134, 141, 147, 152-154, 156-158, 171, 180, 227, 261-262, 264, 273, 288
Schirmer, *Hauptmann* Gerhard, 43, 60-61, 80, 91, 121, 164, 202, 204, 211, 235, 242, 257, 259, 287
Schlenski, Bruno, 123, 135, 138
Schmickl, *Gefreiter* Hans, 82, 162
Schneider, *Oberfeldwebel*, 131, 135, 149
Schröder, *Oberjäger* Heinrich, 179, 205-206
von der Schulenburg, *Hauptmann Graf*, 80, 161, 164, 175, 181
Schulz, *Major* Karl Lothar, 43, 65, 79-80, 83, 91, 104, 121-122, 161, 164, 172, 175, 180-181, 184, 188, 191, 198, 200-204, 211, 214, 220, 234, 241
Simon, Ernst H., 85, 166, 169, 191, 229, 234-235, 243, 282
Snowden, 2nd Lieutenant, 55, 57-58
Spang, *Leutnant*, 117, 121
Spurr, Private Reg, 65, 67, 193-194
Spyridakis, G., 72, 107
Strauch, Adolf, 60, 80, 235-236
Stromathias, Sergeant, 175, 188
Student, *General* Kurt, x-xi, 102, 233, 242-243
von Suttner, *Gefreiter*, 51, 284

Tessenow, *Oberjäger* Otto, 205-206
Tidmarsh, Captain E.T., 223-224
Tost, *Obergefreiter* Ernst, 205-206
Tsagkarakis, Major Emmanuel, 74, 77, 167, 179, 188, 200, 203, 220-221, 272, 280

Tweedie, Lieutenant John, 123, 131
Tzoulakis, Major Michael, 74, 85, 87, 90, 176-179, 189, 206, 211

Vamvoukakis, Odysseas, 61-62, 64, 89
Vardis, Sergeant, 99, 108
Vogel, *Hauptmann*, 229, 232, 234
Vogler, *Hauptfeldwebel* Hermann, 97, 281
Vosshage, *Gefreiter* Heinz, 142-144
Voutirakis, *Gendarmerie* Sergeant, 166, 176

Walther, *Major* Erich, 43, 94, 100, 104-105, 108, 122, 127, 129, 135, 218-219, 257, 259
Wanke, *Oberjäger* Karl, 124, 142-143
Wittmann, *Oberleutnant* Albert, 112, 121, 129-130

Zeimbekis, Apostolos, 265-267

## INDEX OF PLACES

25th of August Street, 184, 187, 190, 192, 195, 208, 266-267
62 Martyron Avenue, 82, 90, 211

Aegean Sea, ix, xi, 13, 36
Agios Dimitrios Church, 184, 186, 189, 191, 193-194, 205
Agias Ekaterinis Square, 179-180
Agioi Deka, 204, 222-224, 229, 232-233, 249
Agios Ioannis (East Hill, or 'Blüchersberg'), 34, 49-53, 55-56, 107, 113, 116-119, 121, 123-125, 130, 135, 139-141, 143, 145-146, 149, 219, 247, 259, 273
Agios Konstantinos Cemetery, 72-75, 138
Agios Minas Cathedral, 175, 180, 269-270
Agios Myron, 60, 62, 166, 178, 205
Agios Titos Church, 90, 175, 178-179
Ai Lias Hill (Hill 296, or 'Apex Hill'), 61, 202, 226, 234-237, 239, 242-244, 259
Albanian Front, 69, 90-91, 184
Alexandria, 19, 209, 222, 246, 254-255
Amnissos, 38, 53, 113, 121, 124, 147, 150, 166, 241
Amnissos Hill, 152, 154, 156, 158-159, 218
Anastasakis wood factory, 90-91
Anopolis (Anapoli), 99-100, 107-108
Archanes, 211, 216, 234, 237, 280
Argos, 13, 61
Asia Minor, 176, 178, 184, 216
Athens, ix, xi, 13, 24, 52, 83, 91, 93, 150, 206, 209, 233, 236, 242-243, 260, 269, 281, 287-288

Berlin, 105, 284
Bulgaria, ix, 164
Buttercup Field, 37, 44

Cairo, 19, 242
Chania, iv, ix-xi, 16-17, 27, 31, 33, 61, 65, 176, 217, 219, 224, 265, 280-281
Chanioporta (West Gate), 31, 67, 69, 79, 82-86, 88, 90, 161-163, 166-167, 169, 171, 173, 175, 179-181, 189, 193, 204, 206, 208, 211, 220, 247, 256, 268
Charlies, 34, 37, 42, 44, 53, 55, 124, 244
Cheretis Metohi, 223-224
Corinth Canal, ix, 24, 61
Crete, i, iii-iv, ix-xi, 13-14, 16-22, 26, 32-36, 41-42, 47, 51, 53, 55, 61-62, 69, 71-72, 74, 77, 80-84, 89, 91, 94, 96-97, 101-103, 105, 138, 158, 164, 167, 178, 183-184, 200, 203, 206, 209, 211, 215-217, 222-223, 232, 238, 243, 246-247, 249, 251, 254, 260-261, 269, 272, 275, 283, 285-288
Customs building, 84-85
Czechoslovakia, 284-285

Deilina, 65, 91, 121, 166
Dermatas Gate, 169-170
Dia, 22, 37, 51, 103, 242
Dialynas Building, 16, 76-77
Dikaiosynis Street, 74, 76, 175, 202
Dortmund, 24, 83

Eastern Front, 21, 61, 80, 105, 201, 268
Egypt, x, 19, 223, 226, 249, 255, 284-285
Eleftherias, 83, 175
Eleusis, 27, 209
Elspe (Lennestadt), 82-83
Episkopi, 99-100, 107-108, 111
Euboea, 13, 22
Evropis Street, 193-194

Fortress Kali, 13-14

Galatas, iv, 19, 27, 280
Galazia Poulia Tavern, 156, 158, 227, 260
Gazi, 65, 91, 121, 164, 176, 233
Georgantas, 176, 189
Giofyros River, 60, 69, 83, 85, 87, 90-92, 121, 166, 198, 211, 213-214
Gournes, iii, 14, 27, 94-96, 98, 100, 103-105, 108, 111-112, 119, 149, 158, 205, 224, 233, 242, 246

Gouves, 99-100, 107
Gyali Kiosk, 161-163, 166-167, 193, 203

Hamburg, 61, 157
Heraklion Airfield, 46, 51, 113, 120, 130, 137, 150, 226, 233, 235
Heraklion Guard HQ, 14, 16, 74, 76-78, 168, 175, 177, 202-203, 220-221
Heraklion War Cemetery, 136, 150, 276-277
Hill 67 (Stavromenos), 60, 64, 91, 164, 198, 211, 220, 224, 229, 232-233
Hill 107, 102, 119
Hill 182 (Koprena), 34, 55, 121, 133, 215, 218-219, 226, 234
Holland, 24, 26, 33, 41, 47, 61, 80, 82, 105, 117, 139, 172, 260
Hotel Gallia, 181, 184, 187, 190
Hotel Minos, 184, 187, 190

Ioniki (Ionian) Bank, 184, 187, 191, 195
Italy, 21, 61, 80

Kainourgia Porta (South Gate), 77-79, 90, 166, 175, 193, 206, 265
Kako Oros (Evil Mountain), 14, 17-18, 59, 69, 99, 103, 109, 150
Kalokairinou Street, 172, 179, 258, 264-265, 267, 269
Kaminia, 65, 85, 90-91, 121, 166, 169, 198, 206, 208, 211
Kanli Kasteli (Prophitis Ilias), 27, 203
Karteros, 18, 34, 112, 117, 139, 149-150, 153, 156, 158, 226-227, 229
Karteros River, 56, 113, 117, 123
Karteros Valley (East Wadi, or East Beach), 17-18, 37-38, 48, 50, 53, 55-57, 59, 99, 121, 123, 126, 128-129, 131, 135, 145, 200, 215, 218-219, 226
Kasos Strait, 209, 251
Katsabas, 34, 37, 39, 41-42, 233, 250, 272
Kavalakis, 176-177, 189
Kitriki juice factory, 85, 87-88, 211
Knossos, 19, 69, 74, 138, 150, 187, 206, 208, 215, 222, 233, 235, 246, 249, 261-262
Knossos Hotel, 187, 208
Konstantinidis Brothers raisin factory, 172, 179-181
Konstantinidis' house, 62, 184, 186-188, 192-193, 198, 203
Kopsas, 103-112, 224
Kopsas Hill, iii, 14, 94, 98-100, 105
Koules, 169, 175, 181-182, 184, 190, 197
Krousonas, 60, 62, 65, 187, 206, 249

Lasithi (West Crete), 76-77, 272
Leningrad, 81, 105
Lesvos, 13, 184
'Liontaria' Square, 200-201, 265, 267
Liopyrakis building, 189, 192, 195

Mahis Kritis Street, 82, 85
Maleme, iv, ix, xi, 29, 34, 41, 94, 119, 205, 209, 219, 242, 247, 280-281, 283
Maleme Airfield, xi, 27, 31, 233
Maleme War Cemetery, 47, 96, 101-102, 106, 117, 151, 160, 277
Mastabas, 31, 65, 67, 69-70, 72-73, 75, 77-80, 85, 91, 166, 217, 222
Mediterranean Sea, 19, 22, 209, 250, 252, 254-255, 287
Megara Airfield, 23, 27, 242-243
Meintani, 175, 221, 265
Mesampelies, 74, 75
Messara, 223, 280
Metaxas Line, ix, 13-14, 22
Middle East, ix, 221
Milos, xi, 41-42, 96, 209
Monte Cassino, 105, 138
Mount Jouhtas, 46, 226
Mount Stroumboulas, 44, 64
Municipal Customs (Dimotikos Foros) building, 82, 84

Narvik, 20, 31
Nea Alikarnassos, 37-38, 40-41, 43, 247, 272
Normandy, 81, 164
North Africa, ix, 35, 81, 123
Norway, 41, 61, 82, 105

Olympia Hospital, 52, 260

Palestine, 19, 238
Panagitsa (Holy Mary), 72-73, 75
Pananion Hospital, 83, 91, 161, 164, 198, 200, 211, 215, 221, 268, 270
Peloponnese, ix, 13, 16
Piraeus (Athens), 87, 90-91, 209, 281, 285
Piraeus Bank, 87, 90
Platia Strata, 172, 175, 189, 264
Poland, 21, 61, 284
Prassas, 50, 150
Prison Valley, 21, 217
Psilorites Mountain, 187, 247

Raisin Co-operatives Union of Crete factory, 167, 203
Rattling Bridge, 113, 116, 123, 218-219

Rethymnon, iv, ix-xi, 27, 33, 65, 169, 204-205, 208, 272, 277
Russia, 21, 61

Salonika, 13, 22, 281, 288
Sfakianakis Metochi, 62, 65-66, 231-232
Souda, iv, ix, xi, 27, 208, 247, 280-281
Souda Bay, 16, 19, 58, 222
Spilia, 211, 222, 234, 237
Stendal, 22, 24, 81, 281, 284

Talos, 85, 88, 211
Tanagra Airfield, xi, 27, 94, 284
Therissos, 65, 67, 69, 80, 91, 121, 166, 169
Topolia Airfield, xi, 23, 27, 29-30, 32, 36, 94
Town Hall, 175, 184, 201
Tsalikaki, 60-62, 80, 121, 211, 214, 224
Tymbaki, x, 222-224, 233, 246, 249

Valestra Street, 172-173
Venetian walls, 65, 85, 161-162, 189, 198, 220-221, 265, 272
Vienna, 24, 82, 284
Villa Ariadne, 19, 138, 222, 249, 261-263
Voutes, 60, 62

Xeropotamos, 33, 90

Yugoslavia, ix, 34, 288

## INDEX OF BRITISH & COMMONWEALTH MILITARY UNITS & FORMATIONS

14th Infantry Brigade, x, 34, 38-39, 41-42, 46, 69, 233, 245, 249

Argyll & Sutherland Highlanders (1st Battalion), vi, x, 204, 222-224, 229, 249, 287
2/4 Australian Infantry Battalion, x, 37, 44, 48, 124, 150, 215, 226, 236, 259, 287
Black Watch Regiment (2nd Battalion), vi-vii, x, 19, 34, 37, 48-49, 51, 53, 55, 57-59, 67-68, 117, 119-121, 123-124, 130-131, 135, 142, 193, 204, 215, 220, 229, 236-237, 244, 246-248, 251, 254-255, 259, 287-288
Leicestershire Regiment (2nd Battalion), x, 193, 204, 215, 233-234, 249
York & Lancaster Regiment (2nd Battalion), x, 19, 34, 56, 65, 67, 74-75, 82, 117-118, 135, 141, 150, 188-189, 193-194, 204, 222, 233-234, 246, 249, 255, 287

'C' Heavy Anti-Aircraft Battery, Royal Marines x, 35
7th Australian Light Anti-Aircraft Battery x, 35
7th Medium Regiment, Royal Artillery x, 38, 204
15th Coastal Regiment, Royal Artillery x
23rd Light Anti-Aircraft Battery, Royal Marines x, 35
156th Light Anti-Aircraft Battery, Royal Artillery x, 35
234th Medium Battery, Royal Artillery x, 35, 37-38

## INDEX OF GREEK MILITARY UNITS & FORMATIONS

Greek Army, ix-x, 13, 91, 99, 103, 176, 184, 214, 216

Heraklion Military Command, 76-77, 85, 167, 181
2nd Greek Military Command, x, 214, 220, 234

V/5th Division 'Crete', ix, 17, 69

3rd Greek Infantry Regiment, x, 67, 69-70, 74-75, 80, 166, 181, 211, 217
7th Greek Infantry Regiment, 31, 69-70, 80, 175, 211, 237
43rd Greek Infantry Regiment, 17, 44, 91, 272, 280

Heraklion Regimental Depot Battalion, x, 14, 16, 83, 90, 211

*Gendarmerie*, x, 62, 72, 74-75, 77-78, 85, 96, 99, 108, 166-167, 175-176, 179, 187, 198-199, 211, 272
Heraklion Guard, 14, 16, 74, 76-79, 85, 167-168, 175, 177, 179, 181, 188, 200, 202-204, 220-221

## INDEX OF GERMAN MILITARY FORMATIONS & UNITS


*Luftwaffe*, viii-xi, 13-14, 18, 22, 31, 42, 92, 121, 127, 138, 161, 203-204, 209, 214, 223, 226, 229, 231-234, 246, 251, 269-270

*VIII Fliegerkorps*, x-xi, 31
*XI Fliegerkorps*, x-xi, 27, 29, 59, 108, 199, 204

*Gruppe Dunz*, 38, 40, 43
*Gruppe Mitte*, xi, 27
*Gruppe Ost*, xi, 27
*Gruppe West*, xi, 27, 94

*FschJgRgt.1*, xi, 14, 20-24, 26-27, 29-31, 33, 37-38, 40-43, 45, 48, 50-55, 60, 65, 67, 69-70, 72, 78, 80- 83, 85, 90, 92-94, 96, 98, 100, 103, 105, 111-113, 120-123, 125, 127-128, 130-131, 142, 148-150, 154, 158-159, 161-164, 166-167, 169, 172, 179-182, 191, 200, 205-206, 211, 214-215, 218-219, 226, 229, 232, 234-235, 241, 243, 258-260, 267-268, 272, 282, 284
*I./FschJgRgt.1* 43, 94, 96, 104-105, 109, 119, 121-123, 125, 133, 137, 159, 161, 218-219, 235, 259, 273
*II./FschJgRgt.1* 37, 44, 55, 100, 113, 121, 123, 133, 150, 161, 200, 205, 229, 259
*III./FschJgRgt.1* 37, 43, 65, 67, 69, 79-80, 85, 91, 121, 161, 164, 166, 169, 195, 204-205, 211, 214, 220, 224, 229, 234-235, 266
*FschJgRgt.2* ix, xi, 27, 43, 60-62, 64, 121, 164, 205, 211, 224, 229, 231, 235, 259
*II./FschJgRgt.2* 27, 60-62, 80, 91, 121, 164, 204-205, 211, 214, 220, 229, 234-235, 259, 266
*FschFlaMGBatl.7* 27, 37-38
*FschSanAbt.7* 23, 27, 30, 33
*Kampfgruppe* Burckhardt 54, 56


## INDEX OF GENERAL & MISCELLANEOUS TERMS


*Der Adler*, 226, 228
Allies, ix, 17, 49, 69, 80, 178

Balkan Wars, 184, 216
Bofors [gun], x, 34-35, 89, 123, 131
Bren Carrier, 48, 50, 52, 55, 59, 117, 223-224, 229, 231

CREFORCE, ix, 222
Cretan Resistance, 14, 69, 72, 176, 206, 217, 261, 269, 287

German Cross in Gold, 81, 105

HMS *Ajax*, ix, 246
HMS *Dido*, 246, 251, 254-255
HMS *Glengyle*, 222-223
HMS *Imperial*, 246, 249
HMS *Kimberley*, 246-247
HMS *Orion*, xi, 246, 251, 253, 255
HMS *Perth*, 209-210, 253
Hurricane [aircraft], 226, 233-234

Iron Cross, 47, 105, 172, 272, 284

Ju-52 [aircraft], 30, 32-33, 36-37, 41, 44, 46, 79, 84, 89, 96-97, 101-102, 144, 242-243, 260
Ju-87 Stuka [aircraft], 17, 34, 58, 67, 138, 141, 166, 251, 253

Knight's Cross, 18, 24, 26, 33, 61, 80, 105, 127, 129, 226-227, 260

Matilda [tank], 37, 131, 134-135, 142, 153-154, 159, 166, 215, 217-218, 222, 224, 231

Operation 'Merkur', x, 20
Operational Instruction No.11, 244-245

'Red Alarm', 34, 36